Political Creativity

Reconfiguring Institutional Order and Change

Edited by

Gerald Berk, Dennis C. Galvan, and Victoria Hattam

PENN

UNIVERSITY OF PENNSYLVANIA PRESS

PHILADELPHIA

Published by
University of Pennsylvania Press
Philadelphia, Pennsylvania 19104-4112
www.upenn.edu/pennpress

Printed in the United States of America on acid-free paper
10 9 8 7 6 5 4 3 2 1

Library of Congress Cataloging-in-Publication Data
Political creativity : reconfiguring institutional order and change / edited by
Gerald Berk, Dennis C. Galvan, and Victoria Hattam.—1st ed.
    p. cm.
Includes bibliographical references and index.
ISBN 978-0-8122-4544-8 (hardcover : alk. paper)
    1. Political science—Research—Methodology. 2. Political sociology—
Research—Methodology. 3. Creative ability—Political aspects—Case studies.
4. Social institutions—Case studies. 5. Public institutions—Case studies.
6. Organizational change—Case studies. I. Berk, Gerald. II. Galvan, Dennis Charles.
III. Hattam, Victoria Charlotte.
    JA76.P59275 2014
    320.01′9—dc23
                                                                    2013026521

Contents

Part III. Time

Introduction

Beyond Dualist Social Science

The Mangle of Order and Change

The game's afoot in institutionalist research. As institutionalists grapple with change, diversity, innovation, indeterminacy, creativity, and surprising assemblages of institutional artifacts, some have come to question the implicit structuralist foundations of their research and turned elsewhere for help. The catalog is big and growing. Among other traditions, institutionalists have turned to social studies of science, action theory, ecology, narrative knowing, poststructuralism, constructivism, postcolonialism, pragmatism, theories of entrepreneurship, religious studies, and economic anthropology. This volume assembles a group of political scientists, whose only obvious commonality is their restlessness with structuralism and their commitment to alternative intellectual traditions to animate their research. By gathering this heterogeneous body of work together, we hope to shift these alternative traditions from the margins to the center of the discipline and in doing so advance a positive research agenda. The contributors work on a wide range of empirical problems—from unions in Russia, Islamist economics, and global supply chains to industrial policy, political consulting, and civil rights in the United States—and draw on many different theoretical traditions to analyze the cases at hand. Despite our apparent differences, we share a common project: to reconstruct institutionalism so it can better inquire into the genuine "mangle," as we call it, of human creativity, surprising assemblages, and political possibilities we see in our research.

Although we share the recent interest in institutional change, the work represented in this volume should not be confused with the recent efforts to theorize change, which retain the false duality of structure and agency.[1] Whereas those projects seek to soften the distinction between institutional structure and human agency with concepts like "layering" or "ambiguity," we work toward concepts that circumvent the distinction and direct research toward the mutual constitution of action and context in everyday practice. Where other projects catalogue the structural gaps in rules, roles, or routines, which enable agency, we investigate the political creativity through which people in plural settings experience and practice rules and roles. Where those projects typologize mechanisms of institutional change, we probe the ways in which order and change are constantly intertwined.

We have shifted our attention to these phenomena and ways of thinking not because we have an aesthetic or political preference for voluntary action, political fluidity, or creative possibility, but because we've found structuralist efforts to make sense of institutional diversity and change intriguing, but ultimately dissatisfying.[2] Although we appreciate the proliferation of mechanisms of institutional change, we worry that existing accounts remain descriptive and cumbersome and endanger the principles that made structuralist approaches to institutions elegant and useful. Although we also acknowledge recent efforts to theorize institutional change by appealing to actor interests fixed in structures beyond institutional borders, we worry that this turn undermines a key institutionalist insight—namely, that institutions shape interests. And although we appreciate the efforts to acknowledge the ways that institutional constraints on action are "softened" by phenomena like "institutional drift," "loose coupling" between parts, or "transposition" of functions, we worry that they leave the antinomy of structure and agency, which has confounded institutionalism, intact.[3] That is, they do little to overcome the widespread, but often confusing, observation that it is impossible to know what actions to focus on without reference to institutional structure, but in a world of plural institutions, multiple instruments, or cultural disputes over the meaning of rules, it is impossible to know exactly which institutional instruments are relevant without reference to action. Instead, the authors in this volume have found useful ways to circumvent the increasingly unproductive distinctions between order and change, structure and agency, or institutions and interests. Doing so requires the elaboration of theoretical positions that refuse the relentless splitting of structure, agency, and change.

Political Creativity

As editors, we have taken inductive license from the expansive theoretical roaming and the rich empirical research in this volume to suggest that the lingering structure-agency dualisms in political science might be overcome by attending to political creativity, a concept intended to capture both the pervasiveness of change as well as the deeply embedded nature of social action. Political creativity is at once not determined by background conditions and yet constituted through extant social relations. Institutional rules and roles, cultural heritage and historical memory situate actors in contexts, which inform action not as guide, constraint, or script, but as the raw material for improvisation and transformation. In this volume, action is not rote playing from sheet music, nor are improvisational riffs predictable from gaps in the score. Instead, we find actors who constantly mess with the score in unexpected and unauthorized ways, rearranging it with each performance. The creativity of situated action is a kind of recomposition.

What then of power and creative action? The turn to creativity by no means eclipses inequality and asymmetrical social relations. The question is not whether power is present, but rather where it is manifest, how it circulates, and how to study it. From a political creativity perspective, power is best understood relationally as social practices through which subjects and subjectivities, institutions and authority are established, challenged, and reconfigured. Power does not inhere in formal conditions. Rather power is secured though the ongoing negotiation of people, places, and things into provisional assemblages that accord meaning to position. A final aspect of power as a practice needs to be mentioned, namely the temporal disorder of things. Historical particularity is at once everything and nothing as elements are drawn both from the materials at hand and from temporally and spatially distant sources. Tracing this unruly process of political creation and attending to the ways in which new configurations privilege some relations while disadvantaging others takes us to the heart of political change.

Attending to power as relational practice requires that we shift the analytic lens from identities, institutions, and material conditions, often assumed to structure political action, to focus instead on the *interplay* of political elements over time. Attending to dynamic interactions is key. It is not easy to train one's eye on dynamic, fleeting micro or partial interactions rather than stable roles, rules, and routines. It requires skills more frequently associated with historians, novelists, ethnographers, and psychotherapists than those in the social sciences. Difficult as this is, we avert it at our peril; without such skills we are likely to misread political situations. Joan Scott's critique of E. P. Thompson's *Making of the English Working*

Class serves as a cautionary tale. Thompson's error, Scott makes plain, was his failure to appreciate the gender coding and relational dynamics of the multiple responses to industrialization. As a result, Thompson mistook the masculinist self-narrative of skilled male workers at face value, thereby replaying the very power relations he aimed to analyze.[4]

While the notion of political creativity, and the subtending concepts elaborated below, grow out of political science, the editors and contributors to this volume follow the lead of numerous scholars beyond political science who have explored creative action. We look, for example, to the work of sociologist Hans Joas, who seeks to recover creativity from an intellectual history that marginalized it to rational and normative action.[5] We look to organization theorist Karl Weick, who notes that successful managers never exercise power by holding fast to rules, roles, and routines. Instead they play with organizational structures like improvisational jazz artists—they know the score well enough never to faithfully reproduce it. Likewise, anthropologist Jean-Loup Amselle reveals how, under colonial regimes, ethnic categories function not as scientific classifications of language or lifeway, but as sites for ongoing negotiation and contestation between subject peoples and imperial administrators. Finally, Michel de Certeau escapes structure-agency splits by attending to *The Practices of Everyday Life* in which acts of reading, speaking, and walking are likened to renting an apartment and making it habitable. As Certeau puts it, "It transforms another person's property into a space borrowed for a moment by a transient. Renters make comparable changes in an apartment they furnish with their acts and memories; as do speakers, in the language into which they insert both the messages of their native tongue and, through their accent, through their own 'turns of phrase,' etc., their own history; as do pedestrians, in the streets they fill with the forest of their desires and goals."[6] These scholars, and many others, have inspired our work. Prior to collaboration, however, our efforts remained scattered across many academic programs and research sites. A significant part of the project's goal was to bring this diverse group together to see if we might more effectively specify analytic tools needed to rethink order and change.

The volume's ambition, then, is to elevate political creativity from a residual problem to a research program. Seen as a residual, there is little more to say than when deterministic, probabilistic, or stochastic explanations of politics fail, free will provides traction for a contingent explanation. Seen as a research program, political creativity jettisons the duality of free will and determinism (or necessity and contingency) for an investigation into the relationships and processes that situate creativity and are, in turn, reconstituted by it. This involves a good deal of careful conceptual and empirical work. Political creativity blurs the analytic boundaries intended to keep order, agency, and change from mingling. In our approach, order is not so orderly and change not so intermittent. Agency, if one remains attentive to it, can be found at every turn. Change is ever present, enacted every day, by those who find themselves in empirically identifiable, complex situations (the raw material for creative action). It makes a tangle, or a mangle, if you will, of neat distinctions that have kept agency apart from order, and change confined to small locations in time and space.

We take a deliberate risk with the term "mangle" for two reasons. First, where some may see a mess or destruction, we see the many imaginative and provocative ways the authors in this volume reconfigure conventional relationships among agency, order, and change. It is chaos only if one reifies these distinctions. Second, we draw on historian of science Andrew Pickering, who calls scientific practice a "mangle," because it shifts our understanding of science from the rarified image of positivist practice to an "open ended," "emergent" process of dialogue or transaction between people, machines, and nature. In his view, "the mangle of practice" is a "convenient and suggestive shorthand" for seeing "science as an evolving field of human and material agencies reciprocally engaged in a play of resistance and accommodation in which the former seeks to capture the latter."[7]

Once we accepted that political practice continually makes a mangle of institutional order, tightly bounded agency, and change confined to critical junctures and structural gaps, we identified three conceptual threads running through the research chapters; highlighting these conceptual moves has allowed us to reimagine agency as relationality, order as assemblage, and change as the politics of time. Although these issues are often intertwined, we take editorial license to organize the volume around these three themes by clustering the chapters according to their strongest accent. Doing so, we hope, will cultivate a research program on political creativity.

Relationality

Political creativity occurs through relational processes, in which people respond (or not) to one another's tinkering, creative projects, experiments, deliberations, and interpretations. In doing so, they learn from one another, reinterpret background conditions, adjust their identities, realign them-selves in relation to others, and experiment anew. Relationality overcomes the structure-agency distinction by setting both in motion. From this per-spective, neither the features of institutions—rules, roles, symbols—nor the identities or interests of actors have meaning apart from the changing roles they play in relationship to one another. As Margaret Somers writes, in relational analysis "cultural concepts and categories that appear to be autonomously defined by their attributes are historically shifting sets of relationships that are contingently stabilized."[8] Political creativity, in other words, is a relational process that continually perturbs and temporarily sta-bilizes the salient features of people and things.

Thus, instead of holding the characteristics of institutions and actors constant in order to make causal inferences, relational analysis puts those features in play and conceptualizes the processes by which their relation-ships evolve. Unlike dualist analysis, in which institutions and actors are the primary units of analysis, in relational analysis the dynamic, unfolding process of interplay among people and institutions becomes the primary unit of analysis. As sociologist Mustafa Emirbayer puts it, the former con-ceptualizes "things" (actors and structures) by their attributes and explana-tion specifies and tests the mechanisms by which they "inter-act." The latter conceptualizes the processes by which people and people and things "transact" with one another and explanation traces the empirical processes that alter and temporarily stabilize their significance. Where "inter-action" produces correlation, "transaction" produces "mutual constitution."[9]

Instead of isolating independent institutional (exogenous) variables to explain action and change, a relational perspective asks how institutional features and inhabitants form relations of mutual determination and flux. Relational analysis, for example, is less concerned with how symbolic sys-tems shape cognition than about how dynamic relationships among people and symbols alter identities, power relations, and creative projects. It is less concerned with how institutional features endow inhabitants with capaci-ties to act than with the way relationships between actors (re)shape creative projects and possibilities. People, places, and things attain explanatory sig-nificance not from their place in background settings, but from their rela-tionships situated in time.

Attention to relationality alters the way we understand power. Although inequalities in access to material and symbolic resources are observable, their values are continually fabricated and reassembled by the interplay among people and things. Power is a relational process, in which the weak and strong are mutually constituted by the ways they make sense of and mess with unequal resources in light of the interpretations and actions of others. Often—not always—history bequeaths repertoires of interpretation and experimentation asymmetrically, so that some people take their privilege to act creatively more for granted than others. Power must be studied by tracing those relational processes empirically; it cannot be inferred from empirically observed inequalities in institutional roles, schemas, or resources.

We draw inspiration for relationality from a variety of empirical and disciplinary settings. In social studies of science, Bruno Latour, Andrew Pickering, and others have conceptualized science as a relational practice, in which explanation traces the mediating processes and controversies through which nature, scientists, technologies, and publics interact. These unpredictable processes involve ceaseless rounds of "tuning," "fact making," and "translation."[10] Closer to home, we have been inspired by Dvora Yanow and Peregrine Schwartz-Shea, who have brought the relational insights of science studies to bear on interpretive methods in the human sciences.[11] In political sociology, Elisabeth Clemens has unpacked the primordial category of groups through relational analysis. Groups are a historical accomplishment, born through mutual interplay and reappropriation; their interests emerge relationally from the transposition of social models of identity to political competition.[12] Gary Herrigel, Michael Piore, Charles Sabel, and Jonathan Zeitlin have shifted our attention from unitary accounts of Western industrialization as an exclusively economic process to the relational composition and interweaving of heterogeneous industrial forms, which are coconstituted with politics and society.[13] In political theory, a lively debate over liberalism and difference has revealed how liberal universalism has always been in historical relationship with remote and inscrutable others. Anne Norton reveals the gendered and bodily nature of the liberal subject—closed and sovereign for men, open and subjected for women. Uday Mehta locates an "anthropological minimum" in classical liberal texts, which infantilizes colonial subjects, rendering them unfit for liberal sovereignty.[14] The authors in this volume engage these scholars and others through deep empirical work. In doing so, they adopt, revise, and invent concepts useful for tracing and analyzing relational processes. One might keep an eye open for the many relational terms that permeate the substantive chapters, among them the "mutual constitution of rules and

identities," "recomposition," "mutual learning," "political reconfiguration," "coevolution," "habituation and dehabituation," and "political
work."

Assemblage

A growing body of institutionalist literature questions the fetish of order,
the finality of lock-in, the rigidity of cognitive schemas, and the marginality
of agency.[15] Our approach builds on these insights to suggest that orders
are partial and multiple: despite the best efforts to craft a rule, role, or
routine for every situation, no institution is able to contain the wily proliferation of human action. As a result, institutions contain multiple, overlapping elements, offering more than one template for any given situation. In
this space, actors have room to dismantle orders, select useful parts, combine them in new ways, and produce what some have called hybrid, recombinant, or syncretic institutions.[16] Thus, where others think in terms of
order and structure, we think in terms of assemblages and processes of
assembly. This entails empirical observation of three kinds of creativity:
making order, shoring it up, and smoothing over its messiness.

First, making order involves creative work. Actors are situated in political regimes, economic relations, cultural tropes, and identity patterns that
are not constraints, but raw materials for present action. Prior orders are
decomposable—we must take them apart, because "situations are never
twice the same,"[17] and so prior patterns of action never quite fit today's
challenges. Rummaging through a junkyard to find the right part, we turn
over and examine many raw materials, and as Claude Lévi-Strauss's *bricoleurs*,[18] we piece these together to fashion new solutions, which rearrange
the shape of order. We find precedent for this approach in Timothy Mitchell's account of the creative work behind the "appearance of order" in colonial Egypt;[19] in Crawford Young's dynamics of cultural pluralism, which
depend on "innovative acts of creative imagination" working with a "reper-
tory of social roles," to assemble many forms of cultural identity;[20] and in
Goran Hyden's peasants assembling a vibrant informal economy from old
"economies of affection" and new impersonal relations of contract.[21]

Second, order requires maintenance. This too is creative work, the production of new configurations from a repertoire of available resources. As
parcour makes a mangle of urban space, planners craft new channels for
skateboarders: metal knobs, railings, slicker concrete. Innovative use of tax

exemptions and revisions to the tax code are the same game of iterative creativity. Theorists of deliberative empowerment offer a similar argument: new institutions that fail when operated by the rules often succeed when opened up to tinkering from below by empowered creative actors. Archon Fung and Erik Olin Wright show this for community policing, public housing, and participatory budgeting.[22] Peter Evans extends the point to international development, highlighting the failure of "institutional monocropping" and the utility of open spaces for deliberative transformation.[23]

Finally, there is creative work in smoothing over and hiding the mess of assemblage. Failure to do so threatens the legitimacy of orders rooted in widespread geographical diffusion, evolutionary necessity, or hegemony. Hiding creative assemblage is work—ironically, a work of creative assemblage. Here we take inspiration from critiques of naturalized modernity: James Scott's state simplifications are smoothed over by high modernist ethos and authoritarian politics, which naturalize everyday, situational practices ("metis") that might otherwise foster alternate modernities.[24] James Ferguson calls development itself an "anti-politics machine," which (creatively) buried contestation under a façade of necessity.[25] Dominant accounts of the path-dependent nature of American politics require similar creative work to mask the intercurrent institutional layers identified by Karen Orren and Stephen Skowronek.[26]

Contributions to this volume expose the assembled nature of institutional orders. We question the naturalized origins of background conditions that others consider exogenous determinants of action. We unpack how they were made and maintained and their eclectic origins are masked. Our contributors describe assemblage in many ways: syncretic projects, discursive suturing, ecological play, the surprising agency of losers, the unexpected salience of memory, and the political work behind seemingly hegemonic outcomes. Despite these differences, we agree that it takes political creativity to make, maintain, and justify order.

Time

Once you attend to agency and change, questions of temporality come to the fore as acts of creativity entail loosening the grip of the past over the present. The generative capacity of political creativity, it seems, is intimately tied to a shift in temporal sensibility from one in which the past governs the present to one in which there is an unruly interplay between past, present, and future, making it impossible to confidently predict exactly which temporal frame will govern political action. Many of the cases explored below reveal a capacity for imagining new political formations through which the multiple and contested status of temporal norms becomes apparent. As Kevin Bruyneel argues in his chapter in this volume, those who set the clock establish the ground rules of political time. Consequently, those seeking change often contest the prevailing conceptions of time and time itself becomes the site of change.[27]

Contrast the notion of time offered here with views of periodization that infuse much historically oriented political science. Where periodization rests on sequentially ordered eras that are seen as coherent social formations (hence conceptions of the Jacksonian era or New Deal Order), political time mangles the grammar of past, present, and future, attending instead to an unexpected temporal interplay where possible futures rewrite the past. Traditions that are invented and originary status retrospectively claimed or conferred are part and parcel of the contestation of political authority in the present.[28] But more is at stake than notions of sequencing and time being out of joint. The assembled nature of all social formations further confounds orderly notions of change, as shifts from one era to the next rarely occur en masse, but rather are the products of continuous acts of *partial* appropriation and disaffection. What then counts as a political element available for reconfiguration? Can the elements be enumerated in advance? Politics is not particle physics; political elements are not waiting to be identified, but are themselves labile so that what constitutes an element changes over time. The only constant is that reconfigured pieces are always partial and incomplete. Which elements are in play at any moment can only be established through careful empirical research, attentive to the partial and relational nature of things.

Many scholars have been exploring temporality for decades: Raymond Williams raised the issue of the emergent in the 1970s, Judith Butler stressed the importance of holding open the sign queer in *Bodies That Matter*, Stephen Skowronek introduced the nonlinear conceptions of political time in his pathbreaking study of the American presidency; psychoanalysts Daniel Stern and Christopher Bollas have been rethinking psychoanalytic practice as being as rooted in the present and future as it is in the grip of the past; Deleuzians have been stressing lines of flight, while artists and designers have been attending carefully to creative acts of social innovation.[29] All break with linear conceptions of time to explore the ways in which the past is reshaped by the present. History itself is a political formation, shaped and reshaped through interpretation and contestation in the present. Thus, we follow William Faulkner: "the past is never dead. It is not even past." We turn our attention to the processes through which some elements of the past are kept alive, while others remain dormant, resulting in kaleidoscopic processes of change in which time becomes a site of the political rather than an organizing ground on which to stand.

Project Genealogy

We did not begin here. Our collaboration initially was animated by opposition to the lingering structuralism within historical institutionalism and political science. We assembled contributors who shared these concerns and who had reached beyond political science for resources to find ways forward. The path was far from clear. Many forays were undertaken, drawing on different intellectual traditions and geographically dispersed research sites.

Some of our contributors situate politics in language and adopt discursive analysis to make sense of innovative action. Others draw on ethnomethodology and constructivist traditions to sort out ongoing, yet partial, recompositions of narrative and meaning. In several chapters, postcolonial theory informs how creativity occurs through collective processes of remembering and remaking temporal orders. In another, ecological theory informs how plural institutional arrangements situate creativity. A subgroup of our contributors draws on pragmatism, in which context consists of a prior repertoire of socially shared habits, subject to creative recombination as actors deliberate on how to apply the past to changing situations of the present. They find in these traditions a variety of ways to pose novel questions about concrete political processes. How did professionals, with diverse national experiences, assemble a uniform international system of national accounts? How do economic actors in global supply chains innovate and learn? Why do political actors stitch together unlikely combinations of political symbols in ways that seem to fly in the face of conventional associations? What use do revolutions make of old regimes? What kinds of political problems call out for creative solutions?

While many of the contributors began their work with other issues in mind, we share an interest in rethinking the analytics of order, agency, and change. We encouraged open, messy exchange. We listened carefully and tried to unravel each other's key motifs: situation as raw material, cultural meaning as fluid medium of relation, time as political resource, and so on. We took pains to avoid a unitary theoretical framing, encourage dialogue during the editorial process, and provide space for alternative approaches to politics and institutions.

We gradually relinquished critique and turned to a positive research program. The pivot was a difficult one that challenged us to identify common analytical moves across this unruly group. The notion of political creativity captures the contributors' shared interest in the ways people decompose structures into raw material for new configurations of rules, roles, and routines. The subthemes of relationality, assemblage, and time identify the processes through which reconfigurations constantly occur.

Intellectual Neighbors

This volume is situated in a lively neighborhood of ideas and projects on the interaction among order, agency, and change. This district has good historic structures from which we take inspiration, on which we hope to build. Early works in the "new institutionalism," for example, aspired to rethink the relationship between institutional structure and human action. In a foundational work, and an obvious touchstone for this volume, Kathleen Thelen and Sven Steinmo presented institutionalism as a means to transcend the divide between old school structuralism (e.g., Marxism and modernization) and behavioralism.[30] James March and Johan Olsen pursued a similar project, embedding rationality and routine in context-specific logics of appropriateness and processes of experiential learning.[31] Paul DiMaggio and Walter Powell deployed concepts like habitus to understand how organizational structure and cognitive schemas set terms for action without determining its direction.[32] This relational ambition—the promise to explore "how a given institutional configuration shapes political interactions"—made early institutionalism exciting.[33]

As institutionalism evolved, the configurations gradually eclipsed interaction. Path dependency became dominant, helping analysts like Ruth and David Collier locate the critical junctures of labor incorporation that shaped regimes across Latin America[34] and Paul Pierson to theorize how national welfare states locked in diversity despite rational incentives to standardize.[35] Similarly, we learned how national varieties of capitalism persist, because institutional legacies shape incentive structures, firm behavior, and policy orientation.[36] Institutionalism became more a matter of describing the channels that delimited action, and less an account of how this conditioned the interaction of political projects. Change and agency turned out to be particular blind spots.[37] Skeptical of "voluntarist" accounts of agency, historical and sociological institutionalists found themselves ill equipped to explain upheaval, except in critical junctures. In historical, sociological, and rational choice institutionalism alike, lock-in proved an obstacle to understanding research that revealed enormous variability in on-the-ground practice, resulting in new efforts to theorize on-path change.[38]

In 1994, Karen Orren and Stephen Skowronek took a radical step in theorizing endogenous change when they invited students of American political development to move "beyond the iconography of order" to develop complex structural theories of institutions, which could handle more adaptive, routine processes of change. They offered their own theory—"intercurrence"—in which incongruous institutions, formed at different times for different purposes, collided in ways that opened opportunities for creative reconstruction.[39] For the most part, however, institutionalists have been much more reluctant to explore equally sophisticated theories of agency or approaches that circumvent the structure-agency distinction altogether. One exception is Skowronek and Matthew Glassman's recent edited volume, *Formative Acts*, which explores the role of entrepreneurship, leadership, and cultural contestation in American political development.[40] Even so, Skowronek and Glassman are cautious. They note that calls for an agency-based political science have been with us since Arthur Bentley's seminal 1908 work, *The Process of Government*. But they worry that realigning the study of American political development from structure to agency endangers progress in addressing the macropolitical "cultural, temporal, and systemic issues that have traditionally animated research" in this subfield. Indeed, while they acknowledge that Bentley might have been suspicious of the late twentieth-century turn to utilitarianism in political science, they argue that the trajectory from Bentley to rational choice theory is real. So while *Formative Acts* represents a body of work that is a necessary corrective to structuralist accounts of political development, its editors do not challenge the dualist foundations of the subfield.[41]

We think these arguments have not been pushed far enough. To clarify our differences with existing accounts, we discuss James Mahoney and

Kathleen Thelen's *Explaining Institutional Change* at some length.[42] Like us, Mahoney and Thelen question the neatness of punctuated equilibrium models. They, too, see that change is not just limited to critical junctures but can happen more incrementally. They recognize that institutions produce as much ambiguity, uncertainty, and room for innovative rearrangement as order and predictability. They sound like they belong in this volume, and in some ways, they do.

So what's the difference? How does an approach centered on political creativity differ from *Explaining Institutional Change*? Mahoney and Thelen remain committed to explaining change within a framework that makes structures themselves the determinants of agency, and sometimes metaphorical agents. We insist that there is no agency without agents. While structures matter a great deal, they require human agency to build, promulgate, and shore up. These are traceable empirical processes. We thus draw a contrast between a *structuralist* tradition, represented well by Mahoney and Thelen, and this volume. Whereas this volume theorizes the interplay between structure and agency, the tradition in which Mahoney and Thelen work subordinates agency and perturbation to structuralist explanation.

This becomes clear when we consider the four basic steps that make up their account of change. Step one: there are four identifiable patterns of institutional change—displacement, layering, drift, and conversion, identified in previous work by Wolfgang Streeck and Thelen.[43] Although excellent descriptions of the structural shape of changing institutions as agents refashion them, they do not capture every possibility. Moreover, as Mahoney and Thelen concede, many fit in one, big ambiguous box (conversion).

Step two: institutions are nested within other contexts, the structural features of which (veto points and discretion in enforcing rules) determine which of the four kinds of change will ensue. In this reductionist move, when institutional structures cannot explain change, scholars appeal to deeper structures, like constitutional order or the "power-distributional" context. Structure matters, we insist, but not in this anemic way. There is much more to context than veto points or an abstraction like discretionary opportunity. The contributors to this volume reveal a better way to appreciate the richness of structure: follow actors who use, dismantle, and reformulate it. In Ato Onoma's account of how losers unexpectedly reformulate Botswana's land boards, the veto structure changes over the life of the institution and, at any given moment, has very little to do with how actors play on and with these structures.

Step three: classify change agents in a five-part typology—insurrectionaries (think Lenin), parasitic symbionts (think Enron—or Spiderman), mutualistic symbionts (every tax filer who's ever bent the rules, but still pays), subversives (play by the rules but seek to change them from within), and opportunists (support or oppose rules depending on interest). It's wonderful to go beyond dichotomous characterizations of agency like winners and losers, to conceptualize compliance as a scalar variable, and open space for the empirical richness of life within institutions. But the new categories are ad hoc fixes appended to once-parsimonious structuralist theories to account for a proliferation of exceptions to orderliness. Institutional life and agency are too wily for these cages; the boxes are both too big and too small.

Too big: setting aside both formalistic descriptions of how people are supposed to behave in institutions, and formalized accounts of rational behavior, who is *not* a symbiont or an opportunist in making rules work in real life? What institution does not experience conversion, except in the reified designs of those who benefit from pretending institutions actually work as originally designed? A few of these categories capture an enormous range of transformation, because they are just too big.

Too small: oversized catchall boxes (conversion) sit next to much smaller cubbies. Insurrectionaries are a rare, if fetishized, type when we think about change. In this method, when structuralism repeatedly bumps into ill-fitting reality, the boxes proliferate and inevitably undermine the elegance of structural explanation itself.

Step four: correlate types of change agents with types of change (insurrectionaries produce displacement, and so on) and attribute causal relationships to veto points and discretionary opportunity: lots of veto points and discretion yields parasitic symbionts and drift, the opposite yields insurrectionaries and displacement. Here we see how Mahoney and Thelen represent the cutting edge, and strangely, the origins, of institutionalism. The real action shaping agency and channeling change into identifiable pathways lies not in the institutions themselves, but in political-distribution context and the wider veto structure. Institutionalism in political science was born in the 1980s out of frustration with interest-group politics, social structural analysis, and old-school emphasis on formal political structures. Although it has a shorthand new language of veto points and "context," we've come full circle, reading possibilities and types of agency from institutional structure, which in turn depends on interests and wider political context. Mahoney and Thelen give us at once the alpha and omega of structuralist institutionalism.

There is another way, and we offer it here. It's possible to engage the politics of institutions in a capacious manner, attending to their origins, promulgation, maintenance, and transformation, without resorting to multilayered matrices of increasingly complex structural conditions and unbalanced typologies, through which a proliferation of stylized forms of agency take place. Institutions are not such coherent structures, and by themselves, they have no agency. Because agency is not determined by structural openings, change is not limited to forms that fit the geometry of the structural gaps or rule ambiguities.

This demands a bit of a leap for institutionalists, but not a radical one. As Mahoney and Thelen so fully suggest, many scholars have been moving toward a more complex account of rules in use and have begun to acknowledge the innumerable ways people dodge, rework, and redefine rules and roles. Still missing is an account of institutions that forsakes the sharp distinction between rigid structures and constrained agents for a view that conceives both as part of an integrated field of creative action.

The emphasis in this volume on political creativity, relationality, assemblage, and time is neither a radical rejection of structure and the legacy of prior rules nor a swing to untrammeled imagination of new institutions by anyone, anywhere, anytime. This volume theorizes the complex interplay between creative agents and structural resources that give form to identities, institutions, and regimes. It emphasizes the ubiquity of transformative action, the complex incoherence of seemingly coherent institutional orders, and the fluid interweaving of past legacies, present action, and future possibilities inherent in political life. It makes a mangle of order, agency, and change, but a recognizable mangle subject to precise empirical study, description, and theorization.

Architecture of the Volume

The contributions to *Political Creativity* are organized in three parts: "Relationality," "Assemblage," and "Time." Although these themes are present in all of the chapters, we take editorial license to cluster them because authors probe political creativity with different inflections. Presenting these chapters through the themes of relationality, assemblage, and time highlights similar analytic moves that groups of contributors have found fruitful while nevertheless grounding each of these concepts in particular times and locales. We hope this double move of analytic abstraction and deep empirical engagement will advance research on political creativity.

Part I: Relationality

The four chapters in this part explore political creativity through relational processes. They demonstrate how institutions and identities are mutually constituted through complex and creative processes of negotiation, learning, coevolution, recomposition, and alignment. The authors show how transnational production systems, markets, and economic identities are formed simultaneously through interactive projects of creativity; how an American president is bequeathed experimental resources that he mobilizes and reconfigures for industrial renovation; how actors engaged in independent projects of political creativity make order and change simultaneously by aligning, adapting, and learning from one another's projects; and how the coevolution of complex social ecologies produces pressing problems that call out for political creativity, which sets those ecologies on new evolutionary paths. We will take up relationality again in a concluding chapter, which will contrast it to recent work on agency, entrepreneurship, and ideational innovation.

In Chapter 1, Gerald Berk and Dennis C. Galvan unpack their concept of creative syncretism by theorizing the relational processes by which people continually make institutional order and change. Creative syncretism insists that all institutions are made up of multiple features, which can be creatively decomposed and recombined. Berk and Galvan begin with two intuitively plausible observations. There is a difference between the way the weak and the powerful practice creative syncretism. There are different styles of creative syncretism: some are seat-of-the-pants, improvisational recombinations; others are carefully planned. They call the former "ramshackling" and the latter "engineering." Power and style are relational concepts. They describe not the features of people or projects, but the way people experience their relationships to institutions and to one another. While this two-by-two grid sounds like a causal matrix (predicting four types of stasis and change), the authors animate it by tracing the relationships between creative projects. For example, sometimes powerful engineers and weak ramshacklers learn from one another; and at other times, weak ramshacklers turn ad hoc projects into more systematic—engineered— recombinations. Berk and Galvan call the former process "learning" and the latter "repositioning." These are relational processes, which reassemble actors, reshape identities, and combine prior resources. They are illustrated with two empirical examples: the institutional politics of AIDS treatment in the United States and the relationship between the development of Islamic sects and the central authority in Senegal.

Whereas Berk and Galvan focus on the relationship between creative projects among institutional actors (the creative side of political creativity), Chris Ansell shifts the lens to the relationships that situate creativity. He finds in ecological theory a relational architecture to guide research on where to look for creativity and how to analyze it once you find it. Ecological explanation distinguishes the distribution, diversity, and relationality of actors, meanings, and resources. Explanation puts these relations in motion and traces the processes by which they transact.

In particular, Ansell thus finds in ecological theory's processual approach and relational architecture a method to identify zones of juxtaposition of diverse institutional contexts and systems. This "intermediary perspective," he writes, points to the spaces where actors emerge who have "an intermediary role in a chain of relations and [an] ability to arbitrate the relationships between other actors." These zones, where multiple logics, cultural tropes, or cognitive schemas interact, produce "problems that beg for resolution." Ansell demonstrates how ecological relationships situate processes of creative action in three cases: the rise of the Medici family's influence in Renaissance Florence, the relationship between trade unions and city politics in the late nineteenth century United States, and the historical relationship between rival socialists in the French labor movement.

Chapter 3 provides novel insights into globalization by tracing the interplay between multinational corporations and local Chinese subcontractors. Instead of positing a structural division of labor (multinational corporations design and Chinese firms manufacture) and asking how institutional and extra-institutional variables alter that relationship over time, Herrigel, Volker Wittke, and Ulrich Voskamp train their lens on the dynamic interplay of roles and practices. They discover a relationship in which mutual dependence and economic improvement has evolved from negotiated interaction and conscious design. Conceptualizing relational processes, rather than structural roles, they characterize the interplay between multinational corporations and Chinese firms by styles of learning. Early on, when Chinese manufacturers served as apprentices in corporate production systems, they learned *from* corporations of developed countries. Over time, as the Chinese transferred their skills to new markets and a domestic Chinese market emerged, multinational corporations and indigenous subcontractors began to learn *with* one another. Neither Chinese skills nor the domestic market are exogenous variables; instead they are understood as "emergent" relational processes. Skills were negotiated and a unique Chinese "middle market" was recomposed from corporations' home country products and Chinese needs. Increasingly dependent on local expertise and under relentless pressure to upgrade manufacturing and customize products, corporations recomposed formal production systems to learn *with* Chinese collaborators. Like the social theory that informs their narrative, Herrigel, Wittke, and Voskamp name these production systems "pragmatist" to capture the way they intentionally spark reflection, learning, and improvement through formal benchmarking, deliberation, and adjustment.

In Chapter 4, Stephen Amberg explains how President Barack Obama's auto bailout was a creative act situated in a long history of diverse institutions, fluid alliances, and experimental responses to pressing problems. In a debate dominated by free markets and government control, Obama opened novel possibilities for industrial restructuring by recomposing the official causes of the crisis and appointing a task force long experienced in reform. Amberg calls these actions "perlocutionary" because they persuaded industry actors to shift their focus from labor costs and public policy to manufacturing processes: lean production, labor management codetermination, and flexible manufacturing. While Obama's actions were innovative, they recomposed a relational process of reform that went back to the 1960s and 1970s when an alliance of labor, management, academics, consultants, bankers, and government officials began to experiment with industrial policy, comanagement, lean production, and team production. Always a weaker rival to industrial pluralism and southern unitary management, this assemblage of ideas, people, and practices evolved in the Treasury, universities, think tanks, reform unions, investment banks, and experiments like General Motors' Saturn Division. Seen in the context of an ongoing historical process of diverse social relations, Obama's perlocutionary and appointment acts were recombinatory, not revolutionary. They were acts of situated political creativity.

Part II: Assemblage

Chapters in this part accent the assembled and heterogeneous nature of apparent order. They highlight the political work of creative actors who draw on eclectic repertoires of institutional and cultural raw materials to configure new institutional arrangements, ensure their salience as conditions change, and bolster their legitimacy by covering their origins with the patina of evolutionary necessity. In African land law, American political consulting, post-Soviet labor relations, and global accounting norms, our authors' careful empirical work gives the lie to organic structure, agentless order, evolution, and hegemony. Recombinatory craft makes new institutions, even when they seem functionally necessary. Agents of many kinds—including losers—keep them stable and useful. Discarded, poached, or borrowed resources are the very stuff of the creative assemblage that we might mistake for irresistibly dominant or naturally emergent from deep infrastructural forces.

In Onoma's chapter on Botswana, land reform became institutionalized through unlikely means—it was precisely the fissures and ellipses that gave the reform its durability. While conventional accounts trace institutionalization to alignments of economic interest, state formation, or the structural imperatives of modernity, Onoma attributes the success of the land reform to the creativity of losers, from powerful traditional chiefs to ordinary peasants. Botswana's reform sought to equalize the distribution of land (a loss for chiefs) and clarify who has title to which fields (a loss for some peasants, a gain for others). But land boards rarely had adequate information to intervene effectively in localized disputes. After losing vast tracts, chiefs offered to serve as "counselors" to the land boards, enabling them to exert influence over land allocation and solidify social support for reform. When land boards demanded title documents from smallholders, many insisted they had been lost, destroyed, or improperly issued. Land boards acquiesced to what became known as "self-allocation"; in so doing they prevented an outright rejection of the reform as a whole.

Underneath the modernist, orderly patina of Botswana's land reform, Onoma reveals the assemblage of traditional pasts associated with chiefly authority and peasant customs. This kept losers engaged, but also made land boards far less coherent than one would expect from a textbook account of property. In the end, Onoma shows how assemblage was responsible for the success of land reform.

Adam Sheingate too looks beneath the patina of standard institutionalist narratives, which ignore the rise of consultants in the emergence of mass politics in a media age. By the 1941 New York mayoral race, "the father of spin," Edward Bernays, deployed surveys and sophisticated message targeting to ethnically fragmented populations in ways that set the terms for today's political consultancy. Sheingate details how this emerged not out of necessity or intentional design, but through Bernays's own ad hoc, politically creative combination of an early career in the theater, his anxieties about being dismissed as a huckster, his careful reading of Walter Lippmann, and his deployment of a family relationship to Sigmund Freud as justification of his status as a "social scientist." If we see this invention as the natural outgrowth of social change, or treat Bernays's creativity as a response to structural opportunities, we miss the full story of his assemblages, ingenuity, and interplay of temporalities.

Yoshiko Herrera uncovers similarly unexpected political creativity as she takes apart conventional accounts of the System of National Accounts (SNA), the global template for gathering and sharing national economic statistics. By the 1990s, a single accounting template had emerged for an increasingly uniform global economy, replacing the competing Cold War accounting conventions of the West and East. Conventional explanations emphasize how epiphenomenal structures (accountancy) came into alignment with causally significant structures (economic efficiency, material interests, or the power of major countries). Agency is in the structures themselves, or in forces that cause them to align. Herrera dismisses this story for invoking metaphorical agents and ignoring history. Like Sil, she shows how politically creative action in a disorderly and heterogeneous context goes back to the beginning of national accounting, whose origins lay in double-entry bookkeeping, Keynesianism, and Pavel Popov's 1926 interindustry tables for measuring Soviet output. Throughout the Cold War, accountants from both blocs met to plan harmonization of the two dominant and several minor systems. In the 1970s, Hungary produced a hybrid system, which informed the post–Cold War merger of the two systems under World Bank guidance.

Rudra Sil cracks open conventional accounts of passive labor unions in postsocialist Russia. His close examination reveals creative assemblage going back to the communist era, when the labor-state relationship changed from revolutionary watchdog to Stalinist transmission belt to de facto social contract swapping passivity for material benefits. In the post-Soviet era, union survival, not militancy, was the imperative. Creative action came in the form of demands that a new labor code include a minimum wage, guarantees against unfair dismissal, interest for delayed wages, and shop floor rights. Workers, who once benefitted from a communist-era material provision, reexpressed their expectations in the West European language of labor autonomy and social democratic bargaining. The resulting assemblage (Putin-era labor code) reflects creative rearrangements of historic and borrowed institutional resources, not structurally determined docility.

Today's global accounting system is an assemblage that bears the mark of creative action, incremental bargaining and tinkering, which began in the 1920s. Misread as a hegemonic norm, the work of assemblage and temporal interplay disappears between the surface of faux order and agentless evolution.

Part III: Time

Time, for the contributors here, is political. Historical narratives and assertions of causal sequence, claims to legacies and traditions, and acts of memory and disavowal all carry with them political consequences of profound proportions. Adherents to established order and those trying to reconfigure power relations frequently clash over questions of time. Whoever gets to set the clock goes a long way to establishing the political terrain.

Not surprisingly, the chapters in part three engage issues of time differently from each other. Victoria Hattam and Joseph Lowndes document the audacious license with which Condoleezza Rice and other Republican Party officials appropriated past civil rights struggles to authorize the war in Iraq, and in so doing sought to reconfigure the relation between race, party, and foreign policy in the United States. Notions of historical constraint and path dependence are inadequate for explaining Rice's efforts. Having grown up in Birmingham, Alabama, Rice actually knew the four girls killed in the Sixteenth Street Baptist Church bombing of September 15, 1963, and used her firsthand experience of political violence to create a connection between the civil rights legacy and Republican foreign policy in Iraq: we were not deterred by "home-grown terrorists" then, and should not be deterred by resistance in Iraq now. Thus, violence provides a hinge linking past and present—a way of suturing otherwise disparate political moments into an apparently continuous political tradition. This is a particularly vivid example of generative projectivity because of the ways it challenges the weight of the past. It also underscores the composite nature of political ideology and party identification in which multiple elements are sutured together into an apparently coherent political formation.

Bruyneel examines the deployments of time, calendars, and commemoration in U.S. indigenous and racial politics. He argues that one cannot understand African American and indigenous politics through a linear temporal framework, nor must we choose between amnesia and history. The remedy for forgetting is not simply to learn about the past. The past matters, but not simply as an unmediated prefiguring. Past and present, in Bruyneel's hands, are deeply entangled, and *how* we remember is what matters as it sets the ground for current and future political action.

Thus, national calendars and commemoration have great political significance, from the French Revolution's "Year 1" to 9/11. Every elite invocation of 9/11 marks a threshold of refounding for the U.S. social and political order—annual components of the habit-memories that shape citizens' relationship to statist power and national identity. Public commemoration also opens sites for alternative temporalities: Bruyneel unpacks a Wampanoag tribal leader's 1970 speech, banned by the authorities who planned the celebration of the 350th anniversary of the Pilgrims' landing, as a creative reconfiguration of memory that recast historic colonization, contemporary peoplehood, and future justice in ways that the authorities found too subversive to permit.

In the final chapter, Deborah Harrold explores political creativity through the reworking of Islam and economic liberalization in Algeria and Turkey. Rather than assuming a simple opposition between tradition and modernity, Harrold documents the complex interplay among community, identity, and economic change. Even under conditions of state-centered development and partial democratization, the reconfiguration of economic practices and Islamic identity is striking.

Contemporary Islamist politics in both societies reflects heterogeneous formations that bring together rural people, nonelite business interests, small entrepreneurs, and unemployed youth as well as Islamic activists from middle-class and professional backgrounds. These movements are philosophically rooted in nineteenth-century Islamic reformism, a series of creative efforts to meet the Western imperial challenge with an authentically Muslim approach to reason, political order, scientific inquiry, and economic dynamism. Today's Islamic politics in Algeria and Turkey draw from and adapt historic reformist ideas, making it possible to deploy Islamic claims on behalf of newly mobilized populations, especially as electoral practices have become more important in both countries. These movements are hardly fundamentalist efforts to challenge and supplant secular modernity. Through careful ethnographic and historical research, Harrold shows how creative practices have generated vibrant political organizations in which interests and identities are constituted through each other and forged into unexpected political alliances.

This pragmatic, pliable, creative recombination confounds most Western accounts of Islamic culture and politics that, all too often, are framed in globalizing and reductive terms. Rather than continually forcing our assessments of contemporary politics in the Islamic world into the simplistic categories of traditional and modern, we would do well, Harrold shows, to attend to the ways in which historic traditions are thoughtfully reconstituted, transformed, and made useful for projects of change associated with democratization and economic liberalization.

Beyond Disciplinary Divides

While all the chapters collected in this volume are written by political scientists who share a restlessness with structuralism in the discipline, the scholars gathered here aim for more than a parochial intervention in political science. We want intellectual engagement across the disciplinary divides set in place over one hundred years ago when the four classic social science disciplines (economics, anthropology, political science, and sociology) were founded. The intellectual wellsprings of political creativity come from far and wide; a robust research program around political creativity will be cut short as long as it is forced to live within the confines of political science. It is important to acknowledge the institutional constraints within which we work as well as to think of ways to reconfigure our disciplines and our research. Much interesting work has been done on the formation of the social science disciplines, perhaps as a prelude to reworking this same terrain.[44]

How then did the social science disciplines form? Economics was first out of the gate with the national association being established in 1885, followed in short order by anthropology in 1902, political science in 1903, and sociology in 1905. By the first decade of the twentieth century, then, the broad parameters of the social science disciplines were set in place and they remain there to this day. Moreover, the intellectual divisions established at the turn of the last century were rather simple: economics was given authority over questions of economic growth and inequality, anthropology held sway over matters of foreign cultures, sociology's terrain was contemporary societies in the West, while political science was the established authority over power and the state. One might quibble with the phrasing, and note that some disciplinary boundaries have shifted to incorporate new territories, while still appreciating the ways in which the disciplinary cores have proved remarkably resilient. Almost all social scientists continue to work within and struggle against these intellectual boundaries. This intellectual geography is crippling. It forecloses innumerable lines of argument through the creation and maintenance of long-standing disciplinary divides. Students who stray too far afield from the core areas of any program are quietly taken aside and asked if they might not be happier in some other building. The policing of disciplinary boundaries is quiet but persistent. Only the brave at heart stray too far off the grid.

To be sure, there have been important boundary crossings over the last half century: cultural studies, historical sociology, historical institutionalism, feminism and race studies, and rational choice all have traversed multiple fields in innovative ways. In many academic institutions, new programs have been added, syllabi revised, and even fields created (gender studies, critical race theory, rational choice, and behavioral economics come to mind). Despite these efforts at forging cross-disciplinary connections, the disciplines themselves have remained remarkably robust. None have collapsed altogether and no new disciplines have replaced those set in place in the decades bracketing the turn of the previous century.

Political Creativity brings together essays from scholars who have worked outside the order of things for decades. All have attempted to understand specific political problems and questions by roaming far and wide across the disciplines. Most have remained sequestered in small ponds nurtured by adventurous institutions and friends. What is special about the collaboration gathered here is the fact that it brings together a remarkably dispersed group of scholars. Putting the volume together has been an exciting endeavor as synergies and intellectual threads have emerged across our heterogeneous group once the various projects were brought into a sustained conversation. An amplification of the underlying theoretical dilemmas and possible paths forward emerged from the multiyear exchanges that preceded the volume, which allowed us to see larger patterns. The sinews running across the chapters are strong. Attending to the lines of argument around relationality, assemblage, and time opens the way to new analyses of politics unfettered by the strictures of disciplinary divides yet linked through broad intellectual commitments.

Scholars from adjacent social science disciplines will no doubt find that the essays gathered here bear the mark of their specific disciplinary formation even as they strive to move beyond its limitations. Although the chapters remain rooted in their disciplines, we hope that our larger ambition of rethinking the artificial divides that plague the social sciences will resonate with those working in other fields. The precise form of the intellectual reimaging taking place within other disciplines will vary from that explored here, since it will be shaped by the local terrain and the quite particular frustrations and opportunities of their specific locations. Additional encounters reaching across the disciplines are needed to identify points of resonance and disagreement. We hope that this volume might prompt future exchanges.

PART I

Relationality

Chapter 1

Processes of Creative Syncretism

Experiential Origins of Institutional Order and Change

Gerald Berk and Dennis C. Galvan

In this chapter, we argue that the origins of both institutional order and change lie in human creativity. In a previous article, we looked at institutions from the inside out.[1] From that perspective, we showed how people experience institutional rules as bundles of resources available for creative reinterpretation and recombination. We called this process "creative syncretism" and conjectured that it produced institutional order and change simultaneously. In this work, we unpack creative syncretism by conceptualizing the interplay among creative projects undertaken by the powerful and the weak in the name of both seat-of-the-pants problem solving and grand institutional engineering. To make sense of these processes, we need only be careful empiricists, tracing the minute pathways people leave as they respond to one another's creativity.

To facilitate this work, we imagine a spatial grid (or a two-by-two table if you prefer; see Figure 1 below), with people's perceived power to tamper with institutional rules or schemas on the vertical axis, and their purposes in tampering with rules on the horizontal. By role, right, education, or circumstance, some believe they have the privilege to tinker with rules or prior practices. Others perceive messing with the rules or past practices as audacious. Privilege and power anchor the top end of the vertical axis, audacity and weakness the bottom. Regardless of the degree of power, some creative actions are improvised in the moment, while others have a broader agenda of social promulgation. Building on similar conceptualizations in organization theory and anthropology, we call the former "ramshackling"

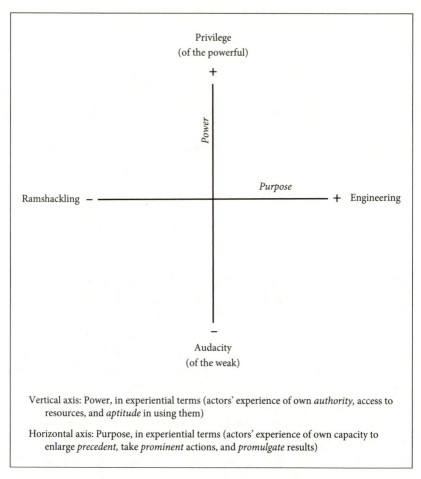

Figure 1. Imaginary grid for mapping creative projects. The vertical axis
shows people's perceived power to tamper with institutional rules, the
horizontal their purposes in tampering with rules.

and the latter "engineering." This grid or two-by-two space, then, is a nice
tool for visualizing a variety of creative projects according to who engages
in them (the powerful or the weak) and what they think they are doing
(ramshackling or engineering).

Like most two-by-two tables, this one is too rigid and static. It's an
imaginary grid, so we ought not make too much of its lines and orderly
right angles. Its true value emerges only when careful empirical work

"animates" the grid. Actors and their creative projects don't sit neatly and permanently in their proper classificatory quadrants. They engage the creativity of other actors. Creativity changes who we think we are, what we think we're doing, and for whom we do it; and so actors shift positions. Tracing this process on the grid involves drawing lines of interplay that cut across quadrants, transgressing boundaries of classification with lines of unexpected connection and transformation. If we trace the interplay of creative projects with care, the grid ends up covered with scribbles. Scribbles are in fact the point. For us, the purpose of a two-by-two table is not to isolate the interaction between causal variables. It is to imagine a space, where we can track the minute and grand forms of interplay among diverse acts of creativity, which, together, produce institutional change and order.

The empirical illustrations we've selected for this essay showcase three forms of interplay among creative projects, which we call "alignment," "learning," and "repositioning." These are relational concepts, which describe how people make institutions by responding to one another's creativity. Sometimes they align multiple creative projects to form novel combinations. At other times, they observe and analyze the work of others and adapt their own compositions in light of what they learn. They also reposition themselves, stepping out of familiar roles and power relations to act as if they have more (or less) skill, authority, and impact than they are supposed to have.

As we have argued elsewhere and in the introduction to this volume, this is quite different from a structuralist account of institutional change. Where structuralists catalog the mechanisms by which people break or alter rules and identify exogenous variables to explain them, we argue that change is a constant artifact of living in and through rules. Seen from the inside—experientially—life in institutions entails ongoing adaptation, tinkering, and retrofitting to keep the rules relevant to the ongoing flow of circumstance. This does not mean that we think that people reconstruct institutions at will—"voluntarism"—or that there is nothing to say other than all the world is in flux. Rather, existing rules, roles, expectations, and traditions matter a great deal—as a repertoire of raw material for tinkering, for not just playing by or against the rules but playing *with* them. Likewise, we find similar creative action behind the orderly, organic, or hegemonic quality of institutions. It takes imaginative, recombinatory tinkering to design, promulgate, and maintain structural order, especially as practice runs far afield of institutional plan. So in this chapter, we insist that a full-spectrum account of institutional order and change carefully traces interwoven projects of human creativity, some by elites, some by the weak, some in the service of improvisation, some for the sake of engineering.

We explore these processes of creative syncretism in five sections. First, we review our earlier work on creative syncretism. Second, we lay out the conceptual underpinnings for our account of privilege and audacity, ramshackling and engineering, mobilizing the work of John Dewey, Michel de Certeau, Claude Lévi-Strauss, and Karl Weick. We then present the imaginary grid as a space for tracking the interplay of processes of creative syncretism. Fourth, we demonstrate how this approach opens novel lines of research using empirical cases from the United States and the developing world: the struggle of AIDS activists to reform federal drug-testing policy in the 1980s, and the shift from confrontation to accommodation between Islamic jihad movements and the colonial state in west Africa. In conclusion, we note how a focus on the interplay of creative projects offers a unified means to make sense of order and change, at the same time rendering institutional analysis more deeply empirical, and more attuned to overlooked forms of political conflict.

What Is Creative Syncretism?

Creative syncretism is a theory of institutional diversity and change. We argue that both are constants. We need not look to historical conjunctures to account for change or at the disordering aspects of history, politics, or conflicts over authority to make sense of institutional diversity. Instead, we begin with a theory of institutions, which makes diversity central to the account of all institutions and makes change a constant feature of institutional action.

Institutions, we hypothesize, are always internally diverse, because they are composed of an indefinite number of features, whose relationship is always being renegotiated. Whether institutions are defined as combinations of rules, taken-for-granted principles, cognitive schemas, or routines, we think it is a mistake to identify particular institutions as comprising a finite set of complementary features. Instead, institutions are better understood as composed of an indefinite number of rules or routines, only some of which are in use at any time. Moreover, we argue that the principles of complementarity are always controversial. There is no single metaprinciple that guides their use or configuration determinately.

To be sure, we also note that not all features or their configurations are up for grabs at any point. Drawing from John Dewey, we argue that actors within institutions settle on "habits," which guide the choice and form of institutional rules or governing principles.[2] But habits, Dewey argues, never determine action, because they are multiple and incongruous and never cover all of experience. Therefore, people inevitably run into problems that habits cannot solve. When they do, they "deliberate." Deliberation, we argue, is a creative act—not readily captured by typical theories of institutional action, such as utilitarian calculation, rule following, or cognitive mapping. Instead, we argue that creative action has three characteristics: (1) it is situated within contexts that provide raw materials, (2) it transforms existing raw materials and contexts through deliberative recombination, and (3) it is a social process with a narrative quality.

First, like institutions, habits are multiple, partial, incomplete, and overlapping. They are not "routines," because no single prior habit or resolution is fully applicable to new circumstances, which constitute new puzzles about "what to do." Moreover, the repertoire of habits is unstable and indeterminate in scope and content. We constantly learn new habits from other locales and times, and add new resolutions to the repertoire with each new action. Habits are the raw material for creativity.

Second, actors *transform* old habits and create new ones through deliberative recombination. We work through in our creative imagination how features of many old habits appear partially relevant to a task at hand.[3] There are no perfect fits. But because habits are decomposable, we use their parts as raw materials to piece together innovative solutions. These are new or recombinant habits. When we act, we also simultaneously craft new or recombined habits in a single motion of creative syncretism. New recombinant habits become the raw material for the next round of problem solving. As a result, transformation happens all the time in creative action.

Third, creative action is sociable and has a narrative quality. Even individual deliberation is social. As George Herbert Mead established, this means that our reflective imagination has a social filter from the very moment we learn to act: we consider possible lines of action and craft new ones in light of how we think others will assess actions, and how they will assess us.[4] Put another way, we make sense of who we are and how we are situated in the social world through narrative. While temporal, our story lines are never linear or determined by the past. Instead, as we craft real resolutions to practical problems, we contribute concrete episodes and vignettes to new, unfolding tales about others and ourselves. Story making underscores the inherent sociability of action: contributing to shared story lines offers meaning that is at once individual (my character acts) and social (my character acts in a tale connected to the actions and reactions of others). Because these story lines are constitutive of cultural meaning, creative action as we understand it is always a cultural process.

In summary, institutions are combinations of an indefinite number of features, and action within and upon institutions is creative. Together we call this account of institutional diversity and change "creative syncretism." This chapter takes a next step by exploring who engages in creative syncretism, to what end, and with what results in terms of the rolling interaction of multiple creative projects.

Setting Up the Imaginary Grid

Pragmatist accounts of creativity date from a period when new institutions of industrial-age modernity were beginning to regularize politics, the economy, and social life. With the midcentury rise of mass media, consumerism, propaganda, and institutionalized conformity, it became easy to treat Deweyan creativity as a fading remnant of a previous age. Dewey theorized the marginalization of deliberative creativity. For him, authoritarian education could teach people to voluntarily surrender their capacity to tinker and instead follow custom, dogma, fashion, or rules bequeathed to them by authoritative sources. Dewey saw this as unusual, exceptionable, and preventable through rigorous critique of educational hierarchies, mindless memorization, and unreflective fealty to orthodox truths.

By the mid-twentieth century, though, Dewey's feared outcome appeared normal. In Weberian terms, legal rationalism had mutated into an iron cage of procedure, domesticating charisma and truncating innovation. Put in a Foucauldian way, modernity entails intricate schemas of disciplinary procedures, regularizing attitudes and dispositions, down to the very movement of the body and orientation of the spirit at work and in play, from sunup to sundown. For contemporary political scientists, large-scale twentieth-century organizations (bureaucratic state, capitalist market, consumption-mediated social and familial world) came to manage mass, heterogeneous societies through a proliferation of standardized codes, roles, and routines. Once, these were understood through grand theories of economic infrastructure or the progressive march of modernization and rationalization. Institutionalism was born from the ruins of such macro-explanation, as a means to nevertheless capture the regularities of human life and the mechanisms that ordered and directed behavior.

Although order and routine seemed ubiquitous, they were never completely rigid or totalizing. Situationists and surrealists defiantly maintained practices of creativity in the face of the industrial regularization of human life.[5] From defense ministries to multinational corporations, managerial elites improvised when routines failed to contain practice.[6] Workers deployed "work to rule" as institutional cannibalism—if order is so complete and rules so determinatively accurate, see what happens when we follow them all, to the letter.[7] Likewise, peasants and the poor found ways to circumvent and redirect even the most ambitious projects of social planning.[8] In the 1970s and 1980s Michel de Certeau interrupted this account of modernity in a way that echoes, and updates, Dewey on creativity. Within what he calls the "strategic" action of totalizing, modern structures, Certeau recognizes that everyday life entails a capacity for disruptive "tactical" action, a function of "consuming," using, and inhabiting these orders.[9] Certeau's strategic action originates from a "spatial position," a place of power. It establishes a sense of the "proper" and seeks to spatially expand that notion of a normative social and cognitive order. Such institutional orders achieve a "triumph of place over time" by organizing the physical arrangement of action in ways that produce approved sequences of behavior and associated forms of consciousness (suburban home for rest and reproduction, freeway for morning transit, office cubicle for production, Starbucks for break, couch 1.5 meters from screen for two to three hours' daily distraction before rest, motorboat out front, reservoir nearby, and chain brewpub or sporting venue at hand for two-day pause from regular schedule). The result is the regularization of sequences of sanctioned behavior, producing a sense of normality and conditioning desire into strategically useful patterns of behavior and life expectation. At the edges of such orders, cranks and artistes occasionally surface with troubled, David Byrne–style questions ("You may ask yourself, well, how did I get here?"). But more often than not, they fade off into their own muted acquiescence ("Same as it ever was"), or meet with casual dismissal.

For Certeau, the cranks are on to something fundamental about how human beings live in and alter totalistic, ordering structures. Even in the most banal acts of consumption (watching television) or seemingly repetitive tasks (commuting, cooking, reading), Certeau identifies an artistry to everyday life, a transformative potential he captures under the label "tactics." Tactical action is creative, improvisational, and transformative, but does not originate from a place of organized power nor seek to establish a heterodox version of a "proper" grid. Instead, tactics poach on strategic institutional orders through guile, wit, and play. In tactical action, we draw on memory—repertoires of past styles and actions—to craft novel actions, compressing and redeploying time to subvert and punctuate a proper spatial order.

Tactics give everyday action its artistry, whether we notice or not. When cooking, even when we think we follow recipes closely, we make subtle alterations with each preparation. When walking in a city, we trace out meandering pathways—drawn here to a storefront window, there to a friendly dog—deforming the grid-like map of authorized pedestrian passage. When we read, we rarely proceed as the author intended, from first to last page, but skim and jump. Our minds wander and we make mental associations to past memories and present moods, so that with each reading we produce in our minds a novel version of any text. When at work, we engage in *la perruque* (the wig): "A worker's own work disguised as work for his employer . . . [it] may be . . . a secretary's writing a love letter on 'company time' or . . . a cabinetmaker's 'borrowing' a lathe to make a piece of furniture for his living room. . . . In the very place where the machine he must serve reigns supreme, he cunningly takes pleasure in finding a way to create gratuitous products whose sole purpose is to signify his own capabilities through his *work* and to confirm his solidarity with other workers or his family *spending* his time in this way."[10]

La perruque is a "coup"—the worker "puts one over" on the employer. Yet for those who look to Certeau for a new blueprint for revolution, tactics have been wrongly dismissed as inconsequential. He calls them, after all, "makeshift things . . . composed of the world's debris." Regarding tactical action, he notes famously, "what it wins it cannot keep." The secretary's love letter or the cabinetmaker's chair built from scraps on company time do not rewrite the rules of employment. But they do effect change, by introducing "things *extra* and *other* into the accepted framework, the imposed order." As a result, "the surface of this order is everywhere punched and torn open by ellipses, drifts, and leaks of meaning: it is a sieve-order."[11]

Like Dewey's account of habit, Certeau's account of strategy and tactics in modern institutions alerts us to the ways in which rules never discipline all experience and experience overflows schemas. In this more complete picture, people live in institutions tactically—opening tears and fissures, which become part of a repertoire of memories available for additional tactics. But as far as Certeau's distinction between strategy and tactics goes in helping us to unpack creative syncretism (and theorize an imaginary grid), we refine his framework in three ways.

First, we insist that tactical, creative tinkering occurs at all levels of institutional life, not just from below. It can be found in the design, promulgation, and most critically the maintenance of institutional orders. Second, we build on the ubiquity of tactical, creative action to explore an interplay of creative processes, disaggregated not by actor, but by how powerful people think they are, and what they think they are doing, when they act creatively. Third, by focusing on the interplay of all creative projects—not just tactical actions by the weak—we can provide a more complete and consistent account of institutions, in which creativity is the constant source of both order and change.

Certeau differentiates strategies as *organizational* action and tactics as *individual* behavior ("a collective mode of administration and an individual mode of reappropriation").[12] We insist that strategic order never happens without managers, architects, planners, and institutional designers who act creatively, just like anyone else. They too mobilize memory, recombine resources, and engage in guile, wit, and play *in the service of* building, maintaining, and elaborating proper relationships in spatial grids. They act like Claude Lévi-Strauss's engineers, who "subordinate each [task] to the availability of raw materials and tools conceived and procured for the purpose of the project." In contrast, the *bricoleur* "makes do" with whatever "oddments" are "at hand."[13] Both are creative actors. Both must find new ways to rearrange the "raw materials" bequeathed by history, context, and culture. While the bricoleur rummages and manages with found objects, the engineer "is no more able than the 'bricoleur' to do whatever he wishes when he is presented with a given task. He too has to begin by making a catalogue of a previously determined set consisting of technical and practical knowledge, of technical means, which restrict the possible solutions."[14] The difference lies in the fact that the engineer proceeds from an end goal or abstract design to "question the universe," and "work by means of concepts," "trying to make his way out of and go beyond the constraints imposed by a particular state of civilization."[15]

We thus borrow Lévi-Strauss's *engineering* to describe creative action in the service of making and maintaining a strategic order. But we separate engineering as purpose from engineering as fixed social role. Engineering is not merely the domain of the educated and powerful, bricolage (ramshackling) the domain of "savages." Rather, as in Figure 1, we insist that the weak and powerful (vertical axis) both ramshackle and engineer (horizontal). We resist the tendency in Lévi-Strauss, Certeau, and most institutional theory to collapse the axes in Figure 1 and imagine that the only meaningful quadrants are the upper right (engineering in service to order by the powerful) and lower left (ramshackling in service to an ephemeral coup by the weak).

This is consistent with work in organization theory on innovation. Karl Weick has shown that sometimes the most effective managers choose bricolage over planning—they improvise combinations of organizational resources to innovate new products, manufacturing processes, or marketing strategies.[16] In practice, managers "design" by "improvisation" rather than plan, following flexible "recipes," not detailed "blueprints." Like jazz musicians or improvisational actors, Weick's managers act in the moment; only in retrospect do they name and formalize what they've done. In Figure 1, the powerful engage in ramshackling (upper left quadrant) in the normal course of doing their jobs.

Similarly, the weak do not just ramshackle; they also engineer. For example, they leverage bonds of trust into informal revolving credit schemes: a half dozen friends or relatives pitch in a few dollars a month, and every month another participant takes the pot to buy something. Sometimes community organizations or local nongovernmental organizations extrapolate informal arrangements into village- or neighborhood-wide systems, with explicit rules, officers, and procedures.[17] The weak thus move revolving credit from ramshackling (lower left) to engineering (lower right).

We have thus drawn from Dewey an account of the underlying creativity of human action. In Certeau, we found an update of Dewey, which shows how everyday creativity remains possible, indeed, ubiquitous, even in the context of high modernism and extensive institutionalization. Lévi-Strauss reminds us that artistry is not the province of the weak but also an ongoing process of making and remaking order. Finally, Weick helps distinguish the power of actors from the kind of creativity in which they engage. The result is a spatial diagram on which it is possible to begin to think more comprehensively about institutional life, the origins of change, and the work needed to make and maintain order.

Creativity on an Imaginary Grid

We conceptualize processes of creative syncretism spatially, on an imaginary grid, which situates people's experience of institutions, understood as bundles of rules, practices, and meanings, in two ways. First, we ask what people think they are doing when they act creatively and thus tamper with rules, roles, and order. They may be solving a problem in the moment for themselves, or they may be trying to reorder things in ways that affect many others. Then we ask who people think they are when they take it upon themselves to act creatively and tamper with rules, roles, and order. People may be audaciously grabbing things they are not authorized to touch, or they may be leading, as leaders ought. The answer to the first question tells us something about the intent and the extent of creative action (am I doing this just for myself and the problem right at hand, or do I have a wider social agenda?). The answer to the second question gets at questions of power. Consistent with our pragmatist and constructivist commitments, these are experiential, not structural, accounts of purpose and power.

On the left side of the horizontal axis, we have improvisation in the moment to help resolve a particular task at hand, without the intent to produce something socially meaningful or transformative. Consistent with Dewey's account of action, Certeau's tactics, and Lévi-Strauss's bricolage, we all sometimes reach for resources at hand and recombine them in an ad hoc, seat-of-the-pants manner to produce a new solution, a new pathway for action. We call this ramshackling. (*Bricolage*, a term that we employ synonymously with *ramshackling*, might for some readers carry Lévi-Strauss's savagery-civilization dichotomy. For Anglophone readers, ramshackling also marks a clearer contrasting metaphor with engineering.) It entails a low sense of *precedent* (is my action part of some continuity with the past?), agnosticism with regard to *prominence* (will others notice what I'm doing right now, in the present?), and limited concern for *promulgation* (can I extend this action to affect what others do?). Ramshackling, consistent with James Scott's *metis*, involves the inductive derivation of technique through actual experience.[18]

"Sense" of precedent, prominence, and promulgation is not reducible to subjectivity. These are matters of relational experience, both our relation with the resources at hand that make up any institution and our relations with other people in an institutional context. When we ramshackle, our handling and use of the resources shape creative solutions: think of Dewey's mason learning what the stone will permit that mason to craft, or Weick's jazz musician gaining a feel for the improvisations made possible by melody, the range and styles of the other musicians, and the responses of the audience.[19] In ramshackling, social relations are horizontal, open, and agnostic. I know others are watching when I ramshackle, but I'm not trying to convince them or change what they do. I produce an "offer," which they may pick up, appreciate, use, or simply ignore.

By contrast, we sometimes engineer, coming to novel situations with a sense that our creative actions are not just for ourselves but for others. Our actions are part of an ongoing trajectory from the past, which others should and will notice, and we believe that the products of our creativity ought to be extended in wide social terms (high sense of precedent, prominence, and promulgation). Engineering combines our basic model of creativity with the conceptualization, scripting, and schematization so central to sociological institutionalism. Engineering, like Scott's *techne*, involves the deductive planning of technique, necessitating systematic reflection and the deliberate evaluation of the nature and results of experimentation.

As in Lévi-Strauss, when we engineer, we relate to the resources by way of planning and prior vision. Our social experience is both more hierarchical and more projective, tuned into questions like who can my actions affect and to what end? To what extent do I need others in order to do what I want? Who will stand in my way, sanction me, or reward me?

To be sure, ramshackling and engineering are ideal types, rarely represented in the world in pure form. And so we conceive of them on a continuum, representing the purposes of creative syncretism, depicted on the horizontal axis in Figure 1.

On the vertical axis, we also conceptualize power experientially (not structurally). We want to know not how formal rules or taken-for-granted schemas allocate power, but what sorts of questions people ask about rules and schemas and how the answers to those questions reveal their experience of who they think they are to be messing with the rules. Think of this as the privilege-audaciousness scale. At the top end, some people perceive that they—as a result of education, status, or social role—are *authorized* to tinker with, revise, and change rules. They believe they have full *access* to the rules in use, those not in use, and others only envisioned. And they are convinced that they have the *aptitude* to handle the rules and other institutional resources, to recombine them in new ways, or to try to maintain them in familiar form. This is not just what they perceive, but how they approach the rules that make up any institution, and how, as a result, they engage others within an institutional field from a position of de facto, taken-for-granted authoritativeness.

But at the bottom of this scale, when people act creatively, this is audaciousness. These are people who do not normally think they should touch institutions, don't know all their elements, and are not qualified to handle the raw materials of institutions or redesign them (low authority, access, and aptitude). When these people act creatively, it's reasonable to ask, "who the hell are they to be messing with the rules?"

This is self-perception intertwined with and discovered through experience, through concrete questions about the relationship between the prior repertoire of practices, habits, or rules and their current situation. These questions, and their answers, have narrative content and help establish roles in experiential and changeable terms. Can I get away with typing a love letter on company time? No one's looking, so I can act audaciously. Should I use my tacit knowledge to rebuild this engine or follow the rules in the repair manual? I'm still saving money by doing it myself, so what the hell, I'll improvise. As Dewey says, the environment intrudes in the answers to questions about skill, about who is authorized to do what.

This grid is a starting point, a space on which to trace out the interplay of creative projects. It is in the interaction of those creative projects, in chains of cumulative, iterative creativity that we find robust accounts of how institutions remain stable and change.

Interplay of Creative Projects

At its most fundamental level, interplay flows from the social, shared quality of the raw materials (the repertoire) that make up any institution. When I act in or on an institution, I make new use of and alter that institution's repertoire of raw materials. When you act subsequently, you draw on this repertoire of raw materials, already altered by my action. Creative projects are thus linked in cumulative chains of recombination and transformation.

Tracing these chains out on the Figure 1 diagram produces lines of genealogical connection, many of them. In this volume, Yoshiko Herrera shows how Hungarian statisticians mixed Soviet and Western systems of national accounting to create their own new protocol for gathering and reporting data. Hungarian innovations were later folded into the UN's official post–Cold War global system of statistical standards, producing a traceable, cumulative chain of creativity.

Building from this basic insight, we identify three specific forms of interplay: alignments, learning, and repositioning. These are not the only possible forms of interplay. Nor are they intended as a typology of ideal types, which produce a range of institutional outcomes. Creative projects interact in sui generis ways in the life of particular institutions. When focused on creative action, the goal of institutional analysis is to produce empirically rich accounts of exactly how institutions emerge, persist, change, and decline by tracing the combination of creative acts that drive institutional life, not to build universal models of the effects of creativity on institutional change.

Alignments occur when actors recognize one another's similar or mutually supportive creative projects. Regardless of the relative power of actors or the goals of creativity, actors may perceive in the creative tinkering of others efforts similar to or supportive of their own endeavors. Political alliances are thus more the result of complementarities between creative endeavors than a function of structural position, identity, or a calculation of interests. In a strikingly surprising example of alignment, recounted in the following section, the U.S. Food and Drug Administration (FDA), which was in the midst of an engineered neoliberal reform, aligned itself with AIDs activists who ramshackled treatment, experimentation, and monitoring from whatever resources they could find. The result was to dramatically alter FDA research protocols and to open regulatory procedure to participation from below by "lay experts."

A second form of interplay involves learning. Many actors in the examples below learn from the creative efforts of others. They observe, compare, take inspiration, and evaluate. This is not mimesis, but genuine social learning, because each instance involves tinkering in novel ways with newly configured resources. Each time creative actors learn they reevaluate their own actions in light of their observations of the creative actions of others. The second case below shows French imperialists learning from Muslim activists: colonial officials vehemently opposed a new Sufi order (Mourides) and sent its founder into exile. Eventually, they learned that a spirituality of hard work was central to Mouridism, and could dovetail with the colonial imperative to increase cash crop (peanut) production. Over time colonial administrators and Mouride leaders aligned their creative projects into a regime of collaboration.

Finally, actors themselves change position or move across the quadrants in Figure 1. Today's ramshacklers become tomorrow's engineers when they recognize that new forms of creativity are possible. Elites who can't fully reconfigure roles or rules may take gains where they find them, through ramshackle improvisation in the moment. This is nonteleological change: there is no necessary evolution from mere ramshackling to more consequential engineering. People move in both directions. Like alignments and learning, repositioning helps account for a particular configuration at any particular time. For example, early AIDs activists were not merely weak ramshacklers, they were criminals who smuggled medicines across the Mexican border and turned large-scale clinical drug trials on their heads. Within less than a decade, many had become "lay experts," who were integrated into the formal, engineering procedures of FDA licensure. The Mouride founder had been a minor cleric, a ramshackler of new interpretations of Islam. Mass conversion by animists turned him into an engineer and Mouride dominance of the peanut economy made him a powerful one.

Illustrations of Interplay

Order and Change in AIDS Research and Treatment

Steven Epstein's study of the politics of AIDS treatment provides an excellent example of the interplay of forms of creative syncretism.[20] He shows how the weak and dying cobbled together a heterodox treatment program from whatever resources they could find. They frayed the dominant institutional practices of pharmaceutical research and regulation. Instead of responding with bureaucratic intransigence or the enforcement of existing rules, the Food and Drug Administration learned from activists and aligned its own creative project with community research from below. The FDA reengineered its authority by opening its doors to participation by "lay experts" and by setting aside large-scale randomized drug trials in favor of learning by monitoring individual treatments. Epstein concludes that creativity, conflict, and interplay did not end with the FDA's realignment, as scientists and activists alike attacked the new procedures for polluting good science and coopting spontaneous action from below.

As the AIDS epidemic began in the early 1980s, treatment was governed by the rules and roles of institutionalized research. Under supervision by the FDA, research scientists in the dominant pharmaceutical companies enlisted physicians to conduct large-scale, multisite randomized clinical trials of new medications. In principle, randomly chosen control groups and randomly administered placebos allowed researchers to isolate the effects of various medications on the progression of the disease and the FDA to make scientifically authoritative decisions.

But AIDS treatment did not follow this or any other institutionalized script. The disease became highly politicized in the 1980s. The evangelical right condemned it as "God's plague" set upon sinning homosexuals. ACT UP (the AIDS Coalition to Unleash Power) became famous for its cultural antics: die-ins, spilling blood on the steps of the FDA, and unfurling campy banners at baseball games ("no glove, no love"). New creative projects, and resulting repositioning, realignment, and mutual learning among creative actors, altered research and treatment in profound ways. This changed the spatial allocation of proper roles for patients, regulators, corporations, and physicians.

The process began with ramshackling among the weak. It was not organizational or movement activists but people with AIDS who looked on with skepticism and rage at the clinical trial processes for new medications. It would be years until drugs became widely available, while gays and lesbians stood by and watched one another die at the hands of a medical establishment and a government that had long stigmatized their sexuality. When they discovered in early 1985 that experimental drugs were available in the *farmacias* of Mexican border towns, "smugglers" began to import them. Their goal was not profit, but distribution, experimentation, and seat-of-the-pants evaluation. "We don't know for sure how these drugs will work," a prominent smuggler told San Francisco's gay community, "but it makes more sense than the next best thing, which is dying without trying anything."[21]

"Buying clubs" emerged in cities where gays had a history of gathering in bars, bathhouses, and political sites. They quickly became places to exchange not only medications but also information. In "guerilla clinics" from San Francisco to New York, people with AIDS began to conduct community-based research of their own. They exchanged information on dosage and response, interpreted their findings, and identified sympathetic physicians willing to work with them. When the FDA approved large-scale tests of the leading AIDS drug, AZT, in 1986, guerilla clinics steered participants to laboratories willing to see whether they were given placebos. Once they knew they were in a control group, study participants dropped out or found other means to get the antiretroviral drugs they needed. When clinic participants learned that AZT might work better when paired with an easily concocted medication (ddC), they enlisted basement laboratories to manufacture it. Basement laboratories and testing placebos contaminated the scientific orthodoxy of randomized clinical trials.

The methodology of randomized clinical trials frayed under the creativity of weak ramshacklers. Once-orderly clinical subjects were becoming unclassifiable agents. Initially, the FDA looked the other way. Regulators judged reports of illicit behavior as episodic and minor. But some scientists began to complain: "cheating" and "noncompliance" undermined "clean data" necessary for reliable inference. Although weak ramshackling hadn't altered the spatial organization of clinical research, it turned it into a "sieve order."

Many activists were unsatisfied with ramshackling. Despite their creativity, the AIDS epidemic accelerated. In 1986, one of the most prominent San Francisco smugglers, Martin Delaney, emerged from the shadows to launch Project Inform to conduct studies on experimental drugs used in the community and publish results in a newsletter: *AIDS Treatment News*. In 1987, activists in New York launched a similar Community Research Initiative, which would aggregate and publish data on the effectiveness of medications in individual cases. ACT UP New York also launched a Treatment and Data Committee. Weak ramshacklers repositioned themselves into weak engineers.

Community research took off in the late 1980s in large part because it aligned with the creative efforts of small groups of community physicians. Like all physicians, they were professionals (elite engineers), who nevertheless ramshackled in order to address the unique combination of symptoms in each case. When they were approached by AIDs activists to participate in their ramshackle clinics, physicians faced a dilemma. They might improve their treatment of AIDs patients by aligning with activists, but doing so put them at risk of FDA, professional, and even legal sanction. Only some had sufficient chutzpah to partner with the insurgents. In doing so, a select group of physicians learned from the case-by-case results of community research and realigned their practice to serve organizations like Project Inform and the Community Research Centers.

Community research became the launching pad for subaltern engineering. By assembling activists, patients, and physicians, organizations like Project Inform began to develop local experts, who challenged roles and research methods. "Lay experts" (as Epstein calls them) criticized large-scale multisite randomized clinical trials as costly "dinosaurs," which would take years to produce "decisive" treatments. They charged the FDA with choosing an excessively slow and unethical clinical measure of improvement, namely, death or opportunistic infections in the control group. Drawing on clinical research from other biomedicines, lay experts proposed the use of "surrogate markers" or biological measures that are assumed to correlate in the long run with overall health benefit (e.g., improvements in blood pressure, metabolic function, weight, cholesterol level). While there were no proven markers for AIDS, lay experts sparked new controversy and research among university, corporate, and FDA scientists.

In 1991 the FDA convened a special meeting of the Antiviral Advisory Committee to consider surrogate markers. Once again, alignments between creative projects generated order and change. The FDA was undergoing its own recomposition. Under the guidance of neoliberal David Kessler, the agency promised to streamline the regulatory process. Despite controversy among scientists, the committee learned from community research and unanimously approved surrogate markers. As mind-boggling as it would have seemed to smugglers, physicians, and guerilla clinicians five years before, the FDA realigned its procedures to incorporate community research. In 1992, the FDA created the Community Constituency Group. Within six months, Kessler announced that all twenty-two members of the group would be included, with full participation rights, in its clinical policy committee for AIDS, the AIDS Clinical Trials Group.

The rules of clinical research and the roles of scientists, doctors, patients, activists, and the FDA changed through creative syncretism. Activists responded to a dire situation with audacity. They cobbled together resources from the gay liberation and women's health movement to create guerilla clinics. They enlisted physicians, monitored treatment protocols, and disseminated their findings, repositioning their ramshackle efforts into carefully worked out (engineered) procedures. For their part, community physicians were torn. At once bottom-up artists and top-down professionals, there was no assurance whether they would defend the existing research and treatment regime or align themselves with community research. A sufficient number of doctors aligned themselves with activists to make community clinics viable. FDA procedures frayed in the face of ramshackling and engineering from below. "Control groups" became unruly. In the midst of its own creative recomposition, the FDA aligned itself with lay experts and experimented with new research protocols and democratic procedures. Everything, it seems, changed.

But change was also elusive. Scientists and activists attacked "lay experts" for polluting "good science" or selling out to oppressive institutions. The hopes of AIDs activists to revolutionize health care remained just that: hopes. Surrogate markers failed to replace large-scale clinical trials for most research, and ACT UP protested lay exclusion from FDA research and licensing proceedings. Epstein concludes that creative projects became no more fixed by the end of his research than they were at the beginning. They did, however, become more diverse and the political process continued.

It would be hard to make sense of this case with mainstream structuralist approaches to institutional change. There was little ambiguity in the rules of large-scale pharmaceutical research. Moreover, the actors with the greatest sense of privilege to modify the rules (pharmaceutical companies, the FDA, and research scientists) had the formal authority to veto community activists and place sanctions on smugglers. To be sure, guerilla clinics opened gaps and fissures in the institutional structures of power. However, there is nothing in structural accounts of institutional change that would predict an alignment between the FDA and community research. Instead, we find in Epstein's narrative a patient willingness to trace the political interplay of daring acts of ramshackling by ordinary people with recombinatory acts of engineering by the audacious and the privileged. The result is a story rich in creative syncretism, in which actions and resources that might go unnoticed in conventional institutional analysis take center stage.

Recrafting Islam, State, and Economy: Mouride Brotherhoods in Colonial Senegal

The relationship between the colonial state in Senegal and Sufi Islamic brotherhoods reveals similar patterns of interplay among creative actors. The French colonial state and a new Senegalese brotherhood, the Mourides, took form around the same time (last decades of the nineteenth century). Ramshackling and engineering, by the privileged and the audacious, shaped each of these institutions and their interaction from the 1880s onward. The result was a remarkably stable relation between alien state and rural religious leaders. This stability helped ground one of the most successful democracies in postcolonial Africa, suggesting a way out of the familiar conundrums of bad governance, chronic poverty, and instability that plague the continent. Tracking the interplay of creative projects shows that Senegal's eventual state-society relations and political economy could not be predicted from structural conditions, resource endowments, imperial institutional ambitions, or acts of agency during critical junctures. To fully understand the way this specific nexus of polity, religion, and economy came to exist, one has to tease apart a cumulative chain of interlocked creative projects.

With the Berlin Conference of 1884, and the rapid imperial division of the continent, France projected its military and administrative power into the interior of Senegal, and beyond, to fulfill its claim to empire and block Britain and Germany. French expansion displaced long-standing local kingdoms, which fell into crisis and collapsed.[22]

But pressure had been building on these kingdoms for decades, especially after the banning of the slave trade in the 1830s. Sufi Muslim clerics saw the dislocation of local "pagan" kingdoms as an opportunity. A number of these weak engineers (Ma Ba Diakhou Ba, El Hajj Umar Tall, Samory Touré) audaciously transformed their scholarly-monastic communities into jihad movements. Through trade with French commercial enclaves, they acquired the weapons they needed for jihad and learned what other Muslims were doing to resist French imperialism. Beginning in the 1860s, Sufi leaders armed their new converts, challenged and overthrew dying animist kingdoms, and for a time blocked French colonial expansion.[23]

The Mourides were one such Sufi movement, but with a difference. By the turn of the twentieth century, the Mourides would eclipse other Sufi orders in size and significance thanks to innovative ramshackling and ensuing repositioning and realignments. Cheikh Amadou Bamba, the founder of the Mourides, initially refused to lead his followers into jihad, preferring seclusion and negotiation to confrontation. His was a minor and mostly forgotten sect, until the conversion to Mouridism of Ibrahima Fall, a leader of the *ceddo* warrior caste in one of the disintegrating animist Wolof kingdoms.[24] The ceddo were a caste of dreadlocked fighters who ostensibly defended their kingdom, but more often pursued private interests, drank heavily, and pillaged villages. They had long been the chief enemy of both the nascent colonial state and the Islamic jihad movements.[25]

When colonial conquest threw the ceddo out of power, Ibrahima Fall saw that the martial way of life of the old kingdoms was dying. He approached Cheikh Amadou Bamba seeking conversion to Islam, redemption, and a new way of life. But he also had the nerve to set terms for his conversion: he would follow Bamba, but instead of praying five times a day, fasting, giving alms, or making pilgrimage, he would express his fealty to Islam only by working slavishly at whatever task Bamba, his spiritual guide, set before him. Bamba accepted this audacious proposal, even though it did not fit with his vision for a righteous Sufi life, the proper order he was making. Soon after, former ceddo in the thousands flocked to Bamba and his Mouride movement, arriving through Ibrahima Fall and his ramshackled, new version of Islamic spirituality.[26] They quickly made the Mourides the largest, fastest growing and most important brotherhood in the region. Fall repositioned himself from discrete, weak ramshackler to key deputy to Bamba, a weak engineer about to become a very powerful one.

Seeing this, the French grew fearful that Bamba posed a new threat, and sent him into exile. This only increased the fervor of his followers, who told stories of his miracles abroad. The French would not let him pray on the boat to Gabon, so he set his prayer mat on the ocean and prayed there. The French secreted a lion into his cell to eat him: Bamba communed with its spirit and tamed the beast.[27] Run-of-the-mill ramshacklers told fabulous tales to keep Bamba's reputation alive even when he was thousands of miles away.

New alignments emerged after Bamba's return from exile to a more pacified Senegal. The French had won militarily, but needed to consolidate administrative control and make the colonies financially self-supporting. They tried with frustration to convince peasants to expand peanut production.[28] Bamba's followers, gathered in rural religious schools where hard work had emerged as the chief expression of devotion, provided the labor needed to make peanuts a viable cash crop.[29] Over time, Mouride leaders creatively reworked religious schools into peanut plantations. A lucrative cash crop economy blossomed, putting Bamba and the Mouride brotherhood on a path to significant capital accumulation.

Although still wary of Bamba and the Mourides, the French colonial state gradually recognized the productive potential of the brotherhood in the 1910s and 1920s. Together Bamba and colonial officials reworked a cautious détente into a new colonial political economy: the Mourides would spread peanut production, exported through French coastal commercial interests, profitable for both. This ensured a measure of rural peace and quiescence. In return, the colonial state would drop its efforts to undermine and displace the Mourides, and eventually would channel infrastructural investment (roads, wells, some agricultural inputs) in the direction of the Mouride zones.

A conventional, structuralist institutionalist account would call this a convergence of interests. We insist it was more. The French colonial state and the Mouride brotherhood both changed over time through mutual recognition of the potentially positive interplay of their distinct creative projects. The French were looking for a way to fund their colony on the cheap, and they needed social peace. While they had feared and had wanted to undermine the Mourides, they came to understand that the brotherhoods were changing, and acted creatively in response to that change. The Mourides at first wanted to be left alone, free from colonial persecution. Bamba and other Mouride leaders came to see the value of turning Fall's novel spiritual devotion into reliable plantation labor. They acted creatively to reengineer the Mouride order into an extremely profitable landowner. This changed how they saw themselves, and altered their perspective on the colonial regime as well, making it possible to recognize and appropriately respond to evolving French imperial policy, and making the deal possible.

Elite and weak engineers found each others' creative projects mutually supportive, and together built interlocked state and religious institutional orders that would endure well after independence. Indeed, in a later episode of elite engineering, founding Senegalese president Leopold Senghor reworked the old colonial bargain with the Mourides, updating it to the needs of the postcolonial order, ensuring forty years of hegemony for his political party. Bamba's successors would go on the radio just before major elections to issue religious edicts for their followers to vote for Senghor's party, while the state massively increased the colonial era infrastructural investment in the towns and villages controlled by the Mourides.[30]

The evolving relationship between the Mourides and the French colonial state traces a number of forms of interplay of creative action. At first local Sufi leaders, weak engineers, learned from the emergent institutional order of the French colonial regime, and crafted jihad movements. Then, Ibrahima Fall proposed a new, audacious form of Muslim spirituality, which when aligned with the efforts of Amadou Bamba, resulted in the rapid voluntary conversion of many former animist warriors and the transformation of the Mourides as an institution. Fall repositioned himself in this process, from discrete spiritual ramshackler to Bamba's lieutenant, a weak engineer. Out in their rural spiritual enclaves, Mouride followers ramshackled their way into peanut farming. Eventually, French colonial officials and Bamba learned the complementarity of their creative institutional projects, and used this alignment to craft what would be the stable and profitable political economy. After independence, Senghor, another elite engineer, renewed and reinvigorated this alignment, to great mutual benefit for himself and the brotherhoods.

Conclusion

This chapter unpacks the theory of creative syncretism. By bringing our earlier engagement with pragmatism into dialogue with more recent theories, we show how creative syncretism is widespread even in the most hostile of circumstances. Everyday actors, from guerilla clinicians to newly conquered peasants, improvise in ways that fray even the most rigidly scientific or imperial institutional orders. But this creativity is not just what the weak do: agency and colonial administrators also recombine institutional resources to buttress order, when practice overflows rules, roles, and routines. Creative syncretism produces order as well as change.

To capture the concurrence of order and change, we theorize the interplay of creative projects among actors who vary in their perceived power to tamper with institutions and their social purpose in doing so. We use an imaginary grid to track the interplay of creative projects. The horizontal axis distinguishes what people think they are doing when they play with the rules: improvisation in the moment (ramshackling) or deliberate redesigns of institutional order, meant to apply widely (engineering). The vertical axis distinguishes perceived power ("who do I think I am to tamper with rules, roles and routines?"). Some think they are naturally authorized to act creatively; others think of such acts as unauthorized audacity.

This imaginary grid makes it possible to trace the vivid, textured, and precise processes of creative syncretism that produce institutional order and change. By following what actors do, we as analysts ("tracers," as Bruno

Latour calls us) scribble all over the grid.[31] Like our actors' practice, scribbling sets aside the conventional assumption that a two-by-two table's dimensions capture the salient aspects of reality. Instead, we argue that in order to capture how people make institutional order and change, we need to track the interplay of creative projects, and doing so inevitably makes a mess of the grid. This is the point. Scribbling adds precision to the idea of creative syncretism, enriches the conceptual tools available for institutional research, and deepens our understanding of how people make both institutional order and change.

Our cases reveal chains of creative interplay. Tinkering by one actor in one moment alters the field for those who follow. We find sociality and narrative, as people observe, align with, oppose, and learn from each other. And we find transformation: as creative action provides experience with handling and rearranging institutional resources, people reimagine themselves, take audacious risks, acquire new skills, learn to move from ramshackling to engineering, bump up against the fact that engineering can never capture experience, and ramshackle again.

If we are serious empiricists, who want to know what happens in the life of an institution (why order? why incremental or conjunctural change?), we need to turn our attention to the way people perturb institutions as they live in and through them. For too long, perturbation of this sort has been dismissed as mere noise. From our perspective (institutions seen from the inside out), it is the initially soft sound of friction, as human experience and human action rub up against rules that don't apply. It is the gently bubbling sound of improvisation and new solutions overflowing the bounds of institutionally defined roles and routines. It is the scratching noise of scribbling on grids.

All of this little noise matters not just because it can add up to a crescendo but more importantly for three other reasons. First, it provides a more complete picture of what happens in institutions when people find solutions to grand and small challenges sometimes through and sometimes in spite of the rules. Institutionalists have become increasingly attuned to the soft rumbling of everyday change, but grope for mechanisms that "make" this change happen, or for three-dimensional images of structural gaps that "generate" this change. Neither mechanisms nor gaps have agency. They are metaphors, which, at best, help us picture what is happening. As empirical social scientists, we ask why not just look at what *actors are doing*? Doing so, we expect, will reveal that the change institutionalists hope to explain comes from the recombinatory, problem solving, tinkering tendency in human action itself. It is an outgrowth of the fact, as pragmatists taught a century ago, that the interplay of context, situation, and skill are simply "never twice the same."

Second, attention to the little noises of people doing things in, with, and to institutions enriches our understanding of institutional stability. Seen from the perspective of creative syncretism, stability is a precise, but shifting, condition of the torn fabric of strategic order, made, punctured, and shored up by tactical creativity. Change is always partial because much creative action is about engineering, not because of path dependency or interest aggregation.

In thinking about the creativity behind order and stability, it helps to recognize that what we do is not *determined* by our power or purpose, but that we are positioned by our own *experience* of power and purpose. Even when we think our status or intelligence entitles us to plan for others, things often don't work as planned, and we have to improvise on the spot, in ways we often hope go unnoticed. Ramshackling of this sort helps make and maintain order. Even when we believe we have no right to make institutions, we improvise in ways that tear at the fabric of order, producing patches of entirely new cloth. The weak contribute to the making (as well as the unmaking) of institutions.

Finally, the little clanking noises of tinkering are the sound of politics. By paying attention to the ways people take apart rules, piece together new roles, or nail gussets to worn-out routines, we discover sites of negotiation, alliance, conflict, and compromise that go unexamined in structural analysis. And by situating political creativity historically and experientially, we can explore how political projects—small and large—emerge from the ways our subjects narrate the sociality of their actions: are they making precedent and doing things in a prominent way that merits promulgation? The answers to these questions are only part of the story. Once we know more about creative intent, we can trace the interplay of projects to see how they make order and change.

Power, then, is a function of experience, not structure. People come to every situation with a sense of their authority over, access to, and aptitude with a prior repertoire of resources. This constitutes their role in an institution. Typically understood as fixed by history, rules, or status, roles have meaningful experiential origins. Through improvisational patching, elites act out of stereotypical role (upper left quadrant) and find themselves in situations where their former sense of aptitude, access, and authority no longer applies (movement down on the grid). Through audacious use of resources, the weak can enact unexpected, socially salient projects (lower right quadrant). Through reflection on one's own creativity (repositioning), one can acquire new authority, access, and aptitude in handling institutional resources. Once fixed roles, understood experientially and enacted through the interplay of creative projects, can change. Power is real and fluid.

Some may embrace our account of power as deeply democratic or emancipatory. But it leaves plenty of room to account for the reinforcement of established roles, domination, and the inhibition of possibilities. What happens in individual cases is not conditioned by the tool: this one "sees" more empowerment and fluidity, while others "see" more stability and control. As analytic devices, creative syncretism, our imaginary grid, and our account of interplay are neutral. They are tools to help us see the human, creative origins of empowerment and oppression in sharper detail.

Still, like the pragmatists and critical theorists who inspire us, we think it critical to acknowledge how, as social scientists, we are situated in the world. We have made choices of what to analyze, of how to think about institutions, of what cases to explore, of what kind of stories to tell. We have commitments as scholars and as people. So we recognize that the approach and the tools offered here are also situated in a truly political world as mirrors: rough sheet metal poorly polished to reflectivity, but mirrors nevertheless. We would not be honest social scientists if we did not admit that we hope our actors will at least glance at the mirrorlike screens we try to hold up and recognize themselves, a bit, in the reflection. If they do, then we hope they might see in new ways what they are capable of.

Chapter 2

Ecological Explanation

Chris Ansell

If, as this volume suggests, reigning theories of institutions have difficulty in explaining institutional change, then new insights might come from *how* we explain things in the social sciences. From that starting point, this essay explores a style of explanation only dimly perceived as a distinctive form—ecological explanation. Although ecological explanation has important and long-standing roots in the social sciences—reaching back at least to the work of the Chicago school of sociology—it is presently much better known as a strategy for explaining the natural world.[1] Natural ecologists adopt a variety of specific explanatory techniques, but are broadly united by the idea that ecosystems are material and biological processes linked together in interdependent ways. Without trying to directly transpose natural ecology ideas or terms directly to the social sciences, this essay explores the broad affinity between natural and social ecologies. The essay then explores how ecological explanation might provide a rich framework for explaining institutional change.

The basic conception of ecological explanation advanced here begins with the idea, to put it in the language of natural ecology, that the form and behavior of any species is shaped by the larger field of action in which it operates—its environment. Yet this is only the first step in an ecological explanation. As a perspective, ecology is founded on a spatial metaphor, which assumes that species and environments are distributed in space, as well as in time. This distributed ecology is composed of multiple species adapting to multiple environments, and to one another. Because of this mutual adaptation, ecological explanation often discovers complex patterns of reciprocal causality generally referred to as "coevolution." Species adapt to specific habitats and to one another, forming interdependent communities bound together by competition, predation, and symbiosis. Species develop niches within these communities. However, a key point is that ecologies tend to be open, rather than closed, systems. A species is affected both by proximate and direct environmental factors, but also by more distal and indirect factors. Historically, natural ecology has tended to assume that "ecosystems" were in equilibrium, but this field has increasingly recognized that open ecologies may be dynamic, nonequilibrium systems.

The analogy between natural and social ecology is not exact, but the basic analytical frameworks are broadly comparable. In the social sciences, we do not generally talk about "species," but instead substitute the idea of different kinds of actors—individual or collective—distinguished by factors like identity, skill, structure, and so on.[2] These actors are distributed in space and time, adapting to each other and to different natural, technological, and institutional environments. They are concretely embedded in particular webs of activity, sociability, control, and resource flows. Through mutual adaptation over time, these actors form interdependent communities—families, organizations, cities, empires—that are in turn linked together into more complex ecologies. Like natural ecologies, however, these communities are not closed systems. They are affected by both proximate, internal conditions, but also by more distal, indirect factors that arise outside the community. Like natural ecologies, social ecologies are entropic, requiring inputs of resources and expenditures of energy (work) to maintain interdependent systems. One of the immediate implications of these ideas is that even equilibrium systems must continuously adapt to local and global change not fully under their control.

As applied to institutions, these ideas are not entirely new. In fact, scholars applying systems thinking to organizations have explored many of these ideas in detail (Herbert Simon, James Thompson, Alfred Chandler, and Karl Weick, among many others). However, this systems thinking has to a large extent focused on how equilibrium systems (e.g., organizations) sustain and support themselves in an open system context. This requires systems to exert control in order to ensure an adequate balance of inputs, throughputs, and feedbacks. And typically, the larger the system, the more extensive and elaborate these controls. While these systems ideas are useful, they are targeted more toward understanding system maintenance or expansion than institutional change. I argue that to appreciate institutional change, we must shift our attention to the wider ecology of adapting actors, giving special attention to four kinds of situations generated by the wider ecology: (1) situations where actors are cross pressured between competing institutional imperatives or control attempts; (2) "interstitial" actors, activities or events that find themselves "betwixt and between" the cracks of existing institutions; (3) "transinstitutional" actors, activities, or events that straddle institutional boundaries; and (4) the interpenetration of institutions. It is in these heterodox situations—often invisible to even open-systems thinkers—that we find powerful sources of institutional change. These situations foster the "situated creativity" described in the introduction to this book.

One of the key features of ecological explanation, as I advance it here, is that it is always multiperspectival. It does not privilege the perspective of a single actor, or institution, or system. Rather, it scans across the ecology, examining it from different perspectives. This multiperspectival approach leads to what I suggest is a characteristic feature of ecological explanation: ecological explanations are typically multiscale or multilevel. As described above, actors are concretely embedded in webs of activity and rooted in specific contexts, which both shape and constrain their behavior and create local problems and opportunities that call for "situated creativity." To understand behavior, we must often focus our observational lens on the fine-grained details of this local embeddedness—peer down into the lived experience of individuals and communities. However, in an interconnected ecology, factors that are more distal and indirect also affect local behavior. To understand the effects of the wider ecology, we have to pan out to a more global perspective—to actors, activities, events, or emerging institutions that link these locally embedded actors and opportunities. Often, certain actors or arenas are in a position to play an aligning and bridging role because they themselves, by accident or design, are multiply embedded in different networks or identities or fortuitously placed at the intersection of flows of critical resources or information. Only by panning out to the wider ecology can we identify these multiply embedded or fortuitously located actors or arenas, to whom power, opportunity, and responsibility flows.

To summarize, ecological explanation begins with an image of actors and activities concretely embedded in space and time. Institutional change arises as the product of heterodox circumstances generated by this ecology, which requires actors to engage in "situated creativity." Explanation focuses on how local opportunities for situated creativity are linked and aligned by actors and emergent institutions who are themselves either multiply embedded or fortuitously located in the ecology. The remainder of this chapter expands on these ideas. But before doing that, I first examine how my version of ecological explanation builds on and departs from related ideas in institutional analysis.

Ecological Thinking in Institutional Analysis

This essay would be remiss if did not acknowledge that some ecological ideas are already well established in institutional theory. Perhaps the best known use of these ideas is the extensive body of work in organizational sociology called "population ecology." Tracing its roots back to a now classic statement by Michael Hannan and John Freeman, the population ecology literature has conducted many studies of the effects of competition on organizational populations (typically interpreted as an industry or sector).[3] This work has been important in organizational theory, but represents only a fairly narrow slice of the explanatory framework I shall describe as being "ecological." Organizational ecologists have recognized this and have distinguished between three different levels of ecological explanation: a "developmental" approach at the level of individual organizations, a "population" approach at the level of industries or sectors, and a "community" level that examines the interaction between populations in a particular region.[4] While organizational ecologists have produced important work at both the individual and the community level, most of their research has been cast at the population level. By adopting a reductionist style of analysis, population ecology has generated important insights into the evolution of organizational populations, but may have also discouraged a wider examination of ecological ideas. The ideas in this essay are cast at the community level of analysis.

Another close cousin of an ecological perspective is the work on "organizational fields," which was perhaps given its classic statement in the work of Paul DiMaggio and Walter Powell.[5] This work built on earlier generations of organizational theory that had begun to shift the level of analysis from studies of individual organizations to the level of interorganizational analysis. The concept of "field" broadly shares with the term "ecology" a "topological" sense of the relationships among a set of interacting elements. As John L. Martin says in his review and defense of this concept, "In sum . . . we may say that a field exists when a set of analytic elements are aligned in such a way that it is parsimonious to describe their current state in terms of position vis-à-vis one another."[6] The concept of "field" has been a productive one in organizational theory, but "field" as a framework for explanation (as opposed to description) has been evasive. While distinctive mechanisms like coercive, normative, and mimetic isomorphism are concrete and powerful, it remains difficult to describe field-level analysis as having a distinctive style of explanation.

Social network analysis is a third area of research that might be labeled "ecological." Network analysis has, for the most part, been a powerful descriptive technology to reveal complex patterns of interrelationship between individuals and institutions. As a descriptive technology, it has a powerful role to play in ecological analysis, as natural ecologists themselves appreciate.[7] It has had less success (which is not to say no success) as a framework for causal explanation.[8] In part, this is a data limitation. Since data is hard to collect, most studies are cross-sectional, making it difficult to establish causality. Social network scholars, however, have produced a wide range of analytical techniques that provide the potential for causal explanation. Ecological analysis can build directly on the relational techniques that social network analysis has developed, because both share a basic relational stance toward social phenomena.

While building on the work of organizational ecology, institutional field theory, and social network analysis, this essay traces its ecological perspective back to a pragmatist perspective on institutions.[9] Some of the early pragmatist institutionalists, notably Everett Hughes, explicitly adopted an ecological approach to institutions.[10] Hughes associated ecological analysis with the struggle of institutions for survival. In this way, his work is a precursor to contemporary population ecology. However, Hughes also stressed that ecology refers to spatial interrelationships and his work clearly focused on what we might today call the "embeddedness" of institutions in communities. He also stressed the contingent character of these relations, suggesting a dynamic view.[11] Understanding institutions as "going concerns"—social orders that strive to persist through time—Hughes regarded their fate to be bound up, in a dynamic way, with the communities in which they were embedded. To persist, these institutions had to continuously adapt to their local ecosystem, which was constantly changing.

While Hughes sketched an early version of an ecological approach to institutions, his work did not really focus on what was specific to ecological explanation. In the remainder of this essay, I shall tackle that task in two ways. In the first section, I shall try to break down ecological explanation into its constituent parts and then identify how institutions can be approached ecologically. In the second section, I will then adopt a more holistic approach, using some of my own past work to illustrate some distinctive styles of ecological explanation.

Basic Features of Ecological Explanation

As will already be clear, I do not advance an account of ecological explanation as specific and well disciplined as that offered by the population ecologists. My account stresses the complex patterning of ecologies and stresses that the heterodox and contingent circumstances that arise out of this complex patterning are the sources of change. Such an account lends itself more to idiographic (inductive and historical) than to nomothetic (deductive covering laws) styles of explanation and theorization. The specifics of an ecological explanation will be as varied as the ecologies it seeks to explain. Nevertheless, four basic building blocks of ecological explanation can be set out: distribution, diversity, relation, and process.

> *Distribution*: most basically, an ecology is a distribution of some set of elements across time and space. The distribution may be a set of actors (ranging from a person to an organization, to a nation-state), a set of meanings (an idea or ideology, language, or musical style), or resources (capital, labor, oil). Sometimes a distribution is interpreted in a statistical sense (a "normal" distribution), but more often it is interpreted as a particular pattern of dispersal across space and time.

> *Diversity*: these actors, meanings, or resources vary along some set of dimensions, and this variation ranges from homogenous (when organisms or conditions are the same) to heterogeneous (when they are different).

> *Relation*: ecological explanation is relational, in that it stresses the relationships between actors, meanings, or resources. Relationships may be conflictual, competitive, or cooperative. But the attention of ecological explanation is less to the specific content of any individual relationship and more to wider or more systemic patterns of relationships. Patterns of connectedness and disconnectedness are critical for understanding an ecology.

Process: an ecology is dynamic and characterized by activities, events, and flows. This dynamism means that the actors, meanings, and resources change their status over time.

Very fundamentally, ecological explanation "explains" by appealing to changes in distribution, diversity, relations, or process. Since this orientation is very general, it is clear that many if not most explanations have some ecological element about them. In fact, it might be hard to imagine explanations that do not appeal to one of these factors. However, the claim here is that these elements are the bedrocks of explanation, which is not necessarily true of all forms of explanation. For example, rational choice theory does not start with these elements as primary ones. It appeals to actor utilities as the bedrock of explanation. Both ecological explanation and rational choice theory may explain by appealing to the distribution or heterogeneity of utilities. But this points to where the explanatory style overlaps rather than to their being identical.

Most ecological explanations are constructed from a combination of these four concepts. Consider the idea of "homophily" in social network analysis. A number of studies have found that people have a tendency to form social relationships with other people who are like them in some basic respect.[12] This idea combines the ideas of diversity and relation. Another example comes from life-cycle analysis, a central concept in the field of industrial ecology.[13] Tracing a product from cradle to grave basically combines the idea of relation and process, demonstrating the relationship through time of a series of events related to a specific product.

Ecological explanation will often construct both the phenomenon to be explained and the explanation itself in ecological terms. In other words, we explain by changes in distribution, diversity, relations, or process. But we may also construct what is to be explained in these same terms.[14] Beyond these basic building blocks of ecological explanation, we can also distinguish different types of ecological explanation based on the granularity of analytical perspective.

Ecological Explanation Is Multiscale and Multiperspectival

Ecological explanation is highly attuned to the interplay between different levels or scales of human interaction. This is a point that stems from two ecological features that stand in some tension with each other: on the one hand, actors are often firmly embedded in local contexts; on the other hand, ecologies are interconnected open systems and local contexts are rarely discretely bounded social units. Ecological explanation must often move back and forth between these perspectives because the local and global interpenetrate in complex ways. It is often the specific mediation between these levels that provides the basis for explaining change.

To develop this argument, I adopt the analytical convenience of describing three different levels of ecological analysis: local context, global system, and an intermediary level that mediates between the two. Natural ecology adopts a similar levels-of-analysis approach to capture the spatial granularity of observation, distinguishing between "patch" and "landscape"—a patch being a small region embedded in a larger landscape and a landscape being composed of many patches. As we shift between levels of spatial granularity, we tend to observe different details, patterns, and time dimensions. These levels of analysis are not ontologically real, but are rather analytical conveniences that help us appreciate different relational and processual scales. When we zoom in to local context, we often see a rich and concrete fabric of social interaction, but we often lose sight of how the local context is embedded in a wider ecology. When we zoom out to the global perspective, detailed patterns of social interaction fall away and we tend to notice the system-level interactions between elements of the ecology.

How does the world look at each of these levels? At the local contextual level, ecological explanation stresses the concrete situatedness of human behavior in webs of relation and activity.[15] A local context (patch) may be interesting because of how it is spatially distributed vis-à-vis other local contexts (e.g., a periphery). But the focus is on the distribution, diversity, relationships, and processes *within* that context. A local context itself is a clustering of certain kinds of actors, relationships, or processes in space or time. A local context may be dominated by a single type of actor (homogeneity) or attract a range of actors (heterogeneity). A contextual perspective treats relationships in localistic terms, stressing the importance of proximity, dyadic ties, and direct interaction. Temporally, local contexts tend either to be studied in a highly contemporaneous fashion (short periods, event focused) or are regarded as repositories for the long-term accumulated experiences of those who inhabit them (e.g., a historical community). Whether the temporal focus is contemporaneous or historical, the emphasis is on the specificity of time as a variable in its own right.

Studies examining why certain regions become high-tech clusters offer an example of this patch logic. In comparison to a range of other patches, a high-tech cluster is a statistical outlier in terms of the local clustering of high-tech firms. In such studies, the question often arises about what is distinctive about this high-tech "patch" that attracts or produces such a high concentration of innovative firms. Annalee Saxenian's book comparing two high-tech clusters, Silicon Valley and Route 128 (outside Boston), offers a good example of this kind of perspective.[16] Although she points to important factors that arise outside these regions (e.g., military spending), the critical factor distinguishing the more successful Silicon Valley from Route 128 is the density and openness of its interfirm networks. Explanation focuses on the distinctive interfirm ecology of each regional patch.

A systemic perspective shifts attention from a specific patch to a wider "landscape" composed of many local contexts. In contrast with the worm's-eye view of the contextual perspective, the systemic perspective adopts more of a bird's-eye view—shifting from a contextual focus on what is happening *within* a patch to an *external* perspective on how the patch relates to other patches and the wider environment. For example, from studying the internal networks and processes of a favella like the "City of God" (a slum community in Rio de Janiero),"we might shift to asking about the processes of spatial segregation that occur as the result of control of capital or space within the urban ecosystem that is Rio de Janiero. Typically, as we shift perspective like this, we abstract away from the concrete embeddedness of social action within any given patch and turn our attention to distributions, diversity, relations, and processes that span *across* (rather than within) different patches or niches. From an emphasis on proximate, dyadic, and direct interactional relationships, a systemic perspective tends to treat any given element in functional terms for the system as a whole. Temporally, a systemic perspective abstracts away from the particulars of contemporaneous or historical time. The "system" itself persists through time, and events or time-dependent processes are considered to the degree that they explain the reproduction or functioning of the system. The focus of a systemic perspective is the global pattern of interdependence among different actors and institutions.

Consider the logic expressed by the work on *Varieties of Capitalism* as an example of a systemic perspective.[17] This work describes two different kinds of capitalist "ecosystem"—liberal market economies and coordinated market economies. The focus is on the firm as the key actor and the key issue is how firms resolve coordination problems they face. In a liberal market economy, firms rely heavily on hierarchy and arms-length market relations to solve coordination problems; in coordinated market economies, firms are more likely to use relational contracting with other economic actors and collaboration with nonmarket actors to handle their coordination problems. Although the key actors are firms, the perspective is ultimately a national economy. Hall and Soskice are clear that these are ideal types and that actual countries may vary along these dimensions. But they also suggest that patterns of relationships among firms will be systemic: "In sum, we contend that differences in the institutional framework of the political economy generate systematic differences in corporate strategy across LMEs [liberal market economies] and CMEs [coordinated market economies]."[18]

Between this contextual and systemic perspective, I also distinguish an intermediary perspective that focuses on the mediation between context and system. While a contextual perspective emphasizes the concrete situatedness of actors and a systemic level focuses on broad patterns of interdependence between actors and institutions, an intermediary perspective zeroes in on opportunities for arbitration that arise from the juxtaposition of contexts and systems. Since this perspective will be less familiar to readers, I offer some ideas about how to interpret each of the four basic ecological concepts (distribution, diversity, relation, process) set out above.

An intermediary perspective on distribution focuses on the boundaries between geographical or functional niches or zones. In natural ecology, this perspective is well represented by the attention to the importance of "edges" as important zones of biodiversity.[19] In social sciences, an important version of this is the work on boundary objects as mediating the relationship between different groups.[20]

An intermediary perspective on diversity might focus on hybridity as a logic by which two different elemental or systemic logics are mediated. A hybrid actor or ecosystem is one that combines characteristics of other types of actors or ecosystems. From an intermediary perspective, it is the combination of logics—not the pure logic—that explains outcomes.[21]

An intermediary perspective on relations often focuses on actors who have an intermediary role in a chain of relations and their ability to arbitrate the relationships between other actors. In natural ecology, this logic is inherent in food chain studies. In the social sciences, we see such logic in studies of brokerage in network analysis.[22]

An intermediary perspective on process will focus on the concept of "transitions" from one biological or ecological state to another. In natural ecology, this might be inherent in studies of reproductive processes or in studies of life cycles. In the social sciences, a parallel might be interest in processes of recruitment to social movements or ritualistic "transitions" like coming-of-age rituals.[23] Another intermediary approach to process is Claude Lévi-Strauss's concept of "bricolage" to describe the process of cobbling together of different tools and resources.[24]

Between Context and System

The context (patch) and systemic (landscape) perspectives reflect often opposing views of action and explanation. Both regard ecologies as historical, but the contextual approach tends to adopt a view of actors as concretely embedded, which as noted earlier lends itself to an idiographic approach to explanation, while the systemic approach tends to abstract away from this embeddedness, stressing the functional relationships among parts of the system and hence tending toward a more nomothetic approach to explanation (idiographic explanation works by holistically enumerating contextual features, often stressing the unique and idiosyncratic qualities of these contexts; by contrast, nomothetic explanation focuses on isolating a few key variables that account for the general behavior of the system—a nomothetic approach treats a context as a "case" that can be explained by a covering law).

In the remainder of the chapter, I focus on an intermediary approach to institutional ecology. Because it calls analytic attention to intercontextual and intersystemic dynamics, it has the virtue of connecting these two different levels of structure and agency. Doing this helps to illustrate some of the style and potential of ecological analysis. I shall also draw a connection with Gerald Berk and Dennis Galvan's concept of "creative syncretism."

An intermediary approach to institutional ecologies suggests that we look for explanations in the forces and factors that mediate between contexts, between systems, and between contexts and system. Thus, the intermediary approach is heterodox in that it focuses on the defining logic of neither a particular context nor an ideal-typical system. It focuses instead on the juxtaposition of different contexts and systems. In this way, it is neither purely idiographic nor nomothetic.

I begin with two cases from my own work, which allows me to more easily schematize this work in terms of the ecological framework I have set out above. The first case is a study (with John Padgett) of the rise of the powerful Medici family as de facto rulers of the Florentine state during the fifteenth century.[25] This study is typically and rightly understood as a network study, which examines the role that marriage, economic, and neighborhood relationships play in the Medicis' consolidation of power. Here, though, I use the case to illuminate ecological explanation.

For at least one hundred years prior to the rise of the Medici as the dominant family of Florence, the city experienced a set of swings between two broad systems for organizing power and politics—a corporatist order dominated by the guilds and an oligarchical order dominated by a small group of high-status families interconnected by marriage and economic ties. This is a landscape view of Florence, describing this urban ecosystem in terms of systemic logics. However, to understand the dynamics that allowed the Medici family and their supporters to disrupt this pattern (producing institutional change), it is necessary to focus down to the patch level of organization and the contextual fabric of Florentine life. As historians have shown, Renaissance Florence was a very localized society, with much of the action taking place at the neighborhood level, where historical alliances and rivalries played out for control of local political support. Marriage between families was one of the cementing bonds of this local society and was the basis for political coalitions, particularly for high-status families (as measured by aristocratic lineage and wealth). By examining the details of this local society—adopting the perspective of individual families—you would find a complex contextually specific calculus for establishing (and breaking) relations with other families. Through strategic marriage ties, families sought to preserve and enhance their social status in the city.

Adopting an intermediary perspective, our focus shifts from competing systems (corporatism versus oligarchy) or context (marriage strategies) to the interaction between them. To do this, we have to add an important historical dimension. In the 1390s, there was an uprising of wool workers known as the Ciompi Rebellion. The wool workers, a lower guild, challenged the oligarchical control of the city. The Medici family stepped into this breach between corporatist and oligarchical systems, offering support and leadership to the wool workers, an act regarded as a class betrayal. After the rebellion was put down, the Medici family was ostracized from marriage ties to other elite families in their home neighborhood of San Lorenzo. The result was a shortage of eligible local marriage partners, pushing the Medici to pursue marriage partners with families in other neighborhoods. As a result, the Medici marriage network transgressed the localism of most elite marriage networks, producing an unusual citywide network. The Medici family, however, continued to do business with people in its own neighborhood, though increasingly with lower-status "new men." In the aggregate, these choices produced a segmented network in which the Medici married people they did not do business with and did business with people they did not marry. Their network placed them in an unusual mediating position. Their marriage network mediated between elite families in different neighborhoods (interpatch); the segmentation of their economic and marriage networks set the Medici family up as the broker of the relationship between supporters from two different class backgrounds (high-status elite families and wealthy, but lower-status new men). This unusual network gave them a powerful organizational base from which to challenge the oligarchical elite.

In this account of political developments in Renaissance Florence, the outcomes are ultimately explained by the Medici family's position betwixt and between context and system. The family's role in the Ciompi Rebellion placed it at the center of the conflict between two system logics—guild corporatism and elite oligarchy. The Medicis' banishment led to the inadvertent creation of a marriage network that allowed them to mediate interpatch politics and to a pattern of segmentation between marriage and economic relationships that allowed the Medici to mediate between social classes.

Ecological Explanation as Coevolution

In this section, I return to the conception of an ecology as composed of multiple kinds of actors (individual and collective), distributed in space and time, and adapting to multiple environments and to one another. One of the interesting implications of this conception is a pattern of coevolution between actors and their environments and between the actors themselves. A change in the behavior or organization of one actor will have implications for the adaptation of other actors, whose adaptation may in turn rebound on the original actor. Change may therefore reverberate through an ecology, producing a complex pattern of mutual interaction and interdependence. Often, new institutions are emergent from these coevolutionary dynamics.

In the example of Renaissance Florence described above, we glimpse some of these coevolutionary dynamics. When the Florentine oligarchy ostracized the Medici, the family had to adapt its marriage strategies. This led it to create the citywide marriage networks that became the basis of its partisan opposition to the city's oligarchy. An important lesson of this case is that the reverberation of coevolutionary adaptations through the urban ecology of Florence led strategic opportunities to flow to particular actors. While actors have to be skillful, creative, and strategic to take advantage of these opportunities—as Cosimo de Medici indeed was—the opportunity itself was partly a product of coevolutionary dynamics.

One of the important features of this coevolutionary perspective is that ecological explanation does not rest on optimizing adaptation to a single fixed environment, but rather focuses on the dynamic interaction between the adaptations of different actors. In this situation, stable situations may arise only when coevolving actors jointly structure environments that lock each other in through a form of reciprocal causality. In institutional studies, this argument has been made by Harrison White in his theoretical analysis of markets as interlocking role structures and by Andrew Abbot in his work on the system of professions.[26]

To further illustrate the implication of this coevolutionary perspective for the emergence of institutions, I now provide another example from my work (with Arthur Burris and Antoine Joseph). The ecological setting is the urban United States during the period between approximately 1890 and 1910, a time when labor movements were growing and party machines were emerging.[27] This was a period of active labor organizing, in which the basic structures of union organization were actively contested. Urban life in the late nineteenth-century United States was ethnically diverse, and workers lived in neighborhoods segmented by ethnicity. Although ethnically based and neighborhood-based electoral mobilization, using patronage strategies, was already common in U.S. cities (in the East and Midwest, in particular), consolidated political machines had not yet emerged. Rather, urban parties were loose federations of ethnic political entrepreneurs, who could deliver the vote in their own neighborhoods. Urban labor organizing during this period threatened these parties, because in some cases unions were able to organize workplace solidarity across ethnic divisions. This inter-ethnic solidarity, in turn, produced cross-neighborhood organization. When unions became active in local electoral politics, this interethnic, cross-neighborhood mobilization threatened the bases of support of ethnic political entrepreneurs. Their countermobilization produced centralized political machines.

Like the tension between guild corporatism and elite oligarchy, this urban political cleavage pitted two systems against one another—a logic of neighborhood-based ethnic mobilization versus a logic of interethnic, cross-neighborhood labor mobilization. However, this polarization was, in turn, overlain by two "systems" of conflict within the world of union mobilization—a conflict between organization around skilled workers (craft unionism) versus organization that united workers across skill divisions (intercraft or industrial unionism). Two critical factors mediated between these two opposing logics. The first was citywide union federations that supported cross-skill and interethnic union organizing. These were in many respects the equivalent of the Medicis' citywide marriage networks, mediating between different workplaces and neighborhoods. These city-based unions adopted a logic of geographically based organizing that was in tension with a strategy of organizing workers into national federations structured along craft or industrial lines.

Thus, from a landscape perspective, labor organizing and ethnic political mobilization in the late nineteenth century confronted a conflicting set of system logics. Understanding the outcome requires awareness of the second critical factor: where workers could organize; this takes us back down to a patch perspective. When workers could organize at the workplace, there were strong incentives for skilled workers to ally with unskilled workers, as well as for workers to organize across ethnic boundaries. However, American employers reacted vigorously to labor organizing at the workplace, often resorting to violence to prevent it. The standard story is that this violent response was supported by legal and political conditions that supported the employers in their quest to keep their workplaces as open shops. The employers' success (which nevertheless varied considerably from workshop to workshop and city to city) ultimately displaced labor organizing outside the locus of the workplace, undermining interethnic and interskill solidarity and reinforcing the value of national craft-based organizing. The consolidation of national trade-based federations, in turn, undermined the electoral threat that city-based union federations posed to the urban ethnic entrepreneurs. Consolidated urban political machines appeared where a threat from citywide, workshop-based labor organizing was followed by consolidation of local craft-based unionism.

This explanation is constructed by focusing on several interpenetrating arenas of action and mobilization: ethnic groups, neighborhoods, cities, and workshops. These arenas were linked and mobilized by contesting institutional logics: patronage-based parties and party machines, industrial and craft unions, city-based union federations and trade federations. This ecology provided the setting for the dynamic coevolution of interdependent institutional logics, beginning with the threat that the mobilization of cross-ethnic and interskill union mobilization posed to patronage-based parties and employers. The threatened groups then adapted by centralizing urban parties and by maintaining open shops. These adaptations weakened industrial unions and city-based union federations, undermining solidarity across ethnicity and skill and strengthening the mobilizing logic of national trade federations. These trade federations withdrew from direct electoral mobilization, ceding the urban electoral terrain to emerging party machines that were now able to consolidate their position in the urban electoral ecology.

In this and previous sections, I have hinted that opportunities for situated creativity arise from the ecological context in which actors find themselves. My account of ecological explanation has placed much more emphasis on trying to describe how ecology shapes these opportunities than on explaining the creative action of actors. In the next section, however, I intend to redress that imbalance by arguing that Gerald Berk and Dennis Galvan's theory of "creative syncretism" offers a perspective that complements an ecological approach. While an ecological perspective stresses the factors that give rise to opportunity, Berk and Galvan show how actors seize and exploit opportunity.

Creative Syncretism as Ecological Explanation

Berk and Galvan have proposed a theoretical framework they call "creative syncretism" for explaining institutional change.[28] In this section, I want to consider their approach, both as a possible critique of the kind of ecological analysis I have just described and as an approach that can complement ecological explanation.

Their concept of "creative syncretism" brings together two different ideas. The first is that human action is creative, a point they derive from pragmatist philosophy. They emphasize that institutional life is a "lived experience" and they counterpose this to depictions of institutional life as "structural constraints on action, temporal pathways of regularity, exogenous mechanisms of socialization, or ingrained patterns of cognition."[29] The term "syncretism" is used to signify the "openness and mutability of seemingly coherent structures," as well as the transgressive and recombinative character of human agency. The idea that brings the creative and syncretic together for Berk and Galvan is John Dewey's concept of habit, which says that rules and practices are not "guides and constraints, but . . . mutable raw material for new action."[30] Creative syncretism stresses the improvisational character of institutional life.

In exploring the larger literature on institutional change, Berk and Galvan closely examine how recent institutional theorizing has grappled with the issue of the ambiguity of institutional life. For example, they point to recent work by Wolfgang Streeck and Kathleen Thelen that points to the "structural gaps" that are created by the layering of institutions. But they note that identifying gaps is not the same thing as providing a theory of how institutions change. They also analyze Karen Orren and Stephen Skowronek's work that focuses on how the interaction of different institutions can generate "structural disorder." But again, they point out that noting this structural disorder does not produce a theory of institutional change, because it has little to say about how social actors will respond to and use this disorder to produce change.

To the extent that the examples just presented emphasize structural conditions, their critique might also extend to the examples described in the previous section. To the extent that those examples relied on a structuralist account of institutional outcomes, Berk and Galvan might point out, they fail to provide a basic understanding of how competing institutional orders generate institutional change. Berk and Galvan, for instance, might argue that Medici family networks are simply relational structures; creative syncretism depends on an account of how the Medici family came to understand and exploit their marriage and economic networks, welding them together to form the basis of a supportive political constituency. In fact, the Medici article does emphasize the Medicis' "robust action"—their ability to use the segmented qualities of their networks to manage the ambiguity of their multiple identities with their different constituencies. However, the account of U.S. labor organizing and ethnic political mobilization comes very close to Orren's and Skowronek's account of the "intercurrence" of different institutional structures.[31]

Berk and Galvan identify several features of "habit" as a basis for thinking about creative syncretism. First, creative syncretism is about skillful use of the materials around us to respond to challenges and opportunities. Second, creative syncretism depends on an understanding of all action as both social and historical. Third, creative syncretism is action-oriented, with people discovering their preferences and ideas through exploratory action. Fourth, creative syncretism is not mindless or automatic response, because "the alignment of skill, rule and material is never exactly the same."[32]

I now suggest that Berk and Galvan's conception of creative syncretism presupposes, but also grounds, an ecological conception of explanation. I suggest that creative syncretism is the model of institutional action that I would associate with an intermediary ecological perspective, and that it has much in common with the accounts of the Medici and urban political mobilization sketched above. Consider Berk's account of Louis Brandeis, a creative syncretist who helped launch the Federal Trade Commission.[33] Brandeis found himself betwixt and between two different systemic logics: a progressive logic of state regulation of industry on the one hand versus a populist logic of preserving competition on the other. As an intermediary between these two logics, Brandeis conceived of a hybrid regulated competition. His conception was a grand narrative, but to understand how it eventually shaped distinct outcomes, it is necessary to look at the contextual details. This shift of focus to context is analogous to moving from the tension between guild corporatism and elite oligarchy down to the concrete local marriage and economic strategies of individual families. For Berk, the analogy is to move the focus onto the detailed cost-accounting strategies of individual firms. Brandeis's idea of regulated competition would have likely remained a political slogan if it had been unable to ground itself in the concrete contexts of individual firms.

How was this syncretic idea of regulated competition made concrete? To place Berk's account in the context of ecological explanation, it is necessary to appreciate the intermediary role that business associations came to play in the development of new cost-accounting practices. Like the Medicis' interneighborhood marriage network or the city-based union federations that linked workers in different urban workshops, the business associations promoted by the Federal Trade Commission mediated between the strategies of different firms. They did this by promoting a specific technology of cost accounting and by promoting industry-wide benchmarking, information pooling, and experimentation. Brandeis's idea of regulated competition was articulated in the context of opposing progressive and populist logics, but the actual implementation of the idea worked by concretely mediating the relations between different firms.

One of the very important features of Berk and Galvan's creative syncretism is that it calls attention to activities that are not really noted and accounted for by other institutional perspectives. The same point might be made for ecological explanation. The interneighborhood character of Medici marriage ties or the importance of city-based union federations would likely be overlooked by standard institutionalist accounts.

The point is that Berk and Galvan's creative syncretists are what they are because they are situated between different systems, straddle different contexts, and generally must mediate between landscape and patch. It may be a more universal characteristic of social actors that they are creative and syncretic, but it is fully consistent with pragmatism that people are often pushed to become creative and syncretic by problems that beg for resolution. To overstretch a bit, Berk and Galvan's description of creative syncretism describes how people behave when they confront problems that beg for resolution; an ecological perspective provides a framework for describing what kinds of problems arise that beg for resolution.

Berk and Galvan's creative syncretism challenges the rule-following notion of institutions. However, their approach may be (mis)interpreted as merely replacing "structure" with "agency"—that is, challenging the dominance of structure by merely stressing the opposing perspective. That is not their intention, but I suspect that is how many will read them. This is because their theory of creative syncretism largely focuses on agents rather than structures.

I illustrate the potential value of joining a creative syncretist perspective with an ecological approach to explanation by again returning to my own work—this time my book on the historical development of the French labor movement.[34] From the 1880s until 1906, the French socialist movement was divided into rival party sects. There were two grand "creative syncretists" during this period who sought to unite the socialist movement through a unifying ideology. The first creative syncretist was Benoît Malon, who advocated an "integral socialism" in the 1880s. The second creative syncretist was Jean Juarès, who also attempted to synthesize the competing ideologies that divided the labor movement beginning in the mid-1890s. The major difference between them was that Juarès succeeded where Malon failed. While it might be possible to argue that Juarès was simply more skillful than Malon, both were creative and talented in their efforts to synthesize opposing socialist ideas. The more important difference between them was the broader ecological context in which each leader preached socialist unity.

During the late 1880s and early 1890s, city-based union federations called *bourses du travail* (labor exchanges) were created in cities across France. These were the same city-based union federations that appeared in the United States at this time, as described in my earlier example. While in the United States these city-based federations helped to unite workers from different ethnic backgrounds, in France they joined workers together who were linked to different party sects. As the bourse movement matured, it began to provide an institutional framework and an ideology (revolutionary syndicalism) for an independent unionism. On the side of the parties, local labor movements built on and imitated the success of the bourses, creating "autonomous federations" in different cities and regions. As with the bourses, this movement to create these autonomous federations was bottom-up and, initially, not a design of the national party sects.

If we now switch our attention to Juarès, we can understand him as operating very much as a creative syncretist. While Juarès had always preached socialist unity, he actually had to discover the operative principles and institutions that would support his rhetoric. He began to appreciate the importance of the autonomous federations as a basis for socialist unity as early as 1900, but until 1904 he failed to understand how the principle of union autonomy from partisan control was the key principle that allowed autonomous federations to survive at the local level. After 1904, he came to understand and adopt this principle. To act as a skillful creative syncretist, Juarès had to deeply understand the ecology that linked the bourses and the autonomous federations. More generally, as I show, Juarès had to learn to throw his weight in some counterintuitive directions in order to cement the underlying union and party structures that would help to consolidate unification. For example, in a contest between the elected party delegates in the Chamber of Deputies (of whom he was one) and the local federations, he had to throw his support behind the federations.

The key difference between Malon and Juarès was that they operated in different institutional ecologies. For Malon, there was little institutional structure to mediate the polarized relations between competing party sects. With the creation of the bourses and later the autonomous party federations, Juarès found an institutional basis for a unified socialist party. But the point is not that these underlying institutional structures are sufficient for explaining unification or that Juarès's speeches were nice rhetorical finishes on a structural explanation. Juarès's leadership was critical for articulating and demonstrating the collective principles that supported the primacy of these local structures. In this account, the structural potential of the bourses and the autonomous federations and the creative syncretism of Juarès were complementary to one another—an example of structure and agency reinforcing one another.

Berk and Galvan's theory of creative syncretism is completely at home in explaining Juarès's success. Like Cosimo de Medici in Renaissance Florence and Louis Brandeis in the early twentieth-century United States, Jean Juarès was a creative and skillful system builder. What is consistent in each of these analyses is that creative syncretists have to work through and with existing institutional ecologies. On the one hand, their own opportunities for creativity and skill were shaped by institutional ecologies, which posed problems for them; on the other hand, to be successful they had to recognize the *potential* of certain institutional structures and learn how to channel them in particular directions. As Berk and Galvan would and do point out, these system builders treated institutions like raw materials whose potential had to be discovered in the course of action.

Berk and Galvan's theory is somewhat less at home in explaining Malon's failure, since Malon too was a creative system-building syncretist. In ecological terms, Malon's failure arose because he had fewer tools to work with than did Juarès. But Berk and Galvan can also use this example to point to a defect in my ecological approach. Had Juarès not come to understand and exploit the opportunities created by his ecology, he could never have articulated the critical principles of the unified socialist movement or have thrown his own considerable political weight in a direction that supported unification. The creative syncretism of Cosimo de Medici, Louis Brandeis, and Jean Juarès is crucial for understanding how the ecology adapts.

To extend this alliance between ecological explanation and creative syncretism, I advance several claims:

1. Although everyone may have the potential for creative syncretism, an ecological approach suggests that some actors will have more need and potential for creative syncretism than others. Creative syncretists are often people who feel cross pressured by system logics, who straddle different contexts, or who must align system logics with local contexts. They may engage in creative syncretism because they need to solve their own problems or because they come to understand the value in solving those problems for others.

2. Creative syncretism suggests that people are creative and skilled in their institutional action, but an ecological perspective suggests that some will be more creative and skilled than others. The Medici family and Jean Juarès had to discover the potentials inherent in their ecologies and then mobilize elements in their ecologies in a way that realized those potentials. A creative syncretist is usually positioned in an ecology in a way that facilitates learning about these potentials and taking advantage of them.

3. If we combine creative syncretism with an ecological perspective, we are therefore led to stress the *positional* opportunities for creative syncretism. Position in an ecology can explain why certain leaders like Medici, Brandeis, or Juarès emerge in the first place as leaders. It might also be used to suggest why certain classes of actors emerge as mediators of broader institutional change movements.

Conclusion

This essay has explored the possibility of utilizing ecological explanation as a distinctive type of institutional explanation, beginning with a relatively inclusive statement of what ecological explanation entails, identifying distribution, diversity, relation, and process as basic orienting concepts. Ecological explanations work by showing how a change in distribution, diversity, relation, or process leads to a change in some feature of institutional life. The essay distinguishes three different levels of analysis on ecological explanation that vary according to the granularity of their analytic attention. A contextual level of analysis focuses on the local embeddedness of actors and action; systemic approaches adopt a wider "landscape" perspective, focusing on patterns of interdependence between actors and action. A third, less well-recognized, intermediary level of analysis calls attention to what lies between contexts and systems. This perspective focuses on boundaries, hybridity, brokerage, and bricolage. The rise of the powerful Medici family in Renaissance Florence illustrates this intermediary perspective. My work on the historical development of the U.S. labor movement serves as an example of the coevolutionary dynamic of ecologies. Finally, examples from Berk's work on Louis Brandeis and my work on French labor history help explore the affinities between this ecological perspective and Berk and Galvan's theory of creative syncretism. While Berk and Galvan focus on the character of action that produces institutional change, the ecological approach describes the broader social environment in which creative syncretism flourishes.

Chapter 3

Governance Architectures for Learning and Self-Recomposition in Chinese Industrial Upgrading

Gary Herrigel, Volker Wittke, and Ulrich Voskamp

For most of its post-1992 rapid industrialization, Chinese manufacturing excelled in global markets as a platform for high-volume and low-cost, export-oriented production.[1] Since China's accession to the World Trade Organization in 2001, however, the fruits of rapid industrialization have been creating home market conditions for very different manufacturing strategies. Successful export-led industrialization has created more sophisticated domestic Chinese demand for a broad array of manufactured goods. In an effort to capture this emergent demand, Chinese producers are shifting their focus toward more advanced production and away from what was traditionally needed (or possible) within the framework of export processing relationships. In particular, they are seeking to leverage their volume production expertise (which involves remarkable flexibility) to move up the value chain into designing and developing their own (increasingly sophisticated) products.[2]

Multinational corporations (MNCs) from developed countries in Asia, Europe, and the United States have responded to the same emergent opportunities in China as the indigenous producers. In order to be competitive, however, MNCs need to enhance and deepen their commitments in China.[3] Global firms need to augment production, engineering, and design capability in China to adapt their products to the technical, regulatory, and cultural characteristics of the Chinese market. They must also train and rely on Chinese workers, engineers, managers, and indigenous suppliers to drive the localization process.

The new dynamics between Chinese firms and MNCs interpenetrate: an indicator of success for increasingly sophisticated Chinese suppliers is to be able to participate in the localizing production networks being established by foreign manufacturing MNCs, while the pressures for localization in China are leading MNC component suppliers and capital goods manufacturers to seek access to indigenous Chinese networks and system consortia. For its part, the Chinese state, mostly at local and regional levels, often supports actors pursuing both upgrading strategies.[4] The result is a complex game of cooperation and competition between foreign and domestic producers, suppliers, customers, and public authorities.

This chapter suggests that this new game is driven by a surprisingly formalized, multidirectional form of organizational and social learning. Industrial players on all sides are constructing formal architectures that aim to systematically disrupt and reconstitute multidimensional communities of manufacturing practice by inducing joint reflection, experimentation, and creativity. These interdependent processes give rise to mutual learning and upgrading all around.

At the least, this is good news for the Chinese. It suggests that doubts about whether Chinese manufacturing can escape the low value and profitability niches of manufacturing value chains are misplaced.[5] The new arrangements aim to cultivate and presuppose the capacity of Chinese producers to collaborate on design, new product development, and increasingly higher-value manufacture.

We also suggest (though will not fully develop here) that MNCs are driving the upgrading process in China in ways that are good for MNC operations generally, including their home markets.[6] MNCs generate recursive effects by globalizing formal learning systems. In the third section we suggest that formalized corporate production systems (CPSs) are emblematic of such formal systems. Originally developed to facilitate innovation and continuous optimization in operations within competitive developed markets, global companies are now extending and adapting CPS principles to Chinese (and other global) operations.[7] Global CPSs create governance architectures that generate reflection, deliberation, and experimentation, which have multidirectional (recursive) consequences for all participants.

The analysis here builds on and departs from much of the sociologically oriented literature on upgrading and organizational learning.[8] We build on this work by emphasizing the significance of producer relations (within supply chains and regional supporting institutions) over technology and other market endowments as preconditions for successful upgrading. However, we abandon its understanding of upgrading as the acquisition of technological knowledge and its (relatively static, structuralist) concern for the specific ties that players have to technology and knowledge-carrying customers and extrafirm institutions. We reject the divide this literature imposes between actors and the context in which they act.

Instead, we embrace the process oriented organizational learning literature's emphasis on relational learning within communities of practice over time.[9] At the same time, we depart from that literature's focus on stability and reproduction, and present a pragmatism-informed perspective on organizational learning that emphasizes the importance of joint inquiry, experimentation, and creativity.[10] We show how firms, rather than unconsciously enacting practices, create "revolutionary routines" that systematically disrupt habits in production and design and force players to continuously reflect on and revise their practices.[11]

In this way, our theoretical orientation is very much in line with the spirit of this volume. We frame our problem as a relational and processual one: Chinese and foreign corporations are understood to be in ongoing, meaningful relations that are recomposed through reflective deliberation in response to challenges that disrupt habitual arrangements. Disruptions occur on myriad levels and processes of recomposition at one level (say in export processing relations between Chinese suppliers and foreign customers) induce changes at other levels (e.g., in the kinds of strategies that Chinese producers pursue both internationally and in their home market). In this way, we regard change as continuous (even as there is pervasive continuity in relations—social relations are complex and not all habitual modes are called into question at once).

Following John Dewey and Hans Joas, we emphasize that disruptions in habitual practice present occasions for joint inquiry about how to resolve the disruption and produce experimental solutions. We also understand actors to be defined by the social relations in which they act, rather than the other way around. As a consequence, social processes of reflection and experimentation cause interrelated actors to rethink their ends and who they are. For us, then, actor "interests" are continuously constructed and reconstructed through social processes of collective inquiry, reflection, and problem solving.[12]

Finally, in what follows we not only apply a pragmatist theoretical perspective to explain the interactive upgrading dynamic between Chinese and foreign firms, we also assert that actors are themselves constructing governance systems that embody pragmatist principles. We follow Charles Sabel, who describes such governance systems as "new pragmatic disciplines." Sabel says:

> We can think of these new institutions as pragmatist in the sense of the philosophy of Peirce, James, and Dewey: They systematically provoke doubt, in the characteristically pragmatist sense of the urgent suspicion that our routines—our habits gone hard, into dogma—are poor guides to current problems. Or we can think of benchmarking, simultaneous engineering, error detection, and the other disciplines grouped under the anodyne heading of 'continuous improvement' as institutionalizing, and so making more practically accessible, the deep pragmatist intuition that we only get at the truth of a thing by trying to change it.[13]

Our pragmatist commitments also question the idea that rules, institutions, or power determine contractual relations. We care less about constraints and opportunities alleged to flow from rule and structural positions than we do about the interactive and recompositional dynamics that mutually dependent players generate through their joint efforts to solve problems. For us, Chinese firms and developed country multinationals are not interacting from positions leveraged by advantages rooted in comparative endowments. Rather, we show how innovation-producing interactions are transforming the terrain on which leverage and endowment can be conceived.

Ultimately, we deploy this theoretical perspective to say something new about contemporary dynamics in China. We make two major points: First, against the skeptics, we show that manufacturing upgrading is actively occurring in China.[14] Second, the chapter outlines how Chinese upgrading involves mutual learning among interlocutors in Chinese firms, foreign corporations, and their supply chains. Learning is achieved through intrafirm and interfirm governance architectures that aim to disrupt shared practices and foster recursive processes of joint inquiry and experimentation. We show that these arrangements allow Chinese producers to compete for business in expanding domestic markets through the development of learning capabilities, while enabling global corporations to enhance their own learning abilities in an effort to gain market share in the same emerging Chinese markets. The result is a highly fluid social and political learning process in which actors continuously redefine their ends and the arrangements they use to pursue them.

Our argument proceeds in three steps. First, we compare our perspective to the existing literature on upgrading and organizational learning. The second section describes the emergent Chinese market and the strategies that both indigenous Chinese and foreign producers follow in order to gain positions within it. Multinationals are shifting their commitments in China by localizing production, design, and even development functions.

The third section shows how efforts to gain position within emergent Chinese markets transform learning dynamics within the community of competitors, as operations in foreign corporations' home countries and their Chinese operations are both redefined. Home operations are no longer simply teachers, their Chinese counterparts learners. Instead, home operations are interested in learning from the experiments that the operations in China are carrying out with the firm's product palette and know-how. In order to capture potential innovation in Chinese practice, firms deploy formal governance architectures, often embedded in CPSs, to induce learning. Such mechanisms combine jointly determined global (intrafirm) standards and metrics (or product designs) with local discretion over implementation in ways that provoke reflection and foster experimentation for adaptation and improvement. In this way, these mechanisms facilitate the recursive multidirectional transfer, transformation, and invention of technological and organizational knowledge between Chinese and foreign corporate actors, as well as across the multinationals' global operations.

Theoretical Framework: Sociological Approaches to Upgrading and Pragmatist Approaches to Organizational Learning

As indicated, our approach builds on the advances that sociological approaches to upgrading have made to our understanding of the development process. This literature moves beyond efforts to explain upgrading processes by incentive alignments[15] and technologically determinist arguments about how the modular characteristics of manufacturing technologies limit possibilities for supplier and emergent firm upgrading.[16] The virtue of the sociological accounts is that they identify specific relations (especially interactive, non-arm's-length relations in supply chains) and environmental conditions (interconnected clusters of regional producers and supporting institutions) as preconditions for successful upgrading that the nonsociological perspectives usually ignore.[17]

This literature's limitation is that it reduces learning to the transfer of specific kinds of technological know-how or knowledge about technologies and products. Moreover, even though it emphasizes the crucial role that multinational corporations play in emergent economy upgrading processes, this literature is guided by structuralist assumptions about power. It assumes that asymmetries in knowledge and capital mean that only one-way flows from foreign corporations to producers in emerging economies are relevant. Consequently, it leaves the possibility that emerging economies have something to teach developed country players undertheorized.

The practice-based organizational learning literature better addresses the processes of learning we observe in China.[18] The sociological literature focuses on discrete nuggets of knowledge and technology, because it presupposes a social terrain in which already formed actors with clear boundaries act within a structure of enabling and constraining rules. By focusing instead on formal and tacit interactive practices—communities of practice—that firms engage in, the practice literature expands the terrain and character of learning: Instead of something actors "learn about" or an external "thing" they acquire, learning is an identity and relation creating process. Learning produces actors as it involves complex and meaningful exchanges that define and redefine roles and capabilities among the interactants. In a companion article,[19] for example, we show that Chinese producer engagement with foreign customers resulted over the last two decades in their integration into transnational communities of practice. Chinese manufacturers learned how to be reliable and competent exporters through interaction with their customers. Customers apprenticed Chinese suppliers by showing them how to meet ever more exacting manufacturing and commercial standards. This was done iteratively, through myriad contracts, audits, supplier quality-assurance encounters, competitor benchmarking, and continuous improvement conferences.[20]

These interactions were not so much about specific technological or knowledge issues as they were about the development of a Chinese firm's ability to learn how to identify the changing production quality and cost needs of foreign customers. Mistakes could be tolerated if the firm gave a sign that it was making corrections. For customers, goodwill and demonstrable learning trumped technological backwardness or a lack of specific know-how. Both of the latter could be more easily mobilized and transferred to a reliable and competent, ever-improving supplier, but competency and learning themselves could not be imposed. They had to develop through the practice of the relationship itself.[21] Crucially, this historical process of meaningful interaction (learning) not only redefined relations between Chinese players and their offshore customers; it also redefined the boundaries, capabilities, and self-understanding of the interacting players themselves. Learning involved political, social, and economic recomposition.

The practice-based theories of organizational learning help explain the first phase of Chinese manufacturing upgrading.[22] By itself, their emphasis on practice and communities of practice integration in organizational learning, however, can't account for the contemporary upgrading dynamics described in this chapter. Their arguments tend on the whole to focus on routine practices and the way in which apprenticeship relations (what Jean Lave and Etienne Wenger call "legitimate peripheral participation") unfold within stable practice arrangements—such as the asymmetric ties between Chinese exporters and their foreign customers. The latter, more knowledgeable and sophisticated producers, taught less experienced (but lower cost) Chinese manufacturers the ropes and gradually integrated them into their global manufacturing practice communities.

Elsewhere we show that the success of this gradual, apprenticeship-based learning process proved self-limiting.[23] Chinese producers found they had competences and ambitions that exceeded their customers' demands. The next two sections of this essay show that awareness of this mismatch between capability and demand in traditional apprenticeship relations has driven both Chinese producers and foreign manufacturers to shift strategy within the Chinese market. Both want market share in emerging Chinese markets for dynamic "middle range" products. We argue that in order to enter these markets rapidly, firms need to disrupt routines and reflect on both the formal and tacit ways in which their practices are organized and their know-how deployed. Uncertainty about strategy, unfamiliarity with new forms of production, and lack of experience with product development and design, moreover, lead producers to encourage experimentation.

These dynamics are a central concern of the pragmatism informed literature on organizational learning. That literature starts with the practice literature's emphasis on action and community, but it further emphasizes the significance of collective reflection and experimentation within organizations when routine practices are disrupted.[24] Although reflection and experimentation contribute to innovation in the community of practice literature, they are not theorized. The suggestion is that reflection and experimentation occur randomly—the result of temporary crises or interruptions in habitual practice. In any case, the mechanisms at work are unclear in the community of practice literature.

By contrast, the pragmatist organizational learning perspective pays systematic attention to the link between the disruption of habitual practices, collective inquiry, and experimental problem solving. It focuses on how collective deliberation emerges and on the way processes of joint problem solving recompose practices and relations in manufacturing communities. Our empirical claim in what follows is that the current period in China has seen a concerted shift toward the systematic provocation of reflection and experimentation in order to disrupt entrenched routines and generate processes of collective reflection that, in turn, yield recursive learning processes. Interruptions in routine that give rise to joint inquiry are not random now; they are systematically and intentionally induced through diverse formal mechanisms.

In contemporary China, reflection- and experimentation-based learning processes stem from foreign corporations' awareness of the limits of their centralized, home-country-developed knowledge, products, and practices. Successful Chinese product adaptation and development forces them to rely on local discretion and competence. Moreover, they can't wait for reflection on the limits of the mother company's products in the Chinese market to occur randomly. They urgently need to induce it.

We argue that multinational corporations accomplish this by deploying formal governance architectures designed to combine joint general goal setting with local discretion. Although there are many variants, we will highlight the way in which CPSs accomplish this. As multidimensional and recursive "constitutional processes,"[25] such governance architectures combine central standard setting with local discretion: relevant global firmwide stakeholder teams establish provisional and revisable central metrics, standards, and product designs that local players then use discretion to implement and adapt to their circumstances. In turn, these monitored local experimental efforts often yield innovation: joint attempts to meet global metrics and create locally competitive products under unfamiliar labor, materials quality, and regulatory conditions, leads all interacting players to interrogate home country products and production practices in ways that induce monitoring teams to reflect on the adequacy and optimality of their own routines, both at home and in other global locations. As Sabel points out, this interactive multilevel experimentation and monitoring makes the tacit dimensions of routine explicit to all the practice community players and thereby makes it possible for them to systematically alter, optimize, and recompose their practices.[26]

Crucially, pragmatist-learning theorists emphasize that these multilevel joint processes of reflection and experimentation can be creative, yielding innovation and new practice and product ideas.[27] To see how these practices fit into our narrative about Chinese upgrading, it is important to notice that what were once more asymmetric relations of apprenticeship or "learning from" relations, where reflection and experimentation were at most random and reactive incidents, are in this way transformed into pro-actively induced, systematic, multidirectional, recursive, mutual learning or "learning with" relations.

To summarize, our emphasis on process, habitual practice, collective reflection, and problem solving in response to disruption are all core dynamics of pragmatist social action theory.[28] They make it possible to interpret industrial dynamics in China as recompositional and social learning processes that occur over time. Following Sabel,[29] we are not simply interpreting events through a pragmatist lens, we are also arguing that the actors we observe are themselves constructing governance mechanisms that operate according to pragmatist principles: contemporary CPSs aim to induce reflection and re-examination of practices in the interest of innovation and optimization. Collective self-reflection and monitoring, systematically imposed by formal procedures, leads to social learning (self-transformation), creativity, and continuous organizational and strategic recomposition. The third section outlines the dynamics of these new forms of learning relations and describes the development of various constitutional mechanisms for the organization and governance of this new kind of learning.

Changing Product Strategies in a Changing Chinese Domestic Market: Competition Between Multinational Corporations and Chinese Producers for the "Middle" of the Market

New foreign manufacturer engagement in the Chinese market is shaped not only by the quantity but also by the changing character of demand.

Contemporary Chinese customers demand products with distinctive characteristics. They want either technologically less sophisticated versions of products foreign manufacturers offer in developed country markets or high-end products with specific modifications to accommodate Chinese preferences, regulations, standards, and differences in resource inputs. In the former (more quantitatively significant) case, foreign corporations can't compete with native Chinese producers by modifying and selling older or outdated versions of their current equipment because Chinese producers easily copy such technologies and underprice foreign producers.[30]

In order to take advantage of the emergent sophistication of Chinese consumers, then, foreign companies in the automobile, automobile component, and complex machinery sectors that we studied modify and reconceive their current technologies or even develop entirely new products to address the incipient needs of Chinese customers. The aim is to reduce sophistication and narrow product functionality. For German firms, in particular, this means learning both how to design less durable products that can be easily maintained and to manufacture them with simpler production technologies and less skilled labor. These modifications directly address the needs and usage norms of Chinese consumers and make the product more affordable than the versions sold in the foreign manufacturer's home markets. The sweet spot for foreign corporations is a midrange market above the highest-volume, lowest-quality commodity segment and yet below the highest-quality, most-sophisticated technologies typically sold in developed markets. Chinese customer desires for such products exceed native Chinese producers' abilities to produce them, so there is a legitimate market opportunity for foreign firms.

There are countless examples of this sort of midmarket product. Take the case of computer numerical control (CNC) technology for machine tools and other steerable capital goods. Japanese and German producers of CNC units cannot sell their highly complex highest-end controllers to machine tool and other capital equipment producers very widely in China. Instead, they succeed there by selling specially designed "simple" CNC controllers. As one German manager told us, "There are millions of conventional machine tools in China that can be easily converted to simple CNC machines if they are provided with the right kind of controller."

Interestingly, neither the Japanese nor German producers could sell older versions of their entry-level controllers in China. Knockoffs of older designs already existed in the market at price points the foreign producers could not match. Instead, they developed entirely new "simple but sophisticated" controllers that integrated new electronics into a simpler delivery unit designed specifically for Chinese customers' needs. Indigenous Chinese producers did not have the electronics know-how to compete with the new products. Crucially, in order to more quickly and efficiently supply demand at a competitive cost, foreign manufacturers produced the new controllers locally in China, using indigenous designers (who cooperated with designers in the home location), less complex production technologies, and Chinese suppliers.

One might ask: why would the Japanese or German companies bother to invest in less than cutting edge business? Interviews with firm representatives reveal that companies need to establish their brand positions in China so that it will be possible to grow in that market. Foreign producers regard it as inevitable that the current midmarket niche ultimately will be overrun by rapidly improving indigenous producers. But the more sophisticated the technology becomes, they believe, the slower the process of indigenous learning will become. If these foreign corporations can establish their brand position in this emerging market, they're betting that the market will grow toward their strengths.

In many cases, rather than designing a wholly new machine or component for the Chinese market, firms redesign existing offerings to make their features and prices more appropriate for Chinese customers. Peter Marsh of the *Financial Times* has been following this phenomenon and he quotes a manager at Mindray, a producer of medical devices and patient monitoring systems: "'We look at what parts we can standardise, where we can reduce the level of technical sophistication without comprising quality, and in what instances we can substitute software for electronic components,' says Joyce Hsu, Mindray's chief financial officer. The result, she says, is often a low-cost product that may not have so many features as an equivalent piece of equipment made in western Europe or the U.S. but which satisfies requirements in hospitals—in China and elsewhere—that are trying to cut back on costs."[31]

A German automobile supplier who has been part of our *"Globale Komponenten"* study has followed a similar strategy for the design and delivery of internal frames (front ends, engine cradles, etc.) for its customers in China. Even when the firm wins a bid on a global component that will be built into the same automobile model in Europe, North America, and China, materials, component designs, and manufacturing procedures still differ in each market. In China, the company uses a different quality steel and welds the front end with less innovative and high-quality techniques than it uses for customers in Europe. The China product is more primitively manufactured and is less complex, durable, or capable of the performance expected in the European variant.

We found producers in many different machinery and automobile component sectors undertaking these sorts of quite substantial product and production modifications (reconceptualizations), including firms making power drives, turbines, gear units, transmissions, and woodworking machinery. Importantly, modifications like these are most conveniently done in China, even when there is substantial cooperation with home country designers. Chinese engineers understand customer requirements, local regulations and standards, and the quirks of local materials. And local production managers have an active sense of labor capabilities and the realistic costs of running complex Western production machinery in the Chinese context.

Such moves on the part of foreign firms, of course, create opportunities for local Chinese suppliers to become integrated into the newly recast production strategies. Foreign manufacturers need local suppliers because the volumes for castings or stamped metal frames for a controller or the front end of an automobile or the cab of a construction machine made in China simply overwhelm the operations of suppliers back in the home market. It is not simply that such distant suppliers are already busy with production slated for home region customers; transportation costs make home country components too difficult to justify. This encourages component-producing multinationals to invest in China to offer their customers a "global footprint." But it also provides an opportunity for indigenous Chinese producers to enter into newly emerging, and more sophisticated, supply chains with foreign manufacturers. In any case, many capable Chinese suppliers have emerged who are chafing at the limits of their old export processing routines and are in a position to take advantage of such business.[32] In cases where capable suppliers were difficult to identify immediately, multinational customers could work with local suppliers to improve their production quality.

The Volkswagen experience in China illustrates one way this interconnected upgrading process takes place.[33] For decades, Volkswagen produced only the modest and outdated Santana in China, in organizationally and technologically minimalist production locations. But toward the end of the twentieth century, when the company recognized that a market for its luxury brand Audi was emerging with the growth of a wealthy class in China, and that demand growth was too robust to service with German exports, the company erected production and assembly facilities in China that mirrored those in Germany. Its aim was to produce a Chinese Audi A6 identical in quality to the A6 manufactured in Germany.

While working to achieve this goal, Audi recognized that Chinese customers actually wanted an A6 with particular characteristics unwanted by German (and other European and North American) consumers. For example, Chinese consumers wanted limousine-like sedans with significantly more legroom (thirty centimeters) than existed in German versions. Incorporating such design changes within an integral architecture like the A6's entailed corresponding changes in materials quality, component machining, in-house system assembly, and the character of local supplier relations. Audi engineers, planners, and purchasing teams could not manage all of these changes from Germany. Therefore, local Audi engineering, production and supplier quality assurance personnel had to be upgraded to facilitate working together with the home country actors to manage the changes.

New and old orientations to the Chinese market can often be seen together, like geological sedimentations, in German operations in China. At our visit to the Volkswagen/Audi/First Automobile Works Joint Venture in Changchun, for example, alongside old equipment still in use for the Volkswagen Jetta, were brand new assembly lines with flexible automation and materials handling workstations that had been specifically designed for Audi's local Chinese assembly needs. The equipment was highly automated, but distinctive in its ability to handle radical variety: different versions of the A6, Golf, Jetta, and Bora were assembled there. Although German engineers were involved in the design of this equipment and supervised its implementation, the ramp-up process soon revealed that Chinese engineers and maintenance and setup specialists were required to implement, maintain, and operate this quite sophisticated equipment.

Audi's traditional German suppliers—including Bosch, ZF, and Hella—were also forced to adjust to the design changes introduced into the A6 (and other Volkswagen models) in China. Since the changes were China-specific, it made sense for these suppliers to implement those changes locally, in their Chinese operations as well. These changes then forced all of those producers to alter their external sourcing strategies to incorporate more local Chinese suppliers. This process, in turn, led Audi suppliers to implement the kind of modifications in material usage and manufacturing engineering and technology described above in the case of our German front-end supplier. Characteristically, once the expanded Audi China production complex proved successful, it made further innovation possible. Volkswagen used its Chinese competence to transform the Jetta into the Bora, a simple yet sophisticated hybrid model that mimics characteristics of the Jetta and the company's simpler Polo model.

The Organization of Mutual Learning: Systematically Disrupting Routine and Inducing Reflection, Experimentation, and Creativity Within and Among Firms

The last section showed that foreign and indigenous manufacturers are altering their strategies and commitments in the Chinese market. Rather than simply purchasing component inputs from Chinese suppliers, or running sleepy low-tech operations producing anachronistic technologies, foreign firms are developing serious Chinese production and design operations to compete in a dynamic and rapidly changing market. Indigenous producers, for their part, are eagerly casting off their apprentice relations and engaging foreign customers in more collaborative, design-intensive, and high-value-added business.

We argue that these changes have given rise to a new multidirectional learning dynamic within multinational corporations and between them and their Chinese suppliers. Remarkable about the stories related in the previous section is that the upgrading processes have a snowball quality: the transfer of capability fosters indigenous competence development that in turn creates additional possibilities that require still more competence transfer and indigenous competence development. We observe that much of this process is not random or an expression of a "natural" development path. Rather multinational manufacturers and the indigenous Chinese producers they interact with are systematically inducing and optimizing learning through the procedures they deploy to combine (global) products, standards, and metrics with disciplined local discretion. Continuous adaptability and innovation, driven by experimentation and learning, is essential for competitiveness in the Chinese market. Moreover, multinationals view the learning and innovation taking place in their Chinese operations as a source of global advantage that can benefit operations elsewhere. As a result, the formerly one-way learning relations characteristic of communities of manufacturing practice in earlier phases of Chinese upgrading are giving way to recursive, multidirectional, mutual learning relations based on joint reflection and experimentation.

The paradigmatic mechanism used to generate these new mutual learning dynamics is the formal CPS that manufacturing firms increasingly deploy throughout their global operations. Examples include the ACE system at United Technologies, Formel ZF at ZF, the Siemens Production System, the Volkswagen production system (known as "the Volkswagen Way"), and the Caterpillar Production System, among countless others.[34] Some, mostly smaller multinationals, like the woodworking machinery producer in our *"Globale Komponenten"* case studies, stop short of branding their corporate systems but nonetheless self-consciously deploy extensive formal procedures that mimic many aspects of the CPSs in larger global corporations.

Many of the companies we interviewed not only infused all their operating practices with the formal procedures of a CPS, they also maintained elaborate continuous improvement teams (CITs) that were charged with the responsibility of spreading the CPS gospel throughout the global organization. These teams teach employees lean production, team collaboration, and realistic target setting, while providing consulting services and reengineering input to teams, departments, and production cells to help them implement new forms of organization and practice. In the German automobile components and complex machinery sectors, CITs were among the most globally active players within the firm.[35]

CPSs establish group-based goal setting and monitoring procedures that systematically induce collective self-observation, problem diagnosis, and problem solving experimentation among all players throughout a firm's value chain. In such systems, internationally composed team negotiations typically establish common global company-wide product designs, quality standards, cost targets, and manufacturing procedures. Crucial in these arrangements is that the targets or standards (or, in cases of simultaneous engineering, the designs) are sufficiently general to allow for considerable local discretion in implementation. Actors in specific markets are encouraged to experiment with adapting the standards, targets, and procedures to local conditions. Local players, however, are not given carte blanche to deviate from common targets. Rather, they are required to justify their decisions to the central teams and provide elaborate quantitative and organizational evidence for the local superiority of their modifications. The possibility of discretion gives local players incentive to experiment and be innovative, while the requirement of justification (and continuous monitoring and dialogue with skilled and interested teams in other locations) wraps processes of local experimentation with discipline.[36]

These formal systems of joint goal setting, local discretion, and mutual monitoring aim to generate positive learning spirals of local adaptation and global improvement, product optimization, and innovation. Product norms and standards and the metrics for local targets are explicitly and continuously (re)constructed by relevant stakeholders in production—manufacturing teams, design teams, customer-focused teams, and purchasing teams, often with the input of CIT players. Teams are constituted at the local level and at the global corporate level and they are interdependent: the success of the local players relies on central actor input while at the same time the success of the central actors depends on local player success. At regular, formally prescribed intervals (and more frequently on an informal basis in between), deliberation between central and local actors generates continuous, mutual self-analysis among production stakeholders.[37]

In effect, having team actors in different locations jointly reflecting on their mutual activities makes practices in each location transparent to all players—the tacit features of local actions are made explicit. Local discretion combined with joint scrutiny induces disruption of routine and causes teams in the plants to experiment with designs, materials, and production organization. The multidirectional learning generated by this process is recursive, in the sense that the output from one application of a procedure or sequence of operations becomes the input for the next, so that iteration of the same process produces changing results.[38] Deviations from central designs and practice made by local teams must be justified to their central counterparts. When the changes are accepted they are then themselves formalized and turned into standard local practice. The new local "standards" are, in turn, benchmarked by higher-order teams within the organization against similar practices in other areas. Where appropriate or possible, adjustments are made elsewhere, which then results in the creation of new higher-order standards and targets. The dialectical logic of jointly negotiated central standards leading to local discretion with public justification (peer review)leading to recursive adjustment of central standards creates a continuous process of experimentation and optimization within the firm that globalizes learning across the entire multinational corporation.

Interestingly, although these systems rely heavily on formal procedure—metrics, standards, writing things down—technology plays only a secondary role in the arrangement of the governing relations (facilitating data collection and monitoring, for example). Indeed, in practice, such systems can be surprisingly low tech. For example, the *"Globale Komponenten"* project's woodworking machinery producer managed transfer of machinery production to its Chinese (and central European) manufacturing locations with what it called a "cookbook" system. German production teams took pictures of each discrete step in the home plant machining processes to be transferred abroad—including machine layout (tools and fixtures), individual setups, tool positioning, transfer procedures, and work organization. The pictures were then annotated with instructions for setup procedures, machining speeds, work rhythms, and expected output for each stage in production and assembly flow. These "cookbooks" were then sent to the company's Chinese operations, along with the blueprint designs for the machines, to guide the construction of all woodworking machine models in the Chinese manufacturing operations.

The "cookbook" or detailed instruction manual functioned as a set of very specific guidelines, but local players were empowered to use discretion while implementing them. The implementation process allowed for any number of local design and procedural modifications in manufacture: the reduction or enhancement of product functionality, the excision or addition of steps in the production process, and substitution of materials were all fair game as the local players sought to adapt the home firm's designs to Chinese regulations, consumer interests, and competitive cost conditions. But local modifications had to be justified to the exporting multifunctional teams and managers that originated the cookbook. The firm noted acceptable changes, took new pictures, and constructed a local instruction manual. If the changes implemented locally improved the way machines were produced, then the German teams embraced the local innovation, photographed the new procedures, and integrated them into the home manual.

Because the "cookbook" is a detailed deconstruction of a machine into literally hundreds of discrete manufacturing operations, it was possible for home country players to selectively adopt small alterations made in China for their own use at home, even as the overall character of the specific Chinese machinery model diverged from the one that the company was manufacturing back in Germany. In this way, the formal process of systematic stakeholder monitoring of the cookbook created a recursive multidirectional process of organizational learning that combined disciplined local innovation and product adaptation with openness to innovation in global design and manufacturing processes.

Significantly, these formal translocational learning practices are also deployed, in modified form, to govern relations between customers and suppliers. Instead of providing a formal manual of pictures and instructions for how to implement and adapt proprietary machinery and operations, multinational customers provide Chinese suppliers with clear targets for cost, quality, and delivery time for a part or component that the customer and supplier design together. Both parties observe the progress of the supplier relative to the target, and, in cases where targets are missed, both immediately seek to identify the reason and work toward a resolution. When successful, such formal collectively self-analyzing relations produce learning and continuous upgrading, for both the customer and the supplier, not only across Chinese supply chains but across entire global production networks.[39]

We observed such relations in a variety of firms. Take the relations between a German gear unit manufacturer and its Chinese supplier of aluminum housings. In this case, the Chinese supplier did both casting and machining for the German subsidiary (the latter in part on machinery that had been transferred from the German company's home plant). In both cases, the customer specified broad production quality and cost targets. Formal audits and regular joint procedure review with the customer took place: engineers from the German company's Suzhou plant regularly visited the Chinese supplier as did skilled workers from the gear producer's German plants. The aim was to help their Chinese counterparts set up the new machinery and understand how to solve problems generated in aluminum housing machining.

These interactions yielded a number of jointly agreed on deviations from original customer designs and practices, in particular regarding materials used in molds, casting techniques (more skilled laborer input, less automation), and even the maintenance procedures for the German company's former machinery. In order to optimize the changes, the Chinese supplier upgraded its own manufacturing engineering and design capabilities (an expense it was encouraged to incur, not only by its German customer but also by the regional Chinese government, which gave tax breaks to firms increasing design capacity). The resulting supplier improvements helped the German company maintain its quality and cost targets, while simultaneously stimulating ideas to adapt the overall gear unit designs to facilitate entry into a new user market—Chinese omnibus manufacturers. Perhaps most significantly, the company took ideas for machining-process modification introduced in China and used them to experiment with the setup of similar processes in its Russian and Indian subsidiaries. This successful mutual learning, moreover, created the possibility for additional, more challenging design-intensive collaborations between the German company and the Chinese supplier in the next contract round.

The are obvious benefits to Chinese manufacturing suppliers (and, in reverse, to Chinese customers working with foreign component suppliers or capital goods suppliers) from this sort of mutual learning activity. It allows Chinese producers to break through the self-limiting structures of the older unidirectional export processing community of practice. The benefits to foreign companies, however, may appear to be more ambiguous. On the one hand, the new relations produce mutual learning, and consequently, multinationals gain the ability to improve not only local Chinese operations but also similar operations in other locations as well. On the other hand, if their Chinese collaborators are becoming such successful and sophisticated learners that they provoke learning processes within their foreign customers, isn't there a danger that the Chinese will abandon the collaboration with the foreigner and manufacture the product on their own? That is, aren't multinationals worried about losing intellectual property, and hence market presence to their increasingly sophisticated Chinese collaborators?

Our interviews uniformly revealed that foreign manufacturing corporations in China engage in these recursive collaboration, learning, and upgrading relations despite the fact that they could not guarantee retention of intellectual property in the relationship, especially not in any long-term sense. Moreover, foreign managers in automobiles and complex machinery sectors broadly acknowledged that their indigenous Chinese employees (managers and skilled workers) were gaining knowledge of proprietary products, technologies, and procedures, and some were taking what they were learning and deploying that knowledge for their own ends.

The same was true of suppliers. Successful collaborators were looking to establish ties with other potential customers that explicitly leveraged what they learned in their relationship with the multinational corporation. In most interviews, foreign managers viewed these dynamics as inevitable and, after a certain point, nonpreventable. All players acknowledge, moreover, that this is true despite what most observe to be continuous improvement in the ability of Chinese authorities to protect property rights.

Why do foreign manufacturers nonetheless proceed with these types of mutual learning relations? They do this because the emerging Chinese competitive and strategic conditions are becoming similar to those in the manufacturers' home regions. Competitive pressure for continuous innovation, cost reduction, and change drive most relations in the global marketplace. Regardless of the property right quality, in relatively mature complex manufacturing sectors based on integrated product architectures, there are few guarantees that a given product or technology will maintain an advantageous position in any market for very long. Rather than orient their systems around protecting technology and product designs, then, firms continuously improve and transform designs to match changing customer needs and identify new customers. Global manufacturing arrangements and relations with suppliers are in this sense strategic, formally governed systems focused not on making specific products but on constructing collaborative, continuous learning processes that drive competence expansion, innovation, and self-transformation.

The Japanese and German CNC controller manufacturers noted above are exemplary of the larger trend. Their long-term market strategy is not to produce simple but sophisticated technologies (such as CNC units) but to be recognized by consumers as reliable and quality manufacturers in their industry (e.g., computer automation equipment). Such firms believe that if they can create dynamic learning relationships in China, they will be able to leverage the global technological know-how that they have in automation equipment, gear units, or woodworking technologies to make those relations continuously and reliably competitive in the dynamic and expanding Chinese market. The idea is to establish dynamic learning capabilities in China that can, in turn, participate in emergent global learning and innovation operations. This strategy promises more return in the long term than one that seeks to protect market share of any particular product model or generation in a specific national market.[40]

Conclusion

This essay describes contemporary Chinese manufacturing upgrading as a multidirectional, interactive, recursive, and learning-driven process. Far from a technological cul de sac, the experience of export processing and participation in transnational supply chains in a broad array of cases has helped Chinese producers learn international best practices in manufacturing. This manufacturing upgrading process has created increasingly sophisticated demand for manufactured products within China itself, and this new demand gives rise to new forms of competitive and cooperative market dynamics among both indigenous Chinese and foreign multinationals seeking to service that (impressively large) new kind of demand.

We argue that this new market situation has been associated with a shift to a new, more dynamic multidirectional and recursive form of mutual learning among Chinese producers and global manufacturers. Chinese engineers, and skilled workers working in rapidly upgrading foreign subsidiaries and their suppliers are helping those companies understand how to adapt their products to the specificities of the Chinese market. Foreign manufacturers are radically altering their commitments to the Chinese market by developing more capacious engineering, design, and organizational capabilities and practices in their subsidiary operations. Key mechanisms for this transformation are the recursive, team-based, mutual learning processes generated by the formal procedures in CPSs. Such systems create global learning spirals by imposing systematic interaction between local discretion and global standards. Though highly competitive (and hence, like any market process, capable of producing losers), our story suggests that the larger dynamic of interaction between Chinese players and multinational corporations has many surprisingly mutually beneficial dimensions.

We can't help pointing out that our story is, at least from one point of view, highly ironic. Initially, the worry about the engagement of developed countries with China was that offshoring and outsourcing relations would involve the loss of competence to China or a shift of home country competence away from manufacturing.[41] Our research shows, however, that these worries are misplaced (or perhaps overtaken by events) in the automobile and complex machinery sectors. Current Chinese engagements systematically foster recursive mutual learning spirals that recompose global knowledge and practice flows across all locations within the multinational. As a result, Chinese operations supply foreign firms' home country product development and production processes with useful benefits. The benefits are likely to be all the greater, moreover, as the gap between Chinese and developed country market sophistication narrows—in part, as a result of the mutual learning processes that this chapter outlines.[42]

In many ways, our ability to point to the ironies in the previous paragraph shows the affinity between our pragmatist analysis and the antistructuralist commitments that animate this volume. The skeptics and worriers we criticize here reason from the undeniable structural observation that asymmetries exist in China's relations with developed country players. Yet while they believe structural asymmetries in resources, competence, and endowments constrain and enable individual strategies, we highlight the mutual dependencies and shared understandings linking asymmetrically aligned players in the flow of social process.[43] The players we describe do not occupy positions in a structure from which they strategize under constraints. Rather our actors are meaningfully interrelated in ongoing processes of negotiation and adjustment regarding the design of products, the scope of markets, the extent of capabilities, the range of training needs—and much more. Social actors mutually recompose their relations as they are disrupted by problems that cannot be resolved through habitual interaction modes or by unilateral action. This process recasts how players understand the context in which they act, their roles within it, and their possibilities for future action. Far from being determined by a structure of rules and endowments acting behind their backs, this process of social deliberation recasts the rules and structure.

Hierarchy and asymmetric access to resources exist in our analysis, and are even reproduced, through the ongoing interaction. But learning and upgrading recomposes self-understanding and sense of possibility for the interacting parties. As they learn and become more capable of increasingly challenging design and engineering tasks, Chinese producers seek to insert themselves in global supply chains and in their own domestic markets in new ways. In response, multinationals change the way they conceive of their Chinese counterparts. They become both potential new partners as well as unexpected competitors in the domestic Chinese market. These actors were once settled in one-way apprenticeship relations, but ongoing interaction along these lines transformed the meaningful character of relations between multinationals and Chinese firms and created the conditions for recursive learning dynamics. In this way, relations are redefined despite the continued existence of endowment asymmetries. The key is that the meaningful dimensions of the asymmetries and the range of action possibilities are recast. Upgrading in China among indigenous producers and foreign manufacturing operations there is driven by reflective and creative processes of social action.

Chapter 4

Reconfiguring Industry Structure

Obama and the Rescue of the Auto Companies

Stephen Amberg

The federal government's rescue of General Motors and Chrysler in 2008–2009 was a dramatic reminder that a liberal state can exert plenary powers to stem a public crisis by controlling the primary agents. Yet federal action came at a moment when social science debates about how institutions shape change had reached a point where government intervention is less significant than the ways that agents are able to innovate from institutional routines.[1] The successful auto bailout raised questions about the evolution of government-market relationships and the capacity of government to improve on market outcomes. The U.S. auto crisis began in the late 1970s when foreign-based companies rapidly increased their share of the domestic market. Since then, debates have asked whether U.S. companies could adopt the new "best practice" evidenced by these market successes. Would competitive forces force them to adapt or would bureaucratic constraints vitiate successful adaptation? Yet this binary frame is upended by the observation that the best practice model of auto manufacturing associated with Toyota was a fairly recent invention in Japan, some key elements of which date only from the 1970s just before Toyota decided to extend its organization in the United States. Moreover, Toyota modified its system to accommodate American conditions because adaptiveness is one of its key qualities. The Obama administration played a crucial role in helping GM and Chrysler autoworkers and managers make a successful adaptation. It did so not by privileging market forces or denying organizational interests and still less by government fiat. Instead, the Obama administration seized an opportunity to build on decades of growing experience with industry restructuring to enable government officials to govern the alliances in auto manufacturing that already were engaged in reform.

There is an important dimension of codetermination to institutional life, which is obscured in the public debate by the polar images of government takeover versus free market and in the professional literature by an overemphasis on structural limits on action that undervalues the creative work that agents do every day. The auto rescue demonstrated that agents could extend their capacity for fomenting social cooperation to solve economic problems to a greater degree than these views allow. In contrast, I present a pragmatist analysis that builds on the distinction between a logic of orientation and a logic of practice.[2] The logic of orientation for the autoworkers and managers for several decades in the mid-twentieth century was the image of mass production (or Fordism). In the 1980s, workers and managers increasingly became reoriented to a new logic associated with the Toyota production system (known as lean production). These orientations are models that agents share that guide their work together in the project of manufacturing automobiles, but the models do not determine the practice of the agents. The logic of practice emerges because the actual situations at work are more complex than models can encompass and because the background conditions for production organization are not fixed. Adaptation depends on agents' assessments of their options and on the political conditions that support (or not) the authority of agents to take creative action.[3] By the time the Bush and Obama administrations bailed out GM and Chrysler, the companies' managers and unionized employees had already made dramatic improvements in manufacturing practice. The auto rescue was less about the exogenous forces of global market competition and a controlling state and more about the accession of a knowing political coalition that empowered the reformers to pursue their goals. The institutional presidency was an important resource for the U.S. auto industry's adaptation.[4]

The remainder of the chapter is organized in the following way. The second section develops the pragmatist argument. A key issue is the status of institutional structures in agents' work and conversely how agents may restructure the conditions they find themselves in through their projects. American institutions have supported multiple forms of social and economic organization. The third section discusses the heyday of Fordism to show that the primary agents oriented themselves to the logic of mass production manufacturing, but that this logic generated boundary problems that led to heterodox practices. The fourth section shows that when Japanese competitors arrived and their challenge became understood as a powerful alternative system of production—lean production—the American auto companies and autoworkers as well as others sought to learn how to adapt the new principles in diverse American conditions. Three alternative narratives emerged to explain the ways auto governance was changing and should change. The Saturn experiment illustrates the reform process at work. The fifth section shows that there were multiple credible interpretations of the 2008 crisis and that President Barack Obama encompassed some of their themes in a broad vision of restructuring. The sixth section sets out how Obama's rescue package restructured the industry, what it changed and what it continued, and what the rescue may augur for the long-run survival of the U.S. auto companies and the United Auto Workers (UAW). The final section sums up the argument about the surprising reform capacity of the American polity.

Innovation Beyond Institutional Constraint and Shocks

Institutions bound situations for agents, but most institutional analyses emphasize how boundaries constrain rather than provisionally stabilize. Peter Hall and David Soskice developed a typology of national governance that focused on how distinctive sets of institutions shape labor-management relations, corporate governance, education and training, and interfirm relations. Firms tend to adapt their strategies to the forms of coordination supported by their country's institutions. These institutional sets create complementary expectations among the agents in each institution about the actions of the others. The coordinating institutions establish distinctive national strategies of competition as well as disincentives for countries to converge on the "one efficient way" as imagined in neoclassical economic models.[5] Hall and Soskice proposed two basic types, "coordinated market economies" like Germany and Japan, whose institutions favor stakeholder negotiations and long-term commitments, and "liberal market economies" like the United States, whose institutions favor arms-length contracting and asset switching.[6] Kathleen Thelen has argued that governance evolves along a path established by historical class political alliances that empower specific institutions of coordination, which are operated to sustain the goals that the alliance has set.[7]

Consider a problem with the institutionalist concept of national governance in the American case and how it can shift our analysis to creative action in institutional politics. The United States operated not one but two (at least) governing types. There was the New Deal type that was associated with workplace pluralism and collective bargaining, antitrust monitoring of large corporations, and social insurance. There also was the southern type that was associated with unitary management; authoritarian political structures, including white supremacy; "right to work" laws that created strong disincentives for union organization; and minimal public services. The national Democratic Party held these regional types together, but the price of southern alliance was segmented rather than national rules.[8] The Taft-Hartley Act of 1947 specifically declared two different goals for national labor policy and supported two different regionally based ways to practice labor-management relations during the New Deal era.[9]

Karen Orren and Stephen Skowronek take institutional multiplicity and complexity as the key to political development.[10] Institutions are conceived not as complementary but as potentially clashing because they were created at varying times to achieve diverse purposes. Wolfgang Streeck and Kathleen Thelen account for evolving governing patterns by such mechanisms as drift and exhaustion and by official strategies to cope with complexity by accommodation, settlement, layering, and redirection.[11] Structural change results from exogenous shocks. But if there are competing institutions that have authority to respond to a shock, more than one solution seems possible because there is plausibly more than one problem to solve and more than one set of rules. Which problem to solve and how to do so would appear to be as much a product of agents' changing their ways of thinking about inherited commitments and institutional rules as it is a product of negative environmental feedback.

Pragmatist constructivism starts with human action—roughly how the agents assess their situation and create new habits.[12] Real agents "think" their institutions as they act. They perceive the situation they are in, interpret for themselves what it is and imagine what their interests could be, and organize with others to revise commitments and reform the rules in ways that enable them to achieve them. The boundaries between exogenous and endogenous, structure and agency, lose their constraining force. For example, when agents perceived a new challenge from global competitors in the 1980s, some officials in North and South initially responded in routine ways, but others began to change their economic development strategies.[13] Japanese and German firms became attracted to the South rather than the North with its dense network of manufacturing expertise and infrastructure. The United States offered two sets of rules to foreign manufacturers, one for the North—with its contentious pluralist labor management and higher taxes—and one for the South, where managements were given a freer hand. Why not choose the profit-subsidizing South and gain a competitive advantage over the American auto companies? Yet as eager as southern officials were for foreign investment, the location of high-performance work organizations in the South became a challenge for southerners, beyond the latter's expectations, to rethink what they were doing.[14]

The scholarly question is how people may be able to pursue new projects in a world in which what people do is already institutionalized. Reformers (presidents among them) create a discursive context in which agents can imagine how to recombine their relationships in ways that could make them more effective in the new context than they were in the old.[15] Projects can take on a new meaning and reconstitute commitments in a new organization. The policy question in 2008–2009 was how federal officials could use public authority to help GM and Chrysler (and Ford) to prevail. The Obama administration's objective was to manufacture high-quality products in the United States that were attractive to consumers while employing American workers in conditions that sustain a middle-class lifestyle. The administration connected itself with the industry by employing individuals at its Presidential Task Force on the Auto Industry who were familiar with the debates about industrial relations, corporate governance, and industry restructuring—the practical discourses of organizational life. It narrated a new history that contrasted selected past practices with current performance and with superior practices demonstrated by more successful organizations, such as Toyota. The administration engaged some parts of the primary agents' common project— the manufacture of cars for a profit and a livelihood—and brought new authority for changes in the rules of play into the discussion. The administration had the authority to be there and compel other agents to participate, but it announced it would lead rather than command.

The Practice of America's Production Systems

Autoworkers and managers always were cognizant of the conditions in which they pursued their projects rather than players following routines.

During the mid-twentieth century the core institution of auto governance was pluralist labor-management relations. The operation of pluralism depended on stable political background conditions that included inter-regional alliances cemented by Democratic Party dominance of Congress and by the leading position of the United States in the world financial system.[16] Auto managers, union leaders, workers, industrial relations experts, government regulators, members of Congress, and others all were engaged in various ways in managing the industry during a long course of profitable development from the 1930s to the 1980s. But the production system was fragile rather than robust because the primary players who worked directly for the companies could not control the boundary conditions that otherwise seemed to promise stable relationships and growth. They always assessed their options for improving their performance vis-à-vis each other and in the marketplace. The interactions between governing institutions, organizational relationships, and individual action are complex and require vision and choice in everyday life.

The dominant orientation for the primary agents was the image of mass production, which facilitated their relationships and gave meaning to their actions. The common orientation supplied knowledge about how production was organized; a shared language of auto work; a habitual rhythm to hourly, daily, and yearly work cycles and contract terms; and expectations about the similarity of conditions and action across companies in the industry. There was an appropriate organization for the factory, clearly marked roles, and obvious performance metrics. These relationships were codified by rules, but the stability of relationships required effort and renewal because boundary conditions were much less amenable to such organizational control.

Thus mass production was taken to be characterized by certain facts of technology and economies of scale that required bureaucratic hierarchy, extreme task specialization, and strict control of the pace of production. Each employee's role was regulated by rules that described precisely what each of thousands of jobs entailed, how the jobs were linked with one another for purposes of promotion and layoff, what pay rates applied, and many other conditions of specific workshops. In the logic of orientation, operational decisions were reserved to managers, and the union had no say in decisions about technology, product strategies, supplier relationships, marketing, and investment. The evaluation of a worker's performance was driven by the overriding fact that the integrated quality of production diminished individual contributions to car building. National contracts specified annual increases in everyone's wages through cost of living allowances and productivity gain sharing. Health and pension benefits were piggybacked on national tax and welfare policies.[17] The wage and work rules stabilized factory life and contributed to the companies' ability to realize volume sales to sovereign consumers.[18]

These routines depended on the actions of many others beyond the factory. Fiscal and monetary policies underwrote increasing incomes for consumers at large, but they did not end business cycles and specific policy debates. The National Labor Relations Board managed the union duty of fair representation in cases of race discrimination and the right of employees not to join a union.[19] The U.S. strategy of global hegemony defined domestic consensus, but it also committed the United States to large foreign military expenditures and unequal trade relations, which created chronic monetary and trade problems. Increasing returns to scale led to rising industrial concentration and dislocated workers. Union wages created disparity between those in the core firms and those on the margins, many of whom were members of minority groups and southerners, while guaranteed wages in the core contributed to inflation.[20] Wage-price inflation aggravated the pursuit of the U.S. role in the world. So throughout the 1960s, Democratic administrations intervened in collective bargaining negotiations and corporate price making, imposed capital controls, and manipulated government commodity inventories and wage and hour rules.

The performance metrics in the industry also had characteristic problems that stimulated a search for modifications. Workers were ensconced in a bureaucratic hierarchy that discouraged their individual contributions, diluted craft skills, and undermined consent. Workers were pressed to work quickly to achieve volume; slowing down to ensure a better product could be penalized. The situated nature of consent was revealed when workers stopped working during strikes. The UAW bargained for time away from work—vacations, personal days off, voluntary overtime, early retirement, and generous attendance rules—and it collaborated with university experts and managers to implement "quality of work life" programs in the 1970s based on behavioral theories of the firm in order to humanize work and improve job satisfaction.[21]

In short, workers, unions, and managers collaborated to fashion the practical meaning of Fordism to enable the auto companies to profit and autoworkers to make a good living. But in the late 1970s the Japanese auto import surge began. The U.S. companies began to miss their performance targets and Chrysler was saved from bankruptcy by a federal bailout in January 1980.

Americans Reorient to Lean Production

The newly competitive automobile market is associated with the success of the "lean" Toyota Production System. In lean production, a company orchestrates collaborations among a network of suppliers in a disciplined process of tightly coordinated manufacturing and continuous improvement.[22] Firms' hierarchies are flatter—there are fewer managers and white-collar staff—and production workers have greater responsibilities for product flow and quality.[23] Toyota promises to create a work environment that enables employees to be the most productive of the highest-quality product they can. The goal is "reliability of delivery rather than sheer volume."[24] When Toyota began to manufacture in the United States, it started to modify its system and integrate the company's principles of manufacturing with practices that American workers and managers were used to.[25]

Three narratives of practice shaped Americans' perceptions of the lean challenge. Presented here as ideal types that are stylizations of empirical materials, they outline the range of choices that agents considered and acted on.[26] I label them "industrial pluralism," "unitary management," and "codetermination." Industrial pluralism is stylized from the historical practice of New Deal policies that supported pluralistic labor management in the factories, regulated monopoly, and the Keynesian welfare state. Unitary management references the historical practices of southern state economic development and labor management as well as the Reagan revolution of neoliberalism. Codetermination references Toyota in Japan or BMW in Germany, but it is stylized and not a reference to the codetermination law in Germany. It also references historical American collaborative decision making in garment manufacturing, toolmaking, building construction, and printing.

The narratives all surfaced in the debates about the government bailout of Chrysler in 1980. First there was the emerging neoliberal critique of New Deal governance related to stagnant stock share prices, which was stimulation for the corporate governance theory of shareholder value (a

referent for unitary management). Shareholders are the primary constituency for the management of the corporation and maximizing their return
on investment is the primary objective.[27] The theory justified aggressive
action to increase share prices in the short run. Chrysler's management was
one that came under intense investor pressure in the 1970s to boost its
share price and dividend. By 1979 the company was virtually insolvent.
However, the company was saved by the federal bailout, which also preserved New Deal industrial pluralism. The contested notion was that Chrysler was too big to fail. To New Dealers, big could be efficient and valuable
for consumers and the public interest could be secured against "big business" power through regulation. Yet the very success of the Chrysler bailout
was considered a terrible threat at the Heritage Foundation, National Taxpayers' Union, the Business Roundtable, Citicorp, and Lehman Brothers
Kuhn Loeb because it violated the market test for firms.[28]

The bailout also was problematic from the perspective of codetermination. Merely guaranteeing loans to Chrysler, as President Jimmy Carter did,
and requiring proportional financial sacrifices from the stakeholders was to
hope that the structural conditions between industry and market would be
restored so that no changes in the relationships among the stakeholders
had to be made and every group could continue to defend its interests.
Proponents of restructuring argued that the pre-1980 market conditions
were not going to return, product market instability was permanent, and
pluralistic industrial relations was no longer a competitive format. But
rather than turn to unitary management as the alternative, they proposed
flexible forms of industrial organization based on union-management partnerships. The terms of this debate were "quality circles," "management by
stress," "employee involvement," "empowerment," "flexible specialization," "strategic choice," and "high performance work organizations."[29]
However, in the New Deal narrative of pluralism, partnership invited management cooptation of workers in the company's plans, and in the unitary
management narrative, it represented an attempt to undermine management by imposing social and political goals on the firm.

The Chrysler bailout debate was settled politically by the victorious
Reagan coalition. Where automobile industry organization showed its vulner-
ability to exogenous change and where the New Deal government demonstrated the political quality of the boundary conditions when it bailed out
Chrysler, the market fundamentalism aroused by President Ronald Reagan
made a fetish of the boundary.[30] The administration's main concessions to

the auto industry were negative: to block increases in fuel economy and compel Japan to limit auto exports. The Japanese auto companies responded by investing in the United States. In 1982, the Federal Trade Commission officially declared the auto markets competitive when it ended its five-year antitrust investigation of auto manufacturing.[31] The companies and the union ostensibly were on their own.

Some leaders in the UAW and the companies began to reorient themselves to lean production. There was growing appreciation of the potential of networks of collaboration, organizational skills, online teamwork, and external research in place of the uniform economic space of Fordism. Lean reformers were encouraged by outside consultants, but inside their organizations they made up factions that faced opposition.[32] Reformers expended time and effort to start new projects, the value of which depended on outcomes, which took time to appear and define, and some reformers were defeated or retired along the way. The companies disintegrated by spinning off parts production into independent companies, a shift that evolved into a prolonged process of learning how to manage decentralized production networks.[33] The UAW reopened its contracts and made wage concessions in the early 1980s, which sparked bitter dissension and useful debates about the meaning of industrial change and therefore about what workers' interests were in change. The Big Three automakers (GM, Ford, and Chrysler) each formed joint ventures with Japanese companies.

The most ambitious project was the joint venture initiated in 1982 by the UAW and GM to introduce industry best practices at Saturn. Saturn's organizational principle was "joint" union-management operational responsibility in contrast to the bright-line distinction associated with the image of mass production.[34] They located Saturn in Tennessee, a right-to-work state with nonunion Japanese factories. The labor agreement created the joint Strategic Action Council, whose mandate was company-wide issues and long-term planning and relations with all stakeholders; the Manufacturing Action Council, which included the plant managements and the UAW local president and all the vice presidents who served on the local bargaining committee; work units of about a dozen employees with elected leaders that operated as self-managed work teams (with authority for assignments, schedules, working to budget, quality, housekeeping, inventory control, and repairs); modules made up of several work units grouped according to location, product, and technology, to which two advisors were appointed by the union and company; and decision-making committees

for business units composed of modules for each of the plants that manufacture the major components (body systems, power train, and vehicle systems). Hundreds of local union members were assigned to modules that
normally were the province of managerial staff, such as operations management, supplier selection, financial analysis, and strategic planning. What
emerged at Saturn was "co-management."[35] The Tennessee factory became
one of GM's most efficient and flexible manufacturing sites and its cars
beat almost all the competition for customer satisfaction in the 1990s.

Skill development and pay systems also diverged. All new Saturn workers received training in their job tasks as well as a broader array of organizational skills, such as teamwork processes, decision making, problem solving,
conflict resolution; the history of the union-management relationship; and
business tasks, such as budgeting, scheduling, quality control, record keeping, engineering and job design, experimental design, and data analysis.[36]
About 20 percent of workers' pay was performance based, because the lean
logic was that employees were given significant control over their work and
responsibility for high performance. Saturn workers' pay partly depended
on meeting benchmarks for quality, cost, schedule, profitability, and
volume.

For many unionists, the UAW gave up core commitments. Saturn
promised job security only for 80 percent of the workforce and it violated
seniority rules in assignments. The pay system undermined long-settled
notions about equality. The workers' right to elected representation was
undermined because advisors were appointed, which distracted union leaders from their roles as advocates for worker interests. Opponents argued
that workers could not be held responsible without authority over strategic
planning, product decisions, and engineering, all of which were under the
control of the top management until the local forced the issue. On the
management side, objections were muffled by corporate hierarchy and
the lack of independent representation for white-collar staff. At the corporate level in Detroit, the chief advocates for Saturn met resistance from vice
presidents of the other product divisions that competed with Saturn for
investment funds. Saul Rubenstein and Thomas Kochan argued that the
signal failure of Saturn was the failure to develop leadership to cultivate
"continuous improvement" by ongoing benchmarking. This is something
that GM's top managers failed to support.[37] In the Saturn local, objections
led to contested elections. But once new leaders took office and new positions were created to handle grievances and the pay formula was revised to

make it more like that elsewhere in the company, the core of the innovations continued—comanagement and joint self-managed teams.

Saturn demonstrated the value of the new labor-management model, but it did not address all of the problems; it could not. The Clinton administration's labor law reform debate came to an end when the Republican Party won control of the Congress in the 1994 election.[38] The Saturn experiment was isolated within GM and then suspended. Comanagement was not the only possible strategy for the company and the union. The company invested heavily in automated production technology, which contributed to a financial crisis in 1992 and a reduction in funding for Saturn. This crisis led it to close twelve factories and the UAW to demand job security to the point that it lobbied to move the next generation Saturn product to Delaware, where GM had just closed a plant.[39] Finally, the company shifted its strategy to trucks and SUVs in the 1990s, which avoided head-to-head competition with foreign firms and which turned out to be very profitable until about 2005.

While the primary agents were activated, the U.S. government had come under the sway of the unitary management narrative that prioritized the capital-allocating functions of managers and investors over all other functions and stakeholders. The electoral background conditions were reflected in the industrial landscape, where battles raged between companies and unions in the 1980s and 1990s over company restructurings, most of which were lost by the unions. Autoworkers could see that contractual security was more important than ever because the political environment was hostile to unemployed workers, including even autoworkers who took buyouts.[40] The American-based companies' market share was cut to half from 1980 to 2008. The UAW's membership shrank from 1.5 million members in 1979 to 392,000 in 2009. At the same time, the companies made a lot of money during most of those years after 1980 and a shrunken cohort of workers made a good living. Yet before the Great Recession began, the American companies had all begun to lose huge amounts of money. In 2008 they were teetering on the edge of bankruptcy.

Narrating the Crisis

President George W. Bush announced on December 19, 2008, that $17.4 billion from the Troubled Asset Relief Program fund would be used for emergency loans to GM and Chrysler, plus about $7 billion for their finance companies, Chrysler Financial and GMAC.[41] In January and February 2009, GM and Chrysler submitted business plans to the Treasury that had been required by the December loan agreements in order to ask for additional federal aid. President Obama's auto task force declared the plans unacceptable, gave each company a new deadline for better plans, and then, when it got them, led each company into a managed bankruptcy. The federal government committed an additional $8 billion to what was by then Chrysler-Fiat and $30 billion to the new GM.[42]

Unlike in the 1980 bailout of Chrysler, President Obama mobilized his administration to transform the industry. The president said, "decade after decade, we've seen problems papered over and tough choices kicked down the road, even as foreign competitors outpaced us. . . . Now is the time to confront our problems head-on and do what's necessary to solve them."[43] Obama drew on the expertise embodied in the networks that helped bring him to power and he used his position to promote a narrative of the crisis and solution. Obama's narrative was a critical resource for restructuring because the complex situation engendered multiple alternative interpretations that expressed themes of pluralism, unitary management, and code-termination. Obama assembled some of these themes into a broader vision of a renewed American economy and he decisively favored the reformers in the companies.

Opponents of the bailout argued that the marketplace had determined that the companies were losers. The *Wall Street Journal* argued in December 2008 that American consumers did not need the American-based companies because they already had decided to buy Japanese cars.[44] A chart accompanying the *Journal*'s editorial illustrated the dramatic shift in sales between American and foreign-based companies, but the chart showed only cars. The editors surely knew that many American consumers switched to trucks and SUVs (which are built on a truck chassis) in the mid-1990s. Car sales peaked in 1986 while total vehicle sales continued to climb. At the time of the *Journal*'s editorial, the American-based companies had a 51 percent market share. In 2008 consumer demand collapsed for all companies, domestic and foreign. The annual production capacity of domestic plus foreign auto companies in the United States was about 17 million vehicles in 2008, but consumer demand dropped in early 2009 to an annual sales rate of under 10 million. That is why even Toyota lost money.[45] A related theme appeared in the argument that regulators had failed to resist interest group pressures from the auto companies on fuel efficiency. Political influence—the capture of the regulatory institutions by the industry—stymied consumer interests, but now the government should compel Detroit to produce electric cars. Obama articulated a link between the auto rescue and rebuilding the economy that aspired to shift the rescue to a broader conception of innovation and security. The administration acknowledged the changed composition of the product market: it pressed the U.S. companies to sharply reduce their production capacity, but the president promised that "the United States of America will lead the world in building the next generation of clean cars."[46] The American Recovery and Reinvestment Act of February 2009 included subsidies for purchasers of electric cars as well as for developers of battery technologies. In April 2009, President Obama set out "five pillars" for a growing economy: new rules for financial firms, investments in education to "make our workforce more skilled and competitive," investments in renewable energy industries, health-care reform, and long-term fiscal prudence.[47]

It was equally important to change the work orientation of the primary agents. To management and industrial relations experts, the unpredictability of consumer demand suggested that manufacturing flexibility—process—rather than particular products was the key to viability.[48] The foreign companies had a more diverse product mix and a flexible factory organization that could handle instability and, thus, their bottom lines were not affected as much.[49] The potential for quality improvements if the companies shifted from their old mass production orientation to volume was detailed in studies by scholars associated with the International Motor Vehicle Program at MIT, the Wharton School of the University of Pennsylvania, the University of Michigan's Center for Automotive Research, the Michigan Technology Institute, Case Western, and the Brookings Institution.[50] Their argument was that the failure to manufacture high-quality vehicles led the U.S. companies to discount prices and seek fleet sales. A strategy that emphasized cost reduction would lead to more production shifted to Mexico.[51] Improved quality could raise prices and profits. Workers and plant managers had shown that they could adapt lean production techniques, but the commitment of corporate leadership was still problematic. The quality argument became incised in the cost-reduction plan of the Auto Task Force.[52] Product and process quality was a goal of teamwork among workers and managers, manufacturers, and suppliers. The administration replaced top managers, invested in suppliers, and placed limits on outsourcing.[53]

Bailout opponents in the U.S. Senate argued that the crisis proved the superiority of the South's unitary management model because the crisis was precipitated by the UAW's push for wages that drove up the cost of vehicles to noncompetitive levels.[54] In fact, in 2007 the UAW made major concessions in collective bargaining agreements to bring wage rates down sharply for certain categories of jobs and cut costs.[55] As a result, GM's average hourly costs were about $50 compared to $47 at Toyota.[56] The greater difference between union and nonunion companies was the "legacy cost" of sixty years of public policy support for employer-based health and pension benefits.[57] The 2007 auto contracts addressed the health care costs by creating "voluntary employees' beneficiary associations," which allowed the companies to buy out their long-term obligations with short- and medium-term payments to a union-controlled benefits fund. These contractual obligations to the voluntary associations and the strategic purpose they served in the long-run revival of the companies were transformed in the rescue into a 55 percent union ownership stake in Chrysler and a 17.5 percent stake in GM.[58] But the antipluralists invoked the image of the vindicated South, whose resistance to the New Deal had now been proven correct. The *Wall Street Journal* argued that the foreign-based companies "made sure not to get saddled with" employee benefits by locating in what it called "investment-friendly states. The South proved especially attractive, offering tax breaks and a low-cost, non-union labor pool." It emphasized that "Mississippi, Alabama, Tennessee and South Carolina—which accounted for a quarter of U.S. car production last year—are 'right-to-work' states where employees can't be forced to join a union."[59] Yet the southern narrative of opposition to federal intervention in markets was never about opposition to government intervention per se; it is specifically federal intervention that might upset state-level social policy that earns southern scorn.[60] Soon the opposition leader, Senator Bob Corker (R, TN), was compelled to update his perception of industry organization because networked auto suppliers served both union and nonunion manufacturers, and therefore the union would survive, but he vowed that "the UAW will get their wages rationalized to where we are paying exactly the same, not a penny more, to what the transplants are making."[61]

When Obama stipulated that best practice was the nonunion auto companies in the American South, it may have seemed to abandon the New Dealers' commitment to pluralist industrial development, but this was not a simple vindication of the old South's unitary management. Instead, the meaning of the regional differences was given a new interpretation by Obama because his administration articulated a different lesson from the crisis. It was not the southern employers but the Japanese who perfected the bundle of manufacturing techniques that create high-performance work organizations. When Obama emphasized a new spirit of factory teamwork to satisfy public needs, this was no acceptance of the New Deal binary but, instead, something like the transcendence of it.[62] Teamwork is a challenge to GM and the UAW, but it is also a challenge to historical southern social and labor institutions and the companies that have grown up under their protection. The president of the UAW, Bob King, who took office in June 2010, stoutly praised the transformations of the union's relationship with the American companies and put the transplants on notice that, now, the unionized companies had best practices that exceeded their own in the area of employee representation. The UAW promised to aggressively seek unionization at the nonunion companies.[63] Auto manufacturing will survive in the United States, but how will it be oriented?[64]

The crisis debate drew on the three ideal types, but practice exceeded the models. The Bush administration violated its principles and the Obama administration was presented with a task it never sought. The auto task force became the superintending authority for the auto agents who had already demonstrated their capacity for reform in the old regime, who were now engaged in more radical reforms whose long-term outcomes are not known.

The Auto Industry Rescue

The White House helped the companies fulfill what the Detroit Three had not been able to accomplish alone. The task force drew on the new expertise in industry restructuring that had developed since the 1970s in management consulting, investment and private equity banking, university research centers, and think tanks, and it had the political leverage to make those knowledge resources available to the industry agents who were willing to become partners to achieve their goals. The rescue was nominally headed by Timothy Geithner because the Treasury managed the relief funds and by Lawrence Summers at the National Economic Council, but the task force was run by a staff led by private equity bankers and industry restructuring experts from the private sector. Steven Rattner became the chief of staff and

Ronald Bloom was the deputy chief. Rattner was a private equity banker and managing partner of Quadrangle; before that he was deputy chairman of Lazard Freres. He was an active New Democrat Clinton supporter. Bloom got his start with Lazard Freres and later formed an investment firm with Eugene Keilin and worked on projects at large companies, such as U.S. Rubber and Eastern Airlines, before going to work for the United Steelworkers Union to help restructure the steel industry.[65] Lazard was the advisor to the UAW during the auto rescue. In addition to the Lazard alumni, the task force relied on management consultants and finance specialists from Boston Consulting Group, McKinsey Global Institute, and Rothschild. The Auto Task Force did not run the factories or pick products and set their prices, but an internal report advised the president that it would be deeply involved in picking the leadership teams in the companies.[66]

The administration's restructuring plan included four main elements:

- Keep automobile manufacturing a viable sector in the United States. The benchmark is Toyota. The administration set goals for each company for employment in the United States.
- Unions would survive as partners of the restructured auto companies once they agreed to substantial worker concessions on pay and health benefits.
- Reorient labor-management contracts to break down the bright-line distinction between management and labor to focus on strategic and production cooperation among workers and managers.
- Once labor costs were reset and the size of the companies was adjusted, discourage the managers from competing on the basis of further labor cost-cutting and shifting production to Mexico.

Rattner, Bloom, and their colleagues assumed the strategic planning function just as they might have in a private restructuring. They superintended the players—the creditors, government agencies both domestic and foreign, the board of directors, the chief executive, and the union leadership. They made clear that continued financial support was contingent on progress.[67] The task force's "viability assessments" focused on adjustments to product mix and design, manufacturing flexibility, purchasing, and dealer networks.[68] The task force left it to the original equipment manufacturers to push the suppliers for quality.[69]

The administration's monitoring was informed by the post-1970s debates, but the president gave codetermination a greater voice.[70] The Treasury was primarily concerned about protecting the "commercial" interests of the taxpayers' investments and loans to the companies. As the General Accounting Office later reported to the Congress, "Treasury developed several principles to guide its role [according to which] Treasury plans to oversee its financial interests in a commercial manner. . . . Treasury officials stated that they . . . would make an appropriate determination to maximize the taxpayers' return."[71] Treasury resisted "external pressures to focus on public policy goals" such as "job retention." The Treasury's view was that the government should have the same goals as those that companies are supposed to have toward their investors—now including citizens-as-investors—the primary of which is to maximize shareholder value. This view is what officials believed made Treasury's actions not political.[72] Even Rattner had doubts about the application of shareholder value to GM, in part because he was impressed by the new capabilities at the factory level.[73] Whatever the government did—including increasing shareholder value— was a commitment to a social vision. In a critical meeting about whether to save Chrysler, the task force was split and the Council of Economic Advisors was opposed. The president made the decision to save the company and workers' jobs despite a "commercial" argument that a Chrysler liquidation would help GM and Ford survive.[74] The agreements between the U.S. Treasury and the auto companies stipulated goals for future domestic production and employment.[75]

The administration saved the union by seeking better collective bargaining agreements and it preserved *most* of the pension and health benefits for incumbent employees and retirees. The auto companies themselves resisted the unitary management assumption that they should fight the union on benefits because "these guys you're dealing with are the ones who build your products."[76] The administration gave new authority to the internal alliances around UAW president Ron Gettelfinger, who fought to save jobs, but who also agreed to convince members about the new strategic cooperation. Starting pay was cut dramatically and performance-based pay may increase over time.[77] Hundreds of job classifications were collapsed to make job assignments and responsibilities more flexible. The companies and UAW folded production worker jobs into two classifications, team member and team leader; the task force pushed to reduce skilled trades jobs into two or three classifications. Union members agreed to a no-strike clause.

These changes earned strong opposition from some autoworkers, but most members voted for the changes.[78]

The government rescue re-created the consumer market. Contrary to commentary that consumers would shun government-controlled companies' products, the American companies thrived. *Wall Street Journal* stories about GM's initial public offering of stock typically included the refrain that the company badly needed to escape the taint of "government motors" in order to win back consumers. But the bailout did not harm the company's popularity with consumers. The rescue drew intense attention to the American companies. Consumers' curiosity led them to discover the great strides the companies were making in their products' quality.[79] The J. D. Power & Associates quality study in summer 2010 showed that domestic makes' reliability outperformed all others for the first time in twenty-four years, except for certain luxury models, and the Detroit Three had regained market share.

Yet the general economic crisis was worse than the president's advisors predicted in 2009 and, as with many of the president's ideas, including his one-time support for the Employee Free Choice Act, which might have aided unionization in the South, legislative proposals were blocked by Republicans or watered down, as happened with the Graduation Initiative to boost technical education at community colleges.

Conclusion

The auto industry rescue revealed a codetermination dimension in American politics that is different from interest group adjustment and market-based, corporate-led coordination. First, the institutional presidency may empower a president to act creatively when his authority is enhanced by the broader network that brought him to office. In Obama's case, the presidential coalition included significant new resources from private equity banking and management consulting, which had been developing new capabilities since the industry policy debates of the 1980s. These groups extended support services to the White House for the restructuring and enabled the mostly successful rescue. The president excelled at governing the industry's alliances.

Second, workers and managers in the companies have choices to make every day in their work with others in a structured project (manufacturing automobiles in a particular way) that orients their cooperative action to get the work done. The logic of practice counts more than the rules that regularize their interactions when problems inevitably arise. The agents must perceive what the new situation is and confer about how to handle it. In this pragmatist conception, organizations are always evolving in some degree. When the Japanese suddenly showed up in the late 1970s, the U.S. auto companies and the UAW greatly accelerated the exchanges of information and strategies across the alliances of workers and managers. This learning process included partnerships between each of the U.S. companies and a foreign auto manufacturer. While the primary agents were activated, the political background conditions of the Reagan years authorized unitary management and reinforced the boundaries between state and economy and workers and managers. It was only when the Bush administration acted in the 2008 crisis that the opportunity was created for Obama to reach back in time to reengage the broader reform debate and use his authority to facilitate a partnership of the reformers in the union and companies to restructure the auto industry.

Obama's discursive leadership was perlocutionary because the mode of reform he favored depends on actions by other agents.[80] His goals required further conditions to exist in order to achieve their effects: citizen actions rather than government edicts. Presidents of course are not free agents; they operate in a densely populated organizational environment that includes organizations in the economy as well as political and bureaucratic ones. Yet the president's judgment about what can be changed and what can be redirected to new goals gives substance to his narrative of his place in this environment and helps others perceive their potential role in his governing project if they choose to act. Obama's narrative of the auto rescue went well beyond the industry's financial crisis to project possibilities for energy policy, industry development, health, education, and community building. The industry could be renewed if workers and managers addressed their responsibilities to respond to public demands; the government stood ready to be their partner in this new industry. President Obama set out to recreate a middle-class public that supports a high-performance economy and an effective public sector, but the critical need was to link his discourse of inclusive reform with a political method of public deliberation and action.

PART II

Assemblage

Chapter 5

Animating Institutional Skeletons

The Contributions of Subaltern Resistance to the Reinforcement of Land Boards in Botswana

Ato Kwamena Onoma

"If this is all about creativity, how do you account for continuity and order?" This is a question that scholars who emphasize the role of creativity, agency, and ambiguity in the study of institutions often face. This question arises because these scholars, as well as their critics, who focus more on positive feedbacks and path dependence, often associate creativity, agency, and institutional ambiguity and incompleteness only with processes of institutional change. Continuity and stability are still too often seen as the result of the mechanistic functioning of self-reinforcing institutions. Drawing on the contributions of subaltern creativity to the development of land boards in Botswana, I introduce a dose of ambiguity, agency, and creativity into the process of institutional reinforcement and continuity. My goal is to suggest that the question posed above is based on flawed dichotomous associations between self-reinforcing mechanisms and institutional stability on one hand and between ambiguity, incompleteness, and agent creativity and institutional change on the other. The emphasis on ambiguity, agency, and creativity does not preclude continuity. As indicated by Gerald Berk and Dennis Galvan elsewhere in this volume, the process of institutional continuity can sometimes be the effect of the creative exploitation of the ambiguities and incompleteness of those very institutions just as much as it can be that of efforts by institution builders to reinforce institutions.

In my study of Botswana's Tribal Land Act (TLA) of 1968 and the subsequent creation of tribal land boards in this chapter, I emphasize the role that creative exploitation of institutional ambiguity and incompleteness can play in ensuring institutional continuity. It afforded people who would have otherwise lost significantly because of the TLA and land boards opportunities to comply with the new institutions in ways that they found less distributionally disadvantageous. This lessened their preference for institutional change. It whittled away grievance against these institutions, thus reducing the tendency of institutions to "disadvantage subordinate groups to the point that they organize and come to identify with one another, thereby increasing their power and capacity to break prevailing institutional arrangements."[1]

While the land boards were incomplete in many ways and were also characterized by ambiguity, of particular relevance here is an imbalance between the knowledge that board members needed to perform their functions of adjudication, documentation, allocation, and land-use planning and the knowledge they actually had and could acquire with reasonable effort given their resources. This gap made them susceptible to societal actors who cleverly exploited such institutional ambiguity and incompleteness to curb some of the more distributionally unfavorable aspect of the new land regime. They tricked land boards into allocating them lands and documenting and recognizing land that they had acquired without the consent of the land boards. This obviated the need for them to stridently oppose and seek the overthrow of what would have otherwise been a very disadvantaging institutional arrangement. But this trickery also brought peoples' interests under the purview of land boards and so contributed to the perpetuation and better performance of the boards over time by giving them an opportunity to improve their information systems. Better land information systems were critical to the ability of land boards to allocate land, document interests, and resolve land disputes in informed ways. Further, better information systems ultimately limited the extent to which societal members could violate land board allocation rules.

The chapter is divided into four sections. In the section that follows immediately I lay out the two sides to a debate over the roles of agency, creativity, and institutional ambiguity in the persistence and change of institutions and demonstrate the common assumptions held by the disagreeing parties. This is followed by a section in which I reflect on the flaws of these assumptions that foreground the debate between the two parties by drawing a theoretical link between institutional continuity on one hand and agency, creativity, and institutional incompleteness and ambiguity on the other. I then demonstrate this link through an exploration of the gradual rise of the land boards in Botswana. The field research on which this section is based was done over a period of five months in Gaborone and Central, North-East, Kgatleng, and Kweneng Districts in Botswana between 2003 and 2005.

A Debate and Its Flawed Bases

"If this is all about creativity, how do you account for continuity and order?" One way to respond to this question is to assert that there is not in fact as much stability and continuity as many observers of institutions claim. Scholars who stress a more evolutionary and gradualist theory of institutional change assert that change in institutions is often underestimated because of the focus on big abrupt changes at critical junctures when there is spectacular institutional breakdown and the role of agency in charting change is obvious.[2] This is a relic of the dependence of "much of the institutionalist literature . . . explicitly or implicitly . . . on a strong punctuated equilibrium model that draws an overly sharp distinction between long periods of institutional stasis periodically interrupted by some sort of exogenous shock that opens things up, allowing for more or less radical reorganization."[3] In this outlook the creation and change of institutions occur during critical junctures—relatively brief periods marked by institutional breakdown often caused by exogenous shocks. Breakdown allows for agency and creativity in the choice and molding of new institutional paths. But once these paths are chosen they become locked in through processes of positive feedback and self-reinforcement leading to long periods of stability until exogenous shocks create another critical juncture characterized by breakdown and agency. The emphasis on exogenous shocks in causing breakdowns and allowing for agency at those rare critical junctures is important because institutions are viewed as self-reinforcing and characterized by positive feedback. As a result change has to be caused by forces external to these institutions—exogenous shocks.

Critics rightly argue that this punctuated equilibrium model underpredicts and underperceives change in that it focuses on "exogenous shocks that bring about radical institutional reconfigurations, overlooking shifts based on endogenous developments that often unfold incrementally."[4]

Critics emphasize a view of institutions as potentially susceptible to endogenous change and portray this change as not just limited to the abrupt and cataclysmic changes evident in critical junctures but also including the more gradual and hard-to-perceive little changes that eventually add up to make big transformations over time.[5] James Mahoney and Kathleen Thelen's example of changes in the British House of Lords during the twentieth century gives a very good picture of such change.[6] The basic contention is that if we look beyond so-called critical junctures and understand institutions as susceptible to gradual endogenous change, we will realize that there is indeed as much institutional change as we should expect from an understanding of institutional processes as characterized by ambiguity, incompleteness, creativity, and agency. As I will show below, one can make the same point about the land boards in Botswana. For beyond what seems to be the persistence and stability of these institutions are ongoing acts of minor tinkering by state agents—Berk and Galvan's "engineers"—meant to reinforce these institutions and ensure their persistence and better functioning.

To push the debate beyond this response provided by Mahoney and Thelen one has to note that the debate highlighted above is often based on a tacit agreement by the disagreeing sides on a pair of associations. Institutional continuity and stability are associated with the workings of mechanistic, path-dependent characteristics of institutions, while institutional change is associated with agency, creativity, ambiguity, and incompleteness. In this equation institutional transformation is to agency, ambiguity, incompleteness, and creativity as institutional continuity is to positive feedback mechanisms. Stability, order, and continuity in institutions, in other words, are the *effects* of mechanistic self-reinforcing, path-dependent properties of institutions, while change, disorder, and instability are seen as the effects of creativity, agency, incompleteness, and ambiguity. Often the only difference is that while the punctuated equilibrium scholars limit such creativity and resulting change to rare critical junctures, their critics allow for the operation of ambiguity, agency, and creativity and the resulting change outside critical junctures and on a more pervasive basis.[7]

Works that utilize a punctuated equilibrium approach are explicit in their identification of mechanistic positive feedback mechanisms with institutional continuity and agency with change during critical junctures. Part of the evidence of the acceptance of this dichotomy by even those who embrace gradualism and endogenous sources of change is the fact that much of their work that emphasizes agency, ambiguity, and continuity concentrates on exploring and explaining institutional change. The edited volumes by James Mahoney and Kathleen Thelen[8] and by Wolfgang Streeck and Kathleen Thelen[9] are leading examples of the opposition to the punctuated equilibrium approach. The collections emphasize the role of agency and institutional ambiguity and incompleteness, unsurprisingly, mostly in exploring and explaining institutional change (even if of the more gradual kind) in various institutions.[10] .

The acceptance of this dichotomy is what foregrounds this debate for both parties. It is this dichotomy that makes the coexistence of ambiguity, incompleteness, agency and creativity, and institutional stability remarkable and even unlikely in the minds of many scholars of institutions, regardless of whether they belong to the punctuated equilibrium school or to the more insurgent currents that stress creativity, agency, and ambiguity. It is why adherents of the punctuated equilibrium model believe that they can validly use what they see as the pervasive fact of institutional continuity and stability as evidence against those who emphasize creativity, agency, and incompleteness in institutional analysis. It is also why scholars who emphasize agency, creativity, ambiguity, and incompleteness in institutional analysis often believe they need to produce evidence of change to justify their assertion that these characteristics of institutions are important.

Rethinking the Associations

It is important to undermine this dichotomy by exposing the associations on which it is constructed as false. One has to question the view that institutional stability and continuity are only the effects of mechanistic path-dependent features of institutions; that institutional ambiguity, incompleteness, agency, and creativity have nothing to do with such institutional stability and continuity; and that institutional continuity is in fact evidence of the absence of creativity and agency. In the preface to their edited volume Mahoney and Thelen take an important, if small, step in this direction by suggesting that "Institutional stability is a function not simply of positive feedback but of active, ongoing political mobilization, and institutions are vulnerable to change not just in moments of crisis but on a more ongoing basis."[11] Unfortunately this step remains only a truncated suggestion and they along with their contributors move on to associate agency, creativity, ambiguity, and incompleteness mostly with institutional change of the gradual kind in the rest of the work.

The necessary identification of agency, creativity, incompleteness, and ambiguity with institutional change is flawed, as is the necessary association of institutional stability with a lack of these characteristics. Agency, creativity, ambiguity, and incompleteness can contribute in meaningful ways to the persistence and continuity of institutions. Institutional continuity and stability is sometimes a sign of the presence of the creative exploitation of institutional ambiguity and incompleteness by agents instead of solely being the effect of the operation of mechanistic path-dependent forces. The difficult task is how one goes beyond these general claims to lay out specific causal propositions about the links between agency, creativity, ambiguity, and incompleteness and the persistence and stability of institutions.

I posit one causal proposition here. Where institutional change unleashes distributional conflicts that create losers that are likely to become dedicated to the opposition of these new institutional arrangements, the creative exploitation of institutional ambiguities and incompleteness can allow would-be losers to learn how to live with the new institutions. It enables them to learn how to go along with the times by allowing them to reduce their losses under the new institutional arrangements. This can transform them from people who are likely to oppose and confront institutions to people who creatively exploit ambiguities and incompleteness in, but ultimately conform to, these institutions in ways that end up making the institutions more stable over time.

The ability to creatively exploit the ambiguities and incompleteness of rules, and their interpretation and enforcement, allows these would-be users to interact with new institutions in ways that decrease their losses and so reduce their motivation to seek to reverse, or change the institutions. Once they learn to creatively manipulate the incompleteness and ambiguity of new institutions to what Eric Hobsbawm would call their "minimum disadvantage,"[12] they lose the motivation to oppose and overthrow the institutions. They begin to engage with the institutions in ways not dedicated to their overthrow or drastic transformation. Some actors might even move from being open critics to vocal supporters of the institutions. If we think of this in terms of a combination of the works of James Scott[13] and Albert Hirschman,[14] learning to live with new institutional arrangements through the ingenious exploitation of ambiguities and incompleteness in institutional rules and enforcement reduces the motivation of actors to exit or voice opposition to institutions and increases their willingness to skill-fully manipulate but ultimately show loyalty to the new institutions.

This transition of potential losers is important. Many scholars acknowl-edge that institutions, even where they work to increase general well-being, enhance the power and wealth of some at the expense of others.[15] The distributive politics unleashed by these institutions often frames attitudes toward these institutions, as winners tend to seek to reinforce institutions while losers develop grievances against the institutions, hope for their change, and tend to seek to undermine them. Some scholars have noted that the work of losers bent on overturning what they perceive as a distribu-tionally unfavorable system sometimes contributes to the transformation of institutions.[16] Mahoney and Thelen similarly make the point I quoted ear-lier, that institutional change may happen when disadvantages groups orga-nize and align, gaining power to disrupt prevailing arrangements."[17]

Against this background we can appreciate how the clever exploitation of institutional incompleteness and ambiguity by creative agents is impor-tant if we are to account for why some institutions tend to generate less opposition and so persist over time. The incompleteness and ambiguity of institutions in terms of the letter, interpretation, and enforcement of their "laws" gives would-be losers room to maneuver within the system, obviat-ing the need for opposition to the system. Through the creative exploitation of what is left unsaid by laws, possibilities for multiple and often conflicting interpretations of what is said, and gaps in enforcement, agents can enter institutions and embrace them in ways that are far less distributionally dis-advantageous and that enable them to avoid the high costs of seeking to overthrow institutions. Institutional ambiguity and incompleteness and their creative exploitation by these agents enable them instead to learn to live with these institutions in ways the agents find less costly. This is in many respects similar to the point made elsewhere in this volume by Berk and Galvan.

Of critical importance here also is the effect that such creative exploita-tion has on the designers of institutions. I am here referring to those state agents responsible for designing these institutions that Berk and Galvan refer to as "engineers." The creative exploitation of ambiguities and incom-pleteness by "bricoleurs" (to borrow another of Berk and Galvan's terms, taken from Claude Lévi-Strauss) can motivate the engineers to engage in ongoing tinkering with the institutions aimed at ensuring their survival in the face of challenges. In this sense the story I tell here mirrors the point made by Mahoney and Thelen,[18] that the continuity of an institution does not always mean stasis. Continuity can mask significant gradual change.

The Rise and Rise of Land Boards in Botswana

The southern African country of Botswana gained independence from Britain in 1968 under the leadership of the Botswana Democratic Party (BDP), which has since won all elections and formed all governments in the country. When the BPD released its first National Development Plan that year, it stated its intention to reform the land sector, transform land into a "fully negotiable asset," and give "progressive farmers" greater security "than that available under customary law."[19] The Tribal Land Act was passed in 1968, giving the state and its agents wide-ranging powers to "define and enforce rules on access, use and disposal of tribal land,"[20] which made up about 71 percent of all land in Botswana by 2004.[21] Section 3 of the act made a provision for the creation of land boards to which Section 13 subsequently gave all powers in the management and administration of lands formerly held by traditional chiefs.[22] These land boards have been the main instruments the state has used to achieve its goals of reforming the administration and use of tribal land in the country.

Land boards have gone from strength to strength over time. They were initially marked by uncertainty, the lack of adequate GIS instruments, a paucity of information and information-management skills and tools, and a shortage of trained and representative personnel.[23] By 2004 they had managed not only to survive but also to improve and become stronger over time. Many land boards then boasted record systems that were often computerized, GIS equipment including those for surveying and demarcating lands, staff and board members with higher education levels, and staffed legal sections.[24]

This raises the question of why this institution—once plagued by logistical problems and widely dismissed as inept, unrepresentative, and unfair—has survived and thrived over time. One answer to this question can emphasize continuing efforts by state officials to reinforce the land boards and the story of path dependence and positive feedback that lies behind it. There has been no shortage of state efforts to shore up the land boards. The state created the main land boards in 1970[25] but immediately realized that the reach of such boards and their impact on land administration and management would be limited given the extent of the area that each had to cover. To solve this problem, the state created subordinate land boards in 1973.[26] This creation of subordinate land boards was not a one-time event. Instead the state has deliberately sought to create subordinate land boards in areas that are seen as particularly problematic. It is because of this, for example, that Mogoditshane on the outskirts of Gaborone received a subordinate land board.[27] There were twelve main land boards and thirty-nine subordinate land boards operating across the country by 2004.[28]

In addition to further propagating land boards, state leaders have invested in improving their personnel and logistics.[29] This has partly been done by changing the criteria for those who can be board members and staff to ensure a higher level of skill and representativeness.[30] The state also invested in training board members and staff through the Land Board Training Unit established in the Ministry of Lands.[31] By 2004 training was part of the regular inauguration program for each group of land board members, supplemented with later occasional training sessions.[32] To further buttress the land boards, the government created the Lands Division in the Ministry of Local Government and Lands "to support the Lands Boards by providing them with professional, technical and administrative advice."[33] Land boards earlier had faced significant logistical problems, lacking the tools, equipment, and supplies they needed to carry out their work.[34] The practice of pacing parcels during allocation exercises was not the best way of demarcating clear boundaries. By 2004 the state invested in acquiring GIS equipment for surveying and demarcating plots for many land boards.[35]

In line with this effort at boosting the responsiveness, accountability, and enforcement capacity of the land boards, the state also created the Land Tribunal in 1997. Provided for under the Tribal Land Act of 1968, the Tribal Land (Amendment) Act of 1993 and the Tribal Land (Establishment of Land Tribunals) Order of 1995, the Land Tribunal was established in October 1997 to deal with appeals against land board decisions by aggrieved parties. These appeals were initially heard by the minister for lands, but issues of fairness and long waiting periods of up to five years motivated the creation of the land tribunal.[36] The land tribunals have contributed to the greater responsiveness of land boards by holding them to the letter of the law.[37] The land tribunal has also empowered the land boards. This is partly by augmenting the enforcement power of the land boards. Land boards can lodge complaints at the tribunal if they believe their decisions are not being complied with speedily enough. The land tribunal can then issue an order that is enforced by state agents, just as are all decisions from magistrate courts. The speedy hearing of cases by the land tribunal means land boards no longer have appealed cases hang over their heads for years and hinder their allocation and planning activities.

In many ways, the state's significant continuing investment in reinforcing the land boards demonstrates classic positive feedback effects. The land boards were created by a burgeoning BDP ruling elite that was heavily involved in the cattle sector. The leadership of the party drew from traditional chieftaincy families that were the owners of some of the largest cattle herds in the country. Seretse Khama, the influential leader of the party and first president of Botswana, who oversaw these initial reforms, was the largest cattle owner in the country as heir apparent to the Ngwato throne, the most powerful chieftaincy in the country.[38] The party also drew heavy financial support from other white and black large cattle owners in the country.[39] The TLA, land boards, and associated reforms in the land sector were expressly designed to serve the interests of "progressive farmers,"[40] a group that was dominated by BDP members and their allies, including chiefs.

The land boards furthered the individualized control of former commons land by members of the state elite who were heavily involved in cattle ranching by issuing them certificates of customary land grants and common law leases, which gave them exclusive rights to land for ranching. These certificates, along with the Tribal Grazing Land Policy of 1975, allowed many members of the state elite and their allies to acquire exclusive user rights to large chunks of lands.[41] The common law leases issued by land boards were used by some of these elites as collateral to acquire loans to further their ranching and farming activities.[42] The later involvement of some of these party and state officials in the real estate sector only further tied them to these institutions.[43]

The ongoing provision of these benefits to BDP elites has only increased their interest in further strengthening the land boards.[44] The continual tinkering aimed at further strengthening and ensuring the long term survival of the land boards can thus be attributed partly to positive feedback and path dependence.

From a Subaltern Point of View

But an examination of the land boards from a subaltern point of view tells a slightly different story. The introduction of the land boards and other reforms engendered by the TLA are examples of reforms that many have touted as holding multiple social benefits.[45] Despite these socially beneficial consequences, the land boards had severe distributional consequences that threatened to heap serious losses on many in society. The case of the traditional chiefs is the most clear.

As owners of large cattle herds and as members of chieftancy families heavily represented in the BDP, many individuals benefited economically and politically from the TLA. But the TLA also threatened the institution of chieftaincy. Understanding this requires us to move beyond the traditional categorization of society into neat winner and loser groups. It requires us to realize that because people often have multiple identities and affiliations, institutions can heap both losses and benefits on the same person or group. What a person gains from an institution because of one of her or his affiliations and identities, that same person might lose because of another.

This was the situation with chiefs under the TLA. While the TLA bestowed the benefits highlighted above on chiefs as cattle owners and supporters of a national political party, it significantly threatened their positions as chiefs. The TLA transferred all the *powers* chiefs had over tribal lands to the new land boards. Chiefs stood to lose their most important source of authority. As in many other places in Africa, control of land gave chiefs an instrument they could use to compel obedience and support, punish and deter what they saw as aberrant behavior, and shape the rural economy in what was still a largely agrarian society.[46] While the creation of the land boards stood to curtail chiefs' access to land, in principle most chiefs had secure access to enough land, especially since they were often owners of large cattle herds, and therefore, part of the class that these new land reforms especially sought to aid. When we understand the political role of the control over land, we can appreciate the losses that chiefs stood to suffer under the new institutions. These institutions threatened their control and power, and this, not the quest to get access to land, informed their struggle with the land boards in the ensuring decades.

The government not only passed the law over vociferous objections from chiefs, the attorney general then went on to backtrack on a promise to make chiefs chairmen of the land boards. This provoked the following exasperated response from Kgosi (Chief) Gaborone in the National House of Chiefs: "I seem to think that it was a mere expression without any promise behind it when it was stated that chiefs would become chairmen of these land boards. Although we raise complaints we cannot do anything because the law is already made. We can say that *the powers* have been taken from the chiefs and there is nothing that we can do."[47] It is important to note that Kgosi Gaborone complained that the land boards robbed the chiefs not of access to land or wealth, but of power. In fact this was only one of a series of blows dealt to the power of traditional chiefs in Botswana, and in many other African countries. The House of Chiefs (Powers and Privileges) Act (1965) had curtailed chiefs' authority by consigning them to a newly created House of Chiefs that only played an advisory role;[48] the Chieftainship Act (1965), while limiting chiefs' jurisdiction to only traditional matters, also gave the president and his minister responsible for chieftaincy the power to instruct chiefs and initiate proceedings for their removal;[49] the Local Government (District Councils) Act (1965) gave district councils all of the chiefs' previous taxation and administration powers;[50] and the Matimela Act (1969) wrested control of stray cattle from chiefs.

Chiefs were not the only ones threatened with significant losses under the new system. Ordinary land users stood to lose autonomy over when and where they could get land as land boards sought to exercise more stringent control over allocation. The creation of the land boards had formalized and rendered more bureaucratic an allocation system that was previously simpler and often involved consultation with the local land overseer and neighboring parcel holders.[51] Sometimes it involved no consultation at all, as people moved into areas adjacent to where they or their relatives had been allocated land.[52] People were not always willing to go through the more authoritarian, bureaucratic, and time-consuming process established under the land boards.[53] The inconvenience of waiting for land boards to allocate parcels was further worsened when many land boards began to temporarily suspend allocations and create long waiting lists as they struggled to deal with applications and sort through various problems. People also stood to lose the convenience of deciding where they could acquire land. The land boards often flouted the established custom of allowing people to expand into areas adjacent to where their parents and other family members had land. This meant the inconvenience of family members being dispersed over a wide area along with all the costs of such dispersal. Further, land boards were given powers to cancel customary land rights where people acquired plots irregularly or did not meet development covenants, among other things. Land boards moved to enforce these rules.[54]

These distributional consequences of the new regime sparked a rush by many in society to "shield themselves or their kin from the impact of the implementation of inappropriate entry, partitioning and allocation rules."[55] Members of the new land boards, their relatives, and state officials with whom these board members were connected manipulated the new institutions to gain access to land and secure their rights to land with impunity.[56] The 1991 report of the Presidential Commission of Inquiry into Land Problems in Mogoditshane and Other Peri-Urban Villages revealed how influential politicians and state officials colluded with board members to acquire and secure their rights to land, a practice that started much earlier, just after the creation of the land boards.[57]

Many persons lacking these connections resorted to subverting the authority of the new land boards by occupying and using land without their approval. This practice became known as self-allocation. The appeal of self-allocation reflected the land boards' lack of institutionalization as well as the degree to which they failed to accord with the actual dynamics on the ground. Self-allocators included those who thought they needed land too urgently to wait for land board permission, those who needed land where they thought land boards were unlikely to give them parcels, and those who simply refused to recognize the authority of the new land boards because of what many saw as their unfairness and arbitrariness.[58] There were also those who did not even know that they now needed to apply to the newly created land boards to occupy land. Some had gone through the usual procedure of seeing their chiefs and land overseers, who, eager to continue to exercise their old powers, assented to the allocations.

But for those without the proper connections, self-allocation only magnified potential losses as the offense became a focus of land boards and their state superiors who marked out such practices for draconian punishment.[59] By 2004 the punishment for self-allocation included a heavy 10,000 pula ($3,000) fine, a year in jail, and the seizure of the self-allocated plot and destruction of improvements on it.[60] The drastic measures resorted to by state and land board officials can once again be understood by looking at the political significance of the control of land. Land board members were bent on punishing self-allocation for the same reason that chiefs objected to the creation of the land boards. Board members rightly saw self-allocation as a dangerous threat to the newly acquired power that their monopoly over the allocation and revocation of rights to tribal land gave them. This was power that they could deploy to ends that ranged from the transformation of agriculture and development of the country to building personal political influence and currying economic favors.[61]

Chiefs and other would-be losers under the new system had various options. One was to accept their diminished power quietly. Given the extent of their losses it is understandable that many were not interested in following this path. Chiefs' vociferous opposition to the creation of the boards[62] and the act of self-allocation by many, including land board members and their friends, was itself evidence of people's unwillingness to take the losses lying down.[63] Another route was to oppose and seek to undermine and overthrow land boards and so avoid these losses. Those who took this path would have had to confront head-on the formidable BDP-led state. Kgosi Gaborone's repeated expression of hopelessness in reaction to the creation of the land boards ("There is nothing we can do . . . we can do nothing")[64] encapsulated the caution with which many contemplated this option.

There was a third and less costly path: learn to live with the new institutions. This process involved embracing and engaging with the land boards but doing so only in ways that minimized or eliminated the losses that this otherwise involved. The would-be losers needed to fashion ways to avoid the losses involved in taking on the land boards and their state backers while minimizing the losses involved in accepting land board rules. Learning to live with the land boards involved, to borrow from Hobsbawm, ensuring their "minimum disadvantage"[65] under the new institutions while embracing them.

Learning to Live with the New Dispensation

The land boards, like many other institutions, are typically ambiguous and incomplete in three ways that are of relevance here. They usually leave "much unstated,"[66] leaving room for creative agency. This is particularly true in situations where a uniform institution is meant to govern widely varying social realities. But even the stated is often ambiguous in being open to multiple interpretations, also allowing room for "contestation and debate."[67] Then there is the gap that sometimes exists between the formal provisions of the law and its enforcement, which allows further room for maneuver by agents.[68] It is the room for maneuver afforded by these characteristics of institutions that can be creatively exploited by innovative agents.

Scholars have almost always emphasized the ways in which such creative exploitation of institutional ambiguity and incompleteness is either geared to or inadvertently leads to institutional change. Here I emphasize the role it can play in ensuring institutional continuity. As I argued earlier, it is the creative exploitation of these characteristics of institutions that affords would-be losers the opportunity to comply with institutions in ways that they find less distributionally disadvantageous, thus lessening their preference for institutional change. It whittles away grievance against these institutions, thus reducing the tendency of institutions to disadvantage subordinate groups, as Mahoney and Thelen argue, so that "they organize and come to identify with one another, thereby increasing their power and capacity to break prevailing institutional arrangements."[69] Of particular relevance here is what I noted earlier, an imbalance between the knowledge required by the land boards to perform their functions and the knowledge that board members actually had and could acquire with reasonable effort given their resources. This imbalance made them susceptible to exploitation by clever societal actors. They were imbued with mandates that required extensive knowledge for their fulfillment but they suffered from a severe lack of such knowledge. Among other things, the TLA tasked land boards with allocating land, documenting these newly allocated interests as well as interests that predated the creation of the land boards, and settling land disputes. All of these required local knowledge of land distribution and use and of land disputes. Without this knowledge they were likely to create overlapping claims, struggle to adjudicate and settle disputes, and make poor decisions in the documentation of interests.

The land boards were afflicted with what Susan Wynne describes as an "impossibility to get unbiased historical information about the extent or validity of prior rights in land."[70] The boards were often rich in what Friedrich Hayek calls "scientific knowledge" but lacked what he calls knowledge of "the particular circumstances of time and place."[71] This distinction between two types of knowledge is akin to that drawn by Scott between high modernist "formal, deductive, epistemic knowledge" and "practical knowledge . . . embodied in local practices."[72] To have a shot at successful social transformation, state leaders need to be able to integrate local knowledge into broader plans that will direct the exercise of state power.[73] State officials who lack adequate knowledge of social realities are unlikely to be able to direct state power in their desired ways and toward their desired ends. Even more important is the fact that local agents with such knowledge can redirect state power toward their own ends and in ways that can sometimes diverge from the intentions of state leaders. State leaders were quick to identify this deficiency and sought to solve it by incorporating chiefs (who had administered land for ages and were rich in such knowledge) in the land boards as conduits of such knowledge.[74] For the chiefs this was a golden opportunity to tame and co-opt the land boards, whose creation they had earlier opposed to no avail.

Realizing their inability to confront the state head-on, many chiefs resorted to the politics of knowledge manipulation to redirect the land boards in ways that made them less harmful to the institution of chieftaincy. In this monumental struggle over the power that control over land afforded, chiefs turned to the politics of knowledge. Their goal was to reduce their losses under the new system and so adapt to life under the new regime. Capitalizing on their superior knowledge of local realities, many chiefs asserted authority over land boards and began to exercise through the land boards the same powers over land that they had before the creation of the boards. Also, because many people saw the chiefs sitting on and often playing leading roles on the boards, they met the chiefs outside the confines of land board settings for land allocation and land dispute adjudication.[75] State officials and their land board agents quickly realized the chiefs were outflanking them. In 1984 they stepped in to reclaim the control over land that chiefs had stealthily reappropriated. Acting on the 1977 recommendations of the Inter-ministerial Committee on Land Boards, the government removed all chiefs from land boards.[76]

But this was not to be the end of the story. The basic facts of the imbalance in the possession of local knowledge remained and so state officials could not completely do away with the chiefs. They instead sought to tap their knowledge through other means. The new method was by instructing chiefs to designate ward heads to serve land boards as advisors or land overseers. Ward heads are leaders of wards in various communities and occupy a position below that of chief, working under the chief in whose realm the ward they lead falls. As land overseers, the ward heads' main role is to vet all applications for land rights and guarantee that the lands applied for are not encumbered by visiting the plots and signing off on the application before it is considered by the land board.[77] They also advise land boards on the adjudication of land disputes and the general history of land-use patterns in their area. They typically move around with the land boards during allocation and adjudication exercises to show them the location of plots and offer advice.[78]

Land overseers and the chiefs they represent on the land boards have exploited these new institutional arrangements to claw back some of the control over land that they once exercised. They retain land allocation powers, through a more complex process. A land overseer colluding with an applicant who urgently needs land will sign an application indicating that the land applied for is unencumbered when he knows full well that it already belongs to someone. The land board will then allocate that plot to the applicant, causing "double allocations." This will be discovered once the two owners meet on the plot and report the case to the land board. The discovery of double allocations caused by land boards is an embarrassment that board members dread. When it happens, land boards look incompetent in the eyes of a public that is often already skeptical of their professionalism. They are often eager to keep these cases hidden and readily offer a new plot to the second recipient of the land.[79] Through this means, chiefs and their land overseers allocate land to people who might have had to wait for long periods before acquiring parcels from the land boards.

This clever manipulation of the incompleteness of the land boards' knowledge has made them far less unpalatable to the chiefs. Many chiefs still see themselves as having the ability to significantly influence the allocation of land where they want to through various means. As one chief told me during an interview at the National House of Chiefs, "The passing of the Tribal Land Act was a bad idea. Too much power has been taken from chiefs and some of it needs to be restored. As for the land boards they are all the same. But fortunately, I can still advise them and I have a say because I appoint the land overseer who works with them. In fact I can still give out land and the land board will issue the certificate."[80]

It was not only chiefs who exploited the incomplete knowledge of land boards to learn how to live with the new TLA. Ordinary villagers have also had to learn to live with the new institutions. Their concerns have involved getting land when and where they want it and avoiding the penalty for self-allocation. Like chiefs, they have creatively exploited the institutional incompleteness that land boards demonstrate in their lack of sufficient knowledge of local land matters. The main goal for most of these peasants is to escape punishment for self-allocation and to get the land boards to recognize and document lands they had occupied without land board approval.

As I conducted research with the Mahalapye Subordinate Land Board in Central District in 2004, I noticed that many people came seeking documentation of their land parcels with various explanations for their lack of documents. Some claimed the parcels were given to them long ago by chiefs before land boards were created. Others with plots in areas that are widely recognized to have only been allocated by land boards claim they had received the parcels from land boards but had not been given documents. Land boards early on were known to have allocated land without issuing documents. Others claimed they had been given documents by the land boards who allocated them the parcels but that the documents had been lost. The common causes of the losses were house fires and insects, goats, and cows that eat documents that are not well guarded. Periodic flooding in the Mahalapye-Palapye flood plain was also frequently blamed for destroying documents. The February 2004 allocation exercise in Tshikhiny-ega, Mowana, Xhosa I, and Madiba Wards was dominated by such requests for replacement of documentation.[81]

Land officials faced with these requests were usually very suspicious of and sometimes irate at what they thought were efforts by peasants to fool them into regularizing self-allocated plots.[82] Officials were quick to rightly connect what they saw as the dishonest audacity of these clients to the weak information system of the land boards.[83] While maintaining a good documentation system was one of the state's main reasons for creating land boards,[84] record keeping had been one of the biggest failings of the boards since their creation.[85] Lacking logistics and trained personnel, many at first allocated land with no documentation.[86] Even when boards issued documentation, they did not keep good records, conducted measurements by pacing plots, and produced maps that were just hand-drawn sketches.[87] Many of the land boards I visited did not have functional records before 1990.[88] Where pre-1990 records existed, they were in such a decrepit and disorganized state that they could not be reliably consulted, and some boards had even dumped them in storage areas where they were rotting away.

The land board members and peasants all knew this. So board members tried to stifle peasants by questioning them about which board members or chief made the allocation and when it was done, threatened to consult past board members and staff members, and even inspected plots to see if there were newly constructed fences. But they almost always eventually gave in and documented most of these claims because their lack of records and justifiable reasons to reject petitions meant they were likely to lose if the clients appealed their decisions to the Land Tribunal. While they were often certain that people were seeking to legitimize self-allocation, they were usually powerless to stop it because they lacked the evidence—records—to do so. Land boards had earlier used draconian and often unjustified criteria to clamp down on such applicants.[89] But with the creation of the Land Tribunal in 1997 they became relatively powerless in the face of such stratagems. The Land Tribunal has aggressively tried to hold land boards to the letter of the law, leading to many land board losses.[90] Land boards are less willing to arbitrarily refuse to document suspected cases of self-allocation without hard evidence that they mostly do not have for fear of being humiliated at the Land Tribunal.

A subordinate land board member confided resignation to me: "Self-allocation is a big problem here. We cannot trace old records, but we cannot risk losing at the land tribunal by making a decision based on suspicion without evidence. People in Xhosa I and Tshikhinyega [wards of Mahalapye] always claim floods washed away their land certificates, but when we ask them, their marriage licenses, death certificates, or party membership cards are never destroyed by the floods and fire."[91] Another board member pointed out that "most of the time we know they are lying. We threaten them with the ten thousand pula fine and one year in jail but we have no way of proving that they are lying. Our lack of records forces us to be lenient. We just regularize the claims that they make."[92] An even more despondent board member complained that "people have greed over land. Most of their certificates were not swept [away] by flood. People have cattle brand certificates, birth certificates, [every kind] except their land certificates. The DC [district commissioner] is not complaining about reregistering birth and marriage certificates."[93] Wynne provides evidence of similar exploitation of land boards' information deficiency by villagers in Letlhakeng, also in the Central District to temper their distributional consequences.[94]

Effects on Boards

By tricking land boards into legitimizing their interests, people brought themselves under the purview of land boards and so contributed to the perpetuation and better performance of the boards over time by giving the boards an opportunity and motivation to improve their information systems. Better land information systems were critical to the ability of land boards to allocate land, document interests, and resolve land disputes in informed ways. Further, better information systems ultimately limited the extent to which societal members could violate land board allocation rules. This is not to claim that land boards have acquired "complete information." Given the gap that almost always exists between fluid social realities and maps of these realities, it is doubtful if the possession of "complete information" on a dynamic sphere such as the land market is possible. The information systems of the land boards still fall far short of perfection. But when we look at where they started out, we can appreciate how far they have come. My claim is that people's willingness to bring their interests and transactions to the attention of the land boards without much fear of punishment and loss has contributed significantly to more accurate records. These improved records have enabled boards to be more efficacious and so increased their legitimacy in the eyes of the public, contributing to their survival.

Better records and more thorough documentation have raised the costs faced by those seeking to stay out of the ambit of the land boards. As more people entered the system and had their rights documented, land board documentation acquired more salience in the wider socioeconomy, making it harder for people to not join or oppose the system. Many agencies began to accept common law leases issued by land boards as collateral for loans. These loan givers thus benefited from and become invested in perpetuating the land boards. More important, agencies such as utility companies started to require people to present common law leases and certificates of customary land grant issued by land boards as evidence of interest in properties before they could have services on their parcels. Opting out of or opposing the new tribal land regime has become harder, because of the increasing numbers of people who have *opted into* the system.

For many of these actors, this stepping out of the shadows into the glare of the land boards was only feasible because they found ways to learn to live with the new land boards; they found ways to creatively exploit the ambiguities and incompleteness of the new land regime to avert what would have otherwise been unbearable costs. The specter of losing their lands and houses, paying what amounts to a $3,000 fine, and going to jail for six months or not getting land when and where they wanted it would likely have kept many from coming to the land boards and would likely have made them trenchant opponents of the TLA that created the land boards. Without this possibility of exploitation, many would have more stubbornly exercised the option of resistance to and subversion of the land boards. We do not have to see such resistance and subversion as an option that was open only to powerful people like the chiefs. As the work of Scott has repeatedly shown us, little acts of uncoordinated guerilla-like resistance by lowly peasants can wreak havoc on such grand state projects and turn them into "utter shambles."[95]

Their creative exploitation of the ambiguities and incompleteness of the new institutions enabled peasants and chiefs alike to embrace and adapt to the land boards instead of committing themselves to their subversion and overthrow. The act of contributing to land board records by deliberately bringing their rights, no matter how they were acquired, to the attention of the land boards is a significant contribution to land board information systems and the long-term perpetuation of the land boards. Creative agency combined with institutional ambiguity and incompleteness transformed these actors from would-be big losers and opponents of the land boards into people who faced loses that were not as large and who were thus willing to engage with the land boards in ways that ultimately further strengthened the boards and contributed to their perpetuation.

The clever manipulation of TLA incompleteness and ambiguities has had another effect. The activities of these bricoleurs have provoked responses from institutional engineers eager to reinforce the land boards and ensure their continuity. These engineers have included higher-level state officials as well as land board staff and members. We can see examples of reactive engineering by land board members and staff in the "new tricks" that they began to employ to catch what they saw as dishonest peasants. Realizing that clients were deliberately exploiting the widely known poor nature of land board records to justify claims, board members innovated new methods for sieving through claims. One was the method of close questioning. If claimants assert they were given land by an earlier land board, the present board members ask them to name some of the members of the board that gave them the land. They ask for the name of the land overseer or chief who was working with the board at the time. They will contact past board members to determine if they had allocated land in a particular area. When they realized that they were losing many appeal cases to some of these bricoleurs at the Land Tribunal, many land boards innovated by creating legal sections and employed legal counsel.

Engineers at the higher state level have also responded to the activities of these bricoleurs. The significant investment in improving land board surveying, demarcation, documentation, and record systems has partly been in response to what many officials see as the ignominy of being tricked by what they see as uneducated and ignorant peasants. The speed with which land boards usually sack their land overseers once they think they have enough information and documentation to do without an overseer is evidence of this. The creation of the centralized and digitized Tribal Lands Information Management System is partly meant to nip in the bud the clever exploitation of information gaps in the tribal lands management system by bricoleurs.

We can thus draw from Mahoney and Thelen[96] in noting that the continuity of the land boards in Botswana has not meant their stasis. The land boards have continued to exist and have grown from strength to strength, but they have done so partly through many minor rounds of tinkering by engineers. The land board of today with its survey instruments, digital records, and relatively well-educated staff and membership is not the same as the land board of 1970 with its nonexistent records and staff and membership with little education who demarcated parcels by pacing them. The continuity of the land boards masks significant gradual change aimed at reinforcing the institution. More important, one can say that this tinkering by engineers aimed at reinforcing the land boards is partly due to the activities of institutional bricoleurs who have cleverly exploited the ambiguities and incompleteness of the institution.

Conclusion

This chapter gives us an alternative way of responding to the question often posed to scholars who emphasize agency, creativity, and institutional ambiguity and incompleteness: "If there is so much agency and ambiguity, why do we see so much institutional continuity?" The response we can draw from Mahoney and Thelen[97] pointing out that continuity and seeming stability sometimes often mask significant gradual change is a good one. I demonstrate its relevance when it comes to the land boards in Botswana.

But I also make the point that scholars need not scramble to produce evidence of change and institutional collapse to justify their insistence on creative agency and ambiguity. Institutional continuity is compatible with the creative exploitation of institutional ambiguity and incompleteness. As Mahoney and Thelen note, we need to stop seeing institutional continuity and stability as a function "simply of positive feedback" mechanisms.[98]

One of the implications of this work is a call to reconceptualize ambiguity and incompleteness in the study of institutions. These characteristics of institutions are too often seen as flaws (even if unavoidable ones) that expose institutions to subversion and change even if of a gradual nature. The suggestion here is that there are situations when these characteristics can contribute to saving and maintaining institutions by contributing to whittling away grievance against institutions.

This reconceptualization also has policy implications. Institution crafters should move away from a view that sees institutions as more perfect the less ambiguous and incomplete they are. The effort should not always be aimed at building institutions that are as unambiguous and complete as possible since incompleteness and ambiguity can actually contribute to institutional stability and continuity. Further, the clever exploitation of such ambiguities and incompleteness by agents should not always be viewed as either directed at or inevitably leading to the subversion of institutions. They may be well-meaning efforts by those disadvantaged by new institutions to learn to live with these institutions in ways that do not make the costs of such engagement unbearable.

Chapter 6

Creating Political Strategy, Controlling Political Work

Edward Bernays and the Emergence of the Political Consultant

Adam Sheingate

A central theme guiding this volume is that politics is marked by everyday forms of innovation, what Gerald Berk and Dennis Galvan refer to as creative syncretism.[1] Focusing on this creativity, they argue, offers key insights into the nature and conduct of politics. What at first may appear to be fixed and rigid structures, such as rules and roles, interests and institutions, are in fact multiple and malleable elements of political life. This diversity allows actors to combine and recombine elements in pursuit of their political goals. The payoff from such an analytical move is twofold. First, attention to the structural sources of creative action broadens our understanding of institutions and the nature of political change. Second, rethinking how structures operate as the building blocks of creative action offers a more meaningful account of agency. Structures are not merely constraints on action but are themselves the product of creative practice and problem solving. In sum, institutional change is an ongoing and adaptive process as actors rearrange and redeploy rules and resources almost daily. Agency is central to, rather than a residual category of, institutional analysis.

This alternative, agency-centered account of institutional change offers exciting possibilities for understanding politics. However, most scholars avoid focusing on individual actors because of concerns that idiosyncratic explanations cannot be generalized beyond a particular case. Or, to put it more charitably, a focus on actors may highlight the role of skill in politics but it says relatively little about the character of institutions or the larger structural forces that influence outcomes. These concerns are well founded. If we are to understand the dynamics of politics, we must avoid overly muscular accounts of agency that focus on heroic individuals who somehow escape the shackles of the institutions they inhabit.[2] How, then, are we to proceed?

The answer proposed here is to focus less on the concept of agency and more on actual practice: what actors do and how they do it. I argue that a closer inspection of actors at work not only illuminates how structure provides a substrate for creative action; it also reveals how actors produce structures in the conduct of everyday politics. To illustrate, I examine the origins of political consulting in the United States and its contribution to the rise of a twentieth-century political style of candidate-centered, media-intensive campaigns.[3]

Consultants offer a rich field for studying the interplay of structure and action. As they devise campaign strategies, consultants engage in a process of creative adaptation, combining scientific polling and sophisticated media with local political knowledge and campaign experience. In doing so, consultants help create the very partisan context in which they work. The strength and orientation of individual party attachments strongly influence the behavior of voters, and these same partisan attachments inform the strategic decisions consultants make during the course of a campaign. As they craft the messages of the candidates, the issue positions they adopt, and ultimately the groups of voters that make up an electoral coalition, consultants re-create, reinforce, and reproduce the partisan identities and allegiances of voters. Structure informs action and actions generate structures.

Moreover, the rise of a consulting profession offers key insights into American political development and the transformation of democratic practice during the course of the twentieth century. Today, virtually all political campaigns are managed by professional consultants. The principal tools of contemporary politics—polls and advertising—are provided by consultants as contract services to candidates, parties, and advocacy groups. The top political strategists in both parties, from state houses to the White House, are drawn from the ranks of the consulting profession. It was not always so. In the nineteenth century, elections were more party-centered than candidate-centered affairs. Voter mobilization relied on partisan loyalties and ethnocultural identities rather than individual preferences and issue niches. The work of campaigns was almost entirely in the hands of local agents "experienced in the customs, traditions, and techniques of party competition" rather than a cadre of political consultants who sell an array of services to the candidate.[4] The rise of a political consulting profession that controls the methods and practice of everyday politics is a central feature of twentieth-century American political development.

With few exceptions, however, political scientists have not paid much attention to consulting for the same reason that they have not paid much attention to agency: consultants appear to operate in the realm of skill, contributing to the short-term dynamics of a campaign rather than the broader structural context in which they work. The result, as political scientist Matt Grossman recently pointed out, is a rather large gulf between political practice and political science in the United States.[5] Indeed, there is a striking disconnect between the strategic decisions practitioners deem important for winning elections, such as devising a compelling campaign narrative, and what political scientists emphasize in their research, such as mass partisanship.[6] Part of this disconnect comes from the different goals of consultants and political scientists. As Grossman puts it, "practitioners want to act, whereas scholars want to know."[7] The accumulated political science research on campaigns and elections may explain 95 percent of the variation in voter behavior, a scholarly achievement to be sure, but it is the 5 percent of unexplained variance that consultants believe may decide the outcome of a particular race.

By downplaying the role of practitioners, political scientists misunderstand key features of contemporary politics. For example, explanations of the rise of candidate-centered campaigns tend to emphasize changes in electoral rules (such as primaries), the weakening of party organizations, and technological advances in communication.[8] These developments are critical to be sure, but an emphasis on structure begs the question: how exactly did changes in rules, organizations, and technologies transform political practice? It is tempting to rely on functional explanations: candidates simply adapted to the changing conditions and context of twentieth-century politics. The problem with this argument is that politicians themselves have little concrete evidence about what works in a campaign other than their own experiences as candidates. More problematic still, political scientists have yet to explain why candidates rely on campaign methods that, according to the accumulated evidence, have only minimal effects on the outcome of a race.[9]

What is missing, I argue, is an account of how the techniques of candidate-centered campaigns, such as the use of polling and media, first arose and then became a durable feature of American politics. The answer offered here is that the rise of a consulting profession led to the development and application of new tools and new approaches to the old task of vote getting. Yet this transition was far from smooth. For the techniques of candidate-centered, media-intensive campaigns to take hold, consultants first had to establish themselves as experts in the provision of political advice. It is only in the successful effort to define and defend the political consulting profession that these techniques transformed American politics. In sum, broad changes in democratic practice turn on the methods and tools of every-day politics, what I refer to as "political work," and the rise of a political consulting profession that exercises near complete control of that work.

This focus on the relationship between political work and democratic practice suggests how creative action contributes to the disruption, creation, and maintenance of institutions.[10] As I noted earlier, political consultants engage in a process of creative adaptation as they use sophisticated polling and media to assemble coalitions of voters on behalf of their client. However, even as they work toward the pursuit of office or some other political goal, consultants are also asserting and defending their claim to be experts in the provision of political advice. The creative act of campaigning serves two pur-poses: the construction of a political majority and the control over a domain of work. Together, these twin processes have transformed the character of American politics, giving rise to a candidate-centered style of campaigns largely controlled by a class of political professionals.

To understand this development, it is necessary to examine consultants themselves. However, because the practice is so pervasive today, it is neces-sary to go back to an earlier period when consultants first claimed that their services were indispensable to the modern conduct of politics. In this essay, I focus on the work and writings of one such political consultant, Edward Bernays. Although he never called himself a political consultant (he pre-ferred the term "counsel on public relations"), Bernays advised several political candidates, including Presidents Calvin Coolidge and Herbert Hoover, as well as a wide range of corporate clients and even foreign nations during his long career.

Using a rich archive of published works and personal materials, I describe how Bernays approached the task of crafting a political strategy for his clients. Using modern social scientific tools such as surveys and census data, Bernays identified the distinct social, economic, and racial groups within a population, their identities and affiliations, and the symbols, words, and other emotional appeals that could generate popular support, whether on behalf of a product or a politician. For Bernays, social structure informed political strategy; coalition building was a creative assemblage of voters manipulated by carefully targeted messages.

In the 1930s and 1940s, however, this approach to political campaigns required a fair degree of salesmanship, something Bernays was well equipped to provide. To that end, Bernays worked tirelessly to convince potential clients and the larger public that his techniques were ideally suited to the particular conditions of modern politics. As I make clear in this essay, the emerging field of behavioral social science was a crucial aid in this regard. Combining the art of communication with a new science of human behavior provided Bernays a set of tools and, critically, a way to exert his professional control over the conduct of political work.

In the next section, I examine the career of Edward Bernays in order to explore how Bernays described his work and defended his methods as a public relations professional. I then turn to an examination of Bernays's efforts on behalf of political candidates, paying particular attention to his involvement in the 1941 New York City mayoral race. The ethnic mosaic of New York City politics provided Bernays a rich palette with which to work, and his use of survey research foreshadowed what has become commonplace today: a poll-driven campaign of microtargeting using messages tailored to the identities, concerns, and prejudices of discrete groups of voters.

In the conclusion, I assess the broader implications of Bernays's work, returning to the central theme animating this volume concerning the relationship between structure and creative action. As the case of Bernays illustrates, political consultants create strategies out of the identities and attachments of voters. Anchored to a professional claim, these strategies become persistent features of political practice. More than simply reflecting the skill of a clever consultant, however, the business Bernays helped create contributed to a broader transformation of American politics, altering the way candidates compete for office and, more fundamentally, how they interact with the voters they endeavor to represent.

Edward Bernays: Public Relations Counsel

Edward L. Bernays was a tireless promoter of public relations, and of himself. In tracing the arc of his career, it is sometimes difficult to separate the achievements of Bernays from the residues of his own self-promotion. In spite of this, Bernays left an extensive archive of writings and professional papers that provide substantial insight into the nature of his work. Two themes stand out prominently. First, Bernays thought considerably and worked consistently to establish his credentials as a professional. For Bernays, it was very important to distinguish his work as a "counsel on public relations" from that of a simple publicity man or theatrical press agent (even though their methods were difficult to distinguish from one another). Second, Bernays often underscored the plural quality of contemporary life, something that became a critical component of his public relations strategy whether applied to business, government, or politics. A society composed of multiple groups made it possible to target appeals toward a specific niche or construct a broad coalition depending on the client's need. Pluralism provided the raw material for public relations.

These two elements in Bernays's work, professional recognition and pluralism, were linked by a behavioral turn in the social sciences taking place during the 1920s and 1930s.[11] With its emphasis on the measurement of individual motives, behavioral social science offered Bernays a way to map individual attachments in an increasingly plural society and, simultaneously, sustain a professional claim that public relations provided a scientific approach to the modern task of opinion management. Grounding his work in an academic field gave Bernays a degree of credibility. At the same time, surveys, census data, and other forms of social science research provided Bernays with a set of tools that could be used to craft messages and plan strategies on behalf of various clients. These influences and impulses are evident in a series of books, articles, and speeches by Bernays in which he described and defended his methods and this new profession he hoped to create.

Origins of a New Profession

Edward L. Bernays began his career working as a publicity man and theatrical press agent in New York City. Sitting at the intersection of journalism and advertising, publicity was a growing business in the early decades of the twentieth century. Whether through spectacles designed to capture public attention or a press release written in the form of a newspaper article, effective publicity became an increasingly important way for politicians, businesses, and government to attract the interest and support of the public.[12]

Bernays was among the first to recognize the many and varied opportunities for effective publicity, prompting the author Larry Tye to dub him "the father of spin."[13]

Bernays was particularly adept at turning social and political issues into commercial opportunities for his clients, a tactic he would employ consistently throughout his career. In 1913, Bernays became involved in the production of a play entitled *Damaged Goods* about a man with syphilis who marries and fathers a syphilitic child. The play caused something of a scandal as it challenged contemporary mores about sexually transmitted disease; promoting it was a risky enterprise at a time when Anthony Comstock was the secretary of the New York Society for the Suppression of Vice. In order to raise money for the production, Bernays established a "Sociological Fund Committee," a strategy aimed at attracting reform-minded elites who saw the play as a way to break down societal taboos that inhibited social reform. With the help of Bernays, the play became something of a cause célèbre, attracting the support of John D. Rockefeller, Jr., Franklin and Eleanor Roosevelt, and other notables whose involvement kept Comstock at bay.[14]

Bernays employed a similar strategy of linking commerce and politics while working on behalf of American Tobacco during the 1920s. At a time when a woman smoking was considered a sign of loose morals, Bernays devised a way to increase the feminine appeal of cigarettes by linking the product with the cresting suffrage movement. Evoking the image of the Statue of Liberty, Bernays organized a suffragette march down Fifth Avenue during which women smoking cigarettes called on their sisters to "carry the torch of freedom."[15]

The underlying cynicism in these methods was not lost on contemporary critics, some of whom saw in Bernays's work evidence of a public easily manipulated by words and symbols. One profile of Bernays called him "a stern realist who operates upon the demonstrable theory that men in a democracy are sheep waiting to be led to the slaughter."[16] Another described publicity experts like Bernays as "the medicine man of the industrial tribe, whose spells and incantations work wonders which, like all religious mysteries, are either absurd or incredible when viewed by the rational mind."[17] Criticisms such as these were characteristic in the decade after World War I as revelations about wartime propaganda by the United States and its allies prompted liberal intellectuals to abandon their belief in a rational public capable of deliberative judgment. As historian J. Michael Sproule observes, "the chief moral of the Great War was its demonstration that the modern public was vulnerable to dubious contrivances promoted by political leaders and institutional managers."[18] Postwar commentators saw an uninformed crowd easily swayed by the tools of mass persuasion.

It was Walter Lippmann, more than any other intellectual of the period, who articulated this deepening skepticism toward public reason. In his widely influential 1922 book *Public Opinion*, Lippmann argued that public understanding of issues and events is limited by the fact that individuals cannot apprehend any objective reality that is not experienced personally. Impressions of the world around us were mere pictures in our head, largely painted by others. In fact, painting these pictures was the principal task of the publicity expert, whose appearance Lippmann noted "is a clear sign that the facts of modern life do not spontaneously take a shape in which they can be known. They must be given a shape by somebody."[19] The war illustrated the increasing sophistication of these methods, in particular "the manufacture of consent . . . and the opportunities for manipulation open to anyone who understands the process."[20] Looking ahead, Lippmann anticipated "a revolution . . . more significant than any shifting of economic power" as "the knowledge of how to create consent will alter every political premise."[21] Persuasion was to become the motive force in society, and one in which the persuaders wielded substantial influence in public affairs.

Lippmann's writing influenced Bernays in two respects. First, Bernays came to see his own work selling cigarettes or publicizing plays as manufacturing consent in the manner that Lippmann described. Bernays, himself, played a small role in U.S. propaganda efforts during the war, and the experience left him deeply interested in the psychological effects of propaganda, what Bernays described as "the impact words and pictures made on the minds of men."[22] Inspired, Bernays considered how the techniques he had perfected as a publicity man and press agent had broader applications in politics and government as well as business. In his 1923 book *Crystallizing Public Opinion*, Bernays drew heavily (and freely) from Lippmann's views about the ephemeral nature of public opinion, writing that "the chief contribution of the public relations counsel . . . is his capacity for crystallizing the obscure tendencies of the public mind." But if Lippmann explained why mass persuasion was possible in theory, Bernays sketched out how such work should be carried out in practice. Through his "ability to create . . . symbols . . . [and] to find those stereotypes, individual and community, which will bring favorable responses," the counsel on public relations was capable of "building public acceptance for an idea or product."[23]

Second, Lippmann offered a response to those critics who saw in the work of Bernays and others a cynical attempt to manipulate public opinion. Propaganda, according to Lippmann, was an inescapable feature of contemporary life. In the hands of trained experts, in fact, propaganda could be used as an instrument of democratic practice. Seeing himself in this role, Bernays endeavored to establish himself as a new kind of professional whose skills were indispensable in a modern, complex society. "The growth and importance of this new profession," Bernays claimed, "is due to the complexity of modern life."[24] In contrast to the many liberal critics concerned about the implications of wartime propaganda for democratic government, Bernays argued that far from a threat, "opinion-management is one of the most vital forces today, especially in preserving democracy." The work of the public relations counsel, Bernays later wrote, "is the very essence of the democratic process, the freedom to persuade and suggest."[25]

To sustain his claim that the public relations counsel performed a critical function in a democratic polity, Bernays worked hard to liken his actions to those of other well-respected professionals. According to Bernays, the job of the public relations counsel was "comparable to that of any special counsel in the highly organized society of today, the lawyer, the engineer, the accountant."[26] Describing "Public Relations as a Career," Bernays likened himself to a medical professional: "Just as a doctor examines his patient thoroughly before he . . . suggests a cure, so the counsel on public relations examines every function of his client and studies every symptom of health or disease before he makes a suggestion."[27] Elsewhere, Bernays compared his work to that of a lawyer. Whereas the attorney appeared before courts of law, the public relations counsel worked "before the bar of public opinion."[28]

The Art and Science of Politics

The effort by Bernays to stake out a professional claim for public relations occurred against the backdrop of broader shifts in American politics. By the 1920s, state and local party organizations were in decline as effective instruments of voter mobilization. Civil service reforms sapped many of the tangible benefits parties had previously provided to their supporters. The spread of the direct primary, and especially the presidential preference primary, encouraged a more candidate-centered campaign style. The advent of radio allowed candidates to reach individual voters in a more direct, less-mediated form than previously was possible. Meanwhile, interest groups proliferated, rising in prominence as "crucial conduits of the democratic will." Together these changes contributed to an "advertised style" of politics in which targeted appeals to individual voters emphasizing the personality of the candidate supplanted an older politics of partisan spectacle.[29]

For Edward Bernays and others like him, these changes presented an opportunity to extend the techniques of publicity and public relations, tools that had become commonplace in business, to the new realm of politics. However, doing so required displacing the traditional party workers who, despite their weakened state, retained control over the provision of political advice. Writing in 1928, Bernays observed that contemporary campaign methods were "archaic and ineffective;" they lacked "the expert use of propaganda" needed to "meet the conditions of the public mind." As a remedy, Bernays advised campaign managers to incorporate business methods—public relations, marketing, and advertising—into politics. According to Bernays, "big business is conducted on the principle that it must prepare its policies carefully . . . in selling an idea to the large buying public. . . . The political strategist must do likewise."[30] As one contemporary put it, "a political campaign . . . is a selling campaign. It is a drive for votes just as Ivory Soap advertising is a drive for sales."[31] Whether in the marketplace or the voting booth, individuals expressed their preferences through an act of choosing rendered manageable by the application of technique.[32]

Nor did the utility of public relations end with the election: "campaigning is only an incident in political life. The process of government is continuous," Bernays observed. Consequently, Bernays argued, "the expert use of propaganda is more useful and fundamental . . . as an aid to democratic administration, than as an aid to vote getting."[33] In a 1925 speech to the National Municipal League on "crystallizing public opinion for good government," Bernays insisted that with the right techniques (which only a counsel on public relations could provide), "good government can be sold to a community just as any other commodity can be sold to a community."[34] Anticipating the plebiscitary character of the modern presidency (and the prominent role of political consultants as political aides), Bernays told an audience at the American Political Science Association that a White House advisor, "independent of the various departments and responsible only to the President," was needed to coordinate publicity functions, "so

that the public would receive a constant and integrated picture of government activities."[35]

Critically, this attempt to broaden the business of public relations
hinged on a particular claim of scientific expertise. More than simply an
effort to persuade, professional public relations required a sophisticated
understanding of mass psychology, especially "knowledge of the workings
of public opinion."[36] To that end, Bernays considered himself a practitioner trained in the science of human behavior. As he put it, "the development of history, sociology, psychology, social psychology, journalism,
advertising and politics has made possible the work of a new type of
technician, whose function it is . . . to deal intelligently with the group
mind."[37] Explaining this new "science of propaganda," Bernays described
his work as "applied sociology in the broad field of influencing public
opinion."[38]

In part, linking public relations to a behavioral social science was an
explicit attempt to garner credibility for this nascent profession. A nephew
of Sigmund Freud, Bernays drew on his uncle's fame to build up his own
credentials as an expert in mass psychology. Meanwhile, Bernays cultivated
relations with leading social scientists of his day such as Harold Lasswell,
whose research on propaganda gave rise to the academic study of mass
communications, and Pendleton Herring, the Harvard professor and head
of the Social Science Research Council.[39] Bernays was also acquainted with
Harwood Childs, a Princeton political scientist who taught a course on
public opinion and was a founding editor of the journal *Public Opinion
Quarterly*. Bernays even contributed a preface to Childs's 1934 book *A Reference Guide to the Study of Public Opinion*, in which Bernays praised Childs
for "the development of important facts and ideas, and the distribution of
them to those people and organizations equipped to make use of them."
Childs lauded him in return, writing in his acknowledgment that Bernays
was a "genius" able "to bridge the chasm between laboratories of academic
endeavor and the world of practice."[40]

Claiming expertise in an esoteric field of knowledge is a characteristic
strategy of professions seeking occupational control. Academic disciplines
confer power and prestige, helping to legitimize professional work. As sociologist Andrew Abbott observes, professions often try to expand their turf
by claiming that their particular branch of knowledge offers new and better
solutions to some problem or task. Knowledge becomes "the currency of
competition" as professions try "to annex new areas [and] to define them

as their own proper work."[41] Social scientific appeals sustained a professional claim that public relations should be a core element of democratic
practice.

While extending professional control over political work, however, Bernays faced a more immediate task. In 1936, Bernays learned from his
accountant that he faced a 4 percent tax on business income in the state of
New York unless he could claim a professional exemption, defined by the
state as "any occupation or vocation in which a professed knowledge of
some department of science or learning is used by its practical application
to the affairs of others."[42] Drawing on his network of academic connections,
Bernays published a thin volume in 1937 that contained a list of sixty-eight
different university courses on propaganda, public relations, and related
subjects. Entitled *Universities—Pathways of Public Opinion*, Bernays wrote
that the purpose of the book was to "ascertain broadly the scope of academic attention to the subjects of public relations and opinion management."[43] In fact, Bernays used the list of courses he collected to petition the
state of New York for a tax exemption on the grounds that "leading universities are teaching the subject."[44]

Even if tax evasion was his principal motivation, Bernays was profoundly influenced by the behavioral turn in the social sciences, especially
its insights into the nature of individual identity, group attachments, and
the plural quality of contemporary life. Bernays frequently described the
techniques of public relations in terms of the complex composition of society and the myriad groups to which individuals belong. Bernays wrote of
the "interlapping" nature of group affiliation, by which he meant that individual identity was a composite of various social, political, ethnic, and religious attachments. "Society is made up of an almost infinite number of
groups," Bernays noted, "whose various interests and desires overlap and
interweave inextricably." Out of these multiple affiliations, the public relations counsel will select which of them to appeal to, or which groupings to
combine, in support of a specific purpose or goal. "The ordinary person is
a very temporary member of a great number of groups," Bernays observed,
and "the inconstancy of individual commitments may be accelerated and
directed by conscious effort."[45] For Bernays, propaganda was a tool for
selectively activating or suppressing aspects of individual identity, thereby
creating and recreating group attachments as the need arose. "The public
is, in fact, many publics," Bernays wrote.[46] The creative construction of a
public became the essence of his technique.

More to the point, Bernays firmly believed that the successful management of human behavior, what he called "the possibilities of regimenting the public mind," required a set of scientific tools and instruments for the effective measurement of public opinion.[47] "Just as there have grown up in America experts in city planning and experts in merchandising and experts in selling and advertising," Bernays observed, "so our complex democracy has developed the expert in appraising public opinion and in developing a technique for changing it."[48] Although still in its infancy, scientific polling was beginning to emerge in the 1930s as a powerful tool whose applications extended well beyond the marketing surveys for which it was initially designed.[49] For Bernays, surveys offered great promise as a scientific approach to selling, one that could be applied to politics and government as well as business. Just as marketing surveys disaggregated the buying public into different kinds of consumers, political polls disaggregated the voting public into different kinds of citizens.[50] According to Bernays, "The first thing a sales manager does when he tackles a new sales problem . . . is to study the public to whom he can sell." Similarly, "a survey of public desires, demands, and needs . . . made as scientifically as possible . . . would come to the aid of the political strategist whose business it is to make a proposed plan of the activities of the party and its elected officials."[51] In particular, survey research enabled the political strategist to select "such appeals as will best serve to reach the groups he desires to influence."[52]

In other words, selecting the right message required knowledge of the "group formation of society" and the various cleavages that form along "religious, social, economic, sex, school, political, professional, medical, fraternal, racial, [and] geographic lines."[53] Scientific polling was especially useful in this regard as it could capture and convey the diverse range of opinions in a pluralist democracy.[54] This is reflected in the statistically crude sampling technique of the 1920s and 1930s, the quota sampling method, in which polling samples were drawn using a representative number or quota of respondents from what the researcher deemed to be the relevant groups in society (e.g., gender, class, religion). As Sarah Igo notes, the quota method carried with it presumptions and biases about whose opinion was worth counting, leading to the creative fiction of an "averaged" American in public life.[55] In addition, survey methodology embraced a pluralist assumption about democratic politics: public opinion in a democratic society is the aggregation of individual and group opinions.[56] Polling, in short, became the science of pluralism.

Polling methods not only reified a pluralist conception of democracy, polling became a critical component of political strategy, eventually transforming campaign practice. By focusing on the particular likes and dislikes of the voter, polling marked a transition away from a mode of political mobilization that emphasized the collective expression of partisan loyalties in parades and rallies and toward a new mode of politics that hinged on tailored appeals to the interests, attachments, and affiliations of the individual. As Bernays argued, "The public is not merely made up of Democrats and Republicans. People today are largely uninterested in politics as such, and their interests in the issues of the campaign must be secured by coordinating these with other interests."[57] Surveys effectively mapped this diverse landscape, enabling Bernays to select the appropriate images and symbols "which stand in the minds of the public for the abstract idea the technician wishes to convey." Polling, in other words, was inseparable from media and the targeting of campaign messages. In combining the two, Bernays helped to create the modern craft of campaign consulting, a union between the art of political communication and the science of public opinion.

The 1941 New York Mayoral Race

We can see how Bernays employed these methods in his own work on behalf of William O'Dwyer, the Democratic candidate for mayor of New York City in 1941. Specifically, Bernays used survey research and other social scientific data to craft a media strategy that focused on the personal qualities of the candidate and his appeal to the various ethnic groups that made up the mosaic of New York City politics. New York was fertile ground for Bernays; the city foreshadowed the kind of campaigns that would characterize American elections in the years to come.

Several aspects of New York City politics deserve attention in this regard. First, the sheer size of the city—New York had a population of almost 8 million people in 1940—made campaigning on a citywide basis a logistical challenge. As the population grew, it also spread. Immigrants who once crowded into Lower East Side tenements made their way north to the upper reaches of Manhattan and the Bronx or across the bridges to Brooklyn and Queens. As voters spread out across the city's three hundred square miles, block captains could no longer reach as many voters as they once did. Mass communications replaced face-to-face contact as politicians turned to radio and newsreels, allowing them to "talk to more voters . . .

in fifteen minutes then they could greet in person in weeks of grueling campaigning."[58]

Second, successive waves of immigration since the nineteenth century had created a rich assortment of ethnic groups in the city. With no single group sufficient in size to control a citywide election, mayoral politics hinged on the construction of ethnic coalitions. Political organizations such as Tammany Hall came to dominate the Democratic Party and city politics by attracting the support of the Irish, then Jews, and eventually Italian voters. In the 1930s, however, these alliances became less stable as Jewish voters divided their votes between the Democrats and a succession of smaller, left-wing parties tied to the labor movement. Similarly, the city's Italian community divided its loyalties between the Democratic and Republican Parties, adding further to the complexity of mayoral politics.[59]

A third challenge of citywide campaigning was the declining strength of political machines due to a combination of shifting demographics and the displacement of party functions by a growing welfare state. Passage of the Johnson-Reed Act in 1924 imposed strict restrictions on immigration, resulting in fewer new arrivals to the city. The foreign-born population of the five boroughs peaked in 1930 at just under 2.4 million people, followed by a downturn in immigration that lasted until the 1970s. As a share of the population, immigrants declined from 40 percent of the city in 1910 to less than 25 percent in 1950.[60] As a result, the traditional role of the party machines as a support structure for new immigrants declined in importance, as did the source of strength that had sustained the machine for decades. For those immigrants who did come, along with the city's poor, New Deal–era programs displaced the welfare functions the machines once performed. As Chris McNickle points out in his study of New York City politics, "the implicit contract between district leader and voter, a ballot in return for bread, became harder for politicians to maintain."[61] At the same time, the construction of a welfare state brought increasing numbers of municipal jobs under civil service protections, sapping the strength of the parties as reservoirs of patronage.

New York City politics was changing, making it more difficult to assemble the ethnic coalitions necessary to win citywide elections and rendering traditional forms of political mobilization less effective. It was in this context that William O'Dwyer entered the race for mayor against Fiorello LaGuardia in 1941. LaGuardia's own success illustrates the changing circumstances of New York City politics. First elected in 1934 on a

Republican-Fusion ticket, LaGuardia was a savvy politician who exploited a weakened machine in order to build a powerful if largely personal following. LaGuardia's own diverse background—the son of Italian immigrants, yet born of a Jewish mother and raised an Episcopalian—embodied the diversity of his city, helping him to build a formidable coalition of political support. During his twelve years in office, LaGuardia created a new kind of big city mayor, mixing personal popularity with control over an expanding array of government services. As a result, LaGuardia enjoyed a greater degree of leeway from the apparatus of party than his predecessors. As the mayor was fond of saying, "there is no Democratic or Republican way of cleaning the streets." Notably, LaGuardia's success hinged in part on his alliance with President Franklin D. Roosevelt; both men understood the alchemy of public opinion and executive power.[62]

For his part, O'Dwyer endeavored to use his own compelling biography to construct an electoral coalition that could compete with that of the popular mayor. Born in Ireland, O'Dwyer could count on the support of his fellow Irish New Yorkers and the backing of the Democratic Party. Amid the shifting allegiances of New York City voters, however, O'Dwyer had to distance himself from Tammany Hall if he was to attract the support of independent and weakly affiliated groups, namely Jews. Throughout his political rise, in fact, O'Dwyer remained in, but not entirely of, the Democratic Party. He came to the attention of party leaders as an effective and honest Brooklyn district attorney, gaining notoriety for his prosecution of organized crime. Much like the fast-rising Republican star Thomas Dewey who began his career as Manhattan district attorney, O'Dwyer used his record as a crime buster to build a reputation as an independently minded official untainted by corruption.[63]

In early 1941, the O'Dwyer campaign approached Edward Bernays for his help in devising a strategy for the race. With five weeks remaining before Election Day, Bernays presented the campaign with a set of recommendations. Backed by a compendium of census data, market research, election results, and surveys of New York City voters concerning the issues of the campaign, Bernays devised a campaign strategy that emphasized O'Dwyer's personal qualities rather than his party affiliation. This emphasis on personality suggests a more candidate-focused style of New York City politics. More important, however, the reliance on survey research to create a compelling narrative of the candidate reveals how Bernays sought to create a modern form of campaign management. Foreshadowing the techniques that would become commonplace in American politics, Bernays described his work as "an engineering approach . . . in the planning of and carrying out of the Democratic campaign . . . the engineering of consent."[64]

Bernays emphasized the sophistication of his methods in order to help sell his services. However, the information gleaned from surveys and other social science data also provided Bernays with insights into the complex structure of society, information Bernays used to target messages to the politically relevant groups in the electorate. Describing this engineering approach, Bernays posed a series of questions he endeavored to answer in crafting the campaign.

> What groups and group alignments are there in New York? Where are the independent voters? What is the largest bloc of voters? How and what do the people feel about the two candidates? What lessons are there in the history of past elections? What are the underlying currents and opinions that represent the bases of public opinion and action . . . ? What social, religious, economic and political blocs exist? What kind of leadership is there and what is it trying to do? What is the relationship of the great channels of communication— radio, motion pictures, newspapers—to the situation?[65]

Put differently, Bernays promised to create an effective political strategy by apprehending the complex social structure of the electorate.

Given the multiethnic context of New York City politics, this strategy consisted of a mixture of campaign messages tailored to the concerns and prejudices of different ethnic groups. Among these, Bernays singled out Jewish voters as the critical swing group that could determine the outcome of the election. In particular, Bernays emphasized emotional appeals rather than policy positions when appealing to group sentiments. According to Bernays, "The analysis of attitudes from a psychological standpoint, indicates that large groups of the New York public are swayed by hate and by fear, rather than by a rational approach to the administrative functions of a Mayor. The sense of psychological insecurity . . . has created a situation where the appeals to the public, particularly to the Jewish public which represents the greatest independent vote, must be made upon other than straight municipal issues. They must rest upon gaining acceptance for the belief that the candidate is not anti-Semitic."[66] In addition to Jewish voters, Bernays devised emotional appeals that could sway other ethnic groups.

When O'Dwyer was speaking to Italians, Bernays recommended that he should "stress complete fairness" and nondiscrimination; when speaking to German Protestants, he should "stress personal qualities" such as dignity and honesty; when speaking to Irish Catholics, he should emphasize "personal qualifications" such as O'Dwyer's record on crime. Bernays articulated similar refinements of strategy along economic and geographic lines as well.[67]

Bernays also distilled the survey data he collected into a set of personal qualities of O'Dwyer and LaGuardia, what contemporary consultants refer to as a candidate's "favorables" and "unfavorables." For instance, Bernays recommended that O'Dwyer present himself as a "powerful proponent for democracy" who was staunchly "supporting President Roosevelt." O'Dwyer should "declare and maintain independence of Tammany and all bosses" as well as stress his "liberal attitude towards labor." In order to distinguish himself from LaGuardia and what some critics viewed as a crass style of self-promotion, O'Dwyer should "pledge devoting full time to the job of running New York" and stress his "steady, even-tempered, tactful, diplomatic character." These characteristics formed a platform for the campaign that was to inform every activity of the candidate, "every event, every speech, every release, [and] every action." Bernays even suggested specific speeches for specific audiences that could be delivered in person and on the radio; he recommended visual images through photographs and motion pictures that could "translate the planks of his platform into pictures," and he suggested a series of planned events that would attract media attention, noting that "the more compelling the created circumstances . . . the more likely it is to find a place in the medium." Altogether, Bernays envisioned a "vigorous, strong offensive" that would result in a "building up of the candidate" and "a deflation of the opponent."[68]

Bernays projected a cost of $100,000 for the campaign, $10,000 for consulting fees with the remainder going to media, campaign personnel, and related costs.[69] It does not appear that Bernays ever closed the sale; his direct involvement with the campaign ended with a set of recommendations and a few thousand dollars to cover services rendered.[70] However, O'Dwyer did follow the broad outlines of the strategy Bernays outlined by painting himself as an independent, New Deal Democrat. In the end, O'Dwyer lost to LaGuardia by the narrowest margin in a mayoral race since 1909, a considerable feat given that FDR openly endorsed LaGuardia against the wishes of New York Democrats.[71] Running again four years later, O'Dwyer won easily in a three-way contest. For the first time in more than a decade, LaGuardia was not a candidate for mayor, a fact that aided O'Dwyer's cause, particularly among the Jewish voters Bernays had identified as the key to the election.[72]

The work of Edward Bernays offers a glimpse into American politics in the making. Amid shifting ethnic allegiances, declining party organizations, and a growing New Deal state, politicians encountered an uncertain electoral landscape. Exploiting this uncertainty, Edward Bernays offered a new style of campaign management that applied the tools of social science to the traditional task of vote getting. Ultimately, however, Bernays could not convince the O'Dwyer campaign entirely about the merits of his methods. This fact illustrates that political consulting was still in its infancy in the 1940s; the ward heelers and other traditional purveyors of political advice still retained control over the conduct of political work. This would change in time. During the 2009 New York City mayoral election, political consultants and pollsters received more than $17 million in fees (most of it from Mayor Michael Bloomberg's reelection campaign). More than just a measure of Bloomberg's deep pockets, or the extravagant cost of elections, this figure reflects the extraordinary growth in consulting that has taken place over the past seventy years. Whether at the federal, state, or municipal level, nearly all competitive candidates employ professional consultants to run their campaigns. Their techniques may be more sophisticated, but the modern consultants working today distill social scientific data into political strategies much the same way as Bernays did more than seventy years ago.

Conclusion

Although he would be pleased to see the business of consulting he helped create, Edward Bernays bequeathed much more than just a way to live profitably from politics. As the historian Robert B. Westbrook notes, American politics has become a form of commodity exchange: campaign advertising packages and sells candidates to voters; polling helps package and sell voters to candidates. Political consultants, Westbrook points out, are critical intermediaries in this exchange; of course, their services are for sale as well.[73]

As I have argued, broad changes in the character of American democracy turn on the nature and control of political work. To describe the rise of a twentieth-century political style in the United States is to trace changes in political practice, especially the reliance on polling and media to craft campaign messages. This focus on practice has important implications for scholars of American political development and political institutions more generally. Technology, party organizations, or electoral rules, although important, cannot alone or in combination explain how various marketing techniques came to dominate campaign methods in the United States. In order to understand changes in practice, one must pay close attention to practitioners. Put in the language of institutional change, political development is the product of actors at work.

In the case of Edward Bernays, this creative work operated on two levels. In his effort to create a new profession, Bernays worked to institutionalize a new kind of campaign so that polling and media would become durable features of political practice. Although Bernays and others of his ilk exploited opportunities such as the decline in party organizations or the advent of new technologies, these structural factors alone were not sufficient to convince candidates of the utility of their methods. In addition, political consultants had to displace existing sources of political intelligence, such as party workers. To advance this goal, Bernays creatively put forward a professional claim grounded in a behavioral social science. Relying on a new field of academic knowledge conferred power and prestige, helping Bernays to extend his control over the provision of political advice.[74]

Backed by this claim of professional authority, Bernays and others perfected campaign techniques that created coalitions out of distinct voter groups, often by highlighting the personal characteristics of the candidate. Features of society such as class, ethnicity, or religion were not immutable structures but rather provided the raw materials for political strategy. Social science was not only a way to establish professional authority; in the hands of Bernays, survey research created a particular model of the American voter, one who could be approached much like a consumer, on the basis of psychological attachments to a product and activated using carefully chosen symbols, images, and words.

In sum, Edward Bernays made politics in two senses. First, in constructing a new profession, Bernays changed the character of democratic practice. Today, the political consulting profession is a central feature of the American political landscape because of the authority of its practitioners and the legitimacy of their methods. Second, and at the same time, political consulting provided a conduit through which a social scientific rendering of the electorate transformed how candidates and elected officials viewed the world and the voters they represent. Rather than mobilize armies of partisans as in the nineteenth century, twentieth-century politics turned on the selective activation of identities and allegiances among discrete groups of voters.

It is ironic that so many political scientists overlook the actual practice of politics when almost daily political consultants apply the tools of their academic discipline to create campaign strategies, television advertisements, and direct mailings. Through the rise of a political consulting profession, American social science has transformed democratic practice. Whether this change has been for good or for ill is a subject for another essay.

Chapter 7

Accidental Hegemony

How the System of National Accounts Became a Global Institution

Yoshiko M. Herrera

The System of National Accounts (SNA) is a massively ambitious institutional enterprise that aims to clarify the overall structure and dynamics of a country's economy. As a single standardized system, it is the basis for virtually every comparative economic indicator used today, including gross domestic product. By structuring the content and meaning of aggregate economic information, the SNA makes economies legible to governments, firms, citizens, and external observers, and informs the development of policy and policy assessment.

Yet despite its apparently firm footing as the global institution for national economic data, the SNA is a relatively recent, mid-twentieth-century innovation, and until the 1990s it was not the only choice available to states. In particular, the Soviet Union and other planned economies used the material product system (MPS)[1] and many developed capitalist states such as the United States and France also had their own systems. Today there is near unanimous agreement on the appropriateness of the SNA for all states, despite the persistence of some country-specific practices. Although countries continue to debate the content of the SNA and use certain alternatives domestically, there is no alternative *international* system in use, and national statisticians no longer question the value of a universal, comprehensive international framework for national accounts. Nevertheless, today's ostensible hegemony masks the multiple decision points and diversity of ideas and national interests behind the development and revision of the SNA, a process that led to the "accidental" hegemony of the SNA as a global institution.

Mutual Constitution and Contestation as Creative Syncretism

It is tempting to think of statistical systems as simply mirrors of the economy, where economic structure determines institutional forms. Indeed, this is the basis for Marxist as well as Smithian approaches to national accounting. But as others and I have argued in detail elsewhere,[2] this simple structural approach to national accounts is misleading. Instead, the development of the SNA was marked by a great deal of contestation among national statisticians and the mutual constitution of rules at the national and international levels.

"Mutual constitution" refers to the productive and consequential interaction between norms (or rules) and their followers (actors). In the SNA there is also a spatial dimension, the interaction between international rules and national actors. The SNA emerged as a single framework on the basis of national statisticians from a variety of countries repeatedly working though complex questions about how to measure different aspects of the economy, recombining country and international experiences with a variety of theoretical insights: in this way the SNA is a prime example of creative syncretism.

Moreover, the SNA and its primary rival, the MPS, developed in relation to each other; they were mutually constituting as well. The MPS appeared in association with the revision of the SNA, and the global hegemony of the SNA is integrally tied to the demise of the MPS. Neither of these institutions was developed only by international organizations; the contributions of member nations and mutual learning led to the formalization of both institutions.

Finally, the development of the SNA was not driven by a logic of increasing efficiency or path dependency; it was instead a radical theoretical departure from past practice in its first instantiation. And it is also not a story of exogenous rule development and imposition. The SNA did not appear on the scene as a self-evident set of rules that suddenly constrained or enabled behavior; it was and is a product of discussions about how economic data could and should be compiled. No leviathan oversaw the creation of the SNA and it is not therefore a story of powerful states dictating to everyone else how national accounts should be organized. Instead, it grew out of mutually constituting contributions from individuals and countries at the national, regional, and international levels.

There was extensive variation in national accounting practices among both individual countries and "types" of states (Western, communist, developing, etc.). Some countries in the Organisation for Economic Co-operation and Development (OECD) fought to include their own practices in the SNA or simply maintained their previous ways of doing things. The United States follows its own system of national accounts (the National Income and Product Accounts, or NIPA), which is fully consistent with SNA principles but not exactly the same.[3] France at various points also took an alternative path. Among postcommunist countries there was variation among eastern European states in not only structural conditions and economic reforms but also in their statistical practices and their familiarity with the SNA; not all participated to the same degree.

Over time, the SNA did not stamp out variation so much as find space for it. The most recent 2008 version of the SNA aims to fit every type of economy, and its "satellite" accounts are sites of ongoing decentralized experimentation within the formal structure of the SNA. To understand this amalgamation, it is all the more critical to analyze the fierce debates along the way. In many respects, the 1993 SNA and 2008 update integrated and incorporated the deliberations and are products of opposition and alternatives.

Given today's outcome, however, the coherence of the SNA, like that of many other international institutions, can easily be overstated. As Gary Herrigel argues, the abstraction of coherence "blends out a great deal of anomalous relationships, habits, dispositions, and institutional practices."[4] By remaining attentive to contestation, or the disorder behind the apparent hegemony, we can detect variation in institutional practice and the causes of that variation, but we also have a more complete picture of institutional development and the bases of compliance. Indeed, understanding the SNA as a process of creative assemblage sheds new light on compliance as well as hegemony: as a flexible and constantly evolving structure that grew out of decades of interaction among national statisticians, it is not so much that states follow the SNA as that the SNA has been constructed by key actors to more or less meet their needs. Hence, their compliance with it is actually a product of its origins and is not something they merely followed once the institution was set up.

In mapping the development of the SNA as a hegemonic global institution, I begin with a brief discussion of the concept of national accounts, the SNA as a particular form of national accounting, and the differences between the SNA and the MPS. I then explore the development of the SNA and the MPS in tandem.

National Accounts

National accounts tackle the question of aggregate economic activity and processes within countries. There are myriad ways to define national accounts, but in general they must tackle four fundamental questions:

1. What counts as productive economic activity?
2. How should activity be conceptually categorized and aggregated?
3. How should specific activities be defined and measured?
4. How should data be collected and disseminated?

The first question addresses what is called the "production boundary," that is, what should be included in measures of economic activity? A seemingly easy answer might be, count everything! Or count all production for which money (or a substitute) is exchanged. Current debates, however, reveal that the production boundary line entails conceptual decisions that have serious consequences for what is valued in a society. For example, if a person cleans his or her own house and takes care of children without pay, that activity is not currently within the SNA production boundary. If that same person paid someone else to clean and take care of children, then those activities would count. This issue of household labor has enormous consequences for the documented level of contribution of women to national output.[5] There are numerous more prosaic examples, such as whether antiques should be treated as consumption or investment, where to draw the line between gardening and subsistence agriculture, and whether illegal but monetized transactions, such as the illicit drug trade, should be counted. In resolving such questions, any national accounting system is likely to be influenced by ideas and interests of the day.

The second question on categorization and aggregation, which is aimed at identifying economic actors and organizing types of activity, can be related to the first. If one considers only material output in the production boundary—steel, timber, cloth, wine, and so on—then the type of categorization may reflect industrial sectors. But categorization is also theoretically informed and tied to the goals for which information is to be used. A follower of John Maynard Keynes, who was interested in the relationship between government spending and unemployment, would categorize information differently from the materialist scheme. At the moment, a Keynesian approach based on "institutional sectors" (government, public and private corporations, households, etc.) and their activity (consumption, savings, investment, etc.) reigns, but for much of the history of national accounting before Keynes that was not the case.

Once we have decided what counts as economic activity and how to categorize and aggregate it, we have to figure out how to connect the national accounting framework to data. Here we move from concepts to indicators and reach the potentially mind-numbing technical minutiae of how, theoretically, to count things we agree should be counted. For example, if we included the costs of pollution and its cleanup in the production boundary, how would we count them? What kind of pollution (air, water, ground) should be measured? Even for seemingly noncontroversial issues the question of measurement is not easy. An enormous amount of time has actually been spent on how to treat "free checking" in the SNA, for example. For data to be reliable and comparable, all these measurement issues have to be worked through and agreed upon.

Even if we can agree on the production boundary, the classification scheme, and measurement schemes for all the data, we then have to tackle the actual collection and dissemination of data. Data are typically collected by a national statistics office (NSO) in three ways: by requesting administrative records from other government agencies, through censuses (full enumeration) or surveys (samples) of relevant actors such as firms and households, and through estimation methods carried out by NSOs or affiliates. All three methods require resources, both material and human capital, and the first two methods require a great deal of cooperation and trust. If a country has limited resources, it may not be able to put theoretically sophisticated measurement schemes into place, even if they have been agreed upon. If a government fears the consequences of revealing certain kinds of data—such as data related to military production or other defense spending—it may not want them collected, much less analyzed and published, and that brings up the question of dissemination, which is also subject to resource and political constraints. Hence collection and dissemination of data do not automatically follow from agreement on the principles of a national accounting system by NSOs and governments.

This brief sketch of the fundamental questions in setting up a national accounting system illustrates that there is a significant ideological or ideational component to national accounts. As William Alonso and Paul Starr have argued, statistical systems reflect the societies that develop them; they reflect the values or "presuppositions" of time and place.[6] The production boundary, division into sectors, and aggregation schemes are deeply theoretical, ideological, and political. The way in which national accounts treat these questions is connected to economic theory, to ideas about what matters, and to interests. The measurement, collection, and dissemination approaches are also theoretically informed, but they involve more practical issues, including resources and political calculations.

Development of the SNA up to 1968

Modern national accounting appeared after the Great Depression, and its development is concomitant with the changes in statistics and economics as disciplines more generally, but it also has a number of distinguishing features.[7] First and foremost among these is the systematic application of macroeconomic theory, especially that of John Maynard Keynes, to national accounts. The critical contribution by Keynes was the move away from an entirely empirical approach focused on industrial production and toward the theoretical concepts of income, consumption, investment, and savings and the relationships among them.

A second theoretical innovation in the SNA was the link between national accounting and double-entry bookkeeping, advanced by Irving Fisher and Morris Copeland.[8] Building on this, James Meade and Richard Stone wrote a "white paper" applying double-entry bookkeeping and national accounts to data from the United Kingdom.[9] Stone later went on to become the main architect of the SNA.[10]

There were other intellectual influences as well, including Wassily Leontief's input-output statistics in the 1920s and 1930s.[11] Approximately one hundred countries began doing input-output accounting on the basis of Leontief's work. One of the influences on Leontief's contribution was the analysis of interindustry tables in the Soviet Union, compiled by Pavel

Popov in 1926.[12] These tables were the basis of Popov's very early estimation of national accounts for the Soviet Union in the 1920s, which was later the theoretical and empirical basis of the MPS. The work of Popov, therefore, influenced not only the MPS but also, via Leontief, the SNA.

After World War II, a new statistical commission at the United Nations, the UN Statistical Office (UNSO), was set up and it took action on two important issues early on: national accounts and sampling.[13] Michael Ward notes that "prior to World War II, both probability sampling and national accounting were viewed as somewhat untried and questionable endeavors. Doubts about their relevance and reliability persisted even after the war, despite the successful uses of both approaches by governments in the intervening period."[14] For this reason he calls the UNSO's decision to focus on national accounts "a significant leap of faith."[15] Nevertheless, the UN Statistical Commission advanced both right away: it published the work of Richard Stone on national accounts and set up the Subcommission on Sampling.[16]

The 1947 publication of Stone's work was a milestone in national accounts. Some analysts, such as Frits Bos of Eurostat, considered it the first version of the SNA. The 1947 UN report had two distinguishing features, according to Bos: "First, it contained the first fully elaborated and detailed national accounting system. Secondly, it contained, for the first time, *international recommendations on compiling national accounts*."[17] This 1947 document represented a significant step beyond just sharing national data toward *collective* work at the international level. In addition, one of the key goals of the 1947 report was comparability of data—a goal that remains part of the core mission of all international organizations involved in national accounts today.

Along with the UN Statistical Commission and the UNSO, the Organisation for European Economic Co-operation (OEEC, later, the OECD) played an important role in advancing the SNA. In 1949 it set up the National Accounts Research Unit, directed by Richard Stone, in Cambridge to train statisticians from member countries.[18] That unit produced two early SNA publications in 1951 and 1952.[19] These three publications, the United Nations' 1947 report and the reports from 1951 and 1952 published by the OEEC, gave rise to the first official document on the SNA in 1953.[20] This document contained forty-six pages of explanation and a two-page description of the accounts. Within about ten years of its publication, approximately sixty countries were using the 1953 SNA, but there were significant other developments by individual countries in national accounts that were not reflected in the 1953 version.[21] Despite work at both the national and international levels, it would still be premature to characterize this process in terms of mutual constitution of international institutions and domestic actors.

Stone continued to work on the SNA after the 1953 publication and played a critical role in producing the revised version published in 1968.[22] Ward describes the 1968 version as "a quantum leap forward."[23] The 1968 version was much longer (250 pages, with 12 pages for the accounts) and incorporated other approaches to national accounting—input-output tables, flow-of-funds, and balance sheets—which had existed before the 1953 version but were not integrated into it.[24] It also outlined the basis for price indices that would allow for measurement of aggregates in current and constant prices. One important aspect of the SNA that did not change from 1953 to 1968, however, was the production boundary.

In the run-up to the 1968 SNA, national experiences influenced the international level, but significant variation in national practices remained, and the UN recommendations were just beginning to take hold. There were regional differences, exemplified by the later development of the MPS, as well as the European System of Integrated Economic Accounts (known as ESA) in Europe,[25] and the NIPA in the United States. But even among OECD countries significant variation in national accounting remained. Peter Hill (later an author of the 1993 SNA) wrote not long after publication of the 1968 version, "No two countries tackle the problem of measuring real product in quite the same way and every country has its own idiosyncrasies."[26] In addition, the 1953 and 1968 SNA versions were dominated by the work of Richard Stone and did not reflect, as the 1993 SNA would, a diverse and multinational as well as multi-institutional approach to the drafting of the formal documents.

Development of the MPS

The MPS developed on three levels: at the United Nations, within the Council for Mutual Economic Assistance (CMEA, which was the economic organization for Eastern bloc states organized by the Soviet Union), and in individual communist states. Developments at one level directly affected others: It is hard to imagine the development of the MPS in the absence of comparison projects between it and the SNA. In discussing the achievements of the UNSO Michael Ward lists the SNA as the most significant achievement, followed by the MPS.[27] That is, the core organization behind the SNA, the UNSO, considered the development of the MPS one of its primary accomplishments.

The development of the MPS differs from the development of the SNA in that an informal statistical system for national accounts existed in the Soviet Union and eastern European countries before such practices were formalized in a written document, and the formal documentation of the MPS took a somewhat circuitous route. According to János Árvay, after World War II, when eastern European countries were setting up their statistical systems using the Soviet Union as a model, they did not have access to Popov's model of national accounts from the 1920s.[28] To learn about the MPS, eastern Europeans held bilateral meetings, primarily in Moscow, with Soviet statisticians. Árvay writes, "In this situation the compilation of national balances started in the new socialist countries without an overall description of the concepts and methods; *they relied frequently on the principle of 'learning by doing.'*"[29]

The first general description of the MPS was published by the UN Statistical Commission in 1957, with the approval of all CMEA countries. In response to expressions of interest, the United Nations asked the Conference of European Statisticians (CES) to undertake a comparison project between the SNA and the MPS. At the Sixth CES meeting in 1958, eight countries, four from the East (the Soviet Union, Czechoslovakia, Poland, and Hungary) and four from the West (the United States, the United Kingdom, France, and Italy), were invited to undertake a comparison.[30]

In preparation for that 1958 CES meeting, Czechoslovakia gave the secretariat of the conference two documents: one that described the methodology for national income under the MPS and one that presented the system as a whole.[31] According to Árvay, these two documents, which together totaled twenty-five pages, were translated into three languages, and were the first international presentation of the MPS by the CMEA. Based on these documents and an early version of the SNA, the eight countries were compared.[32] Of this work, Árvay says, "Looking back at this period from a sufficiently long historical perspective, it can definitely be stated that the comparison of the two systems exerted a mutual influence which was perceivable later when the development of the two systems proceeded."[33] Within the Soviet Union, a short formal description of the MPS was not published until 1960,[34] that is, some years after the work on documenting the MPS had begun at the United Nations.

There was another revision of the country comparisons in 1964, when the CES set up the Working Party on National Accounts and Balances at its twelfth plenary session. The Working Party was supposed to represent the CES during the overall SNA revision in the UN Statistical Commission, but it had two additional tasks: (1) to develop a description of the MPS; and (2) to consider "establishing links between a revised and developed SNA and MPS and of drawing up a European statistical program of national accounts and balances."[35] In conjunction with this expanded comparison effort, representatives from all countries of the CES were invited to join the Working Party.

Closely following these efforts in the CES, in 1965 the CMEA countries decided to work toward harmonizing national accounts within the CMEA, and they began further documenting the MPS to produce a revised and more detailed account. Initially different countries were to work on different parts, with the Soviet Union coordinating the effort.[36] After one round, this proved unworkable and the Soviet Union's NSO, Goskomstat, took over, using some country papers as supplements. The CMEA approved a final document at its eleventh session in November 1968, which appeared in Russian in 1969,[37] and was later sent to the UN Statistical Commission, which published it in 1971.[38] With this publication the MPS became officially acknowledged as one of two internationally recognized systems for national accounts.[39] The 1971 UN document resulted from a combined effort by the CMEA countries, which in turn had been instigated or inspired by the earlier work of the United Nations.

The MPS differed from the SNA on all four fundamental questions of national accounts.[40] First, the production boundary for the MPS was limited to *material* production, meaning it did not include services. Second, beyond the production boundary, the classificatory scheme and related macroeconomic indicators of the MPS were fundamentally different from those of the SNA, meaning the MPS did not use the Keynesian categories of analysis, and in lieu of gross national product (GNP) and gross domestic product (GDP), the MPS gave rise to two alternative macroeconomic indicators: "global social product" and "net material product (NMP)."[41] Third, Soviet statisticians frequently counted things using a different methodology, which they did not share, with the result being many indicators with similar names that were not equivalent to those in the West. Finally, data collection and dissemination in Soviet bloc countries relied almost exclusively on full enumeration (censuses) of firm-level data and eschewed the use of sample surveys and estimation techniques used in the West. Minimal publication of both components and underlying data was another hallmark of Soviet bloc statistics.

A prominent Hungarian statistician, László Drechsler, said that "the difference between the SNA and MPS is analogous to the difference between the smallest common denominator and the lowest common multiple in mathematics."[42] He meant that the CMEA countries collected and analyzed much more data than the MPS officially requested but submitted only the required information. In contrast, the 1968 SNA was so extensive that almost no state implemented it fully, but whatever they did do corresponded to the document.

In this way contestation within the CMEA was managed by permitting flexibility beyond the formal requirements of the MPS. Such divergent national practices affected institutions at the international level. Hungary provides one case of pragmatic innovation in this regard. János Árvay describes its practice: "Hungary has always played an active role in broadening the scope and deepening the observation of economic activity, standard of living, external relations within the CMEA Statistical Commission. Wherever it was not possible to reach agreement with the other member-countries, the Hungarian Central Statistical Office followed its own way in developing its own statistical system, while also adhering consistently to the standards approved jointly."[43] It is interesting that in this passage Árvay points out that Hungarians followed the rules and helped the CMEA, but when that did not work out, Hungary "followed its own way."

Indeed, Hungary introduced its own hybrid national accounts system in 1970.[44] This system was consistent with the MPS, allowing Hungary to submit required data to the CMEA, but it also allowed for the compilation of all the macrostatistical aggregates of the SNA.[45] Where there were points of conflict in the two systems, Árvay says that Hungary went with the system recommendations that fit its economic circumstances.

Although Hungary strayed the furthest from the MPS, variation in national accounting practice also occurred elsewhere in the CMEA. In Poland at the beginning of the 1980s the work of the national statistical office was subject to review by an independent government organization.

The four CMEA countries that belonged to the World Bank and the International Monetary Fund (Yugoslavia, Romania, Poland, and Hungary) submitted data based on the SNA. In their own official statistical publications, however, Poland, Romania, and Yugoslavia used only the MPS.[46]

In 1981 the United Nations revised its comparison of the SNA and the MPS.[47] This time the project involved ten countries: eight SNA countries (the United States, the United Kingdom, Japan, Austria, Finland, Peru, the Philippines, and Zambia) and two MPS countries (Hungary and Yugoslavia). By 1986, the CMEA Statistical Commission decided to formally update the MPS. The goal was to produce one document to reflect all the agreed-on changes over the previous twenty years, which would clarify and harmonize the MPS.[48] The group working to revise the 1968 SNA had similar goals. In 1987 the CMEA sent its revised document on the MPS to the UN Statistical Commission, which published it in 1989 in two volumes.[49] Unbeknownst at the time, that was to be the last major document on the MPS ever published by the United Nations.

SNA Revision from 1968 to 1993

The 1968 SNA was initially published in English. By 1970 it had appeared in the other official UN languages. Soon afterward, important economic events led to thoughts of possible changes.[50] The 1973 oil crisis and resulting inflation spurred interest in rethinking the way that national accounts handle inflation; the use of input-output tables that were sometimes a couple of years old became problematic. In addition, the rise of monetarism sparked interest in improved financial statistics and cooperation between central banks and NSOs.

The complex structure of the SNA, however, took time to implement and update and some international organizations such as the World Bank became frustrated at how long it took to get current estimates of GNP using the SNA, especially for developing countries.[51] Because the World Bank wanted information quickly to assess its loans and other development programs, it began doing its own calculations of per capita GNP.

The World Bank, however, had a different mission than the UNSO. Michael Ward, who worked in the data development group of the World Bank for fifteen years, is very critical of the Bank's efforts to help countries construct GNP.[52] Ward asserts that the World Bank was not actually implementing the SNA in various countries; rather it had developed a quicker method of calculating GNP using statistical estimates, sometimes lacking underlying source data. Nevertheless, soon even UN agencies adopted the World Bank's GNP calculations, despite discrepancies between the UNSO and World Bank figures. The result was that the UNSO eventually lost its role as the leading international organization for national accounts.

The differences in goals and practices of the UNSO and World Bank regarding national accounts highlights the point that contestation over national accounts occurred not just between adherents of the MPS and those of the SNA, or between national and international levels, but also among organizations at the international level. It also suggests an important issue in implementation of the SNA, namely that the data demands from international organizations are not homogenous and that international organizations had different, sometimes contradictory, influence on the work of NSOs.

The process for revising the SNA in the 1970s was opened on several fronts, including greater input from developing countries. Michael Ward writes that the UNSO responded to the economic ideas of the time and "adopted a genuinely international policy perspective."[53] In 1975 an "inter-regional seminar" in Caracas focused on implementation of the 1968 SNA. Regional meetings followed in Africa in 1975 and 1979, in western Asia in 1978, and in Europe in 1978 and 1980.[54] For the UN Statistical Commission's twentieth session in 1979, a report on these meetings was prepared. It argued for the formation of an expert group to consider implementation and future work on the SNA. Such a group with representatives from ten countries and some international organizations met in the spring of 1980 in New York. The group decided not to overhaul the SNA but unanimously agreed that some "clarifications" were necessary.

The twenty-first session of the Statistical Commission in 1981 called for a second expert group. Its eleven national and international representatives met in 1982. This group agreed with its predecessor: the SNA needed "clarifications and updating" but not a major revision. However, it took an important step toward further international collaboration in its report: "It is apparent that those international organizations, regional commissions, and specialized agencies that are directly involved in the development of the systems and standards need to be brought together on a cooperative basis. The burden of work can then be shared and conflicting or duplicative efforts can be avoided. In terms of implementing a common set of standards, furthermore, representation of those directly involved is essential."[55]

The 1982 expert group also recommended the formation of a permanent working group, which became the Inter-Secretariat Working Group on National Accounts (ISWGNA). ISWGNA initially included the UNSO, the OECD, and Eurostat; later the International Monetary Fund and World Bank also joined. Further Statistical Commission meetings in 1983 and 1985 returned to the issue of reviewing the SNA and called for "clarification and simplification and harmonization among different international statistical systems."[56] At this point several systems were still in use: NIPA in the United States, the ESA in Europe, and the MPS.

The Inter-Secretariat Group decided to hold eight meetings, with approximately two per year starting in 1986. The first was to review the structure of the 1968 SNA. Six others would address more specialized topics. A final meeting in 1989 would summarize progress in order to prepare a revised SNA for the 1991 Statistical Commission meeting.[57]

The first meeting in 1986 was scheduled ahead of an "inter-regional" meeting of developing country representatives. The meeting addressed the applicability of the SNA to developing countries. Anne Harrison, a core member of the expert group, writes:

> There was unanimous agreement that the concerns of developing countries needed to be reflected in the SNA, and there was a very clear message that all developing countries were not alike; there were greater differences between developing countries than between some developing countries and some developed countries. With this in mind, therefore, it was felt very strongly that there should not be two versions of the SNA, a "full" version for developed countries and a cut-down version for less developed countries, but that a single version should be expounded, capable of meeting the requirements of the conditions in countries at all stages of development. It would be for individual countries to decide how much of the System they could and would implement, given resource constraints and policy considerations.[58]

Some expert group meetings made significant progress toward the goal of greater harmonization in the SNA. For example, it was agreed that the ESA would be rewritten by 1994 in order to be consistent with the revised

SNA. Some other harmonization efforts, however, did not succeed, including the issue of common data classification systems, on which there was lack of agreement with certain international organizations.[59]

By the sixth expert group meeting in March 1988, it became obvious that the group was in the midst of a major revision to the 1968 SNA.[60] Several additional expert group meetings were scheduled, and the target date for the new SNA was postponed until 1993. The group assigned André Vanoli[61] to work with Peter Hill of the OECD and Carol Carson in drafting the final report (the so-called Blue Book). Altogether, from 1986 to 1992 the expert group met fourteen times, with five sessions in Europe, six in the United States, one in Moscow, one in Zimbabwe, and one in Mexico.[62]

The United Nations and the OECD in 1989–1990 both reacted to events and influenced the course of action taken by countries. The issue of integration of the SNA and MPS or further linkages between the two systems came up at the February 1989 yearly meeting of the UN Statistical Commission. According to Árvay, "During the discussion of these items unexpectedly a sensitive question was raised which had been politely and carefully avoided for thirty years. The representative of Hungary proposed that instead of explaining the differences and creating shorter or longer bridges between the two systems the Statistical Commission should take definite measures for the *integration* of the two systems."[63]

The UN report from the meeting declares, "The work on SNA/MPS links . . . had entered a new phase. The main objective was now the achievement of substantial progress in convergence of the SNA and MPS, with the ultimate goal of integrating the two systems."[64] Also in 1989, at a UN Economic Commission for Europe meeting in Geneva, some CMEA participants suggested an integrated system, rather than two separate systems. The move toward the integration of the two systems was a significant departure from the recognition of two distinct systems, which had been in place since 1971.

It is worth noting that there were several possibilities for dealing with different national accounting systems: comparisons, integration, or replacement of one system with another. The publication of the revised MPS by the United Nations in 1989 suggested further comparison was the likely course; the meetings in early 1989, however, proposed integration—that is, the merging of the two systems. As it turned out, replacement of the MPS by the SNA is what actually occurred, but as late as 1989 that outcome was not at all clear.

The expert group meeting on December 3–7, 1989, in Moscow, had particular relevance for the future of the SNA as a single system, although the results of the meeting reflected the real ambiguity at the time in the relationship between the SNA and MPS. The meeting had been intended to explore further linkages between the SNA and MPS, and at the meeting the group concluded a number of harmonization agreements that entailed changes to both systems. This work on both systems suggests that the idea of integrating the two systems was still in play, despite such major political events as the fall of the Berlin Wall less than a month before the meeting.[65]

A more radical change in the meeting's agenda, however, was the recognition that the revised 1993 SNA would need to be able to accommodate *all* types of economies. According to Harrison, "suddenly and unexpectedly there was a requirement that the Blue Book should adequately cover the conditions in centrally planned economies."[66] Such an expansion of the SNA was a very significant departure from the initial plans for the SNA revision, but it was also compatible with the use of both systems by CMEA countries. So while an important change for the SNA, it was not yet the end of the MPS.

From 1990 to 1992 a great deal of work went into drafting the SNA Blue Book, revising the draft, and getting comments from other ad hoc groups, including a series of regional commission meetings throughout 1990. A complete draft was presented in September 1992 at an interregional meeting in Mexico, where more than sixty countries commented on the draft.[67] The Statistical Commission approved the revised draft in February 1993 and it was published in December 1993, first in English, then in other languages.

The 1993 SNA reflected the institution's role as a universal system. The 1968 SNA had a separate chapter for developing countries, but the 1993 SNA integrated such concerns into the core document, and was much more detailed than previous versions (over seven hundred pages). It also emphasized flexibility: although the framework is supposed to be applicable everywhere, it recognized that the specific conditions of a country might necessitate extensions and the use of so-called satellite accounts.[68]

The 1993 SNA had "approximately 100 significant changes from the 1968 version."[69] In addition, the 1993 SNA had much greater integration with other international institutions for economic data.[70] However, despite vigorous debates, the 1993 version made only minor adjustments to the production boundary, leaving the pressing issues of the environment and household labor for the future.

Unlike the 1953 and the 1968 versions, which were mainly written under the direction of Richard Stone and primarily reflected the experiences of developed countries, the 1993 SNA incorporated the views of experts from all types of economies during the revision process over the course of the fourteen expert-group meetings and regional conferences.[71] Like the MPS, the 1993 SNA resulted from contestation, debate, and mutual learning among those who crafted the revised draft and participated in the process.

The End of the MPS

It may seem as though the end of the MPS was a foregone conclusion, the result of the revolutions of 1989 and the collapse of the Soviet Union in 1991. Although those political events did have an enormous influence on a range of CMEA institutions—including the existence of the CMEA itself—the historical record on the MPS is more complicated.

Árvay comments that no one foresaw the rapid demise of the MPS and its replacement with the SNA. He writes, "For the last three decades, up to 1989 the parallel existence and full autonomy of the two systems seemed to be destined to last for ever."[72] Anne Harrison also notes that although the revision of the 1968 SNA had from the start planned to address needs of developing countries, the integration of the MPS and SNA came "quite late in the process in 1989." Yet even that late plan for "integration" of the two systems would not last. Harrison continues, "By the time the 1993 SNA went to print, the pace of reform in most previously planned economies was such that it was clear the SNA would supplant the MPS in a very short space of time."[73]

Just as the MPS had not simply been imposed on the states that used it, its end was a result of decisions at both the international and the domestic levels. A confluence of actions by CMEA NSOs, interactions between state and international representatives, and steps taken by international organizations led to the end of the MPS. It is in this sense that the eventual hegemony of the 1993 SNA was "accidental."

Changes to National Accounts in CMEA States

While the MPS and the SNA were undergoing revision, the Soviet Union
was entering a period of institutional changes that would eventually transform the entire political and economic landscape. Mikhail Gorbachev took
office in 1985, and his perestroika and glasnost programs were well under
way by 1987. Also in 1987, a revolution in Soviet statistics was just beginning. After decades of opposition, the Soviet Union published GNP figures,
albeit not using any recognized methodology, for the first time in its main
statistical yearbook for 1987.[74]

In mid-1988, Goskomstat put out its first official publication on the
concept of GNP, including a definition and five methods for compiling
GNP.[75] In a July 1988 article, Goskomstat officials explained how GNP
would be calculated, based on MPS data, for the next few years, without
suggesting implementation of the SNA per se.[76] The effects of Goskomstat's
actions were not confined to the Soviet Union. Once Goskomstat began
publishing GNP figures, the other countries of the CMEA followed suit, and
some went further. Hungary stopped submitting MPS data internationally
altogether.[77]

Another important factor was what was happening within the Soviet
republics. Perestroika and glasnost had opened the door to officially sanctioned experimentation and discussion of alternatives in a range of institutional areas. There was an explosion of nationalist mobilization in some
Soviet republics in the late 1980s. These republics challenged central
authority in many areas, including statistics. Some republics, such as the
Baltic ones (Estonia, Latvia, and Lithuania) published their own statistics,
including alternative economic data, sometimes in local languages, which
were not based on a standard Soviet methodology.[78] Eventually the Soviet
Union published guidelines in 1989,[79] but the mixed practices among
Soviet republics and CMEA states continued. In addition, by 1989 even
the Soviet Union's state committee for planning, Gosplan, had started to
use GNP growth rates, instead of the MPS-based NMP, in its plan targets.

The End of the MPS as an Internationally Recognized System

By 1990 most of the CMEA countries were in negotiations regarding transition to the SNA, not integration of the MPS and SNA. To assist in this

transition, the CES met in the summer of 1990 in Geneva. In September 1990, the OECD's Centre for Co-operation with the European Economies in Transition (created that March) and the UN Economic Commission for Europe sponsored a meeting in Paris on "Statistics for a Market Economy."[80]

All central and eastern European NSO directors attended both meetings, and at the Paris meeting the directors unanimously pledged to implement the SNA or the European Community version (the 1993 SNA was still being drafted) within two to three years.[81] This Paris meeting seems to mark the end of the MPS as an internationally recommended system. The steps toward "integration" taken during the meetings of 1989 were important, but after September 1990 there was no further discussion of integration of the two systems. Now the discussion involved the timetable for implementation of only the SNA. During 1990–1991 most eastern European NSOs began the transition from the MPS to the SNA. Implementation of the SNA came a bit later in the Soviet Union–Russia but by early 1992, Russia, the successor to the Soviet Union as the leading force behind the MPS, had fully committed to implementation of the SNA, dropping the MPS entirely.

Thus the adoption of the SNA by the Soviet bloc in the early 1990s required a fundamental change in principles and practices. Abandoning the MPS for the SNA meant a thorough revision of the conceptual as well as the physical apparatus of state statistics—something far beyond buying new computers or retraining staff, though those actions were important too. The story of why Soviet statisticians abruptly dropped their commitment to the MPS and decided against any middle path such as integration between the SNA and MPS, a hybrid system such as Hungary had used, the dual use of systems such as in Poland, or simply the delay of the implementation of the SNA until a more stable financial and political system was in place is explained in detail in my book on this subject, *Mirrors of the Economy: National Accounts and International Norms in Russia and Beyond.*[82] There I argue that in order to understand implementation of the 1993 SNA, one has to look at organizational norms within national statistical offices. In this case Soviet statisticians had for decades normatively linked the structure of the economy to the type of statistical system (the SNA for capitalist countries and the MPS for socialist economies). When the economy changed, these statisticians thought the statistical system should also change. Although this may seem to be a case of a structural change in the economy causing an institutional change, it was the conditional norm, not the material consequences generated by the structural change, that made an abrupt switch to the SNA seem appropriate and the natural thing to do.

SNA 2008

In early 2009 the UN Statistical Commission formally approved an official update to the 1993 SNA: the 2008 SNA.[83] This revision is not a conceptual departure from the 1993 version: it was meant to strengthen the 1993 SNA rather than displace it. Moreover, the changes are primarily clarifications and additions that do not conflict with the ongoing implementation of the 1993 SNA.[84]

The SNA required adjustment for two reasons. First, changes in global and national economies since 1993 necessitated consideration of new types of economic activity, primarily related to the globalization of production and the proliferation of new financial services and products. Second, since its inception, the SNA, like all national accounting systems, has continually grappled with how best to account for existing economic activity; as this shared understanding shifts, so too does the SNA. Thus the 2008 SNA revision includes new collective decisions about how to account for economic activity, not merely changes in economic structure.

This collective, problem-solving approach to updating the System of National Accounts was reflected in the process, which formally began in 2003 when the UN Statistical Commission asked the ISWGNA to form the Advisory Expert Group of twenty country experts to begin work on a revision.[85] After gathering input from a variety of sources, the group agreed on a consolidated list of forty-four changes and thirty-nine clarifications by 2007.[86] It then held a series of meetings to discuss and debate the details, all of which is documented online. This revision process reveals that mutual constitution between national statistical offices and international rules remains firmly established.

Flexibility remains an integral part of the 2008 SNA and is reinforced by the use by individual countries' "satellite" accounts—experimental accounts for new areas such as environmental activity. There are also "supplementary" tables and items for use by certain countries. These satellite and supplementary tables are ways for countries to work through specific issues while maintaining collective dialogue and commensurability of the primary accounts.

In this round of revisions there was no discussion of alternative systems.[87] The debate over the 2008 SNA occurred in a context in which it was not only the single international standard for national accounts but an increasingly all-encompassing system of economic statistics harmonized with ever more international standards. The hegemony of the SNA, established in the 1990s after its adoption by the postcommunist states, seems not only secure but likely to expand in reach in coming years.

Conclusion

Looking back at the development of the SNA through various iterations and the rise and fall of the MPS, one sees that at each point there were multiple actors on different levels (international, national, and sometimes subnational) and that the institutionalized systems influenced actions even as they were affected by various actors. This story exemplifies what a constructivist approach to norms, institutions, and institutional change can contribute. Through process tracing we see that it was not simply efficiency or material interests that drove the development and increasing dominance of the SNA—even though efficiency and material interests are undoubtedly enhanced by its development. This narrative also shows that although power differences and larger geopolitical conflicts such as the Cold War permeated the institutional environment of the time, the SNA's development was by no means simply a reflection of the interests of the most powerful states. There were not only competing ideas and interests but a diversity of practices in national accounts. The development of the SNA as a hegemonic institution is therefore a good example of mutual constitution and contestation in institutional development, or in the terms of this volume, creative syncretism or amalgamation.

Chapter 8

The Fluidity of Labor Politics
in Postcommunist Transitions

Rethinking the Narrative of Russian Labor Quiescence

Rudra Sil

Images of disaffected workers rising up against communist regimes—most evident in the case of the Solidarity-led movement in Poland and the 1989 miners' strikes in the Soviet Union—initially spawned hopes that unions could spearhead the emergence of civil society throughout the postcommunist world. Within a decade after the fall of communism, however, a much bleaker picture emerged: "Not only have unions not experienced a rebirth—on the contrary, they have seen a drop in membership—but they have been largely unable to create for themselves a pronounced political role to allow them to shape the postcommunist transformation."[1] Labor throughout the postcommunist world came to be seen as unusually weak, in part because of the behavior of "legacy unions,"[2] unions derived from the official trade union structures set up by the communist party-state apparatus. Although these legacy unions benefitted from the assets, members, and organizational structures inherited from their predecessors, they were thought to exhibit "weak union identities" wedded to preexisting practices of collaborating with state and management to fulfill production targets and preserve labor peace.[3] Studies of individual countries did draw attention to particularities of labor politics in those countries, and a few comparative studies even took note of differences in the extent and modalities of labor activism across postcommunist settings. However, even in these more nuanced studies, the common refrain stressed a powerful connection between the ubiquitous weakness of labor across postcommunist space and the shared legacies of communist-era worldviews and practices.[4]

There is little doubt that organized labor in postcommunist countries has been unable to exert sustained influence in the way that many expected following the collapse of communism. It is also a matter of record that the leading trade union centers have tended to adopt more cooperative postures than have newly formed unions. What is less clear, however, is whether these tendencies are more pronounced in postcommunist settings than in other places where unions are coping with declining membership and growing pressures for labor flexibility in the midst of neoliberal reforms. Also unclear is whether the aggregate measures of strikes and protests point to an exceptionally high degree of labor passivity in postcommunist settings, at least when tracked over longer periods and situated within the broader context of labor's struggles in the midst of globalization. But perhaps most open to question is whether even the most cooperative unions and the least militant workers have been behaving the way they do because of the enduring legacy of norms and practices established in the communist period.

The point of departure for this chapter is a suspicion that the standard narrative of labor quiescence in postcommunist societies is overly static in its characterization of the outcome it seeks to explain and in the deterministic character of the explanation itself. In terms of the outcome, impressions formed on the basis of the initial stages of transition appear to have crystallized into fixed outcomes rather than as snapshots taken in the midst of highly fluid processes of institutional change. This results in a tendency to either ignore or discount growing evidence of local protests as well as subtle changes in the behavior of different unions with the passage of time. In explaining the apparent quiescence of labor, the standard narrative has placed great weight on the behavior of dominant unions, which is thought to result from habits and practices inherited from the function of unions as "transmission belts" for managers and party officials given the supposed absence of separate workers' interests in a classless society. While attention to the influence of the past is laudable and necessary, an overly structured view of the past risks overlooking the questions of whether discrete elements of communist legacies can exert uniform effects on specific aspects of labor relations over time and how these effects might be mediated by labor actors engaging in creative assemblages to ensure their survival in the midst of an uncertain and fluid transition.[5]

Any attempt to correct for these tendencies is likely to result in messier, less structured stories of labor politics within and across postcommunist countries. But it can also give us a deeper understanding of the anxieties, pressures, and imperatives that differently situated labor actors faced as they sought to gain some control over highly fluid circumstances and unfamiliar institutional environments. This chapter takes a modest step toward such a corrective by focusing on the case of Russian labor politics. It was in the Soviet Union that communist-era labor institutions were most enduring and most deeply entrenched, and it is thus in post-Soviet Russia that the narrative of labor quiescence should be most compelling. Indeed, most studies of Russian labor, including ones that are extremely detailed, consistently describe a weak, passive labor movement, led by union officials whose preexisting habits, experiences, and worldviews inclined them to cooperate and bargain with managers and political elites rather than to actively defend workers' interests.[6] This chapter offers a much more complex and messy view of Soviet and Russian labor relations. In this view, the behavior of actors is neither uniform nor merely reproducing past habits and practices; instead it reflects significant political creativity on the part of differently situated actors seeking to survive in the midst of extreme uncertainty.

The first section questions the monolithic image of Soviet labor relations, highlighting the variation in workers' experiences and union officials' behaviors across sectors and over time. The second section examines the early years of the post-Soviet transition—coinciding with the period of Boris Yeltsin's presidency—with a focus on how workers and unions struggled to reconceptualize their roles and relationships in a turbulent environment marked by extreme uncertainty and hardship. The following section focuses on the first years of Vladimir Putin's presidency, viewing the struggle over a new Russian Labor Code (enacted in 2002) as a key step towards the emergence of a more "normal" pattern of labor politics. The conclusion reviews the ways in which the study of postcommunist labor can be made less structured and thus more attentive to the varying forms of agency exhibited by labor actors as initially unfamiliar institution settings become more stable and intelligible.

The Soviet Inheritance—Neither Monolithic, nor Formless

Rethinking the narrative of labor quiescence in Russia begins with the recognition that the putative legacies of the Soviet era were not derived from a fixed, monolithic system of labor relations. Certainly, communism was predicated on an essential harmony of interests in a classless revolutionary society. This in turn engendered certain standardized institutional structures intended to foster close cooperation between workers, unions, managers, and the communist party-state apparatus. Yet this neither suggested a fixed role for trade unions over time nor preempted instances of militant protest by workers in particular locales or sectors.

In spite of Vladimir Lenin's earlier criticism of trade union consciousness, unions that supported the Bolsheviks in the 1917 Revolution were treated as leading agents of the working class and given a significant place in the new Soviet government. The All-Union Central Council of Trade Unions was set up as a unified association of sectoral federations that corresponded to branches of the economic ministries and encompassed regional and factory trade union committees. The trade unions were not viewed as defenders of workers' interests since the means of production were now owned by a "dictatorship of the proletariat." Even so, during the first decade following the Bolshevik Revolution, factory trade union committees were granted significant autonomy as watchdogs over "bourgeois specialists" who had been retained from the old regime to administer production. At the national level, top trade union officials regularly offered opinions concerning working hours, the structure of wages and benefits, and working conditions in nationalized factories. Mikhail Tomsky, head of the trade unions and later a member of the Politburo, proposed measures to prevent the exhaustion of workers in the midst of efforts to adapt Taylorist forms of work organization designed to boost productivity.[7] Thus, the idealized harmony of interests in a classless society did not initially translate into trade unions functioning as passive collaborators of enterprise managers and central planners.

Under Josef Stalin, however, the independent advisory and watchdog roles of the unions were steadily scaled back. Unions were effectively turned into transmission belts for carrying out directives of party leaders and fulfilling the ambitious targets of the first two Five-Year Plans (1928–1938). As the old "bourgeois specialists" were purged and replaced by a new generation of "red directors," factory trade union committees no longer had a role in reviewing the actions of managers. Official party pronouncements and cultural activities heaped praise on "worker heroes" who set production records. But most workers feared the pressures brought to bear by high targets, and the more established workers resented newer workers who came from the countryside and used the official campaigns to secure better positions. Trade unions could do little about this situation as they were now officially charged with assisting managers and planners in maintaining labor discipline and fulfilling plan targets. In view of the anxiety created by Stalin's campaigns against "wreckers" and "saboteurs," many factory union officials did participate in collusive practices designed to help both workers and managers evade excessive scrutiny and ensure access to resources needed for survival.[8] This collusion underscored the absence of an independent official role for unions in defending workers, but would also produce a distinct alternative legacy: the informal arrangements that managers made to allow workers to use enterprise resources to pursue covert earning schemes and obtain nonwage benefits at a time of declining wages and job security.

The post-Stalin era brought yet another shift, this time in the opposite direction. After Stalin's death, overt coercion and high-pressure campaigns gave way to a Soviet-style "social contract": the regime offered material security and improved living standards in exchange for loyalty to the state, labor peace, and efforts to maintain productivity.[9] This understanding, first anticipated in a party program introduced under Nikita Khrushchev in 1961 and later formalized under Leonid Brezhnev in the 1971 Labor Code, guaranteed workers full employment, price controls on basic necessities, and a host of welfare benefits ranging from education to health and recreation. The Code also formally granted trade unions the right to review and challenge dismissals of employees, while also being placed in charge of managing their own network of buildings, schools, clinics, and vacation sites. In practice, while unions did not often succeed in overturning dismissals, they still played a role in the reassignment of employees and ensuring continuity in workers' access to key educational and health benefits. In addition, during the post-Stalin era, the Soviet Union rejoined the International Labor Organization (ILO) in 1956 after a sixteen-year hiatus (it had joined in 1934 but withdrew in 1940). Following the ILO's tripartite structure, Soviet trade unions joined caucuses with other unions in debating labor standards, and officials in the international section of the All-Union Central Council of Trade Union became familiar with key ILO conventions covering such standard issues as the right to organize, collective bargaining, and social dialogue.[10] On the whole, the role of unions during the late Soviet period may be characterized as lying somewhere between that of a pure instrument of political and managerial control (as under Stalin) and that of the active organization that Tomsky had envisioned during the first decade of Bolshevik rule.

Workers in the post-Stalin era, despite the regime's continuing emphasis on labor-management harmony, did not hesitate to engage in acts of protest when they believed that managers or the government were reneging on implied promises. Under Khrushchev, massive protests were triggered in 1962 in Novocherkassk, when the regime attempted to punish the workforce for sagging productivity by increasing the price of basic foodstuffs.[11] These protests prompted the Brezhnev regime to formally codify job rights, standardized benefits, and subsidized prices for basic foodstuffs. Even so, delays in the delivery of wages or other benefits promised by the regime led to work slowdowns and wildcat strikes, as was the case during large-scale strikes in Dnepropetrovsk and Dneproderzhinsk in 1972 as well as a lengthy strike wave in 1980–1981 that involved tens of thousands of workers and halted production in several automobile plants.[12] Later, during the era of glasnost and perestroika, workers became even more sharply critical of the regime in response to Mikhail Gorbachev's initiatives to boost productivity, culminating in the 1989 miners' strikes, which spread like wildfire across the Kuzbass and Donbass regions. Significantly, the strikers were not motivated by any opposition to socialist principles but by a desire to see these principles adhered to more consistently in the form of better working conditions and greater autonomy at the workplace.[13]

Thus, the history of Soviet labor relations cannot be reduced to the role played by unions as transmission belts since the Stain era. Trade unions were not assertive, independent organizations pursuing separate agendas, but their activities went beyond simply implementing directives from above. While workers in many sectors showed no signs of resistance, in other sectors, perceptions that party leaders or enterprise managers were reneging on existing understandings could lead to a wide range of protest actions, even industry-wide strikes.[14] And while official Soviet rhetoric stressed the unanimity of interests in a classless society, there were in fact competing interests that generated both industrial disputes in certain sectors and informal norms and understandings at the level of the enterprise.

Labor Politics in the 1990s: Survival in Turbulent Times

Following the appearance of unofficial strike committees during the 1989 miners' strikes, the Russian branches of the All-Union Central Council of

Trade Unions decided to detach themselves from the Soviet party-state apparatus and become more proactive in dealing with Gorbachev's reforms. In 1990, they reconstituted themselves as FNPR, the Federation of Independent Trade Unions of Russia. The FNPR is regarded as Russia's chief "legacy union,"[15] and its supposed aversion to industrial conflict is seen as a carryover from the communist period and a key reason for the weakness of the labor movement.[16]

Through the mid-1990s, FNPR's composition, behavior, and inability to mobilize labor protest appeared to confirm this view. FNPR's leadership remained firmly entrenched, with most top officials having spent at least a decade as leaders of factory trade unions or branch unions in the Soviet era.[17] FNPR also inherited the bulk of the material assets—in the form of buildings and facilities for health, education, and recreation—that had been under the control of the Soviet-era trade unions. These assets, which were thought to generate an annual income of $300 million,[18] became a means for political elites to exert pressure on FNPR because it desperately wanted to hold on to its inherited resources. This seemed to suggest that FNPR leaders were looking out for themselves rather than defending the interests of rank-and-file workers, a view that became even more plausible when money from social insurance funds once administered by unions was found to have been siphoned into newly created financial structures from which some union officials' salaries were paid.[19] Moreover, FNPR's first chairman, Igor Klotchkov, ended up siding with Duma deputies who refused to accept Yeltsin's decree dissolving parliament until the armed confrontation of October 1993. Those who saw Yeltsin as a committed supporter of democracy and free markets portrayed opponents of his policies, including FNPR, as defenders of the old regime. The steep decline in FNPR's membership—from over 60 million in 1993 to under 35 million in 1999—supported this view, since it suggested that most workers did not see FNPR as willing or able to solve the problems they faced in the new era.[20] Yet this did not mean that workers engaged in independent forms of labor action. Although the vast majority of the workforce confronted falling wages, hyperinflation, and the growing prospect of layoffs, only 357,000 workers (less than 0.5 percent of the workforce) participated in strikes and lockouts in 1992, and just 120,000 workers (less than 0.2 percent of the workforce) in 1993.[21] Moreover, almost all of the striking workers were from two sectors: coal mining and education.[22] All these factors were cited in the making of the narrative of labor quiescence. A closer look at workers' and unions' behavior during the 1990s suggests a more complicated story.

To begin with, there is the static picture of low militancy. Although scholars paid little attention to cross-national data, most observers viewed the aggregate figures for strikes and protests in the first half of the 1990s as "surprisingly" low.[23] This impression remained intact despite the fact that the period from 1996 through 1998 brought a sharp increase in the number of workers participating in strikes and lockouts, with the figure for 1997 alone (887,300) exceeding the combined total for the four years from 1991 to 1994. The figure for 1997 also included over 150,000 workers from sectors outside the usual hotbeds of labor militancy in Russia, coal mining and education.[24] Moreover, cross-national data on the number of working days lost per one thousand workers indicate that the total for Russia during the 1996–1998 period exceeded the combined total for Britain, France, and Germany during the same period.[25] Perhaps because this increase coincided with—and could be attributed to—the unusual problem of persistent wage arrears, it was treated as an anomalous spike rather than as a response to shifting circumstances. Even so, the sharp increase in strike activity should have raised questions about just how passive Russian workers really were, especially considering that strikes and protests have historically come in waves even in more pluralistic Western societies.[26]

The aggregate figures also had little to say concerning the origins and dynamics of highly visible instances of protest in many locales and sectors. These included dozens of hunger strikes, several lengthy lockouts and strikes by thousands of coal miners, teachers, and health workers, as well as a protracted strike by air-traffic controllers that Yeltsin forcefully crushed. As economic reforms threatened the closure of state enterprises, a variety of other forms of protest came into view during the late 1990s, ranging from a blockade of the Trans-Siberian Railroad by miners to attempts at self-immolation in various enterprises and cities.[27] To the extent that such militant protests were not more prevalent, there are at least two observations that do not conform to the story of passivity: some point to workers' desires to remain on the payroll at all costs so that they could continue to obtain nonwage benefits and informal earning opportunities from paternalistic managers, while others note the high degree of confusion among workers over whom to blame for wage arrears or other immediate grievances.[28] There is no need to adjudicate between these two explanations; both are plausible and both underscore the point that whatever labor passivity was in evidence was more than a result of atomized workers being held back by coopted unions acting as they always had.

Turning to the unions, a closer look at the composition of FNPR's leadership reveals that there was significant variation in the background and behavior of senior officials even if they had held key positions within the Soviet trade union apparatus. Some union bosses rose through the ranks of the FNPR more rapidly precisely because of their reputations for acting independently and assertively. Mikhail Shmakov, who became FNPR's new chairman in 1993, came out of what was regarded as one of the most independent and syndicalist regional unions, the Moscow Federation of Trade Unions, which had organized its own mass protests in 1992 in response to price hikes when the rest of FNPR was considering offering support to Yeltsin's shock therapy. In fact, the Moscow Federation issued its own separate draft platform on "Economic Democracy," explicitly calling for collective action by workers to check the power of management and to press for across-the-board increases in wages, including a base subsistence wage.[29] In keeping with this stance, in 1994, Shmakov called for nationwide strikes and rallies just as mass privatization was getting under way and as Yeltsin was promoting a "Civic Accord" to head off social unrest.[30]

Other leaders, too, rose through the FNPR's ranks after becoming known as advocates of workers' rights and living standards. The late Vitali Bud'ko, who was made FNPR vice-chairman by Shmakov, got his start in the Soviet era in the restive coal industry unions. Bud'ko was an active supporter of participants in the 1989 miners' strikes, and in 1993 threatened large-scale strikes to protest the government's plans to drastically cut back funding for state-owned coal mines. Another Soviet-era trade unionist, Evgeny Sidorov, became FNPR's international secretary in 1999, served as a member of the ILO's Governing Body, and became a staunch supporter of the transnational trade union movement. Upon Sidorov's death in 2010, General Secretary Guy Ryder of the International Trade Union Confederation noted, "Evgeny Sidorov played an extremely important role as an international advocate for workers' rights, and in building and maintaining strong relations between the FNPR and trade union centers across the world."[31] At the regional level, Anatolii Chekis, who served as head of FNPR's regional organization in Kemerovo in the 1990s, publicly promised to defend miners who had blockaded the Trans-Siberian Railroad during the "rail wars" of the 1990s.[32] It is also worth noting that Chekis would make a failed bid—backed by Communist Party deputies in the Duma—to challenge Shmakov for FNPR's leadership. And, even though the 1990s witnessed very little turnover in FNPR's leadership, the aging leadership was acutely conscious of the need to attract younger members and leaders. By 2000, FNPR had organized a nationwide network of young Russian trade unionists and set up a quota to ensure that at least 30 percent of delegates to its 2001 Congress would be under the age of thirty-five.[33]

The point is not that most FNPR officials were committed advocates for workers' interests. Many were focused on holding on to their positions and salaries as new managers began to take over at various enterprises. Others resisted market reforms and did not adapt easily to pursuing workers' interests in the new economy. But there is no reason to assume a priori that FNPR's leaders, even those groomed during the Soviet period, would be uniformly ossified and utterly incapable of acting independently following the end of communism. Absent this assumption, any effort to understand the behavior of unions must be more open-ended, with due attention to the constraints and choice situations they faced.

The dynamics within the Russian Trilateral Commission are instructive in this regard. The commission was established in 1992 in line with the ILO's recommendations for a national forum for the promotion of "social partnership" between labor, business, and the state. This would mainly take the form of general agreements that could serve as a basis for bargaining between workers and employers at the enterprise and branch levels. However, the most significant cleavage within the commission in the 1990s was not that between labor and business, but rather between those unions and business associations that wanted to temper radical reforms (FNPR on the labor side and the Russian Union of Industrialists and Entrepreneurs on the business side) and more recently formed organizations that backed Yeltsin's reforms (for example, the white-collar union, Sotsprof, on the labor side and the Congress of Russian Business Circles on the business side). Different labor and business groups used their positions in the Trilateral Commission to improve their positions within their respective categories, and they did so mostly by either supporting or challenging Yeltsin's policies. Thus, FNPR responded to losing its automatic dues checkoff by hardening its resistance to Yeltsin, while newer unions backed him in the hopes of eventually being granted a share of FNPR's inherited assets and membership by decree. Under such conditions, it was hardly a surprise that the

Trilateral Commission failed to produce viable general agreements, or that the few that were signed were ignored or unenforceable.[34]

Thus, from the mid-1990s onward, Yeltsin began to strike bilateral deals with the FNPR. In exchange for behaving more as a negotiating partner in the midst of growing wage arrears and unemployment, FNPR was permitted to retain all its assets and its affiliated primary organizations. Yeltsin, gearing up for a presidential election in 1996, ended up turning away from the smaller, newer unions that had been supporting him, while counting on some restraint from the federation that still accounted for nearly 90 percent of the unionized workforce. The sequence of events—FNPR's intransigence in 1993–1994 followed by increased bargaining with elites beginning in 1995—is significant. It punctures the notion that FNPR's compromises were an extension of past union behaviors, and instead suggests that FNPR leaders were consciously trying to use their still vast membership base at a time of growing economic crisis in order to protect its assets and maintain its position as the most significant component of the labor movement. While this also meant that the inherited assets could be leveraged by political and business elites in the bargaining process, the basic strategy followed by FNPR was not radically different from that being followed by leading European unions that have engaged in compromises to defend their positions in the face of neoliberal reforms.[35]

Alternative unions, for their part, neither acquired greater influence within the labor movement nor managed to distinguish themselves as reliable defenders of workers' interests. Newer unions such as Sotsprof (a mostly white-collar union seen as one of the first truly "free" unions) tended to focus almost entirely on the goal of curtailing FNPR's influence and redistributing its assets. In the process, they threw their support behind policies that were increasingly seen by workers as responsible for wage arrears, rising prices, falling living standards, and growing unemployment.[36] Non-FNPR unions also failed to coalesce into a unified alternative federation as key leaders competed for influence among different constituencies. The best chance for such a federation, the Confederation of Labor of Russia (KTR), was formed in 1995 but immediately became truncated when the leadership of the Independent Miners' Union withdrew and set up a new federation that it could control better (the All-Russian Confederation of Labor, or VKT). The dynamics of this split also underscored the fact that VKT and KTR, although "free" unions in that they had broken away from FNPR, had also inherited the leadership, membership, and organizational structures of preexisting unions entrenched in particular sectors and regions. KTR, for example, relied mostly on unions set up among the Soviet-era dockers and sea-transport workers, and its ability to form a national-level federation was the result of past networks formed by union officials who came from different regions but had been able to form connections at various ports or at trade union conferences and vacation facilities.[37]

Thus, although the labor quiescence thesis places much emphasis on legacy unions operating in their old ways, it is significant that FNPR is not as monolithic as it is made out to be, and that alternative unions failed to distinguish themselves as committed defenders of labor rights. In fact, the behavior of FNPR as well as other unions are at least in part a result of the extraordinary circumstances they confronted. The main components of shock therapy—dismantling central planning, removing most price controls, adopting mass privatization, facilitating bankruptcies and dismissals—were pushed through quickly by presidential decrees. In a rapidly changing environment, unions of all stripes had to find ways to make themselves relevant actors in the eyes of state and business while watching union membership decline and fighting over limited resources. As Walter Connor put it, "Trade unions, especially the FNPR, had barely found their feet in the post-Soviet period; yet the ground was still shifting. Privatization; unemployment; the looming threat of bankruptcies; the inability of the government, except by cranking up inflationary currency emissions, to satisfy demands for cash—all limited the space in which unions could maneuver."[38]

The connection between unions and their membership base also deserves a closer look since it is a core element in the labor quiescence narrative. The sharp decline in membership throughout the 1990s, alongside surveys indicating that workers tended to rely more on managers rather than on unions to solve their problems, has been cited as evidence of the weakness and passivity of labor.[39] However, this inference does not take into account the impact of unions' sudden loss of their automatic dues-checkoff privileges or of their loss of control over the social insurance fund, which was handed over to municipal governments. Until the end of the 1990s, some workers continued to approach their enterprise unions for social benefits.[40] As it became clearer that unions had nothing to do with benefits, workers had no sense of what unions had to offer in their immediate struggle to survive in the face of unpaid wages, sharp rises in prices for basic foodstuffs, and the looming threat of factory closures. Under these conditions, most workers, even those not paid for months, had no reason to risk losing their jobs when simply being on the payroll guaranteed access to nonwage (in-kind) payments and opportunities to engage in informal supplemental earning.[41] Considering the shifting functions of unions and the extreme anxiety generated by the early years of transition, both the workers' initial exodus from unions and their continued reliance on pater-nalistic managers are better understood as survival strategies rather than as a definitive rejection of unions as tools of management.

These observations point to a more complex picture than is evident in stark narratives about Russian labor quiescence during the 1990s. This was a period of dramatic upheavals followed by the rapid introduction of new, unfamiliar institutions and policies. In such a turbulent environment, there is no question that union bosses worried about holding on to their posi-tions and that workers worried about losing access to benefits linked to their workplaces. But these worries are precisely the reason for dispensing with narratives emphasizing the mechanical reproduction of past practices and entertaining the possibility of creative assemblage among pragmatic actors.

Toward "Normalization"? The Politics
Behind the 2002 Labor Code

Although Russia under Vladimir Putin is thought to be less democratic than it was in the 1990s, the period from 2000 onward coincides with the emergence of a more "normal" pattern of labor politics. This shift came into view with the adoption of the 2002 Russian Labor Code. As part of the 1997 negotiations with the International Monetary Fund, the Russian government had agreed to adopt new labor regulations that would replace the old Soviet Labor Code and give employers more freedom. The result was the comprehensively revised 2002 Russian Labor Code, pushed through under Putin, that would regulate dismissals, working conditions, strike pro-cedures, and union representation. What is important here is not the con-tent of the new code but the political struggles that accompanied its adoption. These struggles reflected the emergence of a clearer separation of interests between the trade union movement—despite continuing divisions and disagreements—and business communities pressing the government for more flexibility in managing their workforces and production schedules. The net result was certainly not a victory for the unions, but it could be read as a sort of "heroic defeat"[42] in the sense that labor created enough resistance that state and business had to engage in a protracted period of maneuvering and bargaining to secure the provisions they wanted most.

The first draft of the Code, introduced by the Kremlin in May 2000, immediately provoked widespread criticism from the entire gamut of unions. Although FNPR would later adopt a more conciliatory posture and get criticized for doing so, the major unions initially lined up on the same side on the most contentious issues. They all challenged key provisions, pushed for alternative drafts, and worked to build public opposition to the government draft. In the process, they cited international labor standards and human rights principles as well as Soviet-era regulations concerning dismissal procedures, working conditions, and minimum wages linked to subsistence. The FNPR's regional and branch organizations organized meetings throughout the country to highlight the most problematic aspects of the proposed code, including one that would have given employers the right to decide which unions it would negotiate with. On the business side, too, newer business organizations and the Russian Union of Industrialists and Entrepreneurs (dominated by older groups of industrial elites) joined to back the Kremlin's initial draft on the grounds that it would boost labor flexibility and make their firms more competitive. Whereas FNPR and the Russian Union of Industrialists and Entrepreneurs had once collaborated to oppose some of Yeltsin's policies, now the two organizations were on opposite sides of the debate. In effect, the cleavage between labor and business became more significant than that between pro- and anti-Kremlin factions within each.[43]

Because the final version of the Labor Code was closer to the government's draft than most trade unions preferred, FNPR was attacked by other unions for not backing a more labor-friendly draft, presumably in order to protect its vested interests.[44] However, it is worth noting that this alternative draft had been produced by smaller unions from opposite sides of the political spectrum, the leftist Zashchita Truda (Defense of Labor) and the liberal Sotsprof (Social Trade Unions). These two organizations had little in common beyond opposition to the FNPR's position in the labor movement. And the draft they offered was distinctive mainly because it retained many Soviet-era labor guarantees (including the requirement of union approval for all dismissals) that would have neither passed in the Duma nor satisfied the conditions stipulated by the International Monetary Fund. Considering this, FNPR's refusal to back the alternative draft hardly constituted a betrayal of the labor movement.

FNPR's shifting position must also be considered in terms of the broader political context. Labor had already suffered several defeats before the proposals to revise the Labor Code came up in the Duma. This included a tough battle over the Unified Social Tax, which was adopted by the Duma in 2001 in spite of extensive lobbying against the bill by FNPR.[45] Moreover, the FNPR's political allies in the Duma were also in a state of flux. Whereas for much of the 1990s, the FNPR had relied on Communist Party deputies for support, by 2000, it had turned to the center-left Fatherland–All Russia Party, only to find that the latter was merging with the pro-Kremlin Unity to form United Russia.[46] As a result, the deputies with whom FNPR was beginning to cultivate relations were now under an umbrella party that was supportive of Putin and dependent on the Kremlin in its efforts to gain control of the Duma. There were still Communist Party officials who sympathized with the unions, but FNPR's political effectiveness now depended on bargains with United Russia.[47] Thus, as the struggle over the Labor Code unfolded, FNPR leaders acknowledged that they felt forced to compromise, but they viewed this as a necessary tactical move given the political pressures they were facing as well as the constraints imposed by "normal" market conditions.[48]

In addition, FNPR's claim that it got the best deal it could get under trying circumstances does not ring entirely hollow. Dismissal procedures are now easier, but specific conditions have to be met before long-term contracts can be terminated or before temporary contracts can be renewed (without becoming long-term ones). While the list of permissive conditions is long, the increased specificity accords workers a measure of legal protection not possible in the more open-ended government version. The Code also reduces the proportion of wages that can be paid in kind, and requires employers to pay interest on delayed wages. This shift is significant in that it reduces the scope for informal arrangements at the workplace, making employers more liable for paying official wages on time. FNPR also insisted on a clause tying the minimum wage to the officially determined subsistence level. Although implementing this clause nationwide would have required a separate Duma law on minimum wages, the basic principle of a wage tied to cost of living increases has been invoked in a number of recent labor disputes.[49] While a legal strike is difficult to mount (requiring the support of over half of workers at an assembly attended by two-thirds of the workforce at a firm), larger unions with membership cutting across different professions are in a position to engineer the necessary support to call strikes. Finally, whereas the original government draft allowed management to choose which union to negotiate with, the Code now requires employers to negotiate with whichever union (or coalition of unions) represents at least half of the company's personnel. While this does not bode well for smaller unions, especially those focused on a single profession, it leaves open the possibility of larger unions developing coordinated strategies for collective bargaining across firms and sectors.[50] Thus, even if FNPR may be criticized for not sticking to a more aggressive approach in defending pro-worker aspects of the old Code, its decision to compromise with the government was more a matter of balancing different calculations, including shoring up its leading position in the labor movement.

The battles over the Labor Code also reveal the maturation of some of the alternative unions. The two largest alternative federations, VKT and KTR, began to focus less on undermining FNPR and more on securing their own positions as important unions within particular sectors (for example, mining and metallurgy for VKT and sea-transport workers for KTR). VKT officials went on record acknowledging FNPR's position as a "real" union and pursued selective cooperation with the latter's affiliates on specific issues.[51] Both VKT and KTR, in turn, were able to secure FNPR's support in applying for representation in the International Trade Union Confederation (at the time, the International Confederation of Free Trade Unions). In 2011, the two trade union centers, which had initially split over rivalries between key leaders, formally reunited under KTR's banner, with VKT's former international secretary, Boris Kravtchenko, becoming the new president. In the meantime, the relatively liberal Sotsprof shifted from being a leading advocate of market reforms to adopting a militant posture on the Labor Code. In making this move, it formed a tactical alliance with the leftist Zashchita Truda. Given that neither union stood a chance of becoming leading players in the labor movement, it made sense for them to adopt a more radical posture that, though not politically viable, helped to boost the visibility of these unions within specific locales and industries.

On the whole, the behavior of trade unions since 2000 has reflected both a growing awareness of labor's general interests and competing strategies that reflect the positions of various unions relative to each other. The pattern of larger unions compromising more readily and smaller unions adopting more militant postures is not uncommon in advanced industrial countries. Major unions often failed to block particular policies but engaged in debates and protests mainly as a way of preserving their roles within a given firm or sector. In some cases, established unions exhibited restraint in exchange for locking in marginal gains for workers under difficult conditions. And unions that adopted more radical positions were often the ones that were relegated to the margins of the labor movement.[52]

The battle over the Labor Code also underscores the point made earlier that union leadership does not remain ossified forever. Some of the most visible players in this battle turned out to be individuals who had little or no experience with labor issues in the Soviet era. Two different examples are FNPR's Andrei Isaev and Oleg Shein. Isaev joined a radical labor group called the Confederation of Anarcho-Syndicalists during the late 1980s, began working for a trade union publication, *Solidarity,* in 1991, and became a FNPR official in the mid-1990s. During the late 1990s, Isaev sought to form a broad-based labor movement led by FNPR (Soyuz Truda, or Union of Labor), and later played a key role in moving the FNPR away from the communists and negotiating new alliances with centrist parties. Isaev was elected to the Duma in 1999, played a key role in drafting the compromise version of the Labor Code, and subsequently became FNPR vice-chair as well as chair of the Duma's Labor and Social Policy Committee. Shein, who was a teenage activist critical of Gorbachev's reforms, participated in the 1993 parliamentary revolt against Yeltsin, and later became head of the most militant of the newer unions, Zashchita Truda. His unyielding and vociferous criticism of both the Kremlin and FNPR during debates over the new Labor Code helped him become a popular figure in his native Astrakhan. Shein also got elected to the Duma, where he became another key member of the Labor and Social Policy Committee, albeit one who was more starkly leftist than Isaev.

In the late 1990s, the attitudes of workers toward trade unions also began to change at the margins. With restrictions on informal contracts and in-kind wages in the new code, wage arrears became less widespread and workers were no longer as dependent on paternalistic managers as they had been during the 1990s. With this shift, it is likely that workers, particularly those who opted to pay their union dues, remained members because they were more aware of the new role played by unions in wage bargaining. While union membership continued to drop, the *rate* of decline slowed considerably. Whereas FNPR's total membership plummeted from 60 million in 1993 to under 35 million in 1999 (an average annual decline of over 4 million members over the six-year period), from 1999 to 2009, the figure fell from 35 million to 28 million (an average annual decline of only 700,000 members over the ten-year period).[53] Surveys still show a low level of public confidence in unions (and in most official and civil organizations). But as union membership fell, the level of trust in unions among workers who remained members began to increase, climbing from 16 percent in 1995 to 40 percent in 2001.[54] This also contributed to a slight improvement in the image of unions among the public at large. According to one national survey, the percentage of all respondents who approve of trade unions rose from just 18 percent in January 2006 to 34 percent in July 2012.[55]

Thus, labor politics since 2000 reveals a number of subtle but important shifts. There is now a clearer differentiation of the interests of labor, business, and the state, as seen in the battle lines initially drawn over the revision of the Labor Code. The behavior of FNPR and other unions reveals a greater degree of pragmatism, with more established unions engaging in selective cooperation with each other despite lingering differences on some issues. And despite the low overall trust in unions, those who choose to remain in unions seem to be doing so not out of habit but out of a growing awareness of the role unions can play in collective bargaining. The past has not ceased to matter as a result of these trends; but its significance lies less in the role of Soviet-era unions as transmission belts and more in preexisting understandings about fair wages and job rights.

Conclusion: Beyond Quiescence

The above discussion of Soviet and Russian labor relations neither suggests that a strong labor movement is about to emerge in Russia nor offers a novel explanation of labor weakness. It does, however, call into question the narrative of extreme labor passivity sustained by atomized workers and conservative legacy unions with an inherited penchant for collaboration with elites. This narrative needs to be critically reassessed and substantially revised if we are to gain a better understanding of continuities and changes in labor politics across postcommunist transitions. This chapter suggests at least three areas to focus on in this regard.

First, the extent of labor passivity or militancy across postcommunist settings needs to be reassessed against a wider range of comparative referents, not merely against expectations informed by the behavior of labor movements in some Western countries. One major study correlates more assertive union behavior with more effective collective bargaining in postwar Germany, contrasting this to Russia, where unions were hesitant to use sanctions and threats.[56] Yet taking into account the context of a tumultuous set of economic, political, and social transformations in post-Soviet Russia, it is difficult to ascertain what constitutes a "normal" level of militancy.[57] When relying on aggregate data, there needs to be some accounting for periodic spikes in the number of strikes and strike participants (as during 1996–1998) and for cross-national data that indicate that the number of working days lost in Russia was actually higher than in Germany during the late 1990s and again in 2004–2005.[58] Moreover, even large unions in Western Europe have found it necessary to exercise more restraint and engage in more compromises given the tactical disadvantages they have had to face in the midst of neoliberal reforms and deepening Europeanization.[59] Such observations underscore the need for a more open-ended exploration of what constitutes labor passivity or militancy in postcommunist settings.

Second, while historically minded social scientists need no convincing that the past matters, *how* that past matters is not self-evident. The narrative of labor quiescence assumes a monolithic view of communist legacies, focusing almost exclusively on the docile behavior of official unions in their role as transmission belts for party elites and enterprise directors. Yet it is worth bearing in mind that the functions associated with this role—including unions' obligation to support the production targets of management and administer the social benefits guaranteed to workers—became irrelevant almost overnight with the dismantling of central planning and the transfer of the social insurance fund to municipal governments. At the same time, communist-era labor relations encompassed other features that could—and did—influence aspects of post-Soviet labor politics, as is most evident in the manner in which pro-worker positions were framed in debates over the new Russian Labor Code. These features included unions' roles in reviewing workers' dismissal and coordinating their reassignment, their far-reaching networks facilitated by the All-Union Central Council of Trade Unions' combined regional and branch structure, and their familiarity with international labor conventions, including those relating to tripartism and collective bargaining. These possibilities point to the need to think more expansively about the range of historical legacies that might matter in postcommunist settings—and to adopt a more differentiated view of which legacies are likely to be most durable and consequential in what contexts.

Third, it is necessary to differentiate between the early years of postcommunist transition, which was accompanied by radical institutional fluidity and extreme uncertainty, and later periods, when the institutional environment became more stable and predictable from the perspective of labor actors. In a new, unfamiliar environment, preexisting habits, beliefs, norms, and social practices neither remained immutable nor changed overnight. Instead, what we see is the fitful emergence of recombinant forms of agency among differently situated labor actors as they all sought to adapt their beliefs and strategies to novel institutional frameworks that were not even fully intelligible, let alone stable and predictable. Thus, it should not have been surprising that workers dealing with falling or unpaid wages would be less concerned with unions than with negotiating with managers to retain access to nonwage benefits and informal earning opportunities at their workplaces. Nor is it surprising that legacy unions would bargain hard to protect their inherited assets and their leading position within organized labor, or that alternative unions would pursue their own deals to expand their clout vis-à-vis legacy unions. As institutional environments became more stable and familiar over time, however, workers' and unions' strategies also became more "normalized" in the sense that they reflected a clearer sense of the separation of interests and identities between labor, business, and government. Moreover, all unions have seen the rise of new cohorts of leaders whose experiences as trade unionists are more connected to the political showdowns over postcommunist reforms rather than to communist-era labor relations.[60] These shifts may not have sparked a dramatic rise in labor militancy nationwide, but there is now a more predictable pattern of local-level strikes and community-based protests, driven either by mounting grievances in specific sectors or by regional elites' attempts to mobilize labor to gain leverage in bargaining situations.[61] These observations suggest that the behavior of labor actors cannot be treated as monolithic and static while postcommunist transitions move forward in time.

Those who had been optimistic about a vibrant labor movement and a burgeoning civil society following the collapse of the Soviet Union must have been deeply disappointed with what actually transpired in the 1990s. That this disappointment would inflect the analysis of postcommunist labor is understandable. But the time has come to pursue more open-ended explorations of the motivations and behaviors of labor actors as they cope with shifting institutional environments and opportunity structures. This chapter has taken a small step in this direction by attempting to surface the pragmatic forms of agency that Russian workers and unions exhibited in the midst of a transition that was initially marked by extreme uncertainty but gradually became more stable. The result is neither a story of a "tabula rasa" nor a narrative of passivity induced by communist-era labor practices. It is rather a story featuring creative assemblage by actors carrying certain expectations and understandings while seeking to make sense of turbulent transformations and new institutional environments.

PART III

Time

Chapter 9

From Birmingham to Baghdad

The Micropolitics of Partisan Identification

Victoria Hattam and Joseph Lowndes

In September 2003, national security advisor Condoleezza Rice began lay-ing claim to the legacy of the civil rights movement to authorize the U.S. war in Iraq. The speeches themselves are arresting, as familiar political affinities between race, war, and political party identification are dramati-cally rearranged. The strangeness of the political position Rice is attempting commands attention. Are Rice's efforts to realign Republican foreign policy with a civil rights agenda sincere? Or is the equation of liberation in the American South with liberation in Iraq mere window dressing for the Bush administration's military aims, divorced from deeper political commit-ments? Put differently, to what extent do Rice's speeches present a challenge to the long-standing presumption that civil rights politics goes hand-in-hand with nonintervention as important cornerstones of Democratic Party identification? More important still, what analytic tools are needed to assess Rice's efforts to change the political terrain?

Evaluating the long-term significance of Rice's remarks is no easy task. Scholars and journalists alike have dismissed the Rice speeches as strategic at best, duplicitous at worst. In contrast, we argue that the Rice speeches in particular, and Republican Party race initiatives more generally, harbor a greater political ambition that needs to be reckoned with both politically and analytically. Doing so requires that we rethink social science theories of order and change.

To assess the Rice initiatives, we examine her speeches from three van-tage points. First we focus on the speeches themselves to document the micro-reconfiguration Rice is attempting. Second, we pull back the analytic lens to show that Rice is not acting alone; rather, her speeches are part and parcel of a long-term campaign by Republican Party elites interested in reconfiguring the relation between civil rights and party affiliation in the United States. Third, we highlight the current political reconfiguration via a flashback to the very different views of civil rights, war, and party spelled out by Martin Luther King Jr. forty years earlier. In his famous 1967 speech "Time to Break Silence," in which King finally broke with President Lyndon Johnson over the Vietnam War, we see King creating the very political connections that Rice now seeks to sever. The King-Rice comparison thus stages the making and unmaking of political connections over time. Throughout we attend to issues of reception. Recapturing the cool reception that both Rice and King encountered (receptions that in King's case have largely been forgotten) underscores the ways in which many political commentators, past and present, often underestimate the long-term significance of such acts of political innovation.

Reckoning with the empirical record requires that longstanding political science theories of order and change be rethought. At the end of the chapter, we consider the dominant paradigms of institutional power within political science, namely path dependence and regime change, and show that both are inadequate to the task of explaining Republican Party efforts at reconfiguring race and party in the early decades of the twenty-first century. Where path dependence frames political change largely as historically constrained incrementalism (with occasional exogenous shocks generating intermittent moments of fundamental disjuncture), regime change theorists identify sequential patterns in which backlash and repudiation provide the motor of political change. Neither captures what we take to be the central dynamic of political change: the mix of dramatic innovation achieved through *partial* appropriation and recontextualization. History matters, but not simply as a constraining force, nor as an object of wholesale repudiation. Instead, we attend to small-scale, continuous, partial appropriations, which all too often are passed over or dismissed as unsuccessful. We argue that the kaleidoscopic shifting of political elements is ubiquitous and that such shifting provides the very ground of political change; it is here—at the micro level—that new political identifications and their attendant affiliations are made and remade.

For Rice, and her Republican allies, the past serves as a political resource in which discrete elements from one political era are selectively drawn on and recombined into new political formations. Examining the ways in which Rice reconnects a civil rights agenda from the past with Republican policy in Iraq provides a dramatic instance through which to theorize the micropolitics of partisan change. What becomes clear in the Rice speeches is the way in which disaggregating past political formations allows her to relinquish some political elements while taking others forward, transvaluing them through recontextualization. From our perspective, political change is best understood as *simultaneous* acts of *partial* repudiation and reaffirmation. Political appropriation is central to the act of political reconfiguration, but always involves the *selective* incorporation of extant elements into the new political formation. Exactly which elements are relinquished and which taken forward, and in what particular combinations, cannot be determined in advance. Tracking the process across time allows us to map the analytics of change.

We focus on the Condoleezza Rice speeches not because we see them as causal; after all, Rice has not yet secured the reorganization of race, war, and party that she is attempting. Nor do we want to claim that large-scale change can be secured by a single actor. Rather her speeches matter because they exemplify two aspects of political life that redirect prevailing accounts of change. First and foremost, we see that change in Rice's hands is at once continuous *and* partial, and as such is simultaneously both pervasive but not always cumulative. The difficult, yet essential, task is to attend to the ever present micro shifts with an eye to assessing the possibilities for enduring change.

Moreover, the small recombinations evident in the Rice speeches confound the long-standing academic split between those who attend to everyday practices far from centers of political power and those who look to institutions, elites, and state policies as the centers of both political authority and change. Typically, micropolitical accounts focus on quotidian politics that reside within the heterogeneity of all discourses and practices. However, such accounts often valorize the local while remaining blind to the dynamism of institutional authority and the complexities of power's circulation.[1] At the other end of the spectrum, analysts for whom meaningful political changes are those registered at the level of institutions and regimes rightly point to the way that elite action has disproportionate influence over the political field. Yet such accounts often conceive of coherent hegemonies anchored in reigning institutions, untroubled by novel articulations or internal contestation.[2] The Rice speeches disrupt the elite-local divide because they demonstrate how aspects of both are combined. Unlike the subjects of many micropolitical accounts, Rice is a nationally and internationally visible figure and her speech acts circulate broadly in countless local and elite settings. Yet unlike most elite accounts, the case of Rice signifies the sort of disruption and creative reordering often associated with counterhegemonic politics from below.

In short, what we find especially appealing about the Rice example is the ways in which it forces us to attend to everyday state practices and to the incomplete, yet ever present, processes of change. Her speeches are at once official and personal, tied to the state and deeply linked to local histories, a blend of formal and informal, old and new, familiar and foreign. Making sense of them requires a new analytics of change.

Bodies in Pieces: Reconfiguring Race, Violence, and War

In May 2003, Condoleezza Rice began analogizing civil rights protest of the mid-twentieth century to the "War on Terror" in Iraq. In both, Rice declared, violent resistance accompanied efforts to depose unjust regimes; democracy did not come easily in the South in the 1950s and 1960s and is not coming easily in Iraq now. The lesson to be drawn from the civil rights movement—in Rice's telling—is the importance of fortitude in the face of resistance. Bombings—and the bloody dismemberments they beget—must not deter us from the difficult task of securing democratic reform at home or abroad. The deaths of four young girls in the basement of the Sixteenth Street Baptist Church, night rides of the Ku Klux Klan, and improvised explosive devices in Iraq all must be met with the utmost resolve. Only then can freedom be secured around the globe.[3] In one speech after another, Rice repeatedly draws on two elements to facilitate connections between Birmingham and Baghdad: violence and the foreign. She uses both to animate partisan change by shifting the substantive content of extant party identifications. Put simply, Rice's ambition is to change the contours of what it means to identify as a Republican in the years to come.

Violence, and one's response to it, becomes a hinge for Rice on which she connects Birmingham to Baghdad. Bodies in pieces, in some quite literal sense, shake up extant associations, thereby creating favorable conditions for political innovation. Successful reconfigurations require the severing of old political identifications, and evocations of violence and upheaval signal political rupture in powerful ways.[4] Rice uses violence past and present to call into question long-standing affinities between civil rights and antiwar movements established almost a half century earlier. Should Rice or subsequent political actors succeed, African American identity will no longer be a presumptively Democratic identification, but might be partially revalued and linked in new ways to core aspects of a conservative political agenda.

Interestingly, Rice knew two of the four girls killed in the Sixteenth Street Baptist Church bombing of September 15, 1963. Denise McNair was her "little friend from kindergarten," and Addie Mae Collins was in her uncle's homeroom at school.[5] Time and again, Rice uses this personal connection to claim that she too knows firsthand the horrors of violence, death, and bodily injury. "I remember more than anything the coffins," Rice recalls, "the small coffins. And the sense that Birmingham wasn't a very safe place."[6] Violence past and present becomes the hinge connecting civil rights protest and foreign intervention. When addressing the National Association of Black Journalists in Dallas, Texas on August 7, 2003, Rice makes the link between the Birmingham bombings and Baghdad resistance explicit:

Like many of you, I grew up around the *home-grown terrorism* of the 1960s. I remember the bombing of the church in Birmingham in 1963, because one of the little girls that died was a friend of mine. Forty years removed from the tragedy I can honestly say that Denise McNair and the others did not die in vain. They—and all who suffered and struggled for civil rights—helped reintroduce this nation to its founding ideals. And because of their sacrifice we are a better nation—and a better example to a world where difference is still too often taken as a license to kill.

Knowing what we know about the difficulties of our own history, let us always be humble in singing freedom's praises. But let our voice not waver in speaking out on the side of people seeking freedom. And let us never indulge the condescending voices who allege that some people are not interested in freedom or aren't ready for freedom's responsibility. *That view was wrong in 1963 in Birmingham and it is wrong in 2003 in Baghdad.*[7] (Emphasis added)

Rice, like many before her, identifies civil rights protest as a redemptive moment wherein African Americans held the United States accountable for failing to live up to its "founding ideals." But Rice does not stop here; she *redirects* familiar civil rights narratives by identifying southern resistance as "home-grown terrorism," which allows her to move easily between Birmingham and Baghdad, between civil rights protest at home and war in Iraq. Linking the two, according to Rice, is the moral mission of our time. In short, Rice invokes past civil rights struggles to authorize Bush's freedom rides in Humvees and Bradley tanks in Iraq.

Rice herself acknowledges this repositioning of race and party in an interview with *Essence Magazine* in September 2006.[8] The unidentified interviewer asks Rice why she supports a political party that so many African Americans believe does so little for minorities. Rice replies that the apparent disjunction between her racial identity and party affiliation is a misperception. She claims that in fact George W. Bush has done more for African Americans than is readily acknowledged. The interviewer presses the issue. Rice responds by explaining that the Republican Party has shifted its position on race; how Rice articulates this shift is telling. Moving back and forth between domestic and international concerns allows Rice to link civil rights protest with key components of the Republican agenda, as she does in her speech to the National Association of Black Journalists.

> I think it [the "perception problem" of Republicans as anti–African American] started in 1964 with the reality that the Republican Party did not rally to the Civil Rights Act and the Public Accommodations Act and the Voting Rights Act and instead, adopted the so-called "Southern Strategy." I think that's long dead in the Republican Party and the notion that somehow, you were going to be able to appeal to—to use opposition to civil rights to appeal to a broader constituency, I think that's long gone from the Republican Party. But I think the historical memory probably lasts. And as the President said, you know, the party has some making up to do, but I really wish people would listen to this President.
>
> *Now on the foreign policy side, if African Americans indeed care about Africa, how many African Americans know* that this President tripled—has tripled official development assistance to Africa, tripled after it was flat from Jimmy Carter—since Jimmy Carter, flat and now tripled that assistance.[9] (Emphasis added)

Rice moves quickly from civil rights to foreign aid to reframe the debate. Racial disparities within the United States and Republican efforts to dismantle antidiscrimination policy fade when Rice—who has a Ph.D. in international relations—shifts from domestic to global concerns. The above quote exemplifies the move: Republican opposition to civil rights recedes as foreign aid to Africa is brought into view.[10]

Rice's investment in the international is deep-seated and intense. In her telling, it was a matter of love at first sight. A (London) *Times* profile captures the sentiment:

> A few months later [after realizing her limitations as a pianist] she walked into a class that changed everything: Introduction to International Politics. The topic that day was Stalin and the professor was Joseph Korbel, a former Czech diplomat whose daughter, Madeleine Albright, would later become America's first female secretary of state.
>
> "It just clicked," Rice said. "I remember thinking Russia is a place I want to know more about. It was like love . . . I can't explain it—there was just an attraction." . . .
>
> "I really adored him [Korbel]," Rice said. "I loved his course, and I loved him. He sort of picked me out as someone who might do this well."[11]

The words "love" and "attraction" indicate the deep investment that Rice brings to her work both as a scholar and practitioner of international affairs. For Rice, growing up in Birmingham, Alabama, is intimately connected to her interest and career in international relations. The international, for Rice, offers a different way out of the tortuous racial hatred of her Birmingham childhood; at once an escape, but also more than that. Foreign policy, for Rice, offers the possibility of political transformation. Her turn to international affairs and shift to Republican Party identification, in Rice's telling, were not simply ways of avoiding the pressing issues of racial inequality, but were, in her eyes, a different path for reframing the political options ahead.

In almost all accounts of her upbringing, Rice describes the various ways in which her parents tried desperately to protect her from southern racism; Birmingham, after all, was widely known to be one of the most racially segregated cities in the United States. Faith, education, and piano offered important protections against the scourge of American racism. She was expected to be "twice as good." As the (London) *Times* profile put it, "This was the unwritten yet firm law of Titusville families: to raise children who were 'twice as good' as white ones to gain an equal footing and 'three times as good' to surpass them." Her parents hoped that high expectations and hard work would armor Rice against the harsh forces of southern racism. "My parents were very strategic," Rice recalls. "I was going to be so well prepared, and I was going to do all of these things that were revered in white society so well, that I would be armored somehow from racism. I would be able to confront society on its own terms."[12] Rice did all that was asked and more. Once in college, at the University of Denver, Rice discovered an additional strategy for navigating American racial hatred—international affairs. In many ways, the Birmingham-Baghdad analogy is part of a long-standing pattern for Rice in which she sees the benefits of traversing the domestic-international divide as a vital resource for withstanding—and transforming—racial hierarchies and practices of discrimination.

An internationalist race politics in itself is not new; intellectuals and activists from W. E. B. DuBois to Stokely Carmichael observed the pernicious ways in which the color line ringed the globe. But Rice's internationalism is different. This is no anti-imperialist or Third Worldist critique. Rather, Rice uses civil rights politics to buttress an interventionist, some might say imperial, foreign policy in which the Bush administration strove to impose American-style democracy on the rest of the world. Note what happens when Rice internationalizes the American South—she repositions herself and the Republican Party as staunch allies of sixties civil rights protest. Yet this was not the position the Republican Party took in 1964, nor in 2004. Race and party have been realigned through her re-narration.

Violence and the foreign come together in a dramatic fashion in a speech Rice gave in the fall of 2005, when touring the South with the United Kingdom's Foreign Secretary, Jack Straw. They stopped in Rice's hometown of Birmingham, Alabama, to attend a commemorative ceremony at the Sixteenth Street Baptist Church. Both there and throughout the tour, Rice again uses violence to hinge foreign and domestic politics. In a University of Alabama speech, Rice reconfigures extant political associations. She begins with a familiar civil rights narrative, but moves quickly in a new direction. It is this combination of old and new that requires attention.

> But despite my fond memories of Birmingham as a place where I was, as a child, secure. I also remember a place called "Bombingham"—where I witnessed the denial of democracy in America for so many years. It was, after all, the city of Bull Connor and the Ku

Klux Klan, where blacks were haunted by rebel yells and terrorized by night riders and accused of burning their own homes.

And of course, it was the city where my friend Denise McNair, and three other little girls, were blown up one Sunday morning while they were going to Sunday school at the 16th Street Baptist Church. And it was a town where my father and his friends had to bear rifles at the top of the cul-de-sac in the community to keep nightriders out.

Throughout the South, when I was growing up, the organized cruelty of segregation was embodied in custom, encompassed in law, and enforced through brutality.[13]

Thus far, the speech is familiar—Rice like many others recalls the harsh realities of American racism. But Rice does not stop here. The way she reframes the civil rights mantel is quite amazing:

Across the *empire of Jim Crow*, from upper Dixie to the lower Delta, the descendants of slaves shamed our nation with the power of righteousness and redeemed America at last from its original sin of slavery.

By resolving the contradiction at the heart of our democracy, America finally *found its voice as a true champion of democracy beyond its shores.*

And today, we face the same choice in the world that we once confronted in our country: Either the desire for liberty and democratic rights is true for all human beings or we are to believe that certain peoples actually prefer subjugation.

President Bush has chosen. He believes, as I do, that all people deserve freedom and democracy—[applause]—and he had said, "The liberty we prize is not America's gift to the world; it is God's gift to humanity."[14] (Emphasis added)

In this stunning redeployment, Rice moves seamlessly from opposition to night riders and the Klan to Bush, God, and invasion of Iraq. Note the innovative ways in which empire and Jim Crow are put together, allowing an account of civil rights protest to be hitched to foreign invasion that is redemptive, even anti-imperial.[15]

Along with violence, the presence of the foreign allows Rice greater license to re-narrate the past. Straw's presence allowed Rice to reposition herself and the Republican Party as inheritors rather than opponents of civil rights reform. In doing so, Rice prepares the ground for the reassemblage of race, violence, and party in new ways. Take the foreign element away, and partisan divisions *within* the United States come to the fore—leaving Rice and the Republican Party on the wrong side—as opponents, rather than allies, of civil rights protest and antidiscrimination policy. Interestingly, Rice almost always gave her Birmingham-to-Baghdad speeches in two contexts—while abroad or when accompanied by foreign dignitaries at home. For the most part, Rice did not give her Iraq speech in the mainstream media markets generated from Washington, D.C., or New York.[16]

In speech after speech, Rice takes us from familiar civil rights narratives onto new terrain. By linking previously incongruous elements, Rice reclaims civil rights protest for Republican foreign policy now. Civil rights is no longer presumptively Democratic terrain, as violence and the foreign animate new associative chains, thereby opening possibilities of new political affiliation.

"Pimp My Rights": Rice's Reception

Rice's speeches were not warmly received; most journalists and political commentators dismissed them as insincere. Few considered the speeches a concerted challenge to long-standing political identifications and alliances. Specific criticisms vary, but Rice's remarks generally were met with considerable skepticism. A quick look across the headlines conveys the picture: "Pimp My Rights," "An Incredible Performance," "What Rice Can't See," "Baghdad Isn't Birmingham," and "Black Inclusion or GOP Delusion?"[17] In one interview after another, journalists probed Rice on both her family's, her own, and the Republican Party's commitment to racial equality.[18]

Mary Orndorff of the *Birmingham News* put the issue sharply: "In your speech yesterday [October 21, 2005] you compared the civil rights movement in the American south to America's foreign policy goal of promoting democracy in Iraq and the Middle East. Is that a fair comparison given one was initiated by individual citizens and the other by military invasion?"[19] Throughout the interview, Orndorff probed the apparent contradiction between Republican rhetoric and action. Rice gave little ground. Steve Weisman of the *New York Times* raised the questions of political disjunction and reassemblage more gently by asking Rice when she began "fusing" her own past with the political present.[20]

Rice's claims were unsettling. Many questioned her linking of the civil rights movement with the "War on Terror." But the disconcerting effects of the new associations are better understood as a mark of innovation rather than a sign of insincerity. Had these speeches been met with easy affirmation and applause, they would signal continuity or extension rather than change. The Republican task is to make *new* connections, to reconfigure old political elements into new political associations, and then to find ways to make them hold. These new political associations must congeal in an altered black political identity—one that perceives black interests as being at one with the GOP.

Republicans may ultimately be unable to forge these new links. It is too soon to tell, and there are plenty of reasons to believe that African American identification with Democratic commitments will remain strong for the foreseeable future. Nevertheless it is worth considering her speeches as harbingers of change.

Other Republican Race Initiatives

Rice's reconfiguration cannot be understood apart from a broader effort within the GOP that finally gained traction with George W. Bush's presidential nomination in 2000. Dubbed "compassionate conservatism" by Bush and his speechwriter Michael Gerson, this set of ideas centered on concern for social welfare and inclusiveness largely absent from mainstream Republican discourse. The most notable thing by far about the Republican National Convention of 2000 was its display of multiculturalism from the stage. Prime-time highlights included Oklahoma representative J. C. Watts in a live broadcast from a black church in Philadelphia, an onstage re-creation of a classroom at a mostly black and Hispanic charter school, and a performance by rhythm and blues artist Brian McKnight. General Colin Powell and Rice gave prime-time addresses headlining a list of black and brown guests who spoke of their hard work, faith, and determination. Finally, in Bush's acceptance speech, he spoke of racial and class divides and the United States in a language alien to prior GOP conventions: "When these problems aren't confronted," he said, "it builds a wall within our nation. On one side are wealth and technology, education and ambition. On the other side of the wall are poverty and prison, addiction and despair." Then, appropriating President Ronald Reagan's famous challenge to the Soviet Union at the Brandenburg Gate, he told his fellow Americans that "we must tear down that wall."[21]

Critics pointed out the stark contrast between the diversity on the stage and the almost total whiteness of the delegates in Philadelphia that week. Syndicated columnist Bob Herbert called it a "breathtaking exercise in hypocrisy for them to haul so many blacks before the camera for the sole purpose of singing, dancing, preaching and praising a party that has wanted no part of them."[22] Comedian Chris Rock did a segment of his television show from the convention, premised on the comedic potential of asking GOP delegates how they felt about black people, and black Philadelphians how they felt about George W. Bush.[23] Even the *New York Times* editorial page called the convention "The Republican Party's Exercise in Minstrelsy."[24] Nevertheless the convention's multicultural pageantry cannot easily be dismissed as cynicism.

Unquestionably, the GOP had gained ascendency over the previous thirty years to a great degree by trading on racialized wedge issues such as crime, public assistance, affirmative action, and busing. And yet, as political scientist Steven Teles has demonstrated, "compassionate conservatism" has a policy legacy, albeit in a minor key, reaching back to the Nixon administration, carried forth by Jack Kemp, William Bennett, Clint Bolick, and other modern Republicans who sought to both reclaim and recast the civil rights legacy meaningfully for a conservative political agenda.[25] Bush, it seemed, was turning away from both race-based wedge politics and color-blind alternatives, in order to incorporate racial identification within the party fold. Historian Gary Gerstle has argued that George W. Bush held a strong personal commitment to racial equality, influenced strongly by Latino friends and associates in Texas, and by his evangelical religious faith.[26] During the 2000 campaign, those seeking to reclaim and rework civil rights legacy, rather than repudiate the past, clearly had the upper hand.

Republican efforts at reconfiguring race and party continued after the 2000 election, with Bush appointing a more multiracial cabinet than any president in history. In 2005, Republican National Committee chair Ken Mehlman gave a speech at the annual convention of the National Association for the Advancement of Colored People (NAACP) that departed from, even mildly repudiated, party orthodoxy of the prior three decades. In the speech he said, "By the 70s and into the 80s and 90s, the Democratic Party solidified its gains in the African American community, and we Republicans did not effectively reach out. Some Republicans gave up on winning the

African American vote, looking the other way or trying to benefit politically from racial polarization. I am here today as the Republican Chairman to tell you we were wrong."[27] This message was underscored by Bush himself when he addressed the annual convention of the NAACP on July 20, 2006. In the speech Bush made clear that he recognized the persistent pernicious legacy of slavery in the United States, and affirmed the legacy of the civil rights movement, going so far as to call it "a second founding" of the nation.[28] By acknowledging the unhealed wounds of slavery and Jim Crow, by elevating the civil rights movement to the status of national rebirth, and by conceding his own party's complicity, he abandoned the alternative Republican discourse of color-blind conservatism. As we saw with Rice, he sought to build new associative chains linking African Americans to other key conservative commitments to liberty, opportunity, and faith. "Most of your forefathers," he said, "came in chains as property of other people. Today their children and grandchildren have the opportunity to own their own property." Part of the sin of slavery, then, was the exclusion of blacks from Lockean promises.[29]

The compassionate conservative position is not a singular one; it contains within it different components. But despite the different emphases given, they echo Rice's embrace of the civil rights legacy as an important element of Republican Party identification. Nor should we be disconcerted by the variation. That is how reidentification works: heterogeneity persists even as identifications shift. New political formations are never homogeneous formations held together by centralized strategies and singular logics. The Bush administration's attempt to appropriate the civil rights legacy for the Republican Party was a failure, as evidenced both by the demographic breakdown of the 2008 presidential election, and the current political emphasis of the GOP. Various arguments have been put forth as to why, including conservative resistance within his own party, and the administration's blundered response to Hurricane Katrina, which made his claims less than credible to people of color.

Gary Gerstle argues that, among other things, the pressures of war worked against Bush's multicultural agenda. Certainly Bush's military agenda directed energy, focus, and resources away from other programs and policy initiatives, and yet war may be one place where the civil rights reassemblage may have some staying power, if not in the GOP. At a Pentagon commemoration of King's legacy on January 13, 2011, Defense Department general counsel Jeh C. Johnson, who is African American, said in reference to the continuing war in Afghanistan, "I believe that if Dr. King were alive today, he would recognize that we live in a complicated world, and that our nation's military should not and cannot lay down its arms and leave the American people vulnerable to terrorist attack."[30]

But even within the Republican Party, which at the national level is defined by strident conservative antistatism, the desire for racial reconciliation remains. Two black members to the U.S. House of Representatives were elected in November 2008 on the GOP ticket, both strong conservatives: South Carolina's Tim Scott, who beat one of Strom Thurmond's children in the Republican primary, and Allen West of Florida. West, who became the first Republican to join the Congressional Black Caucus, said, "I think that there are different voices that are coming out of the black community. You had 42 blacks that ran on the Republican ticket this cycle. Fourteen of them made it to the general election and two of us made it to the House of Representatives. So I think that there is a new movement that needs to have a voice in the Congressional Black Caucus."[31] West, a retired army officer and the first Black Republican member of Congress from Florida since Reconstruction, makes a compelling case that new political identifications for African Americans are more readily available. For West and Rice, being black and Republican are newly convergent identifications.

Martin Luther King: Unhinging Civil Rights and War

The reconfiguration Rice and other Republicans have been attempting might be less easily dismissed when compared with Martin Luther King's speeches forty years earlier. In the spring of 1967, King began to speak out against the war in Vietnam. Both his talk at a Los Angeles conference on February 25 and his more heavily publicized address at Riverside Church in Manhattan on April 4 provide dramatic contrast to Rice's position a quarter century later. We can see King laboring to forge the very same connections that Rice later strove to pull apart.

In his Riverside address, entitled "A Time to Break Silence," King sought to link civil rights protest at home and opposition to the U.S. war in Vietnam. Even as late as the spring of 1967, a political affinity between the two political commitments could not be assumed. King's ambition was to create a connection that many liberals and civil rights leaders refused.

Early in the speech he addressed those who questioned why *he* would speak out on foreign policy at all.

> Over the past two years, as I have moved to break the betrayal of my own silences and to speak from the burnings of my own heart, as I have called for radical departures from the destruction of Vietnam, many persons have questioned me about the wisdom of my path. At the heart of their concerns this query has often loomed large and loud: *Why are you speaking about war, Dr King? Why are you joining the voices of dissent? Peace and civil rights don't mix, they say. Aren't you hurting the cause of your people, they ask?* And when I hear them, though I often understand the source of their concern, I am nevertheless greatly saddened, for such questions mean that the inquirers have not really known me, my commitment or my calling. Indeed, their questions suggest that they do not know the world in which they live.[32] (Emphasis added)

For the remainder of the speech, King challenged the prevailing assumption that "peace and civil rights don't mix." By breaking with President Johnson on Vietnam, King hoped to foster a new political position, buttressed by new affinities and identifications.

To be sure, King was not the first civil rights leader to speak out against American involvement in Vietnam: the Student Nonviolent Coordinating Committee and the Congress of Racial Equality had already explicitly opposed the war. But doing so remained a contentious matter. The latter's resolution, for example, was actually tabled after it had been passed, and the other major civil rights organizations had not opposed the war: the Southern Christian Leadership Conference was deeply divided over Vietnam and passed a resolution crafted by Bayard Rustin reaffirming its singular focus on civil rights, while the NAACP and the Urban League both refused to oppose the war.[33] There was no elective affinity between the civil rights and antiwar movements; King and others had to forge the connection.

What associative chains did King put in circulation? Like Rice, King honed in on, rather than avoided, the brutal consequences of bombings and war. King begins his Los Angeles speech, entitled "Casualties of the War in Vietnam," with a graphic account of the "nightmarish physical casualties of war": "We see the rice fields of a small Asian country being trampled at will and burned at whim: we see grief-stricken mothers with crying babies clutched in their arms as they watch their little huts burst forth into flames; we see the fields and valleys of battle being painted with human-kind's blood; we see the broken bodies left prostrate in countless fields; we see young men being sent home half-men—physically handicapped and mentally deranged."[34] Vietnam, King declares, "mutilates the conscience," provoking "all men to rise up with righteous indignation and oppose the very nature of this war. Interestingly, King's biographer, Taylor Branch, asserts that King decided to speak out against the war after reading the *Ramparts* photojournalism essay "The Children of Vietnam" in which numerous images of mutilated Vietnamese children brought home the bru-tality of war.[35] As with Rice, bodily damage uproots old identifications, creating fertile ground for new political configurations.

At Riverside Church five weeks later, King dropped these introductory remarks on physical disfigurement, but did not replace them with notions of hope and unity. Rather he talks instead of the difficult but necessary politics of political dissent.

> Some of us who have already begun to break the silence of the night have found that the calling to speak is often a vocation of agony, but we must speak. . . . And we must rejoice as well, for surely this is the first time in our nation's history that a significant number of its religious leaders have chosen to move beyond the prophesying of smooth patriotism to the high grounds of a firm dissent based upon the mandates of conscience and the reading of history. Perhaps a new spirit is rising among us. If it is, let us trace its movement well and pray that our own inner being may be sensitive to its guidance, for we are deeply in need of a new way beyond the darkness that seems so close around us.[36]

King first acknowledges the "agony" and the "darkness" of the current moment before offering a new way forward. "Smooth patriotism" needed to be replaced by the difficult work of political criticism.

The key link, for King, is the relation between the "weak and voiceless" at home and abroad—including those we call our enemies in Vietnam: "This I believe to be the privilege and the burden of all of us who deem ourselves bound by allegiances and loyalties which are broader and deeper than nationalism and which go beyond our nation's self-defined goals and positions. We are called to speak for the weak, for the voiceless, for victims of our nation and for those it calls enemy, for no document from human hands can make these humans any less our brothers."[37] King goes on to elaborate this shift in identification and the possibilities it raises of learning from the opposition: "Here is the true meaning and value of compassion and nonviolence when it helps us to see the enemy's point of view, to hear his questions, to know his assessment of ourselves. For from his view we may indeed see the basic weaknesses of our own condition, and if we are mature, we may learn and grow and profit from the wisdom of the brothers who are called the opposition."[38] King's appeal to a transnational brotherly identification is followed by a harsh critique of the Johnson administration, which he describes as the "greatest purveyor of violence in the world today"; in a passing remark, he compares the Johnson administration war policies with those of Nazi Germany.[39] His assessment of Johnson's foreign policy is a devastating one, leaving little or no room for accommodation with the president with whom he had worked so closely on civil rights advancement.

Although much of both the Los Angeles and Riverside speeches are devoted to elaborating the process and consequences of seeing the United States through its enemies' eyes, King does not leave his calls for transnational identification there—in Vietnam. At the end of the Riverside address, King explicitly returns to American soil. King himself alerts listeners to the shift in orientation:

There is something seductively tempting about stopping there and sending us all off on what in some circles has become a popular crusade against the war in Vietnam. I say we must enter the struggle, but I wish to go on now to say something even more disturbing. The war in Vietnam is but a symptom of a far deeper malady within the American spirit, and if we ignore this sobering reality we will find ourselves organizing clergy-and laymen-concerned committees for the next generation. They will be concerned about Guatemala and Peru. They will be concerned about Mozambique and Thailand and Cambodia. They will be marching for these and a dozen other names and attending rallies without end unless there is a significant and profound change in American life and policy. Such thoughts take us beyond Vietnam, but not beyond our calling as sons of the living God.[40]

America, for King, is suffering a profound spiritual ailment, manifest in actions both at home and in the world.

King concludes his Riverside address by turning to the "revolution in values" and "reordering of priorities" that Vietnam provokes at home.[41] In Los Angeles, he elaborates the claim in the following terms:

> Let me say finally that I oppose the war in Vietnam because I love America. I speak out against it not in anger but with anxiety and sorrow in my heart, and above all with a passionate desire to see our beloved country stand as the moral example of the world. I speak out against this war because I am disappointed with America. There can be no great disappointment where there is no great love. I am disappointed with our failure to deal positively and forthrightly with the triple evils of racism, extreme materialism, and militarism. We are presently moving down a dead-end road that can lead to national disaster.[42]

King's "triple evils" connecting "racism, extreme materialism, and militarism" begins to establish civil rights and antiwar commitments as integral to Democratic liberalism and to King's ambition to salvage the American soul.

King's Reception

A quick glance across the headlines in April 1967 reminds us that building connections between the civil rights and antiwar movements remained a controversial matter. The *New York Times* editorial was entitled "Dr. King's Error"; other print media echoed the sentiment with similar critical headlines: "A Tragedy"; "NAACP Decries Stand of Dr. King on Vietnam"; "Bunche Disputes Dr. King on Peace"; and Bayard Rustin's earlier column entitled "Dr. King's Painful Dilemma" that anticipated many of the same issues.[43] Both black and white political elites denounced King for speaking out on Vietnam, arguing that linking civil rights and antiwar protest would deflect energy and resources from the civil rights movement. The *New York Times* summed up what it termed King's error by saying, "This is a fusing of two public problems that are distinct and separate. By drawing them together, Dr. King has done a disservice to both. The moral issues in Vietnam are less clear-cut than he suggests; the political strategy of uniting the peace movement and the civil rights movement could very well be disastrous for both causes." The *Washington Post* editorial concluded, "Dr. King has done a grave injury to those who are his natural allies in a great struggle to remove ancient abuses from our public life; and he has done an even graver injury to himself. Many who have listened to him with respect will never again accord him the same confidence. He has diminished his usefulness to his cause, to his country and his people. And that is a great tragedy." Others criticized King for comparing U.S. policy in Vietnam to Nazi Germany and for offering too sympathetic a view of the Viet Cong.[44]

Although we now refer to "the sixties" as if the period were a relatively unified phenomenon, it is worth remembering how much resistance King encountered when trying to bring civil rights and antiwar politics together. King did not call for a merger of the two movements; that was not what he was asking for. But even spelling out the connections and publicly breaking with Johnson over Vietnam was not warmly received. Most thought it was a strategic blunder that would "confuse" rather than create synergies between the two political causes.

Forty years later, Rice labors in the opposite direction—to uncouple civil rights at home from nonintervention abroad. After all, Rice wants to claim the civil rights legacy to buttress Bush's interventionist foreign policy in Iraq. In both instances, we see new political linkages in formation. In 1967 and 2007, the political affinities being created were very different: in both cases, the linkages had to be forged, not assumed, sutured together politically through speech and action. The acts of reconfiguration considered here are the daily practices of regime change.

Rethinking Disorder and Change

Existing accounts of order and change do not capture the political reconfigurations that Rice and other Republicans are attempting. The limits of current accounts lie in the assumptions of social and political coherence that pervade views of both order and change. Typically, scholars have understood political change as a shift from one largely coherent political order to the next. Whether focused on party systems, presidential administrations, or regimes more broadly, most accounts operate with a notion of political change in which shifts from one era to another occur via discrete

moments of disequilibrium. Two accounts of order and change predomi-
nate among historical institutionalists: punctuated equilibrium, in which
path-dependent eras of relative stasis are disrupted by external shocks to
the system; and regime change, in which countermobilizations are formed
within the political system, eventually creating opportunities for large-scale
backlash and revolutionary reorganization. Mapping both of these accounts
of political change allows us to pinpoint the analytic issues we seek to
reframe.

Path dependence, a theory first meant to explain the constraints on
technological development, found its way into the social sciences through
economics, and has been taken up in sociology, history, and political science to explain the directionally determined nature of political action.[45]
Institutions, for path-dependence scholars, are marked by a logic of direc-
tionality that translates into enduring political orders over time. Political
equilibria form, so the argument runs, because the increasing returns to
existing routines make alternative paths politically costly. Timing is everything: historical location sets the parameters of order and change. To be
sure, political transformation occurs, but only at moments when exogenous
shocks render political routines useless, thereby opening the way for new
political calculi to emerge. Depressions, wars, and revolutions disorganize
the political landscape, but new logics soon inhere, committing institutions
to incremental change along the newly established pathways. Political
agency thus is restricted to exceptional moments of upheaval, while institutional logics and incremental change prevail in normal times.

Scholars operating within a path-dependence frame have much to offer.
The hallmark of such work has been careful empirical research in which
historical contexts have been elaborated in exquisite detail so as to reveal
the underlying logics shaping political action. When done well, this scholarship leaves the reader with an acute sense of the historical and institutional
forces in play.[46] Yet the more rigorously this model is imposed, the more it
evacuates politics from political analysis. The role of ongoing agency is
diminished, and meaningful political change relegated to rare moments of
externally induced disequilibrium.[47]

While regime change scholars have largely abandoned the belief in the
tidy, rhythmic, and inevitable shifts in political eras posited by realignment
theorists decades ago, most still hold to the idea that U.S. politics is marked
by discrete periods—or regimes—dominated by specific political interests
and institutional articulations.[48] As in path-dependence accounts, these

periods are cleaved by decisive moments—crises—when politics is open to fundamental shifts. At these junctures, reigning political commitments are repudiated by new regime builders who offer credible narratives that successfully lay extant political problems at the feet of existing regime leaders. Regime builders make bold claims for transformation and act quickly to alter institutional arrangements. The newly configured political landscape holds, and durably so, until regime opponents are finally able to challenge the order.

Although regime theorists also operate within a frame of punctuated equilibrium, their accounts of order and change differ from path-dependence scholars in two important regards: issues of power and endogenous sources of change are placed front and center. A regime, after all, connotes hegemony and as such foregrounds issues of political coherence, articulation, and domination. While precise formulations vary, most regime theorists agree that coordination is vital to the effectiveness of all political formations. Coherence and power replace "increasing returns" as the central political dynamic to observe. When it comes to change, exogenous shocks still play a role, but regime theorists also attend to endogenous sources of change. Repudiation, backlash, and countermobilization pervade regime theorists' accounts of change as the limits of the old order are seen as fertile ground for new political mobilizations.[49] Regime theorists offer a less deterministic account of politics than path-dependence scholars, and rightly direct our attention to the ways in which governing authority frequently generates countermobilizations. But their accounts of change remain limited by their adherence to notions of political order as coherent and stable; the image of change is usually one of internal contestation between relatively coherent, yet opposed political positions vying for power. Even as these theorists allow for internally generated agents of change, they pay insufficient attention to the heterogeneity and contradictory elements that persist *within* contending camps.

Most accounts of twentieth-century American politics generally follow punctuated equilibrium models by adhering to sequential periodization of the Depression and the New Deal Order, followed by the sixties and the Great Society, resulting in a conservative backlash capitalized on by the Reagan Revolution. This sequential narrative—simple and familiar as it is—needs to be rethought. It has shaped our views of American politics past and present in ways that limit and distort. Powerful critiques of order have been offered for decades now. Poststructuralists paved the way, relentlessly revealing the heterogeneity that persists within all social formations. Claims to order and coherence are themselves ruses of power that serve to marginalize and obscure the persistent heterogeneity within. Extended debates within feminist political theory brought critiques of order into mainstream political science via extended scholarly debates over the category "woman" and the benefits and liabilities of mobilizing under this or any sign.[50]

Over the last decade and a half, a parallel debate has emerged among new institutionalists over the status of political order and change. Karen Orren and Stephen Skowronek blazed the trail with their essay challenging the "iconography of order" as the reigning metaphor for analyses of political regimes.[51] Far from operating in lockstep fashion, Orren and Skowronek argue that regimes are characterized as much by fragmentation and internal contention. Political orders are composite formations, with multiple institutions and competing loci of power in which each institution operates in its own political time making issues of alignment key to regime creation. Adam Sheingate, Gary Herrigel, Gerald Berk, and Dennis Galvan extend the argument from regimes to institutions themselves, revealing the competing imperatives that persist within all organizations. Organization goals, rules, and boundaries are open to multiple interpretations, thereby making way for entrepreneurial action and a more constant and endogenous conception of change.[52]

Taken together, the poststructuralist and institutionalist critiques of order have shown that political regimes, institutions, and identities are not coherent or orderly formations. Rather, political identifications are best understood as composite formations, amalgams of discrete elements that have been forged together politically rather than emanations of interior essences or natural affiliations. Organizations, too, are rarely coherent, homogeneous entities, since institutional boundaries, rules, and missions are inherently ambiguous, opening them to competing interpretations.

Poststructuralist and institutionalist critiques of order have dramatic implications for conceptions of change. Regimes, institutions, and subjects are rarely transformed overnight in seismic fashion. Rather, change in all three realms often occurs slowly as heterogeneous elements are continually combined and recombined into new political formations. A more heterogeneous conception of power foregrounds the importance of microprocesses of political change.

Deconstructing order, however, only takes us partway when analyzing change. Certainly, it has transformed our conceptions of order and forced us to rethink change, but prevailing arguments give us too little leverage over the crucial processes of reconfiguration. Accepting change as a piece-meal process, we still need to attend to the ways in which elements are linked politically and given a retrospective air of coherence that garners them political force. Even though heterogeneity persists, it is not always visible: attending to processes through which political affinities are created and sustained is key for analyzing order and change. Political analysis, from our perspective, requires that we denaturalize existing affinities, essences, and identifications. Doing so makes way for a fine-grained analysis of reidentification. Here we use language—specifically chains of association and shifts in them over time—to track processes of reidentification and change.[53]

Attending to processes of reconfiguration, and the reidentifications that they engender, allows us to see the Rice speeches in a new light. Rather than dismissing them as merely tactical or insincere, we consider whether they might not be opening salvos in a long-term process of political reiden-tification. From this perspective, the Rice speeches startle precisely because they change the terms of conversation by unsettling extant associations of political affinity and affiliation. The shock of the new should not lead us to dismiss the speeches as insignificant; it might equally alert us to the ambi-tion of the reconfiguration. The question we want to consider is whether we are witnessing the micropolitics of reidentification rather than a more fleeting effort at strategic campaigning. The Rice speeches invite us to rethink social science assumptions about both order and change.

Micropolitics of Partisan Identification

The Rice speeches mapped above unsettle existing theories of both order and change as transformative shifts from one era to the next. Drawing on poststructuralists' and postorder institutionalists' critiques of coherence, we acknowledge the heterogeneity of all social formations, and begin to appreciate the ways in which Rice's acts of selective appropriation are part and parcel of a constant process of reconfiguration. To be sure, the Rice examples are unusually striking, but the phenomena are not confined to dramatic acts of recombination. The world is constantly in motion through small-scale acts of political reconfiguration. Seen this way, we can begin to attend to the constant processes of partial change.

One last question must be answered: how do we know whether the initiatives Rice and other Republican elites have been taking will accumulate into broad-based change? Put another way, how do we distinguish everyday flux from more significant political change?

The short answer is that we cannot be certain that small changes will adhere one to another, forging broader processes of change. Being alert to the front lines of change means relinquishing the security of knowing when large-scale social transformation has been secured. This sense of uncertainty we feel actually captures an important dimension of politics that often is lost in structural accounts of political change. While older gauges of systemic transformation allow us to mark tectonic political shifts, they are hardly adequate to register the tremors of change. Instead, we must look to different measures of significance if we are to capture the early movements for change. Indeed, we welcome the way in which attending to the micro generates new measures for assessing significance. Attending to small acts of *partial* reconfiguration shifts the markers of success. Rather than ask whether Rice and the Republicans have successfully realigned race, war, and party over the past decade, we ask whether Republican appeals to African Americans have begun to change the underlying terms of political debate. The analytic criteria shift from those of system-wide change as the hallmark of significance to a recognition of partial and incomplete shifts in the alignment of political elements as a more useful and sensitive measure of continuous political change.

Seen from the micropolitics of regime change, the relevant analytic question shifts from one of whether the Republicans have realigned race and party in a systemic fashion to whether Democrats can continue to assume that civil rights politics are presumptively attached to a liberal agenda. Put simply, are familiar lines of political affiliation in motion? If yes, in what ways? Shifting to a micro lens allows us to attend to a wide range of phenomena that get lost in the gross magnification used in existing theories of systemic political change. To be sure the reconfiguration is not complete, but what is equally clear is that the terrain is shifting and we need analytic tools for taking the measure of these small, yet cumulative acts of political appropriation.

The use of the civil rights movement by conservatives was disrupted in 2008 by the election of a black Democratic president, and by subsequent racially charged opposition to this president on the right. Yet that does not mean that Republican attempts to reconfigure race and party are over.

While the racial dimension of conservative anti-Obama sentiment is strong, it is not directed against specific racially defined policies or issues. The Right today is not being built directly in opposition to the civil rights movement as it was when conservatives deployed racially framed issues of crime, welfare, housing, education, and employment to expand the base of the Republican Party. People of color have become celebrated national figures in sports, entertainment, and politics, and the civil rights movement is embraced or appropriated on the right by everyone from Glenn Beck to Newt Gingrich. Although the same period has seen the further isolation and targeting of the black poor through the dismantling of the welfare state and the massive expansion of the prison system, those conservative achievements have made issues of crime and welfare less useful tools for future conservative mobilization. In the current moment the Right is constrained from deploying racial affect, deprived of the political resistance against which it was constructed, and has new possibilities for appropriation that were pioneered by figures like Rice.

Chapter 10

The Trouble with Amnesia

Collective Memory and Colonial Injustice in the United States

Kevin Bruyneel

In politics, time is a structuring force that shapes collective and individual identities, subjectivities, and imaginaries. We can see the role of political temporality in sweeping historical narratives, such as those a nation tells itself about its founding moment and subsequent arc of development, an arc that almost always legitimizes the status of the contemporary social and political order. We can see it in more quotidian forms such as the calendars that organize people's lives and in so doing habituate citizens into annual practices of remembrance, memorialization, and obligation. These examples point to the fact that political time is a construct, not a natural entity.[1] As such, the structuring force of time is open to unstructuring, and here we locate a critical if underexplored site of politics.

Just as political temporality is an inescapable organizing element of a cohesive social and political order, the effort to bring about change involves unstructuring temporalities that serve to preserve injustices, such as those that too seamlessly distance past injustices from those of the present. For example, political conflicts over indigenous claims to territory and sovereignty as well as African American claims for slavery reparations and affirmative action all implicate the active role of the past in the present. To understand issues such as these that engage the politics of time, I argue that we need to pay close attention to the role of memory, specifically collective memory. Collective memory is an underappreciated, yet fundamental component of our political lives, for while a nation without a military may be deemed weak and vulnerable, a nation without a memory does not exist at all. It is through the production of and contestation over forms of collective memory that the structuring and unstructuring of political time occurs. To get at the politics of time you need to go to memory.

This essay will show how important collective memory is to the contemporary politics of historic injustices, to state building, and to the production of nationhood, all of which involve placing politics in and out of time. To this end, the first section of the essay challenges the popular notion that the failure to address prevailing injustices is a result of collective amnesia, of a forgetting of the past. Instead, I argue that the persistence of colonialist and racial injustices is a consequence of collective disavowal and as such a particular production and presence of memory, rather than a lack of memory. To explore the politics of collective memory at greater length, the rest of the essay focuses on the calendar. I see calendars as forms of evidence for understanding politics because they are products of the mutually constitutive relationship between collective memory and the production of political temporality. Calendars have epistemological value as public documents of state building, of nationhood, and of resistances to both. The second section of the essay looks at the politics of calendars in theoretical and historical terms, setting out their importance for state building, nationhood, resistance, and revolution. The final section of the essay then considers the contemporary U.S. context, looking at examples of political resistance and elite consolidation that take as their target the mnemonics of the calendar. I turn first to what I call the misdiagnosis of collective amnesia.

The Liberal Misdiagnosis of Collective Amnesia

The conventional collective amnesia diagnosis generally goes as follows, using the prevalent example of the nation: nations conveniently forget or suppress from their collective memories those aspects of their pasts that do not shed a positive light on the nation—such as colonial and racial violence, territorial dispossession, and enslavement. The purpose of this forgetting is to avoid dealing with the implications of these past actions for the cultural, socioeconomic, and political relations of the contemporary era.[2] If amnesia is the diagnosis, then the cure is to engage in forms of education or general enlightenment that will allow for a remembering of this past, especially by those people who form the more powerful groups of the nation. With the facts of the past brought into the contemporary light, to follow the logic of this diagnosis and cure, the people and the government of the dominant nation can then address and debate them openly and in the interests of justice. I see this as a misdiagnosis of the problem, and thereby claim that the wrong cure has been prescribed.

The diagnosis of amnesia and the cure of remembering are liberal rationalist ways to conceive the problem of, and solution to, racial and colonial domination. The liberal rationalist approach says that if only we all knew better, had all the facts, then these historic injustices would be resolved, or at least we would be on our way to addressing them. Political philosopher Thomas McCarthy explicitly advocates this liberal enlightenment perspective in his essays on the politics of memory that take as their specific subject matter the relationship between the history of slavery in the United States and the contemporary debate about reparations. In these essays, McCarthy looks to collective memory as the path to fulfill the imperative that "a just society must, so far as possible and permissible, right the wrongs of its own past injustices, particularly when their continuing ill effects upon the descendents of those wronged are plain for all to see."[3] And to foster this aim, he "stress[es] the importance of historical enlightenment," meaning that with regard to "recontextualizing the racial issues of today as the latest chapter in the continuing story of slavery and its aftermath . . . the greater the public familiarity with and knowledge of that history, the greater are the chances of effectively interpreting current problems as belonging to its accumulated effects and thus of publicly framing them as moral issues or issues of justice."[4] Through memory McCarthy offers his sense of the political time of the nation, which is structured like chapters in a book, one after the other, continuing and accumulating its effects. He wants the American people to read or reread the first few chapters, to grasp the temporal sequencing through enlightened collective memory that will lead them to see themselves as part of the "latest chapter" of the same book. I agree that we should seek out historical knowledge, but I question the degree to which this avenue serves as a concrete direction for addressing political problems. I wonder if there is enough politics to this approach.

The *cure* of remembering does not adequately deal with the political fact that historical and contemporary interests are constituted by dominant collective memories as presently constructed. In the U.S. context and case McCarthy discusses more historical knowledge is not likely to amend these interests unless there is a direct challenge to the mutually constitutive relationship between identity, power, racial hierarchy, and collective memory. To his credit, McCarthy sees this as a "consideration weighing against" his approach, which he understands to be the e tension of "passion and interest versus knowledge," and he grants that he could be "overestimating the 'cognitive' dimensions of racism—ignorance and false belief, for example—and underestimating its 'noncognitive' dimensions—for instance, the protection of group interests, the maintenance of social dominance, ideological commitments, prejudices, psychopathologies, and the like."[5] He captures the view and critique that I make of the collective amnesia diagnosis. And his response is that his argument and approach "requires only that knowledge and belief have *some* independent force, that they play *some* role in public deliberation concerning racial issues . . . and that an extended debate could have *some* effect on them."[6] While this qualified and careful claim for *some* (his emphasis) influence stemming from knowledge accumulation is defensible as far as it goes, the political question is how far does it go?

Among the many ways in which this amnesiac-enlightenment approach does not go far enough and may be counterproductive lies in the ways that this approach severs or simply does not see the mutually constitutive relationship between collective memory, temporality, and the production of both state authority and nationhood. The liberal rationalist approach seems to accommodate its remedy and insights to fit within, rather than challenge, the prevailing temporal narrative of statist authority and dominant national identity. The amnesia approach does not offer a direct political critique about how the collective memory of the story of dominant nationhood is critical for the production and iteration of racial and colonialist state authority regardless of what other historical knowledge is brought into the conversation. The liberal rationalist enlightenment remedy imagines, fancifully, that light shed on the earliest chapters of nationhood reflects down a linear temporal continuum on the later chapters, and thereby transforms the political interests and subjectivities of contemporary U.S. citizens in a way that makes them amenable to creating a more just society. The argument that light on the past will lead to enlightened action in the present does not see that interests and power relations are secured through a tightly structured relationship between political time and national collective memory.

An unstructuring politics corrective to the liberal rationalist approach requires positing a more practice-based and fluid view of the relationship between political temporality and collective memory. As a substitute for the amnesia diagnosis and enlightenment cure, my second opinion is that the fundamental problem is not a lack of memory but rather the presence of particular productions of memory, even at times an excess of memory. It is in the practices of memory production and disavowal that we can locate the political identities and interests at stake when the question arises about seriously addressing historic injustices such as slavery. The radical political cure is not more historical knowledge on its own, but rather a direct encounter with the commitments, interests, and hierarchies reproduced through the present productions of collective memory. In this regard, I concur with Marita Sturken that American culture "is not amnesiac but rather replete with memory, that cultural memory is a central aspect of how American culture functions and how the nation is defined."[7] The issue at hand is neither forgetting nor collective amnesia simply defined. Rather, as George Shulman puts it, this is a "problem of disavowal, not error or ignorance."[8] The political problem with white majority settler nations such as the United States *is not what they forget but how they remember.*

In terms of the complicated relationship of the past to the present, I conclude this section with the thoughts of Giorgio Agamben on the temporality of state sovereignty, national foundings, and narratives of political development. In the following passage Agamben discusses the "myth of the foundation of the modern city" out of the state of nature as contrived most notably by canonical modern theorists such as Thomas Hobbes and Jean-Jacques Rousseau: "The state of nature is, in truth, a state of exception, in which the city appears for an instant (which is at the same time a chronological interval and a nontemporal moment) *tanquam dissolute.* The foundation is thus not an event achieved once and for all but is continually operative in the civil state in the form of the sovereign decision."[9] In contrast to McCarthy, Agamben refuses the temporal structure and liberal view of collective memory familiar to enlightenment rationality. Agamben's claim that the foundational moment is not a "once and for all" historical event cemented in time but is instead "continually operative" points to the need to interrogate the politics of collective memory. As it concerns the U.S. case, the moment of foundation is perpetually and necessarily reinscribed in the present through the discourse, practices, and mnemonics of state sovereignty and white settler nationalism. The story of state sovereignty and the nation is not written in sequential chapters but rather in texts that fold on top and through each other like a palimpsest in which, most notably, founding moments continually reoccur in the present, not the past. This view of political temporality calls to mind William Faulkner's famous line: "The past is never dead. It's not even past."[10] To better understand the structuring and unstructuring of political time, I examine the calendar as an active site of the politics of collective memory.

Habit-Memory and the Production of Political Time

Henri Bergson, recently elaborated by Paul Ricoeur, offers two useful ways to define memory. These are "*mémoire-habitude* (memory as habit) and *mémoire-souvenir* (memory as distinct recollection)."[11] As Bergson put it, "the past survives under two distinct forms: first, in motor mechanisms; secondly, in independent recollections."[12] Or as Ricoeur defines the habit-recollection distinction, "to memory that repeats is opposed memory that imagines."[13] It is in the practice of memory as habit that I locate the means by which memory serves in the interpellation of citizens as subjects of state authority and as members of the nation, in distinct, if intertwined ways. As it concerns state authority, habit-memory constructs more of a cyclical temporal relationship of citizens to state practices, such as through the motor mechanisms and repetitions of the annual calendar. I refer to state practices rather than *the state* here, for the latter term conveys the image of a static structural entity rather than what I deem the more accurate image of a fusion of governing practices that might be better termed *statism*, to which the role of memory is a critical cohering practice. As to the nation, I claim that the production of nationhood through the calendar begins with the active imagining of recollection memory posited in historical, even linear political time and becomes, through the repetition of the annual calendar, the habit memory of citizens as national subjects. For both statism and nationhood, habit-memory is the structuring force of political temporality, and thus the effort to "dehabituate" the mnemonics of political time should be seen as a form of unstructuring politics. The encounter between the pairings of habituation-structuring and dehabituation-unstructuring is a critical dynamic of the politics of the calendar. I turn now to the production of statism through politics of collective memory and follow that by examining at greater length the ubiquitous and intimate relationship between memory and nationhood, especially for settler societies such as the United States.

The date of April 15 in the United States likely signifies the same thing to most Americans—tax day. The obligation of residents and citizens to pay their tributes to state institutions is invoked not by the polite request or claim of pressing necessity from those representing these institutions. Rather, it is a habitual obligation tied to the turning of the calendar. Whether we pay without complaint, groan and gripe about it, or try to evade or reduce the obligation, "tax day" still stands as a component of the habit-memory of statism in the political temporality of the United States. Imagine a world without the *habit* of tax day, where state actors and institutions are compelled to make particular appeals for resources from citizens and residents every year, or every month, or every ten years. In such a scenario, citizens and residents would witness in every special plea, request, or demand from state actors and institutions the naked iterative processes of state practices seeking to justify authority or compel obligation.

Of course, as it concerns taxation, American state practices do not have to be justified every year; rather, what was at one time an exceptional request or demand has become a habituated and perpetual one, a motor mechanism of annual political time. Ernst Kantorowicz, in his seminal work *The King's Two Bodies: A Study in Medieval Political Theology*, speaks to the historical and theoretical roots of this development in European statism: "By the fourteenth century, or even in the thirteenth, the pretense of an *ad hoc* taxation was occasionally dropped, and the fictitiously extraordinary became the overtly ordinary: public taxation, at least in many parts of the Continent, became synonymous with annual taxation. In other words, taxation, formerly linked to an unrepeatable event, now was linked to the calendar, to the eternally rolling wheel of Time. The state had become permanent, and permanent were its emergencies and needs, its *necessitas*."[14] This discourse of "permanent emergencies" becomes the "new fiction of a *perpetua necessitas* implying . . . the perpetuation of something that, by definition, indicated an exception, some singular condition or some momentary deviation from the rule."[15] But it is not enough to say that the development of "annual taxation" became "linked to . . . the eternally rolling wheel of Time." It is more accurate to claim that statist developments such as annual taxation that transform the ad hoc into the permanent, make contingencies sites of stability, turn fictions into facts, and pummel notable events into barely conscious habit-memories actually serve to constitute the meaning and experience of time in the political sense. This is just one example of why the politics of the everyday calendar is a fertile subject of examination.

Sociologist Eviatar Zerubavel argues that as it concerns the "social time-lines constructed by entire mnemonic communities . . . perhaps the most spectacular site of collective memory in this regard is the calendar." In his research, Zerubavel discovered that of the 191 countries he examined, 139 "celebrate a national birthday commemorating the historic moment at which they became independent," demonstrating that "the birth of a nation is clearly the most significant political event preserved in its collective memory." As well, he found that only 9 countries had national holidays that commemorated events that had occurred between 680 and 1492; thus: "from a strictly calendro-commemorative standpoint, the eighth, tenth, twelfth, and fourteenth centuries are considered practically 'empty' world-wide!"[16] Here we see evidence of the construction of political time around multiple thresholds, that which defines the temporal starting point of the nation and that which demarcates the advent of European conquest of the so-called New World, these being the thresholds of nation and conquest, respectively. These two thresholds matter because we cannot seriously grasp the structuring force of memory in settler nations such as the United States by focusing on the political time of the nation alone. Rather, we must also see it as intertwined with the temporality of conquest that both prefigures and coexists with the settler nation's political time.

As to the political time of the nation, then, the calendrical commemoration of the United States occurs on what is officially referred to as Independence Day on July 4, marking the anniversary of the adoption of the Declaration of Independence by the American colonies in 1776. While this day formally references an extraordinary political moment in the nation's history and was instituted as a form of recollection-memory, it now more commonly signifies to the majority of U.S. citizens and residents the rather ordinary routine of the first long weekend of the summer: a time to plan a backyard cookout, or head out to the campground or the beach; set off fireworks; and, for many to be sure, also raise the national flag or at least buy paper napkins decorated with the national flag or colors. On this issue, in the wake of the 2010 Memorial Day in the United States (the annual day in May to honor U.S. military killed in war past and present), *Washington Post* op-ed columnist E. J. Dionne asked: "Why is it that every Memorial Day, we note that a holiday set aside for honoring our war dead has become instead an occasion for beach-going, barbecues and baseball?"[17] Dionne's implicit claim here is that this holiday no longer stands as an experience of recollection memory but is a practice of habit-memory, a motor mechanism of national subjects. In many ways, he is seeking to dehabituate this memory by compelling a recollection and historical imagining as an unstructuring form of politics that challenges the way habit-memory creates passive and disengaged citizens.

The mutually constitutive relationship between the calendar and habit-memory is especially revealing in the case of July 4 in the United States. The July 4 holiday is formally referred to as Independence Day, but in the everyday American vernacular one most often references the celebration of independence not as such but by signifying the calendar date itself, as in "celebrating the Fourth of July," or just "the Fourth." A date on the U.S. calendar has become the habituated metonym for the political temporality of the nation itself. The political founding moment and the seeming temporal threshold between the before and after of the nation is reproduced annually. "The Fourth" in annual political time means American independence in historical political time. And it is as component of the palimpsest of nationhood imbricated with statism that I conceptually locate the structuring force of the habit-memory of the calendar. Just as the habit of tax day and taxation relieves state officials of having to request or demand resources anew from the citizens as needs arise, the habit of annually re-marking the date of the founding serves to habitually reinscribe the political temporality of nationhood. As well, in settler societies such as the United States, the political time of the nation and the mnemonic practices of statism are interwoven with a political temporality that habituates a narrative of conquest and settlement. We can see the extent of this in Zerabuvel's insight about the dearth of official holidays referring to events in the centuries immediately preceding 1492.

To be sure, the United States did not exist prior to 1492. Nevertheless, the nation has holidays on its calendar that reference the temporal threshold of conquest. The date often cited for such a threshold is 1492, but more generally one should see this threshold as the period of colonial encounter, conquest, enslavement, and early settlement in the first few centuries after first contact but before the national founding moments and events of the United States. The most famous celebration marking the threshold of conquest is the annual harvest festival and now secular holiday of Thanksgiving, which occurs on the fourth Thursday in November in the United

States. The standard Thanksgiving scene is of Pilgrims of the Plymouth Colony sharing a feast with local Native Americans, thus offering a multicultural image of early settler-indigenous relations. The other notable date on the calendar that marks the threshold of conquest is Columbus Day, the annual October holiday in honor of Christopher Columbus, the so-called discoverer of the New World. While these holidays are not without controversy and protest, as I will discuss, they still represent prime examples of the habit-memory more than the recollection-memory of settler statism. *Settler statism* is the term I give to governing practices that secure and maintain the claims of Euro-American settler populations to being "native" to and possessing lands that were seized from indigenous populations by practices of forced expulsion, legal and political marginalization, and mass killing. These settler-statist practices are further constituted and legitimized through holidays that celebrate settlers (i.e., the Pilgrims) and colonial conquerors (Columbus), archetypal figures that both define and occupy the threshold of conquest in the habit-memory of the political time of the settler society. The habituated political time here is thus not before and after the nation but rather before, during, and after conquest, settlement, and enslavement—from Columbus to the Pilgrims and beyond—on a temporal threshold that purports to mark the trajectory toward the creation of white majority settler societies. These calendrical commemorations help turn the extraordinary acts of conquest and colonial incursion into the ordinary habituation, and habitation, of settled liberal citizens. In this way, these routine features of the annual calendar contribute to the production and maintenance of settler sovereignty by making the temporality of conquest and settlement an ordinary feature of the habit-memory of settler nations.

Thus, from April 15 to July 4 to the fourth Thursday in November, we locate in the U.S. annual calendar markers of three distinct yet interwoven habit-memories of, respectively, statism, nationhood, and settler conquest. These habit-memories shape political temporalities as structuring forces on people's lives, but by that very fact these temporalities are also sites for potential unstructuring via the dehabituation of memory. The calendar is a product of efforts at elite consolidation of political time so as to secure statist authority, the meaning of nationhood, and even claims to conquest, as well as efforts to resist these forms of temporal consolidation. As Zerubavel noted, in the calendar we find a "spectacular site" for understanding the role of collective memory in the production of the temporalities that help give meaning and identity to communities, and this is why the calendar and time itself are often hotly contested sites of politics. It is thus unsurprising that revolutionaries have looked to the calendar and to political time as a way to assert and constitute their claim for the transformation of a social and political order.

In his "Theses on the Philosophy of History," Walter Benjamin wrote of the role of the calendar and the politicization of time during the French (Great) Revolution of 1789 and the (July) French Revolution of 1830, respectively:

> The awareness that they are about to make the continuum of history explode is characteristic of the revolutionary classes at the moment of their action. The great revolution introduced a new calendar. The initial day serves as a historical time-lapse camera. And, basically, it is the same day that keeps recurring in the guise of holidays, which are days of remembrance. Thus the calendars do not measure time as clocks do; they are monuments of a historical consciousness of which not the slightest trace has been apparent in Europe in the past hundred years. In the July revolution an incident occurred which showed this consciousness still alive. On the first evening of fighting it turned out the clocks in towers were being fired on simultaneously and independently from several places in Paris. An eye-witness, who may have owed his insight to the rhyme, wrote as follows:
>
> Qui le croirait! on dit, qu'irrités contre l'heure
> De nouveaux Josués au pied de chaque tour,
> Tiraient sur les cadrans pour arréter le jour.
> [Who would have believed it! We are told that new Joshuas at the foot of every tower, as though irritated with time itself, fired at the dials in order to stop the day.][18]

The "new calendar" Benjamin refers to is the Jacobin-devised French republican calendar that replaced the Gregorian calendar in France from 1793 until 1805, and which also had a very brief revival during the Paris Commune of 1871. Among the changes, the new calendar set the French Republic at Year 1, the new year now began on September 21 (the Gregorian calendar date of the proclamation of the republic), and the new calendar excised religious holidays and saints' days, remnants of the vilified

Catholic church. This is the politics of the calendar at its most extreme, and it also demonstrates the role of the politics of collective memory and political time as discussed thus far. To wit: the refounding of France as a republic involved restarting political time at Year 1. On an annual basis, the relocated date for the turning of the new year was an effort to reimagine the political time of the republic in the French collective memory. And the elimination of traditional calendrical commemorations was an effort to dehabituate the French memory of the political time of the ancien régime. This was a distinct act of unstructuring politics. The transformed calendar is a conscious effort to engage the mutually constitutive relationship between politics, history, and memory in order to "explode" *and* to fundamentally reshape the "continuum" of political time by dehabituating the memory of the French public of the time and reimagining it through the temporal act of starting the calendar over, at Year 1. This was not about overcoming collective amnesia but rather an effort to produce new memories in the calendar and actively disavow the mnemonic productions of the discarded regime.

If the French Jacobin calendar, to Benjamin, was an example of what amounts to recollection-memory that reimagined the history and temporality of the French nation as a republic, what he finds subsequent to that is the emergent power of habit-memory. As he looks through the lens of the "historical time-lapse camera" of the annual calendar, Benjamin is chagrined to find a memory that repeats: "And, basically, . . . the same day . . . keeps recurring in the guise of holidays, which are days of remembrance." For Benjamin, the national calendar marks not Gregorian time but political time, "monuments of a historical consciousness." But for him that consciousness had receded by his time of writing in the early twentieth century, decidedly, to the point that he finds not a "trace" of it in "Europe in the past hundred years." To me, this is an unsurprising development, as it reflects the habituation of the temporality of statism and of nationhood; that is, each "recurring" day and year further habituates the temporal political existence and thus legitimacy of state practices and the motor mechanistic rituals of nationhood. In noting this dynamic of habituation we can see one way in which collective memory serves in maintaining stability in political arrangements, authority, and the subjectivity of citizens. Habit-memory helps to consolidate and maintain social and political orders by securing as self-evident, even to the point of seeming naturalized, the temporal status and authority of statism and nationhood. Thus, we can look to collective memory as a way to explain durability in politics. On the other hand, just as importantly, this same lens also reveals possible paths of activism to propel political change by dehabituating habit-memory and reimagining the political time of the nation. The politics of collective memory is thus a way to gain insight into efforts at unstructuring politics through practices of dehabituation that seek to unleash political agency and generate political change.

In this spirit of change, Benjamin's passage ends on a hopeful note for the transformative potential of politics, when he refers to seeing historical "consciousness still alive" in the 1830 July revolution. For Benjamin, the central symbol of this politics is that of rebels shooting at the "clocks in the towers . . . simultaneously and independently from several places in Paris." As the rhyming "eye-witness" observed, it was as if these "new Joshuas . . ., irritated with time itself, fired at the dials in order to stop the day." It appears that on the first day of fighting and without having to coordinate, the *new Joshuas*—the purported new founders of the nation—implicitly grasped the need to engage collective memory and political time in order to shake the public's consciousness into engagement with the politics at hand. In this sense, "shooting at the clocks" is a symbol for the effort to dehabituate collective memory and unstructure the political time that served to consolidate and maintain the legitimacy of the extant social and political order. Along these same lines, then, when contemporary political actors resist and challenge the meaning and practice of calendrical commemorations, we can say that they are taking their own shots at the clock. With this image in mind, I turn to two contemporary examples of politics of the calendar, the first being a form of anticolonial resistance that seeks to fire at the dials to stop the day in order to dehabituate the temporality of colonial conquest, and the second being a noted example of a dominant state actor utilizing collective memory as a structuring force in order to consolidate the temporal boundaries of U.S. state authority and national identity.

From Thanksgiving to September 11:
The Politics of the Calendar

In Plymouth, Massachusetts, the celebration of the 350th anniversary of the arrival of the Pilgrims lasted more than a year, going from September 12,

1970 (the approximate anniversary of the *Mayflower*'s departure from England in 1620) through to Thanksgiving 1971. For one of the earliest events in 1970, the Commonwealth of Massachusetts invited the Wampanoag tribe to provide a speaker for a banquet celebrating the Pilgrims' landing and the first Thanksgiving. The tribe chose Wampsutta, an Aquinnah Wampanoag activist and leader, who also went by the name Frank James. Beforehand, state officials asked Wampsutta for an advance copy of his remarks, and upon reading them decided that his speech was not appropriate for the *celebratory* nature of the event. When Wampsutta refused to read an alternative speech prepared for him by a state official, the event organizers "disinvited" him from the banquet. At this point, he left the event and proceeded to the "hill near the statue of Massasoit, who [w]as the leader of the Wampanoags when the Pilgrims landed in their territory." There, overlooking a replica of the *Mayflower* in Plymouth Harbor, Wampsutta gave his speech to "eight or ten Indians and their supporters."[19]

Here is a selection of key excerpts of the speech, which he had prepared for a mostly nonindigenous, white American audience:

> It is with mixed emotion that I stand here to share my thoughts. This is a time of celebration for you—celebrating an anniversary of a beginning for the white man in America. A time of looking back, of reflection. It is with a heavy heart that I look back upon what happened to my People. . . .
>
> We, the Wampanoag, welcomed you, the white man, with open arms, little knowing that it was the beginning of the end; that before 50 years were to pass, the Wampanoag would no longer be a free people. . . .
>
> What happened in those short 50 years? What has happened in the last 300 years? History gives us facts and there were atrocities; there were broken promises—and most of these centered around land ownership. . . .
>
> You the white man are celebrating an anniversary. We the Wampanoags will help you celebrate in the concept of a beginning. It was the beginning of a new life for the Pilgrims. Now, 350 years later it is a beginning of a new determination for the original American: the American Indian. . . .
>
> We are determined, and our presence here this evening is living testimony that this is only the beginning of the American Indian,

particularly the Wampanoag, to regain the position in this country
that is rightfully ours.

Wampsutta[20]

First, the decision by Massachusetts state officials to reject this speech as
inappropriate for this public commemoration is an example of collective
disavowal. There is no evidence that the speech was rejected because state
officials disagreed with or were unaware of the history as Wampsutta presented it. This is not a case of collective amnesia and thus a lack of memory.
It is a matter of Wampsutta's remarks not aligning with the particular collective memory that the representatives of the white settler nation were
seeking to produce and affirm through this extended series of calendrical
commemorations of the Pilgrims. And in this regard Wampsutta spoke
most directly to and about the production of racialized and colonialist collective memory: "This is a time of celebration for you . . . an anniversary
of a beginning for the white man in America." Here he explicitly calls forth
the threshold of conquest and its constitutive place in the political temporality of white settler rule; this is the beginning for the white settler society.

With his speech, Wampsutta confrontationally engages the politics of
collective memory at a moment when Plymouth, Massachusetts, and the
United States as a whole was celebrating this narrative of the settler-colonial
founding that had by the late twentieth century taken its place in the habit-
memory of American political culture. To recall and adapt Benjamin's
words, Thanksgiving is another example of the "same day that keeps recurring in the guise of holidays," offering little evidence of "historical consciousness" as the tropes, performances, and rituals of the holiday recur like
a motor mechanism, a memory that repeats rather than one that seriously
recollects or imagines. But Wampsutta's words also take a turn toward
problematizing this narrative of the political time of the settler society and
the American nation, two distinct but intertwined temporalities. He does
this by referring to the "white man . . . celebrating an anniversary" and in
the very next sentence asserting that "we the Wampanoags will help you
celebrate in the concept of a beginning." The key here is his construction
of "a beginning" as a *concept*, seeing it as a notion subject to political construction and reiteration, rather than a hard and fast marker in political
time or in collective memory. In this way, Wampsutta is seeking to unstructure American political temporality. Like many indigenous political actors,

Wampsutta refuses to concede to the "white man" the temporality of political life and thus political authority over this land. Wampsutta pivots the tone of the speech from one of loss to one of political intervention by asserting that this is a time for "the beginning of a new life for the original American, the American Indian." In that phrasing he calls forth the threshold of conquest while also claiming a place for indigenous political life in the contemporary moment, contesting the habit-memory that legitimates the sovereign status of the U.S. settler majority.

In all, Wampsutta's speech calls out the racialized and colonialist mnemonics that drive and are habitually reproduced by the calendrical commemoration of Thanksgiving. In so doing, he sheds light on the role of the habit-memory of conquest as a component of the political temporality legitimizing the contemporary status of U.S. statism and nationhood. For Wampsutta, the Thanksgiving and Pilgrim-landing celebration is not fundamentally about white settlers celebrating a beginning consigned to the past. Rather, it is a calendrical commemoration that re-marks that threshold of conquest in the present as a habitually recurring marker of white Euro-American authority in and over this territory. The habituated annual celebration of the Pilgrims makes the past part of the present again, refounding the settler society in the contemporary moment. Granted, this was one speech in front of a very small audience, but I examine it closely to reveal the history and meaning behind the now annual act of indigenous and allied resistance to Thanksgiving that got its start with Wampsutta.

Wampsutta's action began the annual National Day of Mourning that takes place on Cole's Hill, above Plymouth Rock, on every U.S. Thanksgiving. In the words of organizers of the fortieth annual National Day of Mourning in 2009, United American Indians of New England, "Many Native Americans do not celebrate the arrival of the Pilgrims and other European settlers. Thanksgiving day is a reminder of the genocide of millions of Native people, the theft of Native lands, and the relentless assault on Native culture. Participants in National Day of Mourning honor Native ancestors and the struggles of Native peoples to survive today. It is a day of remembrance and spiritual connection as well as a protest of the racism and oppression which Native Americans continue to experience."[21] This is an engagement with the politics of the calendar as a form of resistance. The indigenous activists here are seeking to dehabituate the collective memory that structures the political temporality expressed and further legitimized through U.S. calendrical commemorations. Unstructuring politics here

means that these activists are seeking to fire at the dials in order to politicize
this day, to make a point of political contention the American collective
memory of Thanksgiving as a day that habitually signifies the tropes and
practices of sharing, unity, gratitude, and plenitude. By contrast, to many
indigenous people and their allies, Thanksgiving symbolizes "genocide,"
"theft of Native lands," and "assault on Native culture." As such a symbol,
on the day that the majority of the U.S. population enjoyed a feast, Wampanoag leader Russell Peters said that "instead we decided to fast and show
by contrast our way of remembering our history."[22] Peters puts the politics
and symbolism of collective memory at the center of the meaning of this
indigenous day of calendrical-commemorative resistance; indigenous people fast as a form of remembrance while the white settler nation feasts, they
mourn while the majority of the United States celebrates. In this way, the
National Day of Mourning fires at the dials of the political time of settler
statism, trying to dehabituate the repetitive trajectory of the annual
refounding of conquest and thereby place it into the realm of political contest, which refuses the notion that the "past is dead."

This effort to compel avowal by unstructuring U.S. political time did
not end with the effort to politicize the colonialist and settler practices
subtending the Thanksgiving celebration. In their literature for the National
Day of Mourning, the United American Indians also pointed out that the
U.S. calendrical commemoration of Plymouth and the Pilgrims elides an
earlier marker of the threshold of conquest, that of the Jamestown Colony
of Virginia, founded in 1607: "Here is the truth: The reason they talk about
the pilgrims and not an earlier English-speaking colony, Jamestown, is that
in Jamestown the circumstances were way too ugly to hold up as an effective national myth. For example, the white settlers in Jamestown turned to
cannibalism to survive. Not a very nice story to tell the kids."[23] This reference to "cannibalism" and "surviv[ing]" is to the so-called Starving Time
for the Jamestown colonists, which occurred from 1609 to 1610 when the
Powhatan Confederacy sought to isolate and starve the colonists into leaving. Along with this "not very nice story" of seventeenth-century settler-
indigenous relations, Jamestown is also a central U.S. historical signifier of
slavery. In 1619 the first African slaves to North America were brought to
Jamestown, making the colony a vital port of entry for the slave trade as
well as a thriving slave-based tobacco economy in its own right. The purpose of the United American Indians' reference to Jamestown is to further
dehabituate the collective memory produced through the Thanksgiving

celebration. These protestors see American disavowal not only of the colonialist violence and dispossession that occurred in New England but also of the earlier memory of European colonial settlement and slave trading in the land that would become the United States. This is the threshold of conquest marking both the violence toward and dispossession of indigenous nations and the violence toward and enslavement of African people.

Now, on the surface, one could see the elision of Jamestown from U.S. calendrical commemorations as a case of collective amnesia, rather than disavowal. But to see this as an act of disavowal one need only take note of an effort at elite consolidation of U.S. political time made by a recent U.S. president in the wake of a nationally prominent crisis. On September 15, 2005, in the wake of Hurricane Katrina, which devastated the U.S. Gulf Coast, in particular the city of New Orleans, President George W. Bush gave a televised speech to the nation from Jackson Square in the heart of New Orleans. In the speech, Bush engages in the politics of collective memory when he puts the Katrina tragedy in historical perspective: "In the life of this nation, we have often been reminded that nature is an awesome force, and all life is fragile. We're the heirs of men and women who lived through those first terrible winters at Jamestown and Plymouth, who rebuilt Chicago after the fire, and San Francisco after a great earthquake, who reclaimed the prairie from the dust bowl of the 1930s. Every time, the people of this land have come back from fire, flood, and storm to build anew, and to build better than what we had before. Americans never left our destiny to the whims of nature and we will not start now."[24] Commenting on Bush's first historical referents in this part of his speech, Simon Stow asserts that "it is, of course, clear *whose* ancestors survived at Jamestown and Plymouth."[25] No one could defensibly claim that Bush's construction of the "we" of the "ancestral survivors" of these noted winters includes indigenous people in any meaningful sense, and since African slaves were not part of the "Starving Time" at Jamestown, it is certainly not their descendants *to* whom Bush is speaking and *for* whom he is producing a national collective memory that temporally entwines these noted historical tragedies with the one in 2005.

This mnemonic reference to Jamestown and Plymouth is of particular note given the fact that Hurricane Katrina disproportionately killed and displaced people of color, in particular African Americans. As Stow reads it, "Bush's was a strategy of forgetting whose intended audience [was] not the victims of the storm, but rather those who had to watch it on television."[26] I concur with Stow's assessment of the audience; certainly Bush's concern was to shape the perspective of the U.S. population—majority white—who viewed but were not directly harmed by the Katrina disaster. But for this very reason I do not see this as a "strategy of forgetting"; rather, in the politics of collective memory, it is a strategy of active and productive remembering through the structuring of American political time. I read Bush's discursive effort as productive of collective memory because he does not say "forget" the suffering of African Americans and the poor; in fact, earlier in the speech, he says, "As *all of us* saw on television, there is also some deep, persistent poverty in this region as well. And that poverty has roots in a history of racial discrimination, which cuts off generations from the opportunity of America."[27] Here, Bush is clear about his audience—the "all of us" who experienced Katrina through the television—while also referring explicitly to the race and class components of the crisis, granted, as a transition to advocating conservative solutions (e.g., business opportunity zones). Still, there is not a simple forgetting of race and class going on here. Instead, there is a productive form of remembering through a temporal narrative of the U.S. nation that says, at base: remember who *we* are, and what *we* have been through, from the time of Jamestown and Plymouth onward; *we* are their heirs, and *their* past of tragedy followed by survival is now *our* present. This is an effort to structure political time through collective memory to serve the purpose of elite consolidation of U.S. statist authority and national identity.

The distinction here between forgetting and remembering matters politically because to argue that Bush's speech was about forgetting claims to see a possible path for future leaders to nurture remembrance of the actual victims of the tragedy as a means to pursuing more progressive political ends. This would be the liberal rationalist approach that sees enlightenment through overcoming amnesia as the path toward justice. But the strategy of remembrance is more insidious than that, and more difficult to counter than with the naïve enlightenment approach. In this case, the strategy of productive remembering does not disavow the experience and suffering of the particular victims of Katrina, but rather it disavows that their experience and suffering defines the central narrative of what this crisis means for the nation as a whole. In this regard, given the profound nature of the Katrina disaster and the well-established failure of U.S. state institutions and actors at all levels, Bush's speech should thus be read as an iterative act of refounding, both at the national and statist level.

As it concerns refounding, recall Agamben's words: "The state of nature is, in truth, a state of exception, in which the city appears for an instant (which is at the same time a chronological interval and a nontemporal moment) *tanquam dissolute*. The foundation is thus not an event achieved once and for all but is continually operative in the civil state in the form of the sovereign decision." With justification, one could see Hurricane Katrina as a "state of exception" in the form of the "state of nature"—with state officials and institutions abandoning a city and its people—but then in an instant Bush calls forth the temporal threshold of the Jamestown and Plymouth crises and overcoming as the means of refounding the U.S. community not via the invocation of the borders of political space, these rendered vulnerable and quite literally porous by the crashing waves of Katrina, but rather through reference to the borders, marking points, and narratives of political time. Bush makes "continually operative" the foundation and thus sovereignty of the U.S. civil state by invoking the temporality and the temporal borders of Euro-American settlement on the continent. This "continually operative" dynamic is evident in the way Bush takes those extraordinary moments of Euro-American and U.S. history—Jamestown and Plymouth, the Chicago fire, San Francisco earthquake, the Depression-era prairies—and turns them into the ordinary of American political time, comprising, at once, recollection-memory and habit-memory. With this form of calendrical commemoration, these moments of exception do not undermine the political temporality structuring Euro-American and U.S. sovereignty. To the contrary, the mutually constitutive invocation of an exceptionalist narrative—"Americans never left our destiny to the whims of nature and we will not start now"—turns the mnemonics of tragedy into the contemporary triumph of American nationhood. The deployment of political time was much more critical to this production than was any referent to political space, as it was through collective memory and the invocation of temporality that Bush seeks to consolidate U.S. statist authority and national identity that appeared quite unstructured, even fraying, during and in the aftermath of Hurricane Katrina.

The words of President Bush are an appropriate way to conclude this discussion of the contemporary politics of calendars. This is because in modern U.S. history no political figure has worked as hard to make one day on the calendar stand for so much politically. That day, of course, is September 11, even more commonly referred to as 9/11. Bush's persistent invocation of the calendrical commemoration of September 11, 2001, invoked both the state of exception and American exceptionalism. But in recalling a day that was indeed quite extraordinary, each recurring reference to 9/11 turns the exceptional into the ordinary, the ad hoc into the annual, and the vivid images recalled in the memory of that day into a habituated referent to U.S. statist authority and American national exceptionalism.

In the wake of the attacks, Bush's persistent reference to 9/11 served to reproduce U.S. statism via the invocation, to recall Kantorowicz, of the "new fiction of a *perpetua necessitas* [permanent emergency] . . . the perpetuation of something that, by definition, indicated an exception." And just as the date of April 15 in the United States quickly calls to mind tax day and one's relationship to statism on this account, so now does September 11 call to mind terrorism and national security and thus one's relationship to statism in this regard. In particular, September 11 is a mnemonic device deployed to call forth a highly politicized temporal border in the story of U.S. national identity and statism, and to demand that the U.S. public "never forget" what this border signifies. This temporal border marks, seemingly, the threshold when "everything changed" on that day, as we often heard. But I would suggest that rather than marking this threshold at the year 2001, the invocation of September 11 is fast becoming a component of habit-memory that resides in temporal symmetry with the invocation of Thanksgiving, Columbus Day, and the Fourth in the collective memory of U.S. political culture. All of these calendrical signifiers reside in the American collective memory as, at once, "a chronological interval and a nontemporal moment"—as time and nontime politically, as a moment in historical time we can put a precise date on and, even more importantly, a moment that transcends simple historical time by constituting the more complex narrative of U.S. political time. Each of these calendrical commemorations on their own and in tandem with others habitually rearticulates the practice by which "foundation is thus not an event achieved once and for all but is continually operative in the civil state in the form of the sovereign decision."

What the politics of the calendar concerning September 11 demonstrates is that the politics of time is as important as that of space. The policing of the thresholds between past and present has as much to do with how majority polities seek to ward off and undermine resistance and political demands by marginalized groups as does the policing of the borders between a spatially defined inside and outside. Closer examination of the politics of the calendar can help to reveal the dynamics of collective memory in this regard, be it from the dominant perspective that seeks to habituate the production and practices of statism and nationhood or from the nondominant perspective that seeks to dehabituate and thereby unstructure these productions for the sake of opening and advocating alternative and even antagonistic ways of narrating and reimagining the past, present, and future of collective life.

Conclusion

In his study on the politics of memory, W. James Booth, drawing from Nicole Loraux, asserts that "the political is the final authority over collective memory."[28] However, I wonder if the opposite is more the case, or at least equally so; that is, might collective memory be the final authority over the political? What this essay has sought to show is that by interrogating the production and role of collective memory, we may be able to discern what gets to count as a subject of politics and what does not, and why. To put another way, that which is up for debate and what is not in our political lives may well be shaped by dominant collective memories in a manner that functionally predetermines, or severely limits, the transformative possibilities of political actions. This form of elite consolidation can and does occur through the structuring of the political time of statism and the nation. This dynamic is especially pertinent to the issue of persistent colonial and racial hierarchies and injustices in white settler contexts such as the United States. But to point to this dynamic is not to suggest a closed, impenetrable system. In examining the politics of collective memory, I seek to offer pathways toward unstructuring or seeing as unstructured those dominant political institutions, discourses, and practices that perpetuate, among other things, colonial and racial hierarchies. I make this point not to end on a falsely optimistic note but to suggest that the study of the politics of collective memory may offer as much insight on resistant forms of politics as on those forms that seek to consolidate boundaries and ward off contestation.

Chapter 11

Interest in the Absence of Articulation

Small Business and Islamist Parties in Algeria

Deborah Harrold

Several authoritarian regimes in the Middle East and North Africa were taken down in 2011, but this wave of challenges to strong states missed Algeria. In Algeria, large demonstrations in January 2011 and new efforts at political mobilization were overwhelmed by state security and could not continue. What Algeria lacked were the alliances built in other nations. Algeria's civil war (1993–2000) left deep rifts and mistrust between groups.[1] Profound dissatisfaction with the state and desire for change could not take the place of the political work, underground or in open, of bridging interests and shaping alliances among democratic forces, secularists, feminists, Berber activists, unions, Islamists, socialists, and those willing to challenge the state in the streets. Legislative elections of May 2012 showed voter support for President Abdelaziz Bouteflika and stability, supported by the regime's campaign of vigorous regional spending for the previous year and perhaps voter determination to head off Islamist victory.[2] The Islamic movement in Algeria has produced several parties since the late 1980s, parties that met different fates. In the early 1990s, rapid electoral success for a more radical Islamic party and explicit threats to regime elites encouraged the military to shut down political groups. In the course of the subsequent civil war, a much smaller liberal Islamic party in Algeria was able to gain ground. It became part of the government in 1997, gaining at once the benefits of inclusion and the risks of co-optation.

Islamic politics in Algeria has been studied largely as a political and cultural program, with economic positions assessed as minor or opportunistic.[3] While commitments to Islamic law and social conservatism may be central to Islamist parties' political projects, economic commitments are grounded in religious teachings and address the economic and symbolic interests of supporters. What parties growing out of Islamist movements have sought to do was bring outsiders into political alliances and articulate interests, shaping an Islamic identity that addressed economic interests of nonelites and those excluded from the petro-state's circulation of rent. While parties from Turkey's Islamist movement have become increasingly successful, Algerian Islamist parties have been less successful. As a result, the interests of their constituents remain largely unrepresented.

Beginning in Algeria in the late 1980s, the Front Islamique du Salut (FIS) appealed to smaller and medium-sized private-sector operators, those in the informal economy, urban poor, and a largely Arabic-speaking younger generation. It combined a moral attack on the Algerian state and its military elite as well as a moralized and economic vision.[4] In Turkey, a party emerging out of a diverse Islamist movement has been able to hold together an alliance based on regional business interests and nonelites while advancing largely liberal economic policies.[5] Both sets of parties emerged as soon as the state permitted particular forms of party organizations; the Turkish Islamic movement, older and with more political experience, also responded to repression and tested openings created by the state over time. These two trajectories benefit by comparison because they show the importance of interest articulation for Islamist politics and the effectiveness of Islamist movements in bridging interests on economic policy. More than that, they show the role of Islamist movements in *shaping* interests and identity, connecting actors and sectors to a shared Islamic narrative of nation in which previously excluded and less-valued groups gain new symbolic importance as they gain voice in politics. While the limits set by the state have conditioned the forms, moves, and fates of these parties—authorizing, banning, accepting alliances—the states and their ruling groups also have been transformed. While Islamist movements produce parties that cannot be reduced to economic policies, the economic policies show how these parties engage pragmatic issues and address concrete concerns of their supporters. Economic policies are where Islamist movements and parties bring moral commitments and Islamic interpretations to bear on concrete situations.

Drawing on Islamic reform and renewal before the twentieth century, as well as engaging the concerns of constituents through social welfare and educational engagements, the parties developing from Islamist movements in Algeria and Turkey reflect the consequences of a modernist Islamic identity. Co-opted into the government, as in the case of Algeria, or constituting the government, as in the case of Turkey, these parties show the intense learning and struggle that have reshaped public space and changed the way the state interacts with the opposition. In other words, not only have these parties responded to new possibilities through state openings; they have been part of more fundamental changes in the larger political field and that most powerful institution, the state.

Theoretical Engagements

While theoretical commitments and assumptions determine what we choose to study, how we explain, and what we determine is important, the political world continues to astonish us. Events such as the Arab Spring, Islamist electoral victories, the robust success of the Turkish economy, and the inclusion of Islamists in the Algerian government have challenged analysts. We scholars continually expect too much of theory and commit to its elaboration, while actors and agents of all kinds seek to adapt any rule, structure, or practice to new use. The drive to generalize and overspecify, which insists "we need to know under what conditions," misses the creativity and risk in underground strategies, or the value of persistence and negotiation, of apparent but imperfect compliance.

In Algeria and Turkey, as the state opened strategically to permit new forms of politics (more open elections) and new actors (an opposition, or an Islamic public presence), it was transformed. All is moving: the ideas, identities, interests, and state itself. The theoretical approaches used by scholars pushing the boundaries of historical institutionalism offer ways of recognizing and understanding change outside binary frames of structure and rupture, encouraging us to examine the importance of intellectual work, of the use of history as a resource, of learning how to negotiate structures, of tactics within and around institutions, themselves also undergoing transformation. This approach is particularly useful for considering the Middle East and North Africa, where statist and materialist orientations dominate explanations of stability for scholars, and cultural explanations have been left to more popular accounts.[6] The structure or institutions are transformed; the state is now governed by Islamists, or includes Islamists. While the state always had the potential for greater force, for violence, it has been politicked out of its earlier position through creative use of institutional possibilities.

This chapter is based on fieldwork in Algeria, by others and me, and makes a limited comparison with Turkey.[7] Its understanding of structure and institutions is marked by Algerian and Turkish interpretations and experiences. Algerian scholars are seldom far from Marx, except when they deploy liberal arguments to decenter a deep state and its dominance of the economy.[8] Turkish scholars have been largely formed by the dominant Kemalist ideology, a republican secularism, except where they reflect regional or Islamic counternarratives. Turkish analysts invented the term *deep state* (*derin devlet*). Both national intellectual traditions emphasize enduring institutions, be they colonial or republican or the state-centered economy; for Algeria, change must be rupture.

So the continual expansion of Turkish political space, Hakan Yavuz argues, through expanding education and electoral mobilization, from urban elites to regional elites and rural subalterns, brought an Islamic vernacularized modernity into public space and politics.[9] Daniel Lerner's classic formulation of modernity—drawn from the Turkish case—foregrounded the result of education, political mobilization, and travel from rural areas of local elite control to cosmopolitan and urban settings of citizen participation. The canonical changes of modernization have been supplemented and transformed into something unexpected. The incorporation of Turks beyond a largely secular republican elite brought Islamic commitments back into public space. Islam itself has been reconfigured and renewed as well as carried forward from its early twentieth-century forms. Lloyd Rudolph and Susanne Hoeber Rudolph have emphasized the dense uses made of traditional practices and ideas in the construction of modern and modernist projects; people use traditional forms and ideas to advance themselves in new forums; they deploy traditional ideas to reconfigure the possibilities of modernity.[10] In particular, they reconfigure the possibilities of modernity where they have been shut out, using traditional ideas to bridge divides between people and the possibilities of power, to make alliances, to imagine themselves in new places. Both imaginative creativity and pragmatic strategies are part of the project. The projectivity of politics theorized by Mustafa Emirbayer and Ann Mische is an abstraction of the use activists make of history and tradition, imagining themselves into modernity as themselves, within their history.[11] This process of radical and unexpected change, launched by the addition of culturally particular features to an ostensibly universal modernity, follows the logic Jacques Derrida offers us in the idea of the supplement: that which being added to something may change it, by accretion and by substitution. The Derridian supplement, in other words, is not just an addition but an addition that may transform.[12] Drawing specifically from recent Turkish history, Alev Çinar argues that the Islamist use of the past offers a critique of the contemporary in order to imagine an Islamic modernity.[13]

Algeria's postcolonial state dominated the economy and everything else, sustained by hydrocarbon rents, and obliged everyone to "think structurally."[14] A fairly opaque ruling group, a black box, "les forces occultes," or simply "le pouvoir" or "as-sulta," encouraged more structuralist habits of mind. In Adlène Meddi's wicked little noir novel about Algeria, the terrifying ruling group is known only to itself, and its name is Structure.[15] But the Algerian state has made unexpected openings and gambits: a liberal opening, a democratic opening, a presidential alliance.[16] These events required that the black box split, or at least crack. Power struggles—coups and expulsions, different strategies concerning the economy, or political opening, or Islamists, or different assessments of the past and different visions for the future—have split the state, giving us a black box that surprises.

Despite the size of the Algerian state's hydrocarbon economy, the informal economy remains an object of concern, today a front line of the state's struggle to control the economy. Algerian economist Ahmed Henni noted the relationship between the state and the informal: *L'informal interroge, en réalité, la nature de l'Etat.*[17] This suggests a structuring, a relationship between the state's regulation and the response, but to interrogate is a more flexible interaction. Henni notes that what the informal economy introduces is something outside the state and its logic; the informal introduces and represents a "social logic," the demands and projects of Algerians as consumers, savers, investors. All these empirical challenges and theoretical efforts demand a poststructuralist position: in the end, it's the economy, but it's never the end.[18] "Never bet against the state" is often good advice: but the underground does. Liberalization in the late 1980s proceeded through lack of enforcement as much as new regulation; it was always uneven.[19] The state controls all hard currency transactions, but permitted a black market in hard currency during the war. Structure is continually dominant and continuously evaded.

Michel de Certeau's elaboration of tactics and strategies by which people negotiate or struggle through structures, by using clever tricks, ancient ruses, ways of speaking, appropriating and insinuating—bricolage—makes clear that all these are the normal and continuous ways of operating in and around and through structures.[20] Practices are "a dark sea from which successive institutions emerge, a maritime immensity on which socioeconomic and political structures appear as ephemeral islands."[21] All informal market operators understand their project as bricolage; the word is as natural to them as colloquial Arabic or Kabyle. "Consumers are transformed into immigrants," notes Certeau, writing when Algerians working in France traveled home with a tire in each hand. With his emphasis on bricolage as combat, hunter's tricks, the protean adversary, Certeau reminds us continually that we are dealing with a reflexive and strategic political world in which practices and strategies never cease, as opposed to a world where people struggle within institutional rules.

Islamic Ideas, Islamic Renewal, and a Modern Islamic Identity

Articulating a modern Islamic identity and articulating economic interests have been crucial to the success of Islamist parties. A commitment to modernity and progress is bound into nationalist commitments to education and real economic development. In addition, an Islamic identity has remained important for much of the population. In Algeria, while economic concerns were crucial to voter support for the Front Islamique du Salut, the major Islamist party in Algeria in the early 1990s, the leading spokesmen for the FIS were preachers who appealed to Algerians in terms of Islam's commitment to economic justice and a moral critique against corruption.[22]

What then, is the connection between Islamic appeals and economic policy? In much of the Islamic world, Islamic movements have sustained opposition to authoritarianism in part because of their effective mobilization of economically marginal groups. They have made dramatic electoral gains when elections have been open. They have generally benefited from voters' wish to punish negative economic growth and generally underperforming economies in the 1990s. While some analysts argue that Islamic economics is of little material importance[23] and that the economic policies of Islamist parties are merely opportunist,[24] the relative electoral success of Islamist parties and their support from private economic interests are more than the result of short-term strategic alliances. Islamist parties take policy positions and periodically show their ability to aggregate interests, reaffirming Islamic arguments about the economy.

Islamic Economics

Islamic economics as a modern discourse has been formed by theoretical writings and by practices and policies shaped to meet the demands of Islamic law for financial markets. Abdul A'la Mawdudi[25] and Sayyid Qutb[26] advanced basic positions on Islamic economics that shaped the field beginning in the 1930s. They emphasized Islam as the middle way between communism and capitalism, affirming private property rights while embedding them in social responsibilities; Qutb particularly contributed a strong social justice commitment. The Muslim Brothers, founded in Egypt in the 1929, was a *mass* organization that drew on reformist and popular Islam. The organization also did pragmatic economic work, founding new companies[27] and trying to keep Egyptian workers, factory owners, and rising middle classes in alliance.[28]

Alan Richards and John Waterbury divide the Islamic economic field into two orientations, one focusing on narrow responses to specific Islamic law demands, the other seeking to address the broader question of what Islam demands of the economy.[29] Both the Algerian and the Turkish Islamist parties have subordinated these theoretical orientations to an engagement with political realities and the interests and demands of their constituents. Today's economic discourses relay and reinterpret modern Islamic economics through critique of contemporary ideas and practices. They have contributed to a revaluing of private economic activity, especially smaller-scale activities that had less weight in modernist visions.

The Islamic movement in Algeria dates from the Islamic reform movement in the late nineteenth century and early twentieth that drew on the intellectual antecedents of the Muslim Brothers, the salafi movement. While the term *salafi* suggests a kind of neotraditionalism, as *salaf* refers to pious ancestors, the salafi movement was intensely rationalist and modernist, insisting on reading and interpretation instead of memorization and commentary. Engagement with the challenges to the Muslim world—weakness, backwardness, and imperialism—was a major part of salafi teaching.[30] Begun as an elite movement, the salafi movement expanded though the work of intellectual renewal into broader educational commitments.[31] While salafi commitments sometimes competed and sometimes cooperated with sufi and nationalist sympathies, it is hard to overestimate the importance of this intellectual and educational movement in Islam.

In most Islamic countries there were local intellectuals—organic intellectuals if you will—who engaged with salafi ideas and struggled against their local agents of superstition, ignorance, and imperialism. Some were able to negotiate distinguished careers; others suffered from persecution by traditional religious elites, French colonial authorities, or new nationalists. The Algerian scholar Ahmed Ben Badis (1889–1940) began with a traditional religious education in his home city, Constantine, and traveled to Mecca and Cairo where he met others concerned with reform and renewal of Islam.[32] Returning to Algeria, he committed to teaching in and engagement with the difficult political field of colonial Algeria, founding newspapers and schools. He contributed to a rising nationalist cohort and inspired another generation of reformers and nationalists. He was one of the founders of the Algerian Association of Ulama, an organization that would articulate and consolidate the salafi movement in Algeria.

Algerian reformers founded the Association of Ulama only a year after the Muslim Brothers organization was founded in Egypt. Preoccupied with cultural issues and education, the Association of Ulama did not create a mass political organization like the Muslim Brothers and would have been unable to do so in the French colonial environment, where the field of Islam was intensely policed. Shortly before the War of Independence began in 1954, an Algerian Muslim Brothers group was organized, but it was caught between the constraints of war and the postwar monopolization of authority by the new Algerian state.[33] Within this Islamic field, Algerian reformers devoted considerable attention to criticizing and attacking sufi orders and practitioners, accusing them of superstitious and un-Islamic practices and collaboration. While sufi orders had been at the center of resistance to French power at an earlier historical moment, resistant orders had been destroyed and cooperative ones placed under French control. Although these developments certainly contributed to the creation of Algeria's nationalists, the Association of Ulama's long-term effects might be best seen in the Algerian educational system and in the general constitution of a modernist and rational Islam.[34] In contrast to the Turkish Islamist movement, which has done a better job of incorporating traditionalist and sufi commitments into the larger project, Algeria's Islamist movement has been characterized by rigor and what its opponents see as intolerance.

Electoral Politics: Translating Power, Articulating Interests, Making Alliances, Reshaping the State

Electoral politics translates economic, political, and social power into governance. Parties compete for votes; structured forms of representation produce general governance. Powerful stakeholders—the existing regime, former single governing parties, state bureaucrats, military forces in their diversity—seek to appropriate or overthrow the results of elections, refusing some outcomes and producing others. While opposition parties are shaped by the rules, rules alone do not make them. They win, unexpectedly sometimes, as in Algeria in 1990 and 1992 (they also did well after 1995). They regroup and come back in new forms after repression, interpellating their supporters as well as their opponents with an altered narrative.

In Algeria, electoral politics is barely twenty years old. Elections have been cancelled, nullified, and boycotted. They still suffer from the suspicion of irrelevance. A military-bureaucratic regime,[35] a bunker state,[36] an army state if not a police state,[37] Algeria began its transformation from the top. In the mid-1980s, as oil prices were down, the ruling group began holding in-party seminars on the country's economic difficulties. Through political opening, this group sought to renew its legitimacy and to build public support for economic restructuring. By October 1988, strikes all over the country and demonstrations that turned into short, sharp urban rebellion convinced the regime and most Algerians that change was necessary. New laws permitted new associations, independent from the state. This opening was eagerly seized by all participants and the first open municipal elections were held in 1990.

The most successful party was the FIS, which rapidly outdistanced other Islamic parties with its mass appeal. While most parties were organized around an important individual, the FIS had two major spokesmen: an older academic who projected calmness, Abbassi Madani (1931–), and a passionate preacher, Ali Belhaj (1956–), understood as uncompromising by his supporters and enemies. The FIS had a clear program, a social welfare branch, and an effective organization. Its victories first in municipal elections in 1991 surprised everyone. Subsequent national elections had new rules that sought to reduce FIS power. They did not appear to work and despite the new rules and a large number of arrests, the FIS once again dominated the election, winning a majority of seats for the National Assembly in 1992.

A military-bureaucratic coup banned the party and shut down political opposition. The nation careened into civil war. In addition to fighters supporting the FIS (Armée Islamique du Salut), a new force appeared including fighters returned from Afghanistan, the Groupe Islamique Armé. The Groupe Islamique introduced new savagery, and its main targets included the Armée Islamique and other Islamists. The state fielded a ferocious counterterrorism project and perhaps committed its own war crimes. The casualties are unknown; over 250,000 Algerians may have been killed. By 1997, the Armée Islamique stood down, in response to the continual and apparently inexplicable civilian massacres in rural areas and internal struggles. The regime was relatively successful; the Islamic resistance split into small armed groups that were more focused on extracting resources locally than challenging the state.[38] By 1997, after struggles in the regime, General Liamane Zeroual put together secret negotiations and a national reconciliation program to offer limited amnesty to fighters. It has been a successful policy; fighting has been largely repressed and the level of violence reduced to episodic.

Yet while the violence was still intense, in 1995, the regime initiated new elections. Such is the power of the idea of elections that continuing indefinitely under appointed military leadership was not possible. The Groupe Islamique demanded a boycott, with the slogan "one vote one bullet."[39] While Zeroual won, as expected or planned, the smaller liberal Muslim Brother Party did well, gaining 25 percent of the votes, perhaps due to its ability to gain the votes of former FIS supporters. The Muslim Brother Party was originally known by its acronym HAMAS (often styled "Hamas"), but post-FIS rules banned religious parties and the party became the Mouvement pour une Société de la Paix (MSP). In 1997, in elections for the National Assembly, the MSP gained enough votes (almost 15 percent) to gain a role in the government. So during a war against Islamists, the state took Islamists into the government. By 2004, this party was drawn into the executive branch through a "presidential alliance" that included the former ruling party (the Front National de Libération) as well as a new political party drawn from the Front National that was backed by the military elite, Rassemblement Nationale Démocratique. Through its new role in the presidential alliance, the MSP gained the portfolios of several ministries; since that time it has held the portfolios for the Labor, Agriculture, Fisheries, Commerce, Tourism, and Small and Medium Enterprises Ministries. While the MSP has lost its role as an opposition party in exchange for a very subordinate role in the government, it now has portfolios with the influence and patronage that come from the insider role.

In both Turkey and Algeria, earlier political victories for the parties coming out of the Islamist movement were annulled and political organizations destroyed. Through new organizations and new leadership and by engaging in more politics, these groups entered arenas restricted to them previously. The FIS had dominated public space, threatened feminists and Berber activists, and announced its determination to persecute Algeria's corrupt military elite. While several of its Algerian political opponents remained committed to open politics and supported FIS participation in the face of the coup, the FIS had intimidated and threatened other groups.[40] Its commitment to multiparty democracy was not clear and its willingness to occupy public space warned the regime that it would not be a silent partner in politics. While the AK Party in Turkey (Adalet ve Kalkinma Partisi, or Truth and Justice Party) has been the ruling party since 2002, the Algerian liberal party, the MSP, remains the weakest party in that country's group of three parties. It has never captured the same high level of votes and participation as the banned Islamic front party, the FIS. But through its continued participation and acquisition of ministerial portfolios, the party is expanding access to the state and bringing into the government a different leadership group. These longer-term stories include important interest-based support; they are not merely about strategy and ideology. But ideology concerns interest; commitment and interest need not be regarded separately.

The Turkish case is one of real success; the AK government has been in power for over a decade. While earlier Islamist parties were unable to negotiate the limits set by Turkey's military, the AK Party is assimilating to the Turkish state. It has weathered serious efforts to displace it, including two legal campaigns and two conspiracies based in the military. The Algerian case is one of qualified persistence; the civil war reshaped the Islamist movement. But as cautious insiders, the MSP has more difficulty advocating for its constituents. It is obliged to keep its critique internal to the government. As economic policy is made by the regime with the National Assembly asked to support rather than debate, the MSP cannot both articulate the interests of private sector economic actors and be a strong opposition party.[41]

Algeria's Politicized Economy

The dramatic struggle for the state in Algeria has been a conflict over the cultural orientation of the country as well as a struggle for the state, the direction of the economy, and who should have access to it. Several scholars have marked the importance of material interests; those who were largely excluded from the benefits of the existing order composed the opposition to the state: the small and medium private sector, workers, operators in the informal economy, the unemployed, and a large part of the younger generation.[42] We would have to add to that part of the government that split and sought to transform Algeria's closed and state-controlled economy into a more open one.[43] The struggle over the shape of the state emerged in the late eighties, as the Algerian experiment with state-driven economic development and political centralization gave way to a decade of economic and political liberalization.[44] The state-driven economic model, in place since independence, had emphasized state ownership, heavy industry, foreign expertise, and limited investment in agriculture and consumer goods.[45] Modernity was a major value in this vision of the economy and intellectuals were privileged supporters of the modern state. While some Islamic figures opposed the state's efforts at land reform, for many mobilized Algerians, including intellectuals, students, peasants, and workers, socialist values and modernity were compatible with Islam.[46] Those Islamic figures who opposed the state's pressure against private property through land reform were cast as backward, feudal, unable to be modern.[47]

Islamic institutions were controlled by the state before and after independence. Colonial rulers had appropriated the funds of pious foundations. Mosques were state property and religious functionaries were paid by the state.[48] General postcolonial practice followed this pattern as well. Modernizing authoritarians in newly independent states did not relinquish this control, but there was more dissent or difference in the system. There were Islamic figures who confronted the state and a wider range of views than the model of a state-controlled Islam would suggest.[49]

Before the coup in 1992 that ended the electoral process and banned the FIS, political space in Algeria seemed wide open. The FIS had won

power in municipal elections in 1990, television journalists on state television asked blunt questions of officials, and the press was no less open. Talk
radio allowed Algerians to air their grievances frankly. Between the 1980s
and early 1990s, academics pursued the topic of economic reform with a
vengeance; Berber activism had spread from intellectuals to a mass movement; feminists, communists, and human rights activists claimed public
space. Independent associations of all sorts, including business organizations, tested the possibilities of influence.[50] Islamists expanded from university and popular bases.[51] Algeria's press was lively and critical with dozens
of titles published in French and Arabic. The demonstrations got bigger all
the time. Democracy, or something like it, had arrived. When the army
came back into politics so forcefully in late 1992, politics moved into the
restrained struggle of facade parties and limited opposition, on the one
hand, and the realm of war, on the other.

Against this background of political effervescence, I want to outline cultural orientations and the relationships to social structures that are harder
to trace. Parts of the private sector, some of them well connected to the
state, others less so, have remained unmoved by appeals from a politicized
Islamic movement. Secular or observant, keeping the Ramadan fast or not,
they have not been mobilized on behalf of Islamic parties. Other private-
sector economic operators, in construction or family businesses such as
textile and jewelry and the former mujahid entrepreneurs,[52] have been more
likely to seek Islamic forms for the cultural and interest expression. Private
funds contributed to mosque building in many parts of the country, marking the importance of an Islamic legitimation of private wealth.[53] And the
private sector expanded rapidly in the uneven liberalization of the late
1980s and early 1990s despite severe critique.[54]

Luis Martinez, who has the distinction of having done fieldwork during the civil war, identifies an alliance of the refused between Islamist
activists and smaller private operators, both groups operating under official exclusion and intermittent repression. He distinguishes between the
small private business operators, usually involved in a small family business, and the former mujahidin because the latter have state contacts. He
draws attention to the way some of these mujahid-business figures situate
themselves within traditional Islamic forms of legitimacy. He offers the
example of a man he calls "Hadj Sadok," a former guerilla who has built
a business empire based on his status as a mujahid and on his state contacts.[55] From a trading family before the war of independence, Hadj Sadok

and his brothers began with a home business producing wafers. He expanded his business with family members and appropriated properties from former settlers; state contacts enabled him to diversify into very different areas. His wealth and prominence found Islamic expression. Hadj Sadok had made the pilgrimage to Mecca more than once, hence the title "Hadj." He considered himself obliged to contribute to the building of beautiful mosques, especially from the profits of his Hadj. He bought gold in Saudi Arabia for resale in Algeria, where a state monopoly has created in informal market in gold. He funded a network of young trabendists; as trabendo was the main form of youth employment in the area, this enhanced his importance and his role as a benefactor.[56] Martinez notes that Hadj Sadok's eventual support of the FIS enhanced his legitimacy: "FIS councilors . . . were quick to point out how, in the Koran, trade is encouraged and poverty denigrated."[57]

Not all larger business operators were regarded so favorably. Those who have not demonstrated their social engagement may be regarded as "the Mafia," an accusation that emphasizes their connections to the state that supports their profitability, or less criminally as "the legal trabendists."[58] Economic interest does not create Islamic identification; instead we see a kind of class fracturing based on proximity to or distance from the Algerian state. Discursive struggles that identify a virtuous private sector against that which is cast as opportunistic, parasitic, or corrupt characterize much of Algerian discussion of the economy.[59]

In addition to men like Hadj Sadok, mujahid-business figures, Martinez notes the importance of small commercial businesspeople, "butchers, bakers, grocers, hardware merchants and above all jewelers," in supporting the Islamist political party.[60] Many were already at odds with the state over urban development, as they often lived and worked in buildings on land sold to them illegally (often by mujahid-business operators with contacts with state authorities). And many resented the state's allocation of subsidized goods that they needed for their work. Price controls and bribes to officials who allocated subsidized or monopoly goods (basic foodstuffs as well as gold) forced them to operate in the informal economy; they resented their capricious exclusion in favor of bigger operators. Marginalization, lack of respect, absence of value for the state's vision of the economy, poor treatment from state officials on a daily basis—these mark the relationship between small business and the Algerian state, even well past the state's post-1990 commitment to a more open economy.

Ethnography of Economic Lives

The lives of individuals in one extended Algerian family, encountered in
my own fieldwork in 1993, dramatize the meaning of the abstract terms
"class fragmentation" and "discursive formation." They were from a small
city in western Algeria. Up through the 1980s, the family of brothers had
lived separately, as some worked in other cities, but a multistory villa served
as a family base. Before the Algerian War of Independence, any son with
intellectual aptitude was sent to the Islamic university in Kairowan,
Morocco. The father died after independence and left several children. The
oldest son became a successful public-sector manager. He built the large
villa, three stories, with a small apartment on top for his mother and aunt.
Another son pursued an advanced scientific degree and had a major position with a large state enterprise. Another son went into education. Sofiane,
the youngest son, had less interest in academics. His father purchased a
shop for him in the wholesale candy sector so he would be able to make a
living for himself.

By the early 1990s, the strains on state enterprises, uneven economic
reforms, and uneven hydrocarbon prices restructured the family. The older
brothers, state employees, suffered from the diminished buying power of
their salaries and the general collapse of the underfinanced public sector.
Sofiane's candy business was increasingly profitable. When the public-
sector manager died suddenly, the youngest became the de facto head of
the family, taking increasing financial responsibility for his brother's family
and the others as political and economic changes buffeted the family. Jobs
were lost, people were in hiding. Funds had to be managed and family
members gotten out of the country.

Sofiane, the baby of the family, became increasingly important for his
family as the private sector gained vis-à-vis public-sector employment. In
the language of Algeria's modernist vision, this was absurd. Sofiane had no
business education, no formal financial plan, no business organization, and
no marketing studies.[61] He enjoyed sitting in the door of his shop, looking
out on the world and greeting his acquaintances. His small warehouse was
minimally equipped; his security system was a knife in the cash box. He
preferred to read one Arabic newspaper that has short articles; he is not
interested in analysis, or what he referred to as "more than one version of
the story."

Sofiane had married with an eye to gaining a business asset. He worked through a family member, a teacher, to identify a suitable young woman. Sofiane was very proud of her; she was a mathematics valedictorian as well as a stunning beauty. They did not meet until the marriage was arranged. Outside the home, his wife was never unescorted. She dressed modestly but smartly and wore a modern form of veiling that covered her hair. While Sofiane would not permit his wife to work outside the home, and did not want her to start the embroidery business that she wanted, he did not oppose women working in principle. One of his steady customers was a woman who ran a candy kiosk with her disabled husband. Sofiane thought the world of her and spoke with compassion about their situation. Female relatives sought advanced degrees or worked outside the home, while living in the villa; the family was diverse in social and political commitments.

Sofiane's immediate family preferred Middle Eastern music; they avoided the lively but often suggestive rai music that Algeria is famous for. They did not drink and had little interest in Europe. It was not their cultural model. Nor did they live an imported or intellectual mode of Islam. Sofiane did not read the work of modern Islamic scholars nor participate in politics. Instead, he became increasingly involved in local business, reinvesting funds, seeking profits in an economy where the inefficiency of the banking sector encourages informal and speculative practices. While the older brothers had developed intellectual capital for particular economies, economic policy turbulence and political events greatly reduced the value of their education and put their families at risk. They and most of their children have emigrated, becoming French or Canadian. Sofiane's children will probably remain Algerian, as family assets may be able to underwrite their own private-sector activities. The candy wholesale business, originally seen as appropriate for the least capable son, became the most important factor economically because the larger economy was transformed. Sofiane's cultural vision—patriarchal, arabophone, traditionally Muslim, not oriented toward Europe as the model of modernity—characterizes much of the Algerian private sector.

While Sofiane began with a substantial family investment and good local contacts, a young private-sector operator I met in Algiers in 2012 had a very different story. Tahir used his savings and a partnership to accumulate capital for a small electronics shop that specialized in mobile telephones. In 2000, he passed his baccalaureate exams in Algiers but did not go on to a university. He knew he had to begin work and found a job in a mobile phone store. After a few years of hard work, he benefited from his general intelligence and effective customer relations skills. He had learned the mobile phone business and was well placed in a new consumer area. While Algeria permitted mobile phones later than most nations, and required a complicated process of validating them for security reasons, several competing phone networks made this new service cheap and accessible. Tahir saved money for more than a year, insisting that while he worked hard to save he did not allow money to rule his life. "I had good food, clothes," he said. "And perfume. I do not drink or smoke." He married during that time and has two small sons, Mohammad and Ali. His wife works as a teacher; his mother takes care of their children.

At the age of twenty-five, Tahir acquired a shop in the neighborhood where he grew up. He is well known and respected in the neighborhood. Because of his reputation and contacts, the shop is rented to him on a monthly basis, unusual in a market where owners demand a year's rent in advance for new tenants. Tahir has built his business by running a spotless shop, maintaining a good reputation, and working long hours: "My day: work, 8:30 in the morning to nine at night. Go home. Pray. Sleep. . . . Also, see my children." While he attributes the necessity for hard work to the general situation of "living in the Third World," he marks the importance of religious observance, practice, and culture. He is articulate about his responsibilities in neighborhood as a shop owner; aware of his responsibility to keep an eye on the street and on people. He is thoughtful about his conduct to different types of customers; the older woman who does not understand technology, the teenager with too much money, the young man who needs a reliable phone but not an expensive one. Tahir has something remarkable, his own business. Many of his peers are unemployed. He is modest about his accomplishment, noting only that "one has to take the first step." He does not criticize the unemployed and insists that Algerians will give small and medium amounts of money to the hungry. As for politics, or voting, Tahir insists he has no time, no interest. As far as he is concerned, none of the parties has a platform or a program. He does not vote and does not join business organizations. If he had a problem with the administrative regulations, he would work with people he knows to get it resolved. He attributes correct conduct in business and the idea of leading a balanced life to religious commitments. "Some people get their ethics from their religion, others from their family, others from the law," he said.

"For me, it is religion." The perfume as well comes from an Islamic cultural model, attributed to the Prophet's practice.

Tahir's networks are particular. His shop is located in an area where the MSP has strong support; he lives in an area that was a FIS stronghold. His rapid accession to ownership, his savings partnership, and the kind of business he is in all point to Islamist networks. He had no need for bank credit, and has not relied on family connections, so despite his discretion about his funders and his avowed disinterest in politics he has situated himself in Algeria's informal Islamic business sector.

While Tahir and Sofiane have very different businesses, and bring different skills and orientations to their work, they share a cultural model based on connections, networks, and a larger Islamic cultural frame. Tahir, younger, is more observant in his practice and better educated; they both take family commitments seriously. Both are profoundly estranged from politics, using networks and connections and not articulating a business interest. While Sofiane supports the ruling party, Tahir particularly avoids all formal politics. He has not voted and does not follow political parties. They do not see state programs as relevant to their effort and do not look to political organizations to advance their interests, which are barely articulated.

Islamic Validation for the Private Sector

What did Islamic ideas as interpreted in Algeria and Islamic politics offer the private sector? First, validation, and the prospect of ethical business. Private economic activity was considered suspect under the previous order; *parasitic* and *comprador* were the two most common adjectives associated with private-sector economic activity before the discourse shifted with liberalization efforts.[62] More recent formulations—*nouveau riche, enrichessement facile, fakhur* (excessive display), and *liberalisation sauvage*—have not done much good for private enterprise either. The simplest Islamic formulation upends all this: the Prophet was a merchant.

Second, Islamic ideas about economics, in Algeria, offer less a body of coherent business law than the understanding that Islamic law is compatible with commercial enterprise. It has been compatible in the past, with great Islamic empires; it can be so again, in the future.[63] While bank credit is extremely difficult to obtain, and presents real dangers, the Islamic preference for the joint venture validates the strategies of small actors with small capital.

Third, Islamic views find satisfaction in economics as a value-neutral science. Much of the rank-and-file leadership of the Islamist movement comes from the sciences, engineering, and information sciences. These leaders perceive the character of economics to be scientific and no more antagonistic to Islam than engineering or information systems. The policy head of the liberal Islamist MSP, Kamel Medhi, is an economist, trained in Algeria.

Fourth, the Islamic economic idea as developed in Algeria emphasizes equality as fairness, as equal access, in opposition to corruption. As the Algerian economy has privileged those close to the state, appropriation, theft, and corruption appear to define the Algerian economy. This is far from being an exclusively Islamist critique, as many on the left, secular intellectuals, journalists, and academics, are sharp in their critiques of the Algerian state and economy. *Rent* has become an intensely pejorative term in general political discourse; corruption and the Mafia are continuously invoked. Algeria's Islamist critique is part of a widely shared Algerian political and economic discourse.

Algerian Islamist Parties and Economic Policy

In the early 1990s, when the political field was wide open and Islamists gained significant political control, the economic policy trajectory of the Islamist movement was linked to the existing regime of liberalization, but it also demonstrated some of its own initiatives. Clement Henry and Robert Springborg detail the cooperation between the regime's liberalizers and the FIS, based on a shared commitment to economic liberalization.[64] Monopolies, price controls, and the general inefficacy and exclusiveness of the state-centered economy were explicitly attacked by the FIS, as well as the corruption of the military elite. After the military coup that shut down politics, liberal economists who had worked on behalf of the liberal reforms lost their posts; some felt obliged to leave the country.

While much of the state's liberalization was large scale and ineffective—such as efforts to privatize the public sector that sought large foreign investors[65]—many of the Islamist efforts were pragmatic, local, and immediate.

Each Islamist party developed its own charitable foundation and addressed social welfare needs directly. The parties raised money from private sources, mostly business operators. This was particularly important in the late 1980s and early 1990s, when because of low energy prices, debt repayment issues, inflation, and high food prices, the state was unable to meet social welfare expectations. The regime also cut funds to municipalities where the FIS had been victorious, putting real financial pressure on the new governing party. Drawing on private funds as well as some international funding, the FIS pursued its policies.

The FIS directly encouraged economic activity by organizing the *suq Islami*, large informal markets, and emphasized the involvement of young people.[66] Using private sector construction firms, the FIS built farmers' markets, *suq al-felah*. These might be no more than a large concrete slab to prevent mud, a galvanized metal roof for protection against the sun, and running water and electricity, but they enabled farmers to reach urban customers more easily and gave city residents access to competitive markets for fresh food. The FIS sought help from private construction firms with heavy equipment to move garbage, to help with the repair of parks and to construct playgrounds and soccer fields. Before they were elected, Islamic activists organized after-school activities for children, including tutoring to help students pass their baccalaureate exams. During strikes, Islamic activists organized street cleaning and garbage collection activities. Private funds were also collected to fund group weddings for young people who could not afford to get married.

While the state focused at the level of the large, involving the management of public-sector firms, privatization plans, working with international creditors, and enormous sums of money, the Islamists worked from the other end. If the state had a brief that was largely negative, the Islamists were able to show a dynamic force, generous, active, building things right here, sustaining people one couple, one soccer field, one small business, one farmers' market at a time. With the new suqs, they reminded Algerians that the Arabic language and Islam were connected to a viable economy. The economy was not (only) a matter for technocrats, it was here, now, and in Islamic history; it was their history and their future. Making things happen with donated services and equipment turned individual fortune into social good, especially important as the rapid growth of the private sector and expanding inequality had the potential to create larger social divisions. While the social welfare activities may arguably not be part of *economic* policy, their incorporation of private wealth and involvement of business operators was intended to create social justice as well as mark the possibility and importance of virtuous, individual effort here and now. Given the historical context of top-down, heavy industry development, the economic policies of the Islamist parties were even more important.

Not all of this effort was focused on urban dwellers, although cities are where most of the Islamist supporters lived and where they governed. In my conversations with young Hamas activists in 1993, I met a young agronomist in training who was passionate about remedying the historic lack of investment in agriculture in his country.[67] There is something to Hugh Roberts's assertion that Islamist policies are not "original." But it's not clear that originality is an important aspect of policy compared to engagement and efficacy. Overcoming Algeria's historic tendency to monumental and unattainable goals,[68] taxing the wealth of an informal private sector, welcoming small-scale activities, extending moral legitimacy, and fostering continuous incremental growth and broad participation in the economy, the Islamist economic policies marked a true departure from previous policy and articulated the interests of a diverse private sector.

Conclusion

In both Algeria and Turkey, political parties from Islamist movements sought to bring a broader articulation of interests into policymaking and emphasized the importance of the private sector in its smaller as well as larger forms. They resisted economic models of high modernism that privileged large-scale economic organizations. The Islamic alternative gave pragmatism and flexibility ideological support, and the attention to gaining electoral support pushed these parties toward economic pragmatism. Islamic moral framing legitimized interest and rendered private economic activity meritorious; small-scale economic activity could be seen as a contributor to prosperity and not merely traditional or nonmodern. Identity is being reshaped, not merely articulated. The AK Party in Turkey has been able to keep the support of its core constituents, Anatolian business interests, as well as its poorest adherents, while maintaining liberal and fiscally conservative policies and relief to the poorest.[69]

In Algeria, we see the marginalization or co-optation of all opposition parties and an economic policy characteristic of a petroleum state, with poor income distribution and much spending going toward enormous projects built by foreign firms. While the presidential alliance has incorporated the Islamist movement to some extent, co-optation cannot take the place of representation. Consultation, after all, relies on those already close to the state. And the lack of effective political voice for the private sector and the unemployed enables the regime to continue its state-centered and gargantuan policies that insist on deferring demands. The billion dollar infrastructure projects, for example, instead of providing thousands of construction jobs to Algeria's unemployed youth, rely on Chinese and other foreign labor. The 2009 regulation of imports, between taxation, delays, and the sequestering of capital, contributed to the collapse of thousands of small artisanal manufacturing firms.[70] Both of these sectors contributed to oppositional Islamist parties in the past and now find little voice. Business organizations do not include small businesses that seem to have little means of influence and prefer to work through contacts and personal networks.

Despite the AK Party's success and the co-optation of the MSP, we could give a different account of MSP success if we considered relationships between structures, institutions, and strategies. While the Algerian state's hydrocarbon resources have given it the capacity to structure the economy and politics, its ruling core shifted over the civil war from a policy of eradication to limited reconciliation. That shift was based on a considerable victory over the most violent Islamists but also on the persistence and presence of liberal Islamists and their supporters. The presidential alliance now includes an Islamist party for the first time in Algerian history and that party is knitting itself into the government with its ministers, portfolios, and patronage. Co-optation is one account. But the game has changed, including the role played by the most powerful institution.

The MSP is not the only Islamist party. The FIS has asked to be included as a legal party, a request that was refused. The regime, however, might permit the FIS to operate again if only to damage the MSP and generally divide Islamist commitments among contenders. Also from a Muslim Brothers tradition, Abdallah Jabahallah has formed two Islamist parties since the 1990s. While he has been able to gain seats and voice, the regime has been much less willing to work with Jaballah or include him in governments. In response to political marginalization, he has created unexpected electoral alliances, including working with the Rassemblement pour la Culture et la Démocratie, a Kabyle party historically extremely hostile to political Islam.[71] In February 2011, a former Algerian prime minister, Ahmed

Benbitour, announced a political initiative, Alliance Nationale pour le Changement. In addition to unions and secular groups, Benbitour's Alliance links many small Islamic organizations on behalf of a moderate Islamic commitment. No stranger to politics, Benbitour held several ministerial positions during and after 1999, including finance and industry. He was prime minister in 1999 but resigned the next year in refusal of the regime's effort to run economic policy by decree. An economist with a Ph.D. from the University of Montreal, he stands explicitly for moderately liberal economics, open politics, and peaceful but serious change. By March 2013 Benbitour announced his candidacy for the 2014 Algerian presidential elections. Despite the Islamic organizations in the Alliance and supporting Benbitour, only his enemies would consider him an Islamist. His commitments are profoundly technocratic and liberal, not populist and Islamist. Nevertheless, Ahmed Benbitour has sought to develop something that can span the gap between secularists and Islamists, a liberalism that benefits workers and the private sector. Whatever its fate, it represents another effort to reshape the articulation of identity by offering representation: another move within the rules to change the whole by incremental measures. If the game involving the state and the Islamist movement in the 1990s was a terrible high-stakes game of Chicken, the current game is Battle of the Sexes, where the regime and an Islamist party will seek cooperation despite their very different preferences. As one Algerian businessman, not an Islamist, said, "There will be an Islamist presence in the state . . . there must be." This represents a profound change in the Algerian state, the result of multiple strategies over two decades.

Conclusion

An Invitation to Political Creativity

We hope this book fosters work on political creativity, enlarging it from a residual explanation into a research program. In that spirit, we conclude with two ventures. First, we contrast notions of agency, order, and change with those of relationality, assemblage, and time to underscore what difference it makes to analyze political phenomena through the lens of political creativity rather than through a dualist framework in which structure and agency are kept apart. Although the pairing of two sets of concepts does not fully capture the rich and wide-ranging scholarship in this volume, we find it a useful heuristic to elaborate and nudge the research program we are advocating. We hope these comparisons will sharpen the contrasts and amplify the payoff of focusing on the dynamic and relational analytics contained under the umbrella of political creativity.

Although *Political Creativity* has gone a considerable distance in elaborating the rich theoretical and empirical terrain that might provide the centerpiece of a new research program, we are aware that this is only a beginning. There are many fronts on which such an intellectual venture might be extended. In this vein, in the second half of the conclusion we issue invitations to three groups of scholars with whom we would like to engage. As with all such invitations, this encounter must remain a provisional one in which the exchange will reshape the project itself. As we see it, there are three absences in the book that we regret: political theorists, methodologists, and fellow travelers across the disciplines all have much to offer our discussion. We hope that we have reached out in ways inspiring some to take up the invitations that follow.

Agency

The new institutionalism came to the fore in the 1980s in response to both overly structural and behavioral accounts of politics.[1] Political action, we learned, was neither determined by grand structures—modernity, the mode of production, industrial society—nor the result of individually rational behavior. Instead, concrete institutions, which varied over time and place, allowed for more nuanced accounts of political action. Historical institutionalists, especially, drew our attention to the role of historical contingency, concrete contexts, and multiple institutional influences on political action. But as we saw in the introduction to this volume, the more institutionalists have faced squarely the problem of change, the more (relatively) autonomous accounts of agency have crept back into the study of institutions. Students of endogenous institutional change, formative political acts, and the autonomy of ideas have turned our attention from structure to agency.[2] And in doing so, they have shifted our attention to political leadership, institutional entrepreneurship, and ideational innovation.

The editors and contributors to this volume are sympathetic to the turn to agency in institutional studies. For example, Gerald Berk and Dennis Galvan have written about the role of creative deliberation in politics, Victoria Hattam and Joseph Lowndes have written both separately and together about the important role of everyday cultural contestation in larger patterns of political change, and Adam Sheingate has written on the role of entrepreneurship in institutional change.[3] Nevertheless, we hope this volume will be understood more as a call for a relational, than an agency-based, institutionalism. By this we mean that the study of institutions—or politics more generally—ought to focus on the relational processes, which constitute the political significance of people and things, rather than on the reciprocal causal effects of essentialized structural and agentic variables. This is a subtle but we believe critical distinction that warrants more explanation.

Despite their many differences, the recent turns to endogenous institutional change, leadership, entrepreneurship, and ideational innovation among institutionalists share a common dualist orientation. They begin by asking under what conditions can political actors escape the constraints of context and, in turn, reshape that context. Where rules are ambiguous or institutional mechanisms incongruous or incomplete, actors can exploit those gaps for strategic advantage and ideational innovation. But not just any actors will do. Some are endowed with capabilities others lack: political warrants; extra-institutional authority; individual autonomy; fortuitous locations; or extraordinary skills in marshaling resources, building coalitions, and bargaining. Conceptual attention, in short, is paid to defining and operationalizing structural and agentic variables. In a second move, institutionalists investigate the interaction between those variables. Where actor features "fit" institutional opportunities, agency makes change. Or in more nuanced accounts, like James Mahoney and Kathleen Thelen's taxonomy, institutionalists predict qualitative variations in change by the confluence of structural and agentic variables.[4]

Although many of the contributors to this volume practice a version of agency-based institutionalism, they also draw on a variety of antidualist traditions in social theory and philosophy to transcend the structure-agency distinction through relational analysis. In these traditions, rule ambiguity, cultural pluralism, and the partial nature of all schemas, theories, and norms are durable facts of life, not unusual occurrences in otherwise static and orderly contexts. Human action always involves rule interpretation, tinkering with institutional resources, and assemblage of artifacts. Instead of focusing on the interaction of essentialized variables, they focus on the relational processes by which people and things attain their meaning and are mutually reconstituted through ongoing transaction. As sociologist Mustafa Emirbayer puts it, relational analysis focuses on "dialogic" or "trans-actional" processes by which "actors immersed in the durée of lived experience engage with others in collectively organized action contexts, temporal as well as spatial."[5] In this perspective, agency is inseparable from the unfolding or emergent dynamics of situations. Instead of conceptualizing institutions and actors independently and then attending to their interaction, relational analysis conceptualizes the processes and practices of relations per se that link people, institutions, culture, and situations in time. Note the semantic quality of the relational concepts the contributors develop and use in this volume. Many are verbs or nouns that identify actions. Many begin with the prefix "re" to indicate the processual nature associated with actions rooted in prior habits ("again") but oriented toward an unknown future ("anew"). In this sense, these concepts also prefigure our third category of analysis: time. Among the many concepts in this book that name relational processes are recomposition (Gary Herrigel, Volker Wittke, and Ulrich Voskamp), recombination (Stephen Amberg), political reconfiguration (Hattam and Lowndes), political work (Sheingate), reactive engineering (Ato Onoma), learning (Berk and Galvan), mutual constitution (Yoshiko Herrera), reconstitution (Rudra Sil), reassemblage (Deborah Harrold), coevolution (Chris Ansell), and memory habituation and dehabituation (Kevin Bruyneel).

Consider the differences between agency and relationality in Sheingate's chapter on Edward Bernays. It would be easy to read this chapter as a paradigmatic case of entrepreneurship (a topic Sheingate has written compellingly about in the past). Bernays exploited the opportunities for vote getting left by the progressive reforms that weakened political parties (institutional gaps). He drew on his expertise in public relations and his family's relationship to Sigmund Freud (entrepreneurial characteristics) to combine social science, advertising, and public relations into an authoritative profession. But Bernays's activities overflowed entrepreneurship in ways that belie the structure-agency distinction. Consultancy, Sheingate writes, was a mediating process, which creatively "constructed publics" by forging relationships among voters with fluid identities and multiple affiliations. In order to distinguish it from entrepreneurship, Sheingate calls this creative relational process "political work" or everyday "political practice." Bernays's significance lies not in the fact that he created a new role for professional consultants in modern candidate-centered elections (an explanation of consultancy Sheingate rejects as functionalist), it is that the political work he initiated makes those elections.

Or consider Berk and Galvan's account of creative syncretism. They conceptualize power and creative projects in a two-by-two grid not to predict how interaction between structural and agentic variables causes stasis or change, but as a technique to map the relational processes that simultaneously produce order and change. The Food and Drug Administration did not enlist lay representatives onto advisory boards or introduce surrogate markers into retroviral drug trials because policy entrepreneurs from the AIDS movement or the state found ways to exploit ambiguous rules or overcome institutional constraints. Instead, in the face of diverse and pressing problems, activists and administrators independently launched creative projects, which altered the terrain of possibility for one another. Through observation and learning, they aligned their creative projects and in doing so they not only collaborated on advisory boards and drug trials, they reconstituted their identities as well. Many activists came to see themselves as "lay experts" and the agency's chief commissioner, David Kessler, came to see himself as a champion not only of neoliberal reform but also of participatory democracy.

The processual concept of "mutual learning" also informs Herrigel, Wittke, and Voskamp's account of organizational change in the governing institutions of multinational supply chains. Looked at from a dualist perspective, the structural relationship between multinational corporations and Chinese subcontractors, supply chains look hierarchical. Those in positions of power finance, design products, and set production standards; subordinates carry out their directives; and competition among subordinates ensures compliance. Looked at as a relational process, the first round of supply chain contracts forged provisional apprenticeships, which inevitably produced novel problems and possibilities in Chinese markets. Negotiated from mutual dependencies, a middle-range market for multinational products deepened multinational corporations' reliance on local expertise. The "recomposition" of corporate production systems from apprenticeship (learning *from*) to mutual upgrading (learning *with*) reflected that changing relationship. It is impossible to make sense of this transition—or of the way corporate production systems foster upgrading—by focusing on the interaction between institutional gaps and entrepreneurial agency. It makes no sense to talk about ambiguities, incompleteness, or incongruities in the (hierarchical) apprenticeship system, because they only emerged from a relational process of learning. In addition, mutual learning is not an unintended by-product of ambiguities or gaps in otherwise determinate hierarchical production routines; instead, those "pragmatist" systems are designed to foster improvement through a relational process, which sparks reflection, experimentation, and learning by continually perturbing routines.

Or think about the ecological concept of coevolution in Chris Ansell's chapter. Like Berk and Galvan's two-by-two grid, Ansell draws on spatial metaphors from ecological theory to map the relationships between diverse institutional logics (ecologies). At first blush, ecological theory appears to provide a more nuanced account of structure, in which multiple institutional formations, at different levels of analysis, are normal. Like institutionalists who focus on ambiguities, gaps, and incongruities, Ansell uses ecological theory to identify the boundaries between institutional logics, where creative recombination or syncretism is most likely to occur. And yet, as Ansell makes clear, ecological explanation does not come in the form of causal propositions about the interaction between structure and agency, but in tracing the coevolution of multiple species or ecologies. This is a dynamic process of mutual adaptation. The Medici family, Ansell argues, gained its prominence in fifteenth-century Florence not because it took on the role of mediating entrepreneur in an institutional order rent with conflict, ambiguity, and incompleteness. Rather, the Medicis' support for a guild uprising against oligarchic control of the city set off a series of mutual adaptations among Florentine ecologies (guild, oligarchy, and neighborhood) that resituated the family at the boundaries of various institutional logics and localities. The explanation for the Medicis' authority is relational and dynamic. Adaptive coevolution, not the causal fit between contextual (institutional) and actor variables, lies at the heart of Ansell's analysis.

Order

The counterpoint to agency as relationality is order as assemblage: there is work behind order. Order does not just exist or emerge organically from the structure of the polity or the configuration of social conflict or the needs of the economy. Order exists because people act creatively to make it, maintain it, shore it up, and keep it relevant to changing contexts and conditions.

Political creativity is not limited to the openings in stable political conditions, times of crisis, ambiguities in the rules, or other patterns of uncertainty. In all circumstances, we see political and institutional orders as decomposable structures, machines with many superfluous contraptions and vestigial parts available for dismantling, unauthorized poaching, and reuse. Creative actors are always in a position to disassemble and rearrange this equipment. This tinkering is behind the initial establishment of order as an assemblage of available elements and a response to new conditions. It is also behind the creative work of maintenance to enable order to persist, and processes of reassemblage that produce ongoing change in institutional orders.

Most accounts of the origins of order tend to follow a punctuated equilibrium model.[6] Periods of great openness or crisis are followed by relative stability over longer durations. In unusual moments when order breaks down, or crisis interrupts existing rules, routines, and roles, it becomes possible to rethink regimes, to reimagine the economy, to transform social arrangements. In moments of formative openness, many find much room for creativity, but in these "moments of madness" little attention is paid to the situatedness of action, or the assemblage of order from existing materials.

We take issue with punctuated equilibrium and treat the origins of order the same way we treat ongoing change—as a process of creative assemblage. Formative moments are not so open as some might think. As Sil's chapter shows, the collapse of the Soviet Union was not the critical juncture that many observers initially expected. There was neither a complete rebooting of state-labor relations nor a steady rise of Western-style adversarial union-ism. Yet Sil also parts ways with those who subsequently overstated labor passivity in post-Soviet Russia, attributing it to the legacy of official unions designed to function as "transmission belts" for the regime. Instead, Sil's chapter finds evidence of creative assemblage, featuring a selective recycling of certain Soviet-era expectations and practices within the framework of new institutions of collective bargaining and social dialogue. This creative assemblage was not limited to the mechanical reproduction of old habits by unreflective agents. It included efforts by dominant unions to leverage their organizational structures and resources in a new political environment. It also included a reworking of elements of the post-Stalin Soviet "social con-tract" to accommodate the realities of a new economic environment. These processes of adaptation and reconstruction are most apparent in the compli-cated and contested negotiations that led to a new 2002 labor code. The code was seen as too pro-worker by business and too pro-business by mili-tant labor groups, but it effectively reconstructed a familiar bargain: reduced militancy in exchange for a predictable system of collective bargaining and some acknowledgment of employment stability and subsistence require-ments. The old practices neither disappeared en masse nor provided fixed blueprints for new practices. Rather, they provided fragmentary ideas that could be dissociated from the old Soviet system and transformed into func-tional, serviceable spare parts within a new landscape.

Likewise, for Harrold, even as North Africa experiences upheaval and political reformulation, older Islamic codes of ethics and economic liberal-ization are reworked together. Turkey's Justice and Development Party, for example, is neither atavistically rooted in Muslim traditionalism nor craft-ing a new polity from whole cloth. Its political creativity is well situated in a specific set of inheritances (religious and secular) that can be imaginatively reassembled. Political creativity, then, is not so much beginning anew as it is a reconfiguration of old associations into new assemblages. Through the resituation of some parts of existing practices and traditions in relation to new elements, new social formations emerge. Take, for example, the actions of the Islamic candy entrepreneur who adheres at the same time to old and new practices that for some observers seem contradictory. He does not simply choose between past and present, but rather blends elements of the two. Some aspects of Islamic religious practices are reassociated with emerging market liberalization. The strange bedfellows are gradually fused and the edges smoothed over. Orders are reimagined, not so much through path dependence or repudiation but through more continuous acts of reconfiguration.

Assemblage also changes how we think about the persistence of order during periods of stability. For most institutionalists, persistence results, in this view, from positive feedback loops, lock-in, powerful historical legacies, underlying cognitive schemas, discursive hegemonies, and other imper- sonal forces that set the parameters for action and give predictability and regularity to political and social life.[7] *Political Creativity* accounts for the persistence of order as the difficult work of creative action.

Consider Onoma's account of Botswana's land boards. In the usual punctuated equilibrium mode, we'd expect to find a critical, fluid moment at independence, when the state broke the back of the traditional chiefs and set up new rules, followed by persistence of this institution over time through gradual diffusion and the consolidation of state authority. That's a smooth story that lends itself well to comparative analysis, relying on a set of big, underspecified collective actors (the state) or on completely agent- less, quasi-metaphysical forces (diffusion).

By contrast, Onoma's situated creativity account is very different, and it suggests a much more challenging (but doable) task for those interested in how best practices persist and can be applied in new locales. Botswana's chiefs lost the initial political battle over the land boards, but they were not broken. They reworked themselves into a new landed, cattle-accumulating elite. They coopted the land boards, leveraging their superior knowledge of local tenure relations and ecological conditions. The boards changed to make room for the chiefs. Peasants who stood to lose land gummed up the works with multiple claims, stories of lost title documents, and supporting accounts of personal hardship. They changed the titling program to recog- nize claims formerly considered bogus. Fifty years of orderly persistence of the land boards has very little to do with consolidation or diffusion, and much more to do with the interplay between the creative assemblages wrought by the losers and the creative assemblages of officials who managed the land boards. If you want to know how order persists, you have to carefully identify, follow, and take note of the creative projects that go into making and shoring up order.

Finally, a shift to assemblage builds on and simplifies recent work that recognizes on-path, incremental change, but theorizes it in terms of the partial operation and incoherence of ordering structures.[8] In this work, the focus of analysis is still on the basic attributes of ordering structures—overlapping rule systems, drift in the relevance of codes, the layering of old and new forms, submerged alternatives within single-path processes, and the like. While these structural features both enable and channel the form of action, they also perpetuate a familiar structure-agency dualism.

Political Creativity questions this dualism, and shifts the discussion away from how structures pattern action and make incremental change more or less predictable. Instead of focusing on the origins and persistence of order, we subsume fine-grained description of structural inconsistency and fragmentation within a wholesale, and equally fine-grained, empirical account of structure as providing materials for creative political action. Layering, drift, intercurrence, conversion, and subversion populate a catalog of ways structure permits its own rearrangement. We predict this will become a long, unwieldy list, because distinct forms of creative assemblage will require distinct names. Instead, the turn to political creativity puts a simple, comprehensive account of change underneath this umbrella of assemblage.

Consider Herrera's account of the emergence of a single, global system of national accounting after the Cold War. The story has elements of what appear to be hegemonic diffusion of a standard accounting order (superstructure) to match the new global political economy (infrastructure). But this masks Herrera's rich empirical account of who did what to make, negotiate, and refashion the various competing accounting orders into a uniform global system. The story has elements of layering, drift, and conversion, but these operated neither as "mechanisms" of incremental change nor as descriptions of the conditions under which agency could be applied to the accounting systems. Rather, such terms offer a partial glimpse of what the global systems of accounting looked like before, during, and after people actually messed with them.

For example, early in the development of Western accounting standards, techniques and principles were borrowed from the seminal work of

Pavel Popov in the Soviet Union, transmitted westward by Wassily Leontief. Perhaps this belongs in a category like "subversion," but so much of the meaning of this early cross-fertilization is lost by squeezing it into a structuralist box for describing conditions for on-path change. During the early Cold War, accountants from East and West crossed paths at international conferences, where they learned about each others' techniques, which they then creatively applied back home. The Western and Soviet accounting standards were not evolving on separate paths, but influenced each others' creative assemblage. This might be conversion or layering, but these concepts get in the way of empirical precision and analytic clarity: they block our view of acts of creative agency with unneeded depiction of structure itself. The same point applies to the 1990s effort to harmonize multiple global accounting systems. Herrera's careful account of the deals, trade-offs, and pressures needed to pull this off belies tales of agentless hegemony. True, institutions were intercurrent and multiple, but that condition is a depiction of the starting landscape, without an account of what people did to assemble the final result.

To tell an empirically complete, analytically useful story of how we got one global accounting system, Herrera must set aside both agentless accounts of persistence (hegemony, evolution, or diffusion) and pictures of the structural shapes that open on-path change. Doing so clears space for a thorough account of a century's worth of creative assemblage.

The turn to assemblage illustrated in this volume increases traction on analyses of how institutional and political order emerges, persists, and changes. This is primarily because we assume less. Rather than assuming that order emerges from moments of great openness or remains stable as a result of structural characteristics (underlying alignment of political interests, stickiness of rules, evolutionary or diffusion effects) or changes incrementally as a result of structural defects, we treat the emergence, stability, and transformation of order as empirical questions, asking, "how does this actually work?" We find assemblage and the situatedness of creativity in critical junctures and founding moments. We find that assemblage is needed to maintain the stability of order. And we find that assemblage offers a simpler and more empirically complete account of incremental change than a study of the gaps, inconsistencies, and deformities in institutional structure.

We also note that a shift to political creativity blurs the analytic boundary between institutions and politics. In more dualist ontologies, institutions stand outside human agency, channeling, constraining, ordering it.

Within this view, it makes sense to differentiate the study of institutions and what they do (institutionalism) from the arguably wider question of what people do, how they act, think, justify, within the constraints set for them. One could call the latter politics, and then it's easy to see why so much political science has been institutionalism: because we focus on the important underlying structures (institutions) that condition or determine the near epiphenomenon called politics.

Political creativity confounds the distinction between institutions and politics. Institutions are not extant, persistent orders with agency of their own. They are real and important, but as raw material for relational, recombinatory action, for dismantling, reassemblage, and tinkering. What we do with and to institutions is just as political as what we do in light of them. Politics is informed by how institutions situate action (in Hattam and Lowndes, civil rights and overseas military adventurism are important institutional discourses and practices, key pieces of context, and raw material for creativity). But action also consists of a politics of who messes with these institutions, by what means, to what ends, with what responses and results (Condoleezza Rice's ingenious suturing of 1960s civil rights struggles against racial injustice with 2000s efforts to bring democratic human rights to the Arab world). Seen in terms of political creativity, institutions can no longer be outside or infrastructurally under politics. They are in fact the subject of competing projects of creative reworking, and that contestation opens new research terrain for political science. We need no longer strangely sequester politics from our main analytic concerns.

Change

Questions of change have long been central to political science, the assumption being that once the relevant causal chains have been specified, more effective leverage points for enacting change can be identified, thereby facilitating political intervention of many kinds. Political scientists who appeal to complexity without specifying the prime movers shaping the political formation usually meet with criticism. Explanations that have currency in the discipline are those that cut through complex processes to identify the most powerful causal relations. Occam's razor still reigns as one of the principal criteria for evaluating competing explanations.

Not surprisingly, then, many formative debates in political science have centered around questions of causation: debates over the three faces of power, voter turnout, social revolutions, and the paradoxical relation between liberalism and its exclusions all hinge on competing views of causation and change. The exchange between Walter Dean Burnham and Philip Converse in the *American Political Science Review* in the 1960s and 1970s is a classic case in point. The issue at hand was how to explain the precipitous decline in voter participation in the United States in the early twentieth century.[9] What brought about this dramatic change? Converse and Burnham offered very different explanations and for the most part talked past each other. Where Converse and other behavioral political scientists carefully specified the proximate causes of voter decline—poll taxes, registration procedures, and the Australian ballot—Burnham and fellow historical institutionalists looked to centuries-long macrohistorical forces, such as the sequencing of capital accumulation and suffrage extension during industrialization as shaping voter turnout. The debate between these two schools was powerful and consequential precisely because it encapsulated radically different intellectual traditions, each with very different views of political change, vying for authority within the discipline.

The Burnham-Converse debate rested on deep-seated differences regarding the spatial assumptions undergirding political change. For behavioralists, spatial and temporal proximity was key, while Burnham and other historical institutionalist focused on large scale macro historical trends. Proximity and legibility, for behavoralists, went hand-in-hand; distance was presumed to dissipate causal force. For historical institutionalists like Burnham, Theda Skocpol, Karen Orren, Stephen Skowronek, and others, distance, whether spatial or temporal, was no deterrent to importance. Indeed, historical institutionalists of various stripes labored to document the ways in which processes of institutional and cultural mediation allow political connections to be made and remade with considerable force over enormous expanses of space and time.[10]

Although the Burnham-Converse exchange garnered considerable scholarly attention, their shared assumptions are as instructive as their differences. Both sides presume a temporal linearity—movement along a single time line. There is little or no attention to the mangle of political time in which time itself is subject to contestation. While the scholars in *Political Creativity* draw on a wide range of intellectual traditions to buttress their work, there is a common thread that runs through this section. The chapters gathered here document time and again the intricate processes of mediation and assemblage that confound spatially proximate and temporally linear conceptions of change. The politics of space and time, as Bruyneel shows, do not follow the dictates of the map and calendar, but are frequently reworked, or mangled, into new political formations. Proximity, Hattam and Lowndes, Amberg, and Harrold show, is no guarantee of significance. Partial appropriations and unexpected assemblages in which *pieces* of the past are animated in the present make clear the limits of mechanical conceptions of causation that continue to dominate mainstream political science.

Consider, for example, Hattam and Lowndes's account of Condoleezza Rice's efforts to reconfigure race and partisan identification in the United States. Surely, the past is present throughout her speeches, but not as a heavy-handed constraint on political innovation. Rather what is striking is the audaciousness with which Rice picks and chooses from the past when authorizing foreign intervention in the present. Historical institutionalists' notions of path dependence, punctuated equilibrium, and incremental change are poor guides to analyzing Rice's political interventions. Rather than tracing causal chains from remote to proximate variables, Hattam and Lowndes identify Rice's acts of selective appropriation in order to identify the ways in which she and other Republican operatives try to reconfigure the political landscape by rearranging the political elements. Units of analysis cannot be taken for granted; lines of affiliation and difference are themselves political formations in which variegated elements have been fused into apparently coherent and stable entities. Attending to the heterogeneity that persists within all social formations is the critical analytic task, since these are the elements available for reconfiguration. Doing so is no easy matter; we must relinquish faith in the apparent underlying order of things and look closely at the surface for the suturings.

From this perspective, the political meaning and significance of objects do not inhere in the things themselves, but in the manifestation of quite particular, but by no means enduring, assemblages. Civil rights politics, for example, is no longer viewed as a presumptively Democratic Party issue, because of the Left's political commitments or historical legacy. Rather, Condoleezza Rice's claim to civil rights politics becomes part and parcel of the new Republican agenda as she, and other party officials, seek to forge connections between civil rights, tax policy, and foreign invasion. As Jasbir Puar has argued so powerfully in terms of homonationalism, the political inflection of an issue, identity, or position can be radically reconfigured once welded to different political elements.[11] Change for Hattam and Lowndes is always partial and incomplete in ways that make it difficult to assess the significance of any particular reconfiguration. Gone also are clearly identifiable levers of change, replaced by new tools for attending to the emergent, and for remaining alive to a wide array of change. Importantly, attending to the partial and incomplete nature of change also underscores the heterogeneity and constant movement within all apparently coherent social formations, thereby expanding the domain of the political to ordinary times.

Consider too, the way in which Bruyneel documents the parallel and contested notions of settler and indigenous time. History is not simply one damn thing after another in which we struggle to identify causal sequences. Rather, there are multiple histories vying for position, so that the question being posed not only is one of change but also contains a prior question of what exactly is it that needs explanation? What events are even recognized as events to be explained? Indigenous peoples' political power, Bruyneel asserts, lies precisely in their refusal to abide by settler time. When the Wampanoag tribal leader contests the narrative Americans tell themselves of the Pilgrims' landing, he animates his account by voicing alternative temporal frames. His political intervention is to remember and retell the history of America through a different temporal lens. Throughout, Bruyneel shows that the clock and calendar are themselves vehicles of power that both mask and maintain the legacy of conquest. Recovering competing views of time retrieves questions of power and conquest from the past and returns them to the present, from distant state policies to everyday actions. Telling time, making appointments are actions that reestablish settler time and authority day by day. Past and present are intimately linked, not by long causal chains, but through the reinscription of conquest in our temporal practices in the present. Conversely, the Wampanoags' unsettling of time, remembering differently, repoliticizes the heterogeneity within, making our settler past visible in the present. Change, for Bruyneel, is not so much something that happens over time, although it does that too; the notion of change Bruyneel wants to amplify is one in which we come to see the intricate ways in which settler politics and inequality inhere in our conception of time itself.

Finally, Amberg also disturbs traditional conceptions of industrial and policy change in his analysis of President Barack Obama's auto reform. Typically, institutionalist histories of the auto industry are recounted through oscillations of stability and change. In this narrative, the 1970s marked a crisis in the Fordist regime and a struggle over the future. While some reformers advocated industrial policy, labor management codetermination, and Toyota-style quality production, America got neoliberalism and southern-style unitary management (the order now in crisis again). Amberg shows that this history was never so linear. By drawing a distinction between "logics of orientation" and "logics of practice," he reveals how production regimes are always partial. Fordism was never simply Fordist all the way down. Auto companies, workers, and policymakers inevitably ran into unfamiliar problems that necessitated experimentation, no less in the age of Fordism than in the 1980s or the present. In Amberg's history, the reformers of the 1980s did not disappear; they created new sites for experimentation and practice within a diverse array of organizations: think tanks, reform unions, investment banks, universities, and industrial locations like GM's Saturn division. Obama's auto rescue neither took the industry as he found it nor reinvented it anew. Instead, the president reconfigured prior experiments, personnel, and models to renarrate the causes of crisis, compose a reform task force, mobilize industry and union reformers, and project a future of reinvigorated manufacturing and middle-class prosperity.

Consider the ground we have traveled from Converse and Burnham to political creativity. Gone are the splits between behavior and history, space and time, and empirical and theoretical work. Instead of the intractable debate over where to draw the temporal boundaries to causal explanation, the contributors to this volume redirect our attention to time as a heterogeneous political resource. Like institutions, the past provides a reserve for creativity, in which politics produces novel possibilities through recombinations of the distant and the proximate.

Three Invitations

We close this volume with an invitation for political theorists, methodologists, and intellectual neighbors in political science and other fields to engage the analytics of political creativity. This is by no means an exhaustive list. We call out these three groups because they have been conspicuous by their absence in this volume or because we hope to advance research on political creativity through dialogue and debate.

First, we see this volume as an invitation to exchange with our colleagues who work more on the theoretical than the empirical dimensions of the political. This volume began as a collaboration of scholars concerned with empirical instances of change in American political development and comparative politics. We worked our way to political creativity and the subtending concepts of relationality, assemblage, and time by culling lessons and concepts from the many careful empirical analyses presented in this book. Still, many of the problems, ideas, and emphases in these chapters came from prior roaming and poaching in theoretical terrain. Some of us have gone directly to contemporary theory in political science—Bruyneel to Giorgio Agamben and George Shulman; Hattam and Lowndes to Ernesto Laclau and Michel de Certeau; Amberg to Judith Butler; Berk and Galvan to Pierre Bourdieu, William Connolly, and Roberto Unger; Ansell to the Jane Mansbridge, John Dryzek and John Bohman; Herrigel to Cornelius Castoriadus and Hans Joas; and Harrold to Jacques Derrida. Others have found their way to political theory through capacious readers in our empirical subfields or in other disciplines altogether. Whatever the route taken, we share the hope for a political science that reconnects empirical exploration and theoretical inquiry.

As editors, we have tried to build on that goal by articulating a conceptual infrastructure for political creativity that actively transgresses the theory-empirics divide. We see relationality, assemblage, and the politics of time as analytical terrain on which to embark on a fruitful engagement between theory and empirical research. We note that careful attention to relational creativity in global supply chains allows Herrigel, Wittke, and Voskamp to invent a useful distinction between "learning from" and "learning with"—processual concepts that may be equally useful in probing other forms of hierarchical relations. Or think about how Hattam and Lowndes's reflection on theories of political time allows them to probe the micropolitics of changing partisan identifications through "simultaneous acts of partial repudiation and reaffirmation." This too can provide an orienting logic to help political scientists focus on the mangle of political creativity in their research on regime order and change in other contexts. In these examples, neither the process of theorizing nor of conducting deep empirical work dominates. Both take the broader orientations of political creativity, relationality, and temporality and use them to birth novel interpretations and usable concepts that provide the ability to reach out in a variety of directions. We see many opportunities for generative dialogue with political theorists. We know we have much to gain and hope the fruits are reciprocal.

Second, *Political Creativity* constitutes an invitation to colleagues who have been working in parallel on questions of qualitative and interpretive method. Just as with explicitly theoretical work, method and epistemology have not been the primary concerns of this volume, but reflections on these issues have been in the background of our conversations. Indeed, some of our authors (Sil, Herrera, Hattam, Ansell) bring to this collaboration active engagement on questions of method that help define our invitation here.

Our problem-driven (à la Ian Shapiro) approach to empirical questions of political order, agency, and change has led contributors to deploy a wide range of methods with enormous dexterity. Our authors trace processes of interplay between the creative projects of national leaders and local chiefs in Botswana's land boards, between the colonial governments and the Mouride Brotherhood in Senegal, between multinational corporations and Chinese subcontractors in transnational supply chains, between statisticians across the industrialized world. They unpack the assemblage of cultural symbols in Condi Rice's reconfiguration of race, violence, and foreign policy. They unravel the ad hoc, stitching together of institutional and cultural elements in assemblages that often look natural and unassembled. They follow actors whose relationship to time might seem surreal, if one adheres to a strict linear account of past, present, and future.

The research crafts we've used to examine political creativity are certainly not entirely new, although some may be strange to political science. We invite conversation with colleagues concerned with research craft around at least three techniques that cut through this volume: ethnography, scale, and units of analysis. We don't claim to be scholars of these issues, or to have command of their history and full implications. That's why we invite dialogue with colleagues versed in such issues. But we know we've found these useful as means to make sense of the recombinatory realities our cases present.

First, many in this volume practice ethnographic and archival listening, real, deep listening (to face-to-face informants, and to informants who leave documentary traces) devoid as much as possible of totalizing prior metanarrative, so the subtleties of relational innovation and unexpected assemblage are not drowned out by an analyst's preordained expectation of how these sorts of people in these sorts of situation should normally act. This is not antitheory: it is a call for a kind of theory that can attune the researcher to the complex interplay of many projects of situated creativity. A closely related second skill is attention to processes, changes, actions, and effects that are small, often considered too small to be worthy of political science. Our accounts of relationality, assemblage, and time make it possible to aggregate the significance of chains of small events. But this is impossible if our analytic lenses are set to recognize only the socially macroscopic, the national, the longue durée, or the grand event. Third, we relax the fixity of variables, so that what we do involves dynamic rather than static operationalization. Politically creative actors mess with forms, practices, rules, and relations that, in most political science methods, must be held fixed in order for operationalization to mean anything and for analysis to proceed. Political creativity shows how that which is fixed is ephemeral. So we must learn to look at variables that shift and morph during the life of our analysis. It's the difference between analysis as pencil sketching and analysis as animation.

These skills and the focus on political creativity, relational process, assemblage, and temporality raise a variety of questions. How do we develop nonmechanistic styles of explanation consistent with our account of action, order, and change? Can we build on the skills we deploy to fully articulate what relational explanations should look like in political science? How do the sorts of conceptual and empirical commitments undertaken in this volume intersect with the current debates between qualitative and interpretive political science? We pose these questions and reflect on the techniques we have opportunistically deployed as a way to offer a wide-open invitation to dialogue with colleagues who share similar concerns, but whose expertise lies in reflection on the craft of research itself.

Finally, and perhaps most obviously, this volume invites a dialogue with intellectual neighbors and potential fellow travelers who have been puzzling over institutional change, political entrepreneurship, cultural contestation, ideational innovation, and the distinctions between structure and agency or necessity and contingency. As we noted in the Introduction, the editors and contributors to this volume have roamed outside political science because their research raised conundrums that challenge dualist frameworks in the field. They found political creativity where existing accounts of structure and agency would least expect to find it: among colonial peasants and indigenous peoples who have been forced to accept orthodox modernities at gunpoint; among the powerful, for whom legitimate authority seemed most secure; and in the everyday life of government bureaucrats, statisticians, workers, political consultants, engineers, candy vendors, people with AIDS, and business managers. They found surprising assemblages of supposedly contradictory and incongruous elements: traditional and modern institutions, conservative and liberal ideologies, the discourse of racial hierarchy and emancipatory liberalism, communist and capitalist organizations, hucksterism and professional norms. They found the past was never just the past for Wampanoags, Condi Rice, President Obama, trade unions in Russia, street vendors in Algeria; it became a surprising resource in the making of politics in the present and projecting a better future.

All of the contributors to this volume at one time or another have had to contend with the limits of the discipline for making sense of their research. Familiar notions of order, agency, and change seemed inadequate to the task. The contributors have navigated their way out of these intellectual difficulties through a variety of strategies; the editors have brought them together under a collective research program. If you have shared with us that sense of sitting on unfamiliar empirical terrain, staring into the face of confusing evidence, watching your subjects' actions overflow the constraints of the worlds they inhabit, noticing things go together when they shouldn't, we invite you to consider the shift in perspective we have associated with political creativity. We invite you to consider what it means to pay attention to relational processes of political creativity instead of the interaction between essentialized variables. We invite you to watch carefully how people make strange yet beautiful assemblages out of the ongoing detritus of politics as well as the high-minded aspirations of theories, ideologies, and designs. We invite you to pay attention to the way that creative political actors jump the tracks of time, reassociating past, present, and future in small ways that shift the broader possibilities of politics. We invite you to join the conversation over rethinking order and change through political creativity.

Notes

Introduction

1. John L. Campbell, "Institutional Reproduction and Change," in *The Oxford Handbook of Comparative Institutional Analysis*, ed. Glenn Morgan, John L. Campbell, Colin Crouch, Ove Kaj Pedersen, and Richard Whitley (New York: Oxford University Press, 2011), 87–117; Paul DiMaggio and Walter W. Powell, introduction to *The New Institutionalism in Organizational Analysis*, ed. Walter W. Powell and Paul DiMaggio (Chicago: University of Chicago Press, 1991), 1–40; Gretchen Helmke and Steven Levitsky, *Informal Institutions and Democracy* (Baltimore: Johns Hopkins University Press, 2006); James Mahoney and Kathleen Thelen, eds., *Explaining Institutional Change: Ambiguity, Agency, and Power* (New York: Cambridge University Press, 2009); Karen Orren and Stephen Skowronek, "The Study of American Political Development," in *Political Science: State of the Discipline*, ed. Ira Katznelson and Helen Milner (New York: Norton, 2002); Karen Orren and Stephen Skowronek, "Beyond the Iconography of Order," in *The Dynamics of American Politics*, ed. Lawrence C. Dodd and Calvin Jillson (Boulder, CO: Westview Press, 1994), 311–330; Karen Orren and Stephen Skowronek, *The Search for American Political Development* (Cambridge: Cambridge University Press, 2004); Marc Schneiberg, "What's on the Path? Path Dependence, Organizational Diversity and the Problem of Institutional Change in the U.S. Economy, 1900–1950," *Socioeconomic Review* 5, no. 1 (January 2007): 47–80; William H. Sewell, "A Theory of Structure: Duality, Agency and Transformation," *American Journal of Sociology* 98, no. 1 (July 1992): 1–29; Wolfgang Streeck and Kathleen Thelen, eds., *Beyond Continuity* (Oxford: Oxford University Press, 2005); Kathleen Thelen, *How Institutions Evolve: The Political Economy of Skills in Germany, Britain, the United States, and Japan* (New York: Cambridge University Press, 2004); Kathleen Thelen and Marius R. Busemeyer, "Institutional Change in German Vocational Training: From Collectivism Toward Segmentalism," in *The Political Economy of Collective Skill Formation Systems*, ed. Marius R. Busemeyer and Christine Trampusch (Oxford: Oxford University Press, 2011), 68–100.

2. Gerald Berk and Dennis Galvan, "How People Experience and Change Institutions: A Field Guide to Creative Syncretism," *Theory and Society* 38, no. 6 (November 2009): 543–580; Victoria Hattam and Joseph Lowndes, "The Ground Beneath Our Feet: Language, Culture, and Political Change," in *Formative Acts: American Politics in*

the Making, ed. Stephen Skowronek and Matthew Glassman (Philadelphia: University of Pennsylvania Press, 2007), 199–222.

3. See Campbell, "Institutional Reproduction and Change"; DiMaggio and Powell, introduction; Streeck and Thelen, *Beyond Continuity*; Mahoney and Thelen, *Explaining Institutional Change*.

4. Joan Scott, "Women in *The Making of the English Working Class*," in *Gender and the Politics of History* (New York: Columbia University Press, 1999), chap. 4. See also Sarah Ahmed, "Affective Economies," *Social Text* 79, no. 22:2 (Summer 2004): 117–139; Siobhan Somerville, "Scientific Racism and the Emergence of the Homosexual Body," *Journal of the History of Sexuality* 5, no. 2 (October 1994): 243–266.

5. Hans Joas, *The Creativity of Action* (Chicago: University of Chicago Press, 1997).

6. Karl Weick, *Making Sense of the Organization* (Malden, MA: Blackwell, 2001); Jean-Loup Amselle, *Mestizo Logics: Anthropology of Identity in Africa and Elsewhere* (Palo Alto, CA: Stanford University Press, 1998); Michel de Certeau, *The Practices of Everyday Life* (Berkeley: University of California Press, 1988), xxi.

7. Andrew Pickering, *The Mangle of Practice: Time, Agency, and Science* (Chicago: University of Chicago Press, 1995), 21–27.

8. Margaret R. Somers, "What's Political or Cultural About Political Culture and the Public Sphere? Toward an Historical Sociology of Concept Formation," *Sociological Theory* 13, no. 2 (1995): 136. See also Margaret R. Somers, "Rights, Relationality, and Membership: Rethinking the Making and Meaning of Citizenship," *Law and Social Inquiry* 19, no. 1 (1994): 63–112.

9. Mustafa Emirbayer, "Manifesto for a Relational Sociology," *American Journal of Sociology* 103, no. 2 (September 1997): 281–317. Emirbayer draws the distinction between "inter-action" and "transaction" from John Dewey and Arthur F. Bentley, *Knowing and the Known* (Boston: Beacon Press, 1949), 103–118.

10. Bruno Latour, *Science in Action: How to Follow Scientists and Engineers Through Society* (Cambridge, MA: Harvard University Press, 1987); Bruno Latour, *Reassembling the Social: An Introduction to Actor-Network Theory* (New York: Oxford University Press, 2005); Pickering, *The Mangle of Practice*; Andrew Pickering, "Beyond Constraint: The Temporality of Practice and the Historicity of Knowledge," in *Scientific Practice*, ed. Jed Z. Buchwald (Chicago: University of Chicago Press, 1995), 42–55.

11. Dvora Yanow and Peregrine Schwartz-Shea, eds., *Interpretation and Method: Empirical Research Methods and the Interpretive Turn* (New York: Sharpe, 2006); Dvora Yanow and Peregrine Schwartz-Shea, *Interpretive Research Design* (New York: Routledge, 2011).

12. Elisabeth S. Clemens, *The People's Lobby: Organizational Innovation and the Rise of Interest Group Politics in the United States, 1890–1925* (Chicago: University of Chicago Press, 1997).

13. Gary Herrigel, *Industrial Constructions: The Sources of German Industrial Power* (Cambridge: Cambridge University Press, 1996); Michael Piore and Charles F.

Sabel, *The Second Industrial Divide* (New York: Basic Books, 1986); Charles F. Sabel and Jonathan Zeitlin, "Historical Alternatives to Mass Production: Politics, Markets and Technology in Nineteenth Century Industrialization," *Past and Present* 108, no. 1 (1985): 133–176; Charles F. Sabel and Jonathan Zeitlin, eds., *World of Possibilities: Flexibility and Mass Production in Western Industrialization* (New York: Cambridge University Press, 2002).

14. Anne Norton, "Engendering Another American Identity," in *Rhetorical Republic*, ed. Frederick Dolan and Thomas Dunn (Amherst: University of Massachusetts Press, 1993): 125–143; Uday S. Mehta, "Liberal Strategies of Exclusion," *Politics and Society* 18, no. 4 (1990): 427–454. The Norton and Mehta essays contribute to a rich debate on liberalism and its exclusions in the United States that extends back over many decades and is an extensive one. See also Edmund Morgan, *American Slavery, American Freedom* (New York: Norton, 2003); Michael Rogin, *Ronald Reagan the Movie* (Berkeley: University of California Press, 1988); Toni Morrison, "Unspeakable Things Unspoken: The Afro-American Presence in American Literature," *Michigan Quarterly Review* 28, no. 1 (Winter 1981): 1–34; Eric Lott, *Love and Theft: Blackface Minstrelsy and the American Working Class* (New York: Oxford University Press, 1993); David Roediger, *The Wages of Whiteness and the Making of the American Working Class* (New York: Verso, 2007); Richard Slotkin, *The Fatal Environment: The Myth of the Frontier in the Age of Industrialization, 1800–1890* (Norman: University of Oklahoma Press, 1998); Desmond S. King and Rogers M. Smith, "Racial Orders in American Political Development," *American Political Science Review* 99, no. 1 (2005): 75–92.

15. Orren and Skowronek, "Beyond the Iconography of Order"; Orren and Skowronek, "Study of American Political Development"; Orren and Skowronek, *Search for American Political Development*; Colin Crouch and Henry Farrell, "Breaking the Path of Institutional Development: Alternatives to the New Determinism," *Rationality and Society* 16, no. 1 (February 2004): 5–43; Hokyu H. Hwang and Walter W. Powell, "Institutions and Entrepreneurship," in *Handbook of Entrepreneurship Research*, ed. Sharon Alvarez, Rajshree Agarwal, and Olav Sorenson (New York: Springer, 2005), 179–210; Mahoney and Thelen, *Explaining Institutional Change*.

16. Thad Dunning and Grigore Pop-Eleches, "From Transplants to Hybrids: Exploring Institutional Pathways to Growth," *Studies in Comparative International Development* 38, no. 4 (2004): 3–29; David Stark and Laszlo Bruzst, *Postsocialist Pathways* (Cambridge: Cambridge University Press, 1998); Berk and Galvan, "How People Experience and Change Institutions."

17. William James, *The Varieties of Religious Experience* (New York: Simon and Schuster, 1997 [1902]).

18. Claude Lévi-Strauss, *The Savage Mind* (Chicago: University of Chicago Press, 1996 [1962]), 1–33.

19. Timothy Mitchell, *Colonizing Egypt* (Berkeley: University of California Press, 1988), 63–94.

20. Crawford Young, "The Dialectics of Cultural Pluralism," in *Rising Tide of Cultural Pluralism: The Nation State at Bay?* ed. Crawford Young (Madison: University of Wisconsin Press, 1994), 22–25.

21. Goran Hyden, "Governance and Poverty Reduction in Africa," *Proceedings of the National Academy of Sciences* 104, no. 43 (2007): 16751–16756.

22. Archon Fung and Erik Olin Wright, eds., *Deepening Democracy: Institutional Innovations in Empowered Participatory Governance* (London: Verso, 2003), 3–19.

23. Peter Evans, "Development as Institutional Change: The Pitfalls of Monocropping and the Potentials of Deliberation," *Studies in Comparative International Development* 38, no. 4 (Winter 2004): 30–52.

24. James C. Scott, *Seeing like a State* (New Haven, CT: Yale University Press, 1998).

25. James Ferguson, *The Anti-Politics Machine* (Minneapolis: University of Minnesota Press, 1994), 251–278.

26. Orren and Skowronek, "Beyond the Iconography of Order."

27. Mustafa Emirbayer and Ann Mische, "What Is Agency?" *American Journal of Sociology* 103, no. 4 (1998): 962–1023.

28. See Eric Hobsbawm and Terence Ranger, eds., *The Invention of Tradition* (New York: Cambridge University Press, 1992); and Horace Kallen's account of the formation of the patriotic societies including the Sons and Daughters of the American Revolution in 1890, which he links to the great wave of migration at the end of the nineteenth century, in Horace Kallen, *Culture and Democracy in the United States* (New Brunswick, NJ: Transaction, 1924), 78–80.

29. Raymond Williams, *Marxism and Literature* (New York: Oxford University Press, 1977); Judith Butler, "Critically Queer," in *Bodies That Matter: On the Discursive Limits of Sex* (New York: Routledge, 1993); Stephen Skowronek, *The Politics President Make: Leadership from John Adams to Bill Clinton* (Cambridge, MA: Harvard University Press, 1997); Christopher Bollas, *The Evocative Object World* (New York: Routledge, 2009); Daniel N. Stern, *The Present Moment in Psychotherapy and Everyday Life* (New York: Norton, 2004); William E. Connolly, *A World of Becoming* (Durham, NC: Duke University Press, 2011); Geoff Dyer, *The Ongoing Moment* (New York: Vintage Books, 2005); Jane Futon Suri and IDEO, *Thoughtless Acts? Observations on Intuitive Design* (San Francisco: Chronicle Books, 2005); Johanna Drucker, "Temporal Photography," *Philosophy of Photography* 1, no. 1 (2010): 22–28.

30. Kathleen Thelen and Sven Steinmo, "Historical Institutionalism in Comparative Politics," in *Structuring Politics: Historical Institutionalism in Comparative Analysis,* ed. Sven Steinmo, Kathleen Thelen, and Frank Longstreth (New York: Cambridge University Press, 1992), 1–32.

31. James G. March and Johan P. Olsen, *Rediscovering Institutions* (New York: Free Press, 1998).

32. DiMaggio and Powell, introduction.

33. Thelen and Steinmo, "Historical Institutionalism in Comparative Politics."

34. Ruth Berins Collier and David Collier, *Shaping the Political Arena: Critical Junctures, the Labor Movement, and Regime Dynamics in Latin America* (Princeton, NJ: Princeton University Press, 1991).

35. Paul Pierson, "Increasing Returns, Path Dependence, and the Study of Politics," *American Political Science Review* 94, no. 2 (June, 2000): 251–267.

36. Peter A. Hall and David Soskice, *Varieties of Capitalism: The Institutional Foundations of Comparative Advantage* (New York: Oxford University Press, 2001).

37. Campbell, "Institutional Reproduction and Change."

38. John L. Campbell and Ove K. Pedersen, eds., *Legacies of Change: Transformations of Postcommunist European Economies* (New York: Aldine de Gruyter, 1996); Stark and Bruzst, *Postsocialist Pathways*; Crouch and Farrell, "Breaking the Path of Institutional Development"; Elisabeth S. Clemens, "Lineages of the Rube Goldberg State: Building and Blurring Public Programs, 1900–1940," in *Rethinking Political Institutions: The Art of the State*, ed. Ian Shapiro, Stephen Skowronek, and Daniel Galvin (New York: New York University Press, 2006), 380–443; Schneiberg, "What's on the Path?"; Marie-Laure Djelic and Sigrid Quack, *Globalization and Institutions* (Cheltenham: Edward Elgar, 2003); Douglas North, *Understanding the Process of Economic Change* (Princeton, NJ: Princeton University Press, 2005); Streeck and Thelen, *Beyond Continuity*.

39. Orren and Skowronek, "Beyond the Iconography of Order."

40. Skowronek and Glassman, *Formative Acts*, 2–3.

41. There is reason to hypothesize that Arthur Bentley advocated a relational, not an agency-based or behavioral, political science, which is more in line with the research program of political creativity (at least late in his career). In 1949, he collaborated with John Dewey on *Knowing and the Known*, in which they advocated a shift from a mechanistic to a "transactional" approach to philosophy and social science, which paralleled Albert Einstein's shift to relativity in physics. As we point out in note 9, Mustafa Emirbayer draws heavily on Dewey and Bentley in his efforts to conceptualize and justify a relational, rather than a mechanistic, sociology. See Dewey and Bentley, *Knowing and the Known*; Emirbayer, "Manifesto for a Relational Sociology."

42. Mahoney and Thelen, *Explaining Institutional Change*.

43. Streeck and Thelen, *Beyond Continuity*.

44. See George Stocking, "Lamarckianism in American Social Science, 1890–1915," in *Race, Culture, and Evolution: Essays in the History of Anthropology*, ed. Stocking (Chicago: University of Chicago Press, 1982), 234–269; Raymond Seidelman, *Disenchanted Realists: Political Science and the American Crisis, 1884–1984* (Albany: State University of New York Press, 1985); David Ricci, *The Tragedy of Political Science: Politics, Scholarship, and Democracy* (New Haven, CT: Yale University Press, 1987); Peter Novak, *That Noble Dream: The "Objectivity" Question and the American Historical Profession* (New York: Cambridge University Press, 1988); John Gunnell, "American Political Science, and the Invention of Political Theory," *American Political Science Review* 82, no. 1 (March 1988): 71–87; Dorothy Ross, *The Origins of American Social*

Science (New York: Cambridge University Press, 1992); James Farr, *Discipline and History: Political Science in the United States* (Ann Arbor: University of Michigan Press, 1993); Thomas Bender and Carl Schorske, eds., *American Academic Culture in Transformation* (Princeton, NJ: Princeton University Press, 1998); Robert Vitalis, "Birth of a Discipline," in *Imperialism and Internationalism in the Discipline of International Relations*, ed. David Long and Brian Schmidt (Albany: State University of New York Press, 2005), 159–182; Benjamin Barber, "'The Politics of Political Science': 'Value-Free' Theory and the Wolin-Strauss Dust-up of 1963," *American Political Science Review* 111, no. 4 (November 2006): 539–545.

Chapter 1. Processes of Creative Syncretism

1. Gerald Berk and Dennis Galvan, "How People Experience and Change Institutions: A Field Guide to Creative Syncretism," *Theory and Society* 38 (2009): 543–580.

2. John Dewey, *Human Nature and Conduct* (Amherst, NY: Prometheus Books, 2002 [1922]).

3. Hans Joas, *The Creativity of Action* (Chicago: University of Chicago Press, 1996).

4. George Herbert Mead, *Mind, Self and Society* (Chicago: University of Chicago Press, 1962).

5. Michael Sheringham, *Everyday Life: Theories and Practices from Surrealism to the Present* (Oxford: Oxford University Press, 2006).

6. See, for example, Philip Scranton, "Urgency, Uncertainty and Innovation: Building Jet Engines in Cold War America," *Management and Organizational History* 1, no. 2 (March 2006): 127–157.

7. Alan Fox, *Beyond Contract: Work, Power and Trust Relations* (New York: Faber & Faber, 1974).

8. James Scott, *Seeing like a State: How Certain Schemes to Improve the Human Condition Have Failed* (New Haven, CT: Yale University Press, 1998).

9. Michel de Certeau, *The Practice of Everyday Life* (Berkeley: University of California Press, 1988).

10. Ibid., 25–26.

11. Ibid., 107.

12. Ibid., 96.

13. Claude Lévi-Strauss, *The Savage Mind* (Chicago: University of Chicago Press, 1996), 17.

14. Ibid., 19.

15. Ibid., 19–20.

16. Karl Weick, "Organizational Design as Improvisation," in G. P. Huber and W. H. Glick, eds., *Organizational Change and Redesign* (Oxford: Oxford University Press, 1993); Karl Weick, *Sensemaking and Organizations* (Thousand Oaks, CA: Sage, 1995); Karl Weick, *Making Sense of Organizations* (Malden, MA: Blackwell, 2000).

17. Isabelle Guerín, "Women and Money: Lessons from Sénégal," *Development and Change* 37, no. 3 (2006): 549–570.

18. Scott, *Seeing like a State*.

19. Dewey, *Human Nature and Conduct*, 15; Weick, "Organizational Design as Improvisation," 543–544.

20. Steven Epstein, *Impure Science: AIDS, Activism, and the Politics of Knowledge* (Berkeley: University of California Press, 1996).

21. Ibid., 188.

22. Martin Klein, *Islam and Imperialism in Senegal* (Stanford, CA: Stanford University Press, 1968).

23. Donal Cruise O'Brien, *Saints and Politicians: Essays in the Organization of a Senegalese Peasant Society* (London: Cambridge University Press, 1975).

24. Cheikh Anta Babou, *Fighting the Greater Jihad: Amadou Bamba and the Founding of the Muridiyya of Senegal, 1853–1913* (Athens: Ohio University Press, 2007).

25. Ernest Noirot, "Notice sur le Sine-Saloum, pays de Sine," *Journal Officiel du Sénégal et Dépendances*, April 16, 1892.

26. Lucy Behrman, *Muslim Brotherhoods and Politics in Senegal* (Cambridge, MA: Harvard University Press, 1970).

27. Allan F. Roberts, Mary Nooter Roberts, Gassia Armenian, and Ousmane Gueye, *A Saint in the City: Sufi Arts of Urban Sénégal* (Los Angeles: UCLA Fowler Museum of Cultural History, 2003).

28. Gerti Hesseling, *Histoire politique du Sénégal* (Paris: Karthala, 1985).

29. Donal Cruise O'Brien, *The Mourides of Senegal* (Oxford: Clarendon Press, 1971).

30. Leonardo Villalón, *Islamic Society and State Power in Senegal: Disciples and Citizens in Fatick* (Cambridge: Cambridge University Press, 1995).

31. Bruno Latour, *Reassembling the Social: An Introduction to Actor-Network Theory* (Oxford: Oxford University Press, 2005).

Chapter 2. Ecological Explanation

Thanks to Todd LaPorte, Paul Schulman, Eva Sørenson, Jacob Torfing, and especially Gerry Berk for comments on an earlier version of this essay. Sincere thanks also to Peter Houtzager, whose comments were extensive and substantial enough that I have decided that they are best addressed in a subsequent version of this argument. In general, the essay owes a great debt to the work and teaching of John Padgett.

1. One meaning of the term "ecological" in the social sciences often refers to explanations that emphasize human-environment interactions.

2. An ecological perspective adopts the assumption of "unitary" actors as an analytical convenience and this goes for both individual human beings and for more collective social organizations. Ideally, however, it is ecology "all the way down," meaning that on closer inspection, every unitary actor is an ecology.

3. Michael Hannan and John Freeman, "The Population Ecology of Organizations," *American Journal of Sociology* 82, no. 5 (1977): 929–964. This body of work traced its origins back to the synthetic statement about "human ecology" by Amos Hawley; see Hawley, *Human Ecology: A Theory of Community Structure* (New York: Ronald Press, 1950).

4. Glenn R. Carroll, "Organizational Ecology," *Annual Review of Sociology* 10 (1984): 71–93.

5. Paul DiMaggio and Walter Powell, "The Iron Cage Revisited: Institutional Isomorphism and Collective Rationality in Organizational Fields," *American Sociological Review*, 48, no. 2 (1983): 147–160.

6. John Levi Martin, "What Is Field Theory?" *American Journal of Sociology* 109, no. 1 (2003): 1–49.

7. Stephen R. Proulx, Daniel E. I. Promislow, and Patrick C. Phillips, "Network Thinking in Ecology and Evolution," *Trends in Ecology and Evolution* 20, no. 6 (2005): 345–353.

8. Chris Ansell, "Network Institutionalism," in Sarah Binder, Rod Rhodes, and Bert Rockman, eds., *Oxford Handbook of Political Institutions* (Oxford: Oxford University Press, 2006).

9. Christopher Ansell, *Pragmatist Democracy: Evolutionary Learning as Public Philosophy* (New York: Oxford University Press, 2011).

10. Everett C. Hughes, *The Sociological Eye: Selected Papers* (New Brunswick, NJ: Transaction Press, 1993); Everett C. Hughes, "The Ecological Aspect of Institutions," *American Sociological Review* 1, no. 2 (1936): 180–189.

11. Hughes, "The Ecological Aspect of Institutions," 181.

12. Miller McPherson, Lynn Smith-Lovin, and James M. Cook, "Birds of a Feather: Homophily in Social Networks," *Annual Review of Sociology* 27 (2001): 415–444.

13. T. P. Seager and T. L. Theis, "A Uniform Definition and Quantitative Basis for Industrial Ecology," *Journal of Cleaner Production* 10 (2002): 225–235.

14. One of the challenges for ecological explanation is to establish a clear separation between independent and dependent variables.

15. This is very close to what economic sociologists mean when they talk about the *embeddedness* of action. See Mark Granovetter, "Economic Action and Social Structure: The Problem of Embeddedness," *American Journal of Sociology* 91, no. 3 (1985): 481–510.

16. Annalee Saxenian, *Regional Advantage: Culture and Competition in Silicon Valley and Route 128* (Cambridge, MA: Harvard University Press, 1996).

17. Peter A. Hall and David Soskice, *Varieties of Capitalism: The Institutional Foundations of Comparative Advantage* (New York: Oxford University Press, 2001).

18. Ibid., 14.

19. On the concept of edges in natural ecology, see Leslie Ries, Robert J. Fletcher Jr., James Battin, and Thomas D. Sisk, "Ecological Responses to Habitat Edges: Mechanisms, Models, and Variability Explained," *Annual Review of Ecology, Evolution, and Systematics* 35 (2004): 491–522.

20. Susan Leigh Star and James R. Griesemer, "Institutional Ecology, 'Translations' and Boundary Objects: Amateurs and Professionals in Berkeley's Museum of Vertebrate Zoology, 1907–39," *Social Studies of Science* 19, no. 3 (1989): 387–420.

21. Examples include David Stark, "Recombinant Property in East European Capitalism," *American Journal of Sociology* 101, no. 4 (1996): 993–1027; Bryan Borys and David B. Jemison "Hybrid Arrangements as Strategic Alliances: Theoretical Issues in Organizational Combinations," *Academy of Management Review* 14, no. 2 (1989): 234–239.

22. For example, see Chris Ansell, Sarah Reckhow, and Andrew Kelly, "How to Reform a Reform Coalition: Outreach, Agenda Expansion, and Brokerage in Urban School Reform," *Policy Studies Journal* 37, no. 4 (2009): 717–743.

23. See especially Victor Turner's work, which develops a liminal perspective on process (e.g., Victor Turner, *The Ritual Process: Structure and Anti-Structure* (New Brunswick, NJ: Transaction Press, 1995).

24. Claude Lévi-Strauss, *The Savage Mind* (Chicago: University of Chicago Press, 1966).

25. John Padgett and Christopher K. Ansell, "Robust Action and the Rise of the Medici, 1400–1434," *American Journal of Sociology* 98 (1993): 1259–1319.

26. Harrison White, "Where Do Markets Come From?" *American Journal of Sociology* 87, no. 3 (1981): 517–547; Andrew Abbott, *The System of Professions* (Chicago: University of Chicago Press, 1988).

27. Christopher K. Ansell and Arthur Burris, "Bosses of the City Unite! Labor Politics and Political Machine Consolidation, 1870–1910," *Studies in American Political Development* 11 (1997): 1–43; Christopher K. Ansell and Antoine Joseph, "The Mass Production of Craft Unionism: Exploring the Sources of Workers' Solidarity in France and the U.S.," *Politics and Society* 26, no. 4 (1998): 575–602.

28. Gerald Berk and Dennis Galvan, "How People Experience and Change Institutions: A Field Guide to Creative Syncretism," *Theory and Society* 38 (2009): 543–580.

29. Ibid., 544.

30. Ibid.

31. Karen Orren and Stephen Skowronek, *The Search for American Political Development* (Cambridge: Cambridge University Press, 2004).

32. Berk and Galvan, "Creative Sycretism," 533.

33. Gerald Berk, *Louis D. Brandeis and the Making of Regulated Competition, 1900–1932* (Cambridge: Cambridge University Press, 2009).

34. Christopher K. Ansell, *Schism and Solidarity in Social Movements: The Politics of Labor in the French Third Republic* (Cambridge: Cambridge University Press, 2001).

Chapter 3. Governance Architectures

Thanks to Gerry Berk for editorial help and to Dennis Galvan, Jonathan Zeitlin, Andreas Glaeser, Andy Abbott, Dan Slater, Marc Blecher, and Maja Lotz for comments on earlier versions. Research was funded by the Alfred P. Sloan Foundation and the Hans Boeckler Stiftung.

1. Edward Steinfeld, *Playing Our Game* (New York: Oxford University Press, 2010); Françoise Lemoine, "FDI and the Opening Up of China's Economy," Centre d'Études Prospectives et d'Informations Internationales, París, 2000.

2. Loren Brandt and Eric Thun, "The Fight for the Middle," *World Development* 38, no 11 (2010): 1–20; Peter Marsh, "China's New Formula," *Financial Times*, May 29, 2008, 1–4; Mehdi Shafaeddin and Juan Pizarro, "The Evolution of Value Added in Assembly Operations," *Journal of Chinese Economic and Business Studies* 8, no. 4 (2000): 373–397; Lemoine, "FDI."

3. Brandt and Thun, "Fight for the Middle"; Peter Marsh of the *Financial Times* has been chronicling these dynamics for some time; see Peter Marsh, "Bosch Plans Big Drive into China," *Financial Times*, December 23, 2004, 1; Peter Marsh, "Focus on Deals High up Value Chain," *Financial Times*, April 25, 2011, 1–2; Marsh, "China's New Formula"; Peter Marsh, "Companies Move to Computerise Plants in China," *Financial Times*, June 1, 2005, 1; Peter Marsh, "Emerging Economies Flex Manufacturing Muscle," *Financial Times*, March 14, 2011, 1–4.

4. See Sebastian Heilmann and Elizabeth Perry, eds., *Mao's Invisible Hand* (Cambridge, MA: Harvard University Press, 2011).

5. Steinfeld, *Playing Our Game*; Richard Lester and Timothy J. Sturgeon, "China, America, and the Global Competition for Industry," Industrial Performance Center Working Paper, Massachusetts Institute of Technology, Cambridge, MA, 2003; K. M. Nam, "Learning Through the International Joint Venture," *Industrial and Corporate Change 20, No 3* (2011): 1–53; Daniel Breznitz and Michael Murphree, *Run of the Red Queen: Government, Innovation, Globalization, and Economic Growth in China* (New Haven, CT: Yale University Press, 2011). Our claim must not be taken for more than it is. We do not mean that differences in technological sophistication and organizational practice no longer exist between China and its developing country competitors. That gap is narrowing rapidly, but still exists. We argue that the differences in sophistication constitute a challenge for both Chinese and corporate competitors. As a result, the entire terrain on which the Chinese and corporate strategizing is taking place is rapidly shifting upward in value in a way that increasingly narrows the gap.

6. We develop these recursive effects on home country operations in our report to the Hans Boeckler Stiftung: "Globale Komponentenproduktion—Herausforderungen für deutsche Standorte in globalen Produktions—und Innovationsstrukturen der Zulieferindustrie," Goettingen, Germany 2012.

7. Charles Sabel, "Real Time Revolution in Routines," in Charles Heckscher and Paul S. Adler, eds., *The Corporation as a Collaborative Community* (New York: Oxford

University Press, 2005), 106–156; Steven J. Spear, *Chasing the Rabbit* (New York: McGraw Hill, 2009).

8. For the sociologically oriented literature, see Gerald A. McDermott and Rafael A. Corredoira, "Network Composition, Collaborative Ties, and Upgrading in Emerging-Market Firms," *Journal of International Business Studies* 41, no. 2 (2010): 308–329; G. Blalock and P. J. Gertler, "Foreign Direct Investment and Externalities," in T. H. Moran, E. M. Graham, and M. Blomstrom, eds., *Does Foreign Direct Investment Promote Development?* (Washington, DC: Institute for International Economics, 2005), 73–106; N. Lin, "Building a Network Theory of Social Capital," in N. Lin, K. Cook, and R. S. Burt, eds., *Social Capital* (New York: Aldine de Gruyter, 2001), 3–30. For the practice-oriented literature, see J. S. Brown and P. Duguid, "Organizational Learning and Communities-of-Practice," *Organization Science* 2, no 1 (1991): 40–57; F. Blackler and S. McDonald, "Power, Mastery and Organizational Learning," *Journal of Management Studies* 37, no. 6 (2000): 833–852; Etienne Wenger, *Communities of Practice: Learning, Meaning, and Identity* (Cambridge: Cambridge University Press, 1998); Jean Lave and Etienne Wenger, *Situated Learning* (New York: Cambridge University Press, 1991).

9. Brown and Duguid, "Organizational Learning."

10. Bente Elkjaer, "Organizational Learning with a Pragmatic Slant," *International Journal of Lifelong Education* 22, no. 5 (2003): 481–494; Bente Elkjaer, "Organizational Learning: The 'Third Way,'" *Management Learning* 35, no. 4 (2004): 419–434; B. Simpson, "Pragmatism, Mead and the Practice Turn," *Organization Studies* 30, no. 12 (2010): 1329–1347.

11. Sabel, "Real Time Revolution." See also AnnaLee Saxenian and Charles F. Sabel, "Roepke Lecture in Economic Geography, Venture Capital in the 'Periphery': The New Argonauts, Global Search, and Local Institution Building," *Economic Geography* 84, no. 4 (2007): 379–394.

12. John Dewey, *Human Nature and Conduct*, in *The Middle Works, 1899–1924*, vol. 14 (Carbondale: Southern Illinois University Press, 1922); George Herbert Mead, *Mind, Self and Society from the Standpoint of a Social Behaviorist* (Chicago: University of Chicago Press, 1934); Hans Joas, *The Creativity of Action* (Chicago: University of Chicago Press, 1995); Gary Herrigel, *Manufacturing Possibilities: Creative Action and Industrial Recomposition in the U.S., Germany and Japan* (Oxford: Oxford University Press, 2010).

13. Sabel, "Real Time Revolution," 121.

14. We show elsewhere that upgrading has been occurring over the last two decades in China. Gary Herrigel, Volker Wittke, and Ulrich Voskamp, "The Process of Chinese Manufacturing Upgrading: Transitioning from *Unilateral* to *Recursive Mutual Learning* Relations," *Global Strategy Journal* 3 (2013): 109–125.

15. See Moran, Graham, and Blomstrom, *Does Foreign Direct Investment Promote Development?*

16. Timothy J. Sturgeon, "Modular Production Networks: A New American Model of Industrial Organization," *Industrial and Corporate Change* 11, no. 3 (2002), 451–496; Boy Lüthje et al., *Contract Manufacturing: Transnationale Produktion und Industriearbeit in der IT-Branche* (Frankfurt: Campus, 2002); G. J. Gereffi, J. Humphrey, and Timothy J. Sturgeon, "The Governance of Global Value Chains," *Review of International Political Economy* 12, no. 1 (2005): 78–104; Breznitz and Murphree, *Run of the Red Queen*.

17. R. Gulati, N. Nohria, and A. Zaheer, "Strategic Networks," *Strategic Management Journal* 21, no. 3 (2000): 203–215; B. McEvily and A. Marcus, "Embedded Ties and the Acquisition of Competitive Capabilities," *Strategic Management Journal* 26, no. 11 (2005): 1033–1055; B. Uzzi and R. Lancaster, "Relational Embeddedness and Learning: The Case of Bank Loan Managers and Their Clients," *Management Science* 49, no. 4 2003): 383–399; G. Blalock and P. J. Gertler, "Foreign Direct Investment and Externalities: The Case for Public Intervention," in *Does Foreign Direct Investment Promote Development?* ed. T. H. Moran, E. M. Graham, and M. Blomstrom (Washington, D.C.: Institute for International Economics, 2005), 73–106; N. Lin, "Building a Network Theory of Social Capital," in *Social Capital: Theory and Research*, ed. N. Lin, K. Cook, and R. S. Burt (New York: Aldine de Gruyter, 2001), 3–30. See G. A. McDermott, R. A. Corredoira, "Network Composition, Collaborative Ties, and Upgrading in Emerging-Market Firms: Lessons from Argentine Autoparts Sector," *Journal of International Business Studies* 41, 2 (2010.): 308–329 for an overview.

18. See Brown and Duguid, "Organizational Learning"; Blackler and McDonald, "Power, Mastery and Organizational Learning."

19. Herrigel, Wittke, and Voskamp, "The Process of Chinese Manufacturing Upgrading."

20. Cressida Lui, "Collaboration on Thin Ground: Contract Production Arrangements Between Taiwanese Firms and Their American MNC Customers in the Personal Computer Industry," Ph.D. diss., University of Wisconsin, forthcoming; Breznitz and Murphree, *Run of the Red Queen*.

21. See Jeffrey H. Dyer and Wujin Chu, "The Determinants of Trust in Supplier–Automaker Relationships in the U.S., Japan, and Korea," *Journal of International Business Studies* 42, no. 1 (2011): 10–27; Inge Ivarsson and Claes Alvstam, "Upgrading in Global Value Chains: A Case Study of Technology Learning Among IKEA Suppliers in China and Southeast Asia," *Journal of Economic Geography* 11, no. 4 (2010): 731–752; Brown and Duguid, "Organizational Learning."

22. Herrigel, Wittke, and Voskamp, "The Process of Chinese Manufacturing Upgrading."

23. Herrigel, Wittke, and Voskamp, "The Process of Chinese Manufacturing Upgrading."

24. See Elkjaer, "Organizational Learning with a Pragmatic Slant"; Simpson, "Pragmatism, Mead and the Practice Turn"; Sabel, "Real Time Revolution."

25. Christopher Ansell, *Pragmatist Democracy: Evolutionary Learning as Public Philosophy* (New York: Oxford University Press, 2011).

26. In addition to Sabel, "Real Time Revolution"; see Charles Sabel, "Learning by Monitoring," in Neil J. Smelser and Richard Swedberg, eds., *The Handbook of Economic Sociology* (Princeton, NJ: Princeton University Press, 1994), 137–165.

27. Elkjaer, "Organizational Learning with a Pragmatic Slant"; Simpson, "Pragmatism, Mead and the Practice Turn." See also George Romme, "Making Organizational Learning Work: Consent and Double Linking Between Circles," *European Management Journal* 14, no. 1 (1996): 69–75; George Romme, "Organizational Learning, Circularity and Double Linking," *Management Learning* 28, no. 2 (1997): 149–160.

28. Dewey, *Human Nature and Conduct*; Mead, *Mind, Self and Society*; Joas, *The Creativity of Action*.

29. Sabel, "Learning by Monitoring"; Sabel, "Real Time Revolution."

30. L. Xi, L. Lei, and W. Guisheng, "Evolution of the Chinese Automobile Industry from a Sectoral System of Innovation Perspective," *Industry and Innovation* 16, no. 4 (2009): 463–478; Zejian Li, "The Role of International Technology Transfer in the Chinese Automotive Industry," MMRC Discussion Paper Series No. 269 (Tokyo, 2009), 1–23; Ivarsson and Alvstam, "Upgrading in Global Value Chains"; Breznitz and Murphree, *Run of the Red Queen*.

31. Marsh, "China's New Formula."

32. W. W. Chu, "How the Chinese Government Promoted a Global Automobile Industry," *Industrial and Corporate Change* 20, no. 5 (2011): 1235–1276; Eric Thun, *Changing Lanes in China* (Cambridge: Cambridge University Press, 2006); Li, "The Role of International Technology"; Herrigel, Wittke, and Voskamp, "The Process of Chinese Manufacturing Upgrading."

33. We also saw localization upgrading in visits to auto suppliers, woodworking machinery, and drive train and braking systems producers in the Shanghai and Tianjin regions.

34. See Sabel, "Real Time Revolution"; Spear, *Chasing the Rabbit*; Takahiro Fujimoto, *The Evolution of a Manufacturing System at Toyota* (New York: Oxford University Press, 1999).

35. See Johann Soder, "Ziel: Prozessberater-Pool in allen Feldern aufbauen Produktion: Interview mit Johann Soder, SEW-Eurodrive," *Produktion*, 7, p 27 February 16, 2006.

36. Sabel, "Real Time Revolution."

37. See Romme, "Making Organizational Learning Work" and "Organizational Learning, Circularity and Double Linking," for an interesting theoretical rendering of this dynamic.

38. Charles Sabel and Jonathan Zeitlin, "Experimentalist Governance," in David Levi-Faur, ed., *The Oxford Handbook of Governance* (New York: Oxford University

Press, forthcoming). This understanding of recursivity comes from mathematics and computer science.

39. Ivarsson and Alvstam, "Upgrading in Global Value Chains"; Lui, "Collaboration on Thin Ground."

40. This orientation may be specific to the sectors we studied and may be less characteristic of industries like electronics, where first mover monopolies account for an enormous share of value.

41. Kate Bronfenbrenner and Stephanie Luce, "The Changing Nature of Corporate Global Restructuring: The Impact of Production Shifts on Jobs in the US, China, and Around the Globe," report to US-China Economic and Security Review Commission, Ithaca, New York, October 14, 2004.

42. See Herrigel, Wittke, and Voskamp, "The Process of Chinese Manufacturing Upgrading."

43. On the nondetermining character of asymmetric power relations within multinational corporations and supply chains, see C. Bouquet and J. Birkinshaw, "Managing Power in the Multinational Corporation: How Low-Power Actors Gain Influence," *Journal of Management* 34, no. 3 (2008): 477–508; Stewart Clegg, David Courpasson, and Nelson Phillips, *Power and Organizations* (Thousand Oaks, CA: Sage, 2006).

Chapter 4. Reconfiguring Industry Structure

1. Gerald Berk and Dennis Galvan, "How People Experience and Change Institutions: A Field Guide to Creative Syncretism," *Theory and Society* 38, no. 6 (2009): 543–580; Stephen Skowronek and Matthew Glassman, eds., *Formative Acts: American Politics in the Making* (Philadelphia: University of Pennsylvania Press, 2008); Margaret Archer, *Structure, Agency, and the Internal Conversation* (New York: Cambridge University Press, 2003).

2. Gary Herrigel and Jonathan Zeitlin, "Inter-Firm Relations in Global Manufacturing: Disintegrated Production and Its Globalization," in Glenn Morgan, John L. Campbell, Colin Crouch, Ove Kaj Pedersen, and Richard Whitley, eds., *The Oxford Handbook of Comparative Institutional Analysis* (Oxford: Oxford University Press, 2010), 527–561.

3. Charles Sabel and Jonathan Zeitlin, "Stories, Strategies, Structure: Rethinking Historical Alternatives to Mass Production," in Charles Sabel and Jonathan Zeitlin, eds., *Worlds of Possibility* (Cambridge: Cambridge University Press, 1997), 1–33; Gerald Berk and Marc Schneiberg, "Varieties of Capitalism, Varieties of Association: Collaborative Learning in American Industry, 1900–1925," *Politics & Society* 33, no. 1 (2005): 46–87.

4. Cf. Stephen Skowronek, *The Politics Presidents Make: Leadership from John Adams to Bill Clinton* (Cambridge MA: Belknap Press, 1997).

5. Peter A. Hall and David Soskice, eds., *Varieties of Capitalism: The Institutional Foundations of Comparative Advantage* (New York: Oxford University Press, 2001); Paul Pierson, *Politics in Time: History, Institutions, and Social Analysis* (Princeton, NJ:

Princeton University Press, 2004); Sven Steinmo, Kathleen Thelen, and Frank Long-streth, eds., *Structuring Politics: Historical Institutionalism in Comparative Perspective* (Princeton, NJ: Princeton University Press, 1992).

6. Hall and Soskice *Varieties of Capitalism*; Wolfgang Streeck and Kozo Yama-mura, "Convergence or Diversity? Stability and Change in German and Japanese Capitalism," in Kozo Yamamura and Wolfgang Streeck, eds., *End of Diversity? Prospects for German and Japanese Capitalism* (Ithaca, NY: Cornell University Press, 2003), 1–50; J. Rogers Hollingsworth, "Continuities and Changes in Social Systems of Production: The Cases of Japan, Germany, and the United States," in J. Rogers Hollingsworth and Robert Boyer, eds., *Contemporary Capitalism* (Cambridge: Cambridge University Press, 1997), 265–310.

7. Kathleen Thelen, *How Institutions Evolve: The Political Economy of Skills in Germany, Britain, the United States, and Japan* (Cambridge: Cambridge University Press, 2004). Cf. Thomas R. Cusack, Torben Iversen, and David Soskice, "Economic Interests and the Origins of Electoral Systems," *American Political Science Review* 101, no. 3 (2007): 373–391.

8. Stephen Amberg, *The Union Inspiration in American Politics: The Autoworkers and the Making of a Liberal Industrial Order* (Philadelphia: Temple University Press, 1994).

9. James A. Gross, *Broken Promise: The Subversion of U.S. Labor Relations Policy, 1947–1994* (Philadelphia: Temple University Press, 1995); Stephen Amberg, "Governing Labor in Modernizing Texas," *Social Science History* 28, no. 1 (2004): 145–188.

10. Karen Orren and Stephen Skowronek, *The Search for American Political Development* (New York: Cambridge University Press, 2004).

11. Wolfgang Streeck and Kathleen Thelen, eds., *Beyond Continuity: Institutional Change in Advanced Political Economies* (New York: Oxford University Press, 2005), 1–37; Karen Orren and Stephen Skowronek, "Regimes and Regime Building in American Government: A Review of Literature on the 1940s," *Political Science Quarterly* 113, no. 4 (1998): 689–702; James Mahoney and Kathleen Thelen, "A Theory of Gradual Institutional Change," in James Mahoney and Kathleen Thelen, eds., *Explaining Institutional Change: Ambiguity, Agency, and Power* (New York: Cambridge University Press, 2010): 1–37.

12. See Christopher Ansell's contribution to this volume; Hans Joas, The Creativity of Action (Chicago: University of Chicago Press, 1996), 158; Mary Douglas, *How Institutions Think* (Syracuse: Syracuse University Press, 1986). Cf. Kathleen Thelen, "Beyond Comparative Statics: Historical Institutional Approaches to Stability and Change in the Political Economy of Labor," in Morgan et al., *Oxford Handbook of Comparative Institutional Analysis*, 41–61;

13. Stephen Amberg, "Liberal Market Economy or Composite Regime? Institutional Legacies and Labor Market Policy in the United States," *Polity* 40, no. 2 (2008): 164–196.

14. Steven Greenhouse, "Taking a Vote on Union Construction," *New York Times*, October 15, 2010; Bob McCullough, senior vice president of manufacturing at HEB, speech, (Center for Advanced Manufacturing and Lean Systems, University of Texas at San Antonio, November 12, 2010).

15. A president may draw on the resources that he or she inherits from party politics, developments of institutional authority, and contingent conditions, and on his or her own imagination about how these resources are conditions for what that president wants to do. Skowronek, *The Politics Presidents Make*.

16. Amberg, *Union Inspiration*; John Dunlop, *Industrial Relations Systems* (Carbondale: University of Southern Illinois University Press, 1957); Ira Katznelson and Sean Farhang, "The Southern Imposition: Congress and Labor in the New Deal and Fair Deal," *Studies in American Political Development* 19 (2005): 1–30.

17. Marie Gottschalk, *The Shadow Welfare State* (Ithaca, NY: Cornell University Press, 2000).

18. Harry C. Katz, *Shifting Gears: Changing Labor Relations in the U.S. Automobile Industry* (Cambridge, MA: MIT Press, 1985), 14f.

19. Paul Frymer, *Black and Blue: African Americans, the Labor Movement, and the Decline of the Democratic Party* (Princeton, NJ: Princeton University Press, 2008); Robert Lieberman, *Shifting the Color Line* (Cambridge, MA: Harvard University Press, 1998).

20. Lieberman, *Shifting the Color Line.*

21. Eric Parker, *Inside the Circle: A Union Guide to QWL* (Boston: South End Press/Labor Notes, 1985); Richard Walton, "From Control to Commitment in the Workplace," in *Harvard Business Review* 63, no. 2 (1985): 76–84; Thomas Kochan, Harry Katz, and Robert McKersie, *The Transformation of American Industrial Relations* (New York: Basic Books, 1986); Barry Bluestone and Irving Bluestone, *Negotiating the Future* (New York: Basic Books, 1992), 191–201.

22. John Krafick, "Triumph of a Lean Production System," *Sloan Management Review* 30, no. 1 (1988): 41–52; John Paul MacDuffie and John Krafcik, "Integrating Technology and Human Resources for High-Performance Manufacturing: Evidence from the International Auto Industry," in Thomas Kochan and Michael Useem, eds., *Transforming Organizations* (New York: Oxford University Press, 1992), 209–226.

23. Michael Cusumano, *The Japanese Automobile Industry* (Cambridge, MA: Harvard University Press, 1985); John Womack, Daniel Jones, and Daniel Roos, *The Machine That Changed the World: The Story of Lean Production* (New York: Rawson, 1990).

24. Kazuhiro Mishina, "Making Toyota in America: Evidence from the Kentucky Transplant, 1986–1994," in Robert Boyer, Elsie Charron, Ulrich Jurgens, and Steven Tolliday, eds., *Between Imitation and Innovation: The Transfer and Hybridization of Productive Models in the International Automobile Industry* (Oxford: Oxford University Press, 1998), 99–127.

25. Mishina, "Making Toyota"; Paul S. Adler, Barbara Goldoftas, and David I. Levine, "Stability and Change at NUMMI," in Boyer et al., *Between Imitation and Innovation*, 128–160; Frits K. Pil and Takahiro Fujimoto, "Lean and Reflective Production: The Dynamic Nature of Production Models," *International Journal of Production Research* 45, no. 16 (2007): 3741–3761.

26. Jonathan Zeitlin, "The Historical Alternatives Approach," in Geoffrey Jones and Jonathan Zeitlin, eds., *The Oxford Handbook of Business History* (New York: Oxford University Press, 2008), 120–140; Colin Crouch, *Capitalist Diversity and Change: Recombinant Governance and Institutional Entrepreneurs* (New York: Oxford University Press, 2005); Gerald Berk, *Alternative Tracks* (Baltimore: Johns Hopkins University Press, 1994).

27. Neil Fligstein, "The Rise of the Shareholder Value Conception of the Firm and the Merger Movement in the 1980s," in Fligstein, *The Architecture of Markets* (Princeton, NJ: Princeton University Press, 2001): 147–169; Michael Useem, *Investor Capitalism* (New York: Basic Books, 1996).

28. Robert B. Reich and John D. Donahue, *New Deals: The Chrysler Revival and the American System* (New York: Times Books, 1985), 133–134.

29. Michael Piore and Charles Sabel, *The Second Industrial Divide* (New York: Basic Books, 1984); Parker, *Inside the Circle*; Kochan, Katz, and McKersie, *Transformation*; Paul Osterman, *Security Prosperity* (New York: Century Foundation, 1999); Reich and Donahue, *New Deals*, 135, 251, 268.

30. Paul W. McCracken, "Can Capitalism Survive?" in Herbert V. Prochnow, ed., *Dilemmas Facing the Nation* (Washington, DC: American Enterprise Institute, 1979), 134–152.

31. Norman S. Fieleke, "The Automobile Industry," *Annals of the American Academy of Political and Social Science* 460 (March 1982): 83–91, cited by Thomas H. Klier, "From Tail to Fins to Hybrids: How Detroit Lost Its Dominance of the U.S. Auto Market," [Federal Reserve Bank of Chicago], *Economic Perspectives* second quarter (2009): 2–17.

32. Mike Parker and Jane Slaughter, *Choosing Sides: Unions and the Team Concept* (Boston: South End Press, 1988); Mike Parker and Jane Slaughter, eds., *Working Smart: A Union Guide to Participation Programs and Reengineering* (Detroit: Labor Notes, 1994); Daniel Marschall and Ellen Scully-Russ, "Joint Union-Management Workforce Development Model," in David Finegold, Mary Gatta, Hal Salzman, and Susan J. Schurman, eds., *Transforming the U.S. Workforce Development System* (Champaign, IL: LERA, 2010) 205–236.

33. Josh Whitford, *The New Old Economy: Networks, Institutions, and the Organizational Transformation of American Manufacturing* (New York: Oxford University Press, 2005), 60–75, 99f, 112.

34. Saul A. Rubenstein and Thomas A. Kochan, *Learning from Saturn: Possibilities for Corporate Governance and Employee Relations* (Ithaca, NY: ILR Press, 2001); Joe

Sherman, *In the Rings of Saturn* (New York: Oxford University Press, 1994); Henry Bass, *What Happened to Saturn?* (Merrimack Films, 2007).

35. Rubenstein and Kochan, *Learning from Saturn*, 27, 28.

36. Ibid., 35.

37. Ibid., 50, 118f.

38. Commission on the Future of Worker-Management Relations, *Report and Recommendations* (Washington, DC: U.S. Department of Labor, 1994).

39. Rubenstein and Kochan, *Learning from Saturn*, 109–111.

40. Ruth Milkman, *Farewell to the Factory: Auto Workers in the Late Twentieth Century* (Berkeley: University of California Press, 1997), 93–136.

41. David Rogers and Mike Allen, "Bush Announces $17.4 Billion Auto Bailout," *Politico*, December 19, 2008, www.politico.com/news/stories/1208/16740.html.

42. Steven Rattner, *Overhaul: An Insider's Account of the Obama Administration's Emergency Rescue of the Auto Industry* (Boston: Houghton Mifflin, 2010); statement of Ron Bloom, senior advisor at the U.S. Treasury Department, before the Senate Banking Committee, June 10, 2009.

43. "Remarks by the President on the American Automobile Industry," March 30, 2009, www.whitehouse.gov/the_press_office/.

44. Editorial, *Wall Street Journal*, December 1, 2008; Daniel Griswold and Daniel J. Ikenson, "Blowing Exhaust: Detroit's Woes Belie a Healthy U.S. Auto Market," July 27, 2006, www.cato.org.

45. Annual Toyota sales were off 36.7 percent, Honda 34.7 percent, Nissan 30.7 percent, Hyundai 48.3 percent, and BMW 36.0 percent. Cf. Stephen Cooney and Brent D. Yacobucci, "U.S. Automotive Industry: Policy Overview and Recent History," Congressional Research Service Report for Congress, April 25, 2005, Washington, DC; Stephen Cooney, "Motor Vehicle Manufacturing Employment: National and State Trends and Issues," Congressional Research Service Report, December 27, 2007, Washington, DC.

46. "Remarks of President Obama," March 30, 2009, www.whitehouse.gov/blog.

47. Barack Obama, "The House upon a Rock," April 14, 2009, www.whitehouse .gov/blog; Barack Obama, "The American Graduation Initiative: Stronger American Skills Through Community Colleges," speech, Warren, Michigan, July 14, 2009, www .whitehouse.gov/the_press_office/; National Economic Council, *A Strategy for American Innovation: Driving Toward Sustainable Growth and Quality Jobs*, September 2009, www.whitehouse.gov.; Jared Bernstein, "Chains in Command," June 23, 2009, www .whitehouse.gov/blog.

48. Thomas A. Kochan, Eileen Appelbaum, Jody Hoffer Gittell, Carrie Leana, and Richard A. Gephardt, *Workplace Innovation and Labor Policy Leadership: A Challenge to Business, Labor, and Government* (Washington, DC: Center for Economic Policy and Research, 2009), 1–10.

49. Klier, "From Tails Fins to Hybrids."

50. Susan Helper and Howard Wial, "Putting U.S. Cars on the High Road to Recovery," Metropolitan Economy Initiative 8 (Washington, DC: Brookings Institution, 2009), www.brookings.edu/opinions/2009/0304_auto_industry_wial.aspx; Susan Helper and John Paul MacDuffie, "Better than a Bailout: Here's How to Rescue Detroit Without Forcing Them into Bankruptcy," *New Republic*, December 2, 2008.

51. Robert E. Scott, "Invest in America: Essential Policies Needed to Secure U.S. Jobs and Broadly Shared Prosperity in the Auto Industry," Briefing Paper 233 (Economic Policy Institute, Washington, DC, April 8, 2009).

52. Cooney and Yacobucci, "U.S. Automotive Industry"; Cooney, "Motor Vehicle Manufacturing Employment," 12.

53. Rattner, *Overhaul*, 69–79, 127.

54. Alison Fitzgerald and Jonathan D. Salant, "Toyota, BMW, Hyundai Workers' Senators Oppose Federal Bailout," *Bloomberg*, www.bloomberg.com, accessed November 17, 2008; Emily Pierce and Steven T. Dennis, "Bailout Bill Needs Own Rescue Plan," *Roll Call*, December 11, 2008; Geof Koss, "Congressional Reaction Is Mixed to White House Auto Bailout," *Roll Call*, December 19, 2008.

55. Cooney, "Motor Vehicle Manufacturing Employment," 25–32.

56. "How Deal Can Pull GM Even with Toyota," *Detroit Free Press*, October 2, 2007, and Sean McAlinden, "The Big Leave: The Future of Michigan's Automotive Industry" (University of Michigan Center for Automotive Research, Ann Arbor, November 15, 2007), cited in Cooney, "Motor Vehicle Manufacturing Employment," 30.

57. Teresa Ghilarducci, "The New Treaty of Detroit: Are Voluntary Employee Benefits Associations Organized Labor's Way Forward, or the Remnants of a Once Glorious Past?" (Institute for Research on Labor and Employment, Berkeley CA, 2007), *www.irle.berkeley.edu/events/fall07/symposium/ghilarducci.pdf.*

58. Militants in the union opposed the voluntary associations because future health care needs were not guaranteed. They preferred national health care. See "Ford-UAW 2007 Lowlights," Soldiers of Solidarity at www.soldiersofsolidarity.org, 2007. Jerry Tucker, "VEBAs No! National Health Care Yes!" Center for Labor Renewal, http://www.solidarityeducationcenter.org/?P = A&Category_ID = 24&Article = 183, September 2007.

59. Editorial, *Wall Street Journal*, December 1, 2008.

60. Southern states subsidized the auto transplants. See Good Jobs First at www .goodjobsfirst.org/corporate-subsidy-watch/foreign-auto-plants, 2010.

61. "Further Examining the State of the U.S. Domestic Automotive Industry and Its Overall Impact on the Nation's Economy, the Automotive Workers, and the Companies Involved in the Supply Chain and Their Employees," *Hearing Before the Committee on Banking, Housing, and Urban Affairs.* U.S. Senate. 110th Cong., 2nd sess (December 4, 2008), 101.

62. Amberg, "Liberal Market Economy or Composite Regime?"

63. See www.uaw.org/convention/videos/president-bob-kings-entire-address-35th-uaw-constitutional-convention-6-files. See Bob King, "A UAW for the 21st Century," speech (Center for Automotive Research Conference, University of Michigan, Ann Arbor, August 2, 2010); Jennifer M. Granholm, in "Not Your Father's UAW," *Huffington Post*, August 10, 2010, wrote that King's speech "sent tremors . . . right through Tennessee and down to Alabama and off to Juarez." See also Keith Naughton, "UAW's New President Focuses on Organizing Toyota's U.S. Workers," *Bloomberg Businessweek*, June 17, 2010; Jane Slaughter, "UAW Says It Will Go 'All In' to Organize Foreign-Owned Auto Plants," *Labor Notes*, February 2011.

64. Josh Whitford and Jonathan Zeitlin, "Governing Decentralized Production: Institutions, Public Policy, and the Prospects for Inter-Firm Collaboration in US Manufacturing," *Industry and Innovation* 11 (March–June 2004): 11–44; Timothy J. Sturgeon, Olga Memedovic, Johannes Van Biesebroeck, and Gary Gereffi, "Globalisation of the Automotive Industry: Main Features and Trends," *International Journal of Technological Learning, Innovation and Development* 2, nos. 1–2 (2009): 7–24.

65. Kate Pickert, "Ron Bloom, Obama's Car Non-Czar," *Time*, February 18, 2009; Kathryn Kroll, "Steel May Give Auto Industry Restructuring Roadmap," *Cleveland Plain Dealer*, February 23, 2009; "Meet Obama's New Manufacturing Whiz, Ron Bloom," *Manufacturing & Technology News*, September 17, 2009.

66. Jonathan Alter, *The Promise: President Obama* (New York: Simon & Schuster, 2010), 184.

67. U.S. Government Accountability Office, "Troubled Asset Relief Program: Continued Stewardship Needed as Treasury Develops Strategies for Monitoring and Divesting Financial Interests in Chrysler and GM" (GAO Report to Congressional Committees, Washington, DC, November 2009).

68. "Determination of Viability Summary" for General Motors and for Chrysler, March 30, 2009, www.whitehouse.gov/the_press_office/.

69. Nick Bunkley, "Aid Program for Suppliers Starts with $3.5 Billion in Loans to GM and Chrysler," *New York Times*, April 9, 2009; Susan Helper, "Best Options for the Auto Industry Crisis" (MIT International Motor Vehicle Program, Cambridge, MA, November 20, 2008), lerablog.org; Bill Vlasic, "A Flush GM to Lavish Cash on New Vehicles," *New York Times*, December 7, 2009.

70. Steven Rattner, "The Auto Bailout: How We Did It," *Fortune Magazine*, October 21, 2009.

71. U.S. Government Accountability Office, "Troubled Asset Relief Program," 14, 24–25.

72. Ibid., 12, 24.

73. Rattner, *Overhaul*, 280–281.

74. "U.S. Likely to Sell GM Stake Before Chrysler," *New York Times*, August 6, 2009; U.S. Government Accountability Office, "Troubled Asset Relief Program," 15.

75. Fiat had to agree to produce an engine for a compact car in the United States; Bill Vlasic, "Chrysler Pays Back Rescue Loan," *New York Times*, May 24, 2011.

76. Carol Loomis, "The Tragedy of General Motors," *Fortune*, February 6, 2006; Nick Bunkley, "U.S. to Allow GM to Use Federal Loans to Invest in Delphi," *New York Times*, November 3, 2009.

77. Nick Bunkley, "$4,000 Bonus Checks for GM Workers," *New York Times*, February 15, 2011.

78. "April 2009 UAW-Chrysler Settlement Agreement" and "2009 UAW-GM Modification Agreement," Soldiers of Solidarity, www.soldiersofsolidarity.com, 2009. Nick, Bunkley, "UnionVotes Go Against Cuts at Ford," *New York Times*, October 28, 2009.

79. Bill Vlasic, "Detroit Refueled," *New York Times*, October 14, 2010.

80. James T. Kloppenberg, *Reading Obama: Dreams, Hopes, and the American Tradition* (Princeton, NJ: Princeton University Press, 2011); Judith Butler, "Performative Agency," *Journal of Cultural Economy* 3, no. 2 (2010): 147–161.

Chapter 5. Animating Institutional Skeletons

1. James Mahoney and Kathleen Thelen, "A Theory of Gradual Institutional Change," in James Mahoney and Kathleen Thelen, eds., *Explaining Institutional Change: Ambiguity, Agency and Power* (New York: Cambridge University Press, 2010), 9–10.

2. Amy Bridges, "Path Dependence, Sequence, History, Theory," *Studies in American Political Development* 14 (Spring 2000): 111; Mahoney and Thelen, "A Theory," 2; Wolfgang Streeck and Kathleen Thelen, "Institutional Change in Advanced Political Economies," introduction to Wolfgang Streeck and Kathleen Thelen, eds., *Beyond Continuity: Institutional Change in Advanced Political Economies* (New York: Oxford University Press, 2005), 5–6.

3. Streeck and Thelen, "Institutional Change," 1.

4. Mahoney and Thelen, "A Theory," 2.

5. Marc Schneiberg, "Combining Institutionalisms: Explaining Institutional Change in American Property Insurance," *Sociological Forum* 20 (March 2005): 94; Huseyin Leblebici et al., "Institutional Change and the Transformation of Interorganizational Fields: An Organizational History of the U.S. Radio Broadcasting Industry," *Administrative Science Quarterly* 36 (September 1991): 333–339.

6. Mahoney and Thelen, "A Theory," 1–2.

7. Examples of works that embrace a punctuated equilibrium view are Ira Katznelson, "Periodization and Preferences: Reflections on Purposive Action in Comparative Historical Social Science," in James Mahoney and Dietrich Rueschemeyer, eds., *Comparative Historical Analysis in the Social Sciences* (New York: Cambridge University Press, 2003); James Mahoney, "Path-Dependent Explanations of Regime Change: Central America in Comparative Perspective," *Studies in Comparative International Development* 36 (Spring 2001); Ruth Collier and David Collier, *Shaping the Political Arena: Critical Junctures, the Labor Movement and Regime Change in Latin America*

(Princeton, NJ: Princeton University Press, 1991), ch. 1; Brian Arthur, *Increasing-Returns and Path Dependence in the Economy* (Ann Arbor: University of Michigan Press, 1994), chs. 1 and 2. Insurgent works that also embrace the dichotomy while emphasizing gradual endogenous change and a greater room for agency include Ato Kwamena Onoma, "The Contradictory Potential of Institutions: The Rise and Decline of Land Documentation in Kenya," in Mahoney and Thelen, *Explaining Institutional Change*; Adam Sheingate, "Rethinking Rules: Creativity and Constraint in the U.S. House of Representatives," in Mahoney and Thelen, *Explaining Institutional Change*; Dan Slater, "Altering Authoritarianism: Institutional Complexity and Autocratic Agency in Indonesia," in Mahoney and Thelen, *Explaining Institutional Change*.

8. Mahoney and Thelen, *Explaining Institutional Change*.

9. Streeck and Thelen, *Beyond Continuity*.

10. Streeck and Thelen, "Institutional Change," 9; James Mahoney and Kathleen Thelen, preface to Mahoney and Thelen, *Explaining Institutional Change*, xi.

11. Mahoney and Thelen, preface, xi.

12. Eric Hobsbawm, "Peasants and Politics," *Journal of Peasant Studies* 1 (October 1973): 13.

13. James Scott, *Weapons of the Weak: Everyday Forms of Peasant Resistance* (New Haven, CT: Yale University Press, 1985), xv–xvii; James Scott, *Domination and the Arts of Resistance: Hidden Transcripts* (New Haven, CT: Yale University Press, 1990), 17, 188.

14. Albert O. Hirschman, *Exit, Voice and Loyalty: Responses to Decline in Firms, Organizations and States* (Cambridge, MA: Harvard University Press, 1970).

15. Jack Knight, *Institutions and Social Conflict* (New York: Cambridge University Press); Kathryn Firmin-Sellers, *The Transformation of Property Rights in the Gold Coast* (New York: Cambridge University Press); Terry Moe, "Power and Political Institutions," *Perspectives on Politics* 3 (June 2005): 221–228; Mahoney and Thelen, "A Theory," 8.

16. Elisabeth Clemens, "Organizational Repertoires and Institutional Change: Women's Groups and the Transformation of U.S. Politics, 1890–1920," *American Journal of Sociology* 98 (January 1993): 756; Schneiberg, "Combining New Institutionalisms," 120–121; Marc Schneiberg and Elisabeth Clemens, "The Typical Tools for the Job: Research Strategies in Institutional Analysis," *Sociological Theory* 24 (September 2006): 218.

17. Mahoney and Thelen, "A Theory," 9–10.

18. Ibid., 1–2.

19. Botswana, *National Development Plan, 1968–73* (Gaborone: Government Printer, 1968), 10.

20. Faustin Kalabamu and Siamsang Morolong, "Informal Land Delivery Processes and Access to Land for the Poor in Greater Gaborone, Botswana," Informal Land Delivery Processes Working Paper 3 (International Development Department, School of Public Policy, University of Birmingham, 2004), 48–49.

21. Ibid., 47.

22. Ibid., 47. This was one significant blow among many that the BDP dealt to chiefs' power. Laws such as the House of Chiefs (Powers and Privileges) Act in 1965, Chieftainship Act of 1965, Local Government (District Councils) Act (1965), and Matimela Act (1969) badly eroded the powers of traditional chiefs and subordinated them to state officials. See Ato Onoma, *The Politics of Property Rights Institutions in Africa* (New York: Cambridge University Press, 2010), 93–94.

23. Kalabamu and Morolong, "Informal Land Delivery," 49; Onoma, *The Politics of Property Rights*, 66–72; Botshelo Mathuba, *Report on the Review of the Tribal Land Act, Land Policies and Related Issues* (Gaborone: Government Printer, 1989), 71; Botshelo Mathuba, *Land Administration in Botswana* (Gaborone: Ministry of Lands, 1991); Susan Wynne, "The Land Boards of Botswana: A Problem in Institutional Design" (Ph.D. diss., Indiana University, 1989), 26; John Comaroff, "Class and Culture in a Peasant Economy: The Transformation of Land Tenure in Barolong," *Journal of African Law* 24 (Spring 1980): 107.

24. Onoma, *The Politics of Property Rights*, 66–72.

25. Mathuba, *Land Administration*, 4.

26. Wynne, "The Land Boards of Botswana," 1.

27. Interviews with a deputy land board secretary in Kweneng District, January 27, 2004, and a staff member of the Department of Surveys and Mapping, Gaborone, January 15, 2004.

28. Kalabamu and Morolong, "Informal Land Delivery," 51.

29. Wynne, "The Land Boards of Botswana," 447–457.

30. Botshelo Mathuba, "Opening Address by Permanent Secretary, Ministry of Lands and Housing-Botshelo Mathuba at a Joint Orientation Workshop for New Land Board Members—Ghanzi 26th to 28th January 2004."

31. Mathuba, *Land Administration*, 8.

32. Mathuba, "Opening Address."

33. Ibid.

34. Wynne, "The Land Boards of Botswana," 447–457; Comaroff, "Class and Culture," 107.

35. Interview with a deputy subordinate land board clerk in Kweneng District, March 17, 2004.

36. Ato Onoma, "Mutual Gains from Hostile Confrontations: Land Boards, Their Clients and 'Self Allocation' in Botswana," *Africa Development* 34, no. 1 (2009): 111.

37. Interview with a staff member at one of the main land boards in Botswana, February 2, 2004.

38. Onoma, *The Politics of Property Rights*, 72–75.

39. Ibid., 74–75.

40. Ibid., 65.

41. Adrian Cullis and Cathy Watson, "Winners and Losers: Privatizing the Commons in Botswana," International Institute for Environment and Development and

RECONCILE Briefing Paper (December 2003), 9, 16; Jack Parson, "The Trajectory of Class and State in Dependent Development: The Consequences of New Wealth for Botswana," *Commonwealth and Comparative Politics* 21 (1983): 54; Comaroff, "Class and Culture," 106–110; Louis Picard, "Bureaucrats, Cattle, and Public Policy: Land Tenure Changes in Botswana," *Comparative Political Studies* 13 (October 1980): 314; Jack Parson, "Cattle, Class and the State in Rural Botswana," *Journal of Southern African Studies* 2 (1981): 244.

42. Onoma, *The Politics of Property Rights*, 75.

43. Ibid., 77–78.

44. Ibid., 73–74.

45. See Hernando de Soto, *The Mystery of Capital: Why Capitalism Triumphs in the West and Fails Everywhere Else* (London: Bantam, 2000), for some of the benefits of property rights reforms.

46. Wynne, "The Land Boards of Botswana," 26. For more on the political significance of the control of land, see Martin Doornbos, "Land Tenure and Political Conflict in Ankole, Uganda," *Journal of Development Studies* 12 (October 1975): 65–66; Jean-Philippe Platteau, "The Evolutionary Theory of Land Rights as Applied to Sub-Saharan Africa: A Critical Assessment," *Development and Change* 27 (1996): 52–53.

47. House of Chiefs, *Official Report of the Proceedings of the Thirteenth Meeting of the House of Chiefs Sitting from 5th August to 7th August, 1968* (Gaborone: Government Printer, 1968), 30–31.

48. J. H. Proctor, "The House of Chiefs and the Political Development of Botswana," *Journal of Modern African Studies* 6 (May 1968): 59.

49. Kalabamu and Morolong, "Informal Land Delivery," 25.

50. Ibid.

51. Wynne, "The Land Boards of Botswana," 308–312.

52. Ibid., 318–321.

53. See Richard Werbner, "The Quasi-Judicial and the Experience of the Absurd: Remaking Land Law in North-Eastern Botswana," *Journal of African Law* 24 (Spring 1980), and Comaroff, "Class and Culture," for many of the problems that people had with the land boards.

54. Comaroff, "Class and Culture," 108; Werbner, "The Quasi-Judicial," 144–145. Kalabamu and Morolong list six other reasons for which land boards could cancel rights in "Informal Land Delivery," 50.

55. Wynne, "The Land Boards of Botswana," 26.

56. Comaroff, "Class and Culture," 110; Wynne, "The Land Boards of Botswana," 390.

57. *Report of the Presidential Commission of Inquiry into Land Problems in Mogoditshane and Other Peri-urban Villages* (Gaborone: Government Printer, 1991).

58. See Werbner, "The Quasi-Judicial," 144–147.

59. Ibid., 144.

60. Onoma, "Mutual Gains," 107.

61. Comaroff, "Class and Culture," 108; Werbner, "The Quasi-Judicial," 135–145.

62. Wynne, "The Land Boards of Botswana," 32, 316, 326. Also see the speech of Gaborone at the House of chiefs as reported in House of Chiefs, *Official Report*, 30–31.

63. Wynne, "The Land Boards of Botswana," 26; Onoma, "Mutual Gains," 110–113; Comaroff, "Class and Culture," 110.

64. House of Chiefs, *Official Report*, 30–31.

65. Hobsbawm, "Peasants and Politics," 13.

66. Comaroff, "Class and Culture," 107.

67. Mahoney and Thelen, "A Theory," 11.

68. Ibid., 10.

69. Ibid., 9–10.

70. Wynne, "The Land Boards of Botswana," 5.

71. Friedrich A. Hayek, "The Use of Knowledge in Society," *American Economic Review* 35 (September 1945): 521.

72. James Scott, *Seeing like a State:How Certain Schemes to Improve the Human Condition Have Failed* (New Haven, CT: Yale University Press, 1998), 6.

73. Ibid., 3.

74. Response by the attorney general to a question in the House of Chiefs. House of Chiefs, *Official Report*, 30; Kalabamu and Morolong, "Informal Land Delivery," 51;

75. Onoma, *The Politics of Property Rights*, 96.

76. Mathuba, *Land Administration*; Kalabamu and Morolong, "Informal Land Delivery," 51.

77. Interview with a land board clerk in Central District, February 11, 2004; Wynne, "The Land Boards of Botswana," 368–370.

78. Interview with a land board clerk in Central District, February 11, 2004; Wynne, "The Land Boards of Botswana," 368–370.

79. Interview with a land board member in Central District, February 21, 2004.

80. Interview with a member of the National House of Chiefs in Gaborone, January 29, 2004.

81. This account is gleaned from my observation and participation in the activities of the Mahalapye Subordinate Land Board during its allocation exercises in Mahalapye village in February 2004 and from a series of interviews with a land board staff, February 12, 2004; board member, February 13, 2004; board staff, February 18, 2004; board member, February 20, 2004; and board member, February 21, 2004.

82. Observation of Mahalapye land board and related interviews.

83. Observation of Mahalapye land board and related interviews.

84. B. Machacha, "Botswana's Land Tenure: Institutional Reform and Policy Formulation," in J. W. Arntzen, W. L. D. Ngcongco, and S. D. Turner, eds., *Land Policy and Agriculture in Eastern and Southern Africa: Selected Papers Presented at a Workshop*

Held in Gaborone, Botswana, 14–19 February, 1982 (Tokyo: United Nations University, 1986).

85. Kalabamu and Morolong, "Informal Land Delivery," 49.

86. Ibid., 49.

87. Interview with a deputy subordinate land board clerk in Kweneng District, March 17, 2004, 2004.

88. I visited the Kgatleng, Kweneng, Ngwato, and Tati Land Boards and the Mochudi, Mogoditshane, Molepolole, Mahalapye , Shoshong, Bobonong, and Serowe Land and Subordinate Land Boards.

89. Werbner, "The Quasi-Judicial," 133; Comaroff, "Class and Culture," 108.

90. Interview with a staff member at one of the main land boards in Botswana, February 2, 2004.

91. Ibid.

92. Interview with a land board member, February 20, 2004.

93. Interview with a land board member in Central District, February 21, 2004.

94. Wynne, "The Quasi-Judicial," 5.

95. Scott, *Weapons of the Weak*, xvii. Also see Goran Hyden, *Beyond Ujamaa in Tanzania* (London: Heinemann, 1980), 32, 231; Scott, *Domination and the Arts of Resistance*, 188–189.

96. Mahoney and Thelen, "A Theory," 1–2.

97. Ibid.

98. Mahoney and Thelen, preface, xi.

Chapter 6. Creating Political Strategy

1. Gerald Berk and Dennis Galvan, "How People Experience and Change Institutions: A Field Guide to Creative Syncretism," *Theory and Society* 38 (July 2009): 543–580.

2. Walter W. Powell and Jeannette A. Colyvas, "Microfoundations of Institutional Theory," in *The Sage Handbook of Organizational Institutionalism*, ed. Royston Greenwood, Christine Oliver, and Roy Suddaby (London: Sage, 2008), 276–298.

3. Michael E. McGerr, *The Decline of Popular Politics: The American North: 1865–1928* (New York: Oxford University Press, 1986).

4. Richard Franklin Bensel, *The American Ballot Box in the Mid-Nineteenth Century* (Cambridge: Cambridge University Press, 2004), 294.

5. Matt Grossman, "Do the Strategists Know Something We Don't Know? Campaign Decisions and American Elections," *Forum* 7, no. 3 (2009), article 9, http://www.bepress.com/forum/vol7/iss3/art9, accessed August 19, 2010.

6. John R. Petrocik and Frederick T. Steeper, "The Politics Missed by Political Science," *Forum* 8, no. 3, (2010), article 1, http://www.bepress.com/forum/vol8/iss3/art1, accessed October 20, 2010.

7. Grossman, "Do the Strategists Know Something We Don't Know?" 8.

8. John Aldrich, *Why Parties? The Origin and Transformation of Political Parties in America* (Chicago: University of Chicago Press, 1995).

9. Despite their ubiquity in modern campaigns, for instance, there is little evidence that negative ads work. See Richard Lau, Lee Sigelman, and Ivy Brown Rovner, "The Effects of Negative Political Campaigns: A Meta-Analytic Reassessment," *Journal of Politics* 69 (November 2007): 1176–1209. See also Stephen Ansolabehere, "The Paradox of Minimal Effects," in *Capturing Campaign Effects*, ed. Henry E. Brady and Richard Johnston (Ann Arbor: University of Michigan Press, 2006), 29–44.

10. My understanding of political work is influenced by the concept of institutional work, which examines how creative actors deploy a repertoire of skills that create, maintain, and transform institutions. On institutional work, see Thomas B. Lawrence, Roy Suddaby, and Bernard Leca, "Theorizing and Studying Institutional Work," introduction to *Institutional Work: Actors and Agency in Institutional Studies of Organizations*, ed. Thomas B. Lawrence, Roy Suddaby, and Bernard Leca (Cambridge: Cambridge University Press, 2009), 1–27.

11. Dorothy Ross, *The Origins of American Social Science* (Cambridge: Cambridge University Press, 1991).

12. Adam D. Sheingate, "'Publicity' and the Progressive-Era Origins of Modern Politics," *Critical Review* 19 (2007): 461–480.

13. Larry Tye, *The Father of Spin: Edward Bernays and the Birth of Public Relations* (New York: Crown, 1998).

14. Edward L. Bernays, *Biography of an Idea: Memoirs of Public Relations Counsel Edward L. Bernays* (New York: Simon and Schuster, 1965), 56–57; Stuart Ewen, *PR! A Social History of Spin* (New York: Basic Books, 1996), 158–161.

15. The "torch" parade was only one of several ways Bernays promoted cigarettes among women. In addition, he championed smoking as a way to lose weight, crafting the slogan "reach for a Lucky instead of a sweet." See Tye, *The Father of Spin*, 28–31.

16. Henry F. Pringle, "Mass Psychologist," *American Mercury*, February 1930, 155–156.

17. Ernest Boyd, "Portrait of a Press Agent," *The Bookman*, July 1924, 563–565.

18. J. Michael Sproule, *Propaganda and Democracy: The American Experience of Media and Mass Persuasion* (Cambridge: Cambridge University Press, 1997), 53.

19. Walter Lippmann, *Public Opinion* (New York: Free Press Paperbacks, 1997 [1922]), 218.

20. Ibid., 158.

21. Ibid.

22. Bernays, *Biography of an Idea*, 187.

23. Edward L. Bernays, *Crystallizing Public Opinion* (New York: Boni and Liveright, 1923), 173; Edward L. Bernays, "Counsel of Public Relations—A Definition," January 1927, Edward L. Bernays Papers, Library of Congress (hereafter ELB Papers), box 422.

24. Edward L. Bernays, "Public Relations as a Career," speech, Newark, NJ, June 27, 1934, ELB Papers, box 422.

25. Bernays quoted in Wayne W. Parrish, "He Helped Make Press-Agentry a Science," *Literary Digest*, June 1934, 26; Edward L. Bernays, "The Engineering of Consent," *Annals of the American Academy of Political and Social Science* 250 (March 1947): 113–120, quote on 114.

26. Bernays, "Counsel of Public Relations."

27. Bernays, "Public Relations as a Career."

28. Edward L. Bernays, "Comparison Between the Legal Profession and the Profession of Public Relations," n.d., ELB Papers, box 425.

29. On civil service reforms, see Stephen Skowronek, *Building a New American State: The Expansion of National Administrative Capacities, 1877–1920* (Cambridge: Cambridge University Press, 1982). On the direct primary, see Alan Ware, *The American Direct Primary: Party Institutionalization and Transformation in the North* (Cambridge: Cambridge University Press, 2002). On radio and candidate-centered campaigns, see Gil Troy, *See How They Ran: The Changing Role of the Presidential Candidate* (Cambridge, MA: Harvard University Press, 1996). On interest groups as "crucial conduits," see Brain Balogh, "Mirrors of Desires: Interest Groups, Elections, and the Targeted Style in Twentieth-Century America," in *The Democratic Experiment: New Directions in American Political History*, ed. Meg Jacobs, William Novak, and Julian Zelizer (Princeton, NJ: Princeton University Press, 2003), 222–249 quote on 222. On the "advertised style" of American politics, see McGerr, *The Decline of Popular Politics*.

30. Edward L. Bernays, *Propaganda* (New York: Horace Liveright, 1928), 93, 96. See also Edward L. Bernays, "Putting Politics on the Market," *Independent*, May 19, 1928, 470, 472.

31. Emily Newell Blair, "Another Job for the Supersalesman." *Independent*, March 10, 1928, 222–223.

32. Robert Westbrook, "Politics as Consumption: Managing the Modern Election," in *The Culture of Consumption: Critical Essays in American History, 1880–1980*, ed. Richard W. Fox and T. J. Jackson Lears (New York: Pantheon Books, 1983), 145–173.

33. Bernays, *Propaganda*, 105.

34. Edward L. Bernays, "Crystallizing Public Opinion for Good Government," speech, National Municipal League, Pittsburgh, November 1925, ELB Papers, box 422.

35. Edward L. Bernays, "The Public Relations of the National Government," speech, annual meeting of the American Political Science Association, December 27, 1934, Chicago, ELB Papers, box 423.

36. Bernays, "Public Relations as a Career."

37. Ibid.

38. Edward L. Bernays, "The Science of Propaganda," text of radio address, April 15, 1937, ELB Papers, box 426.

39. Harold Lasswell to Edward Bernays, October 26, 1936, ELB Papers, box 425; Pendleton Herring to Edward Bernays, November 16, 1934, ELB Papers, box 423.

40. Harwood Childs to Edward Bernays, September 29, 1934, ELB Papers, Box 422; Harwood L. Childs, *A Reference Guide to the Study of Public Opinion* (Princeton, NJ: Princeton University Press, 1934), ii–iii.

41. Andrew Abbott, *The System of Professions: An Essay on the Division of Expert Labor* (Chicago: University of Chicago Press, 1988), 54–55, 102.

42. A. Percy Block to Edward Bernays, February 21, 1936, ELB Papers, box 423.

43. Edward L. Bernays, *Universities—Pathways of Public Opinion* (New York: n.p., 1937), 6.

44. Edward Bernays to Henry Epstein, April 9, 1936, ELB Papers, box 425.

45. Bernays, *Crystallizing Public Opinion*, 143, 147.

46. Bernays, "Putting Politics on the Market," 472; Bernays, *Propaganda*, quote on 102.

47. Edward L. Bernays, speech, New York Newspapers Women's Club, October 21, 1930, ELB Papers, box 422.

48. Bernays, "Crystallizing Public Opinion for Good Government."

49. Sarah Igo, *The Averaged American: Surveys, Citizens, and the Making of a Mass Public* (Cambridge, MA: Harvard University Press, 2007).

50. Coleman Harwell Wells, "Remapping America: Market Research and American Society, 1900–1940" (Ph.D. thesis, University of Virginia, 1999).

51. Bernays, "Putting Politics on the Market," 470. See also Bernays, *Propaganda*, 97.

52. Bernays, "Putting Politics on the Market," 472; Bernays, *Propaganda*, 102.

53. Bernays, "Crystallizing Public Opinion for Good Government."

54. Igo, *The Averaged American*, 173.

55. Ibid.

56. Susan Herbst, *Numbered Voices: How Opinion Polling Has Shaped American Politics* (Chicago: University of Chicago Press, 1993). See also Taeku Lee, *Mobilizing Public Opinion: Black Insurgency and Racial Attitudes in the Civil Rights Era* (Chicago: University of Chicago Press, 2002).

57. Bernays, "Putting Politics on the Market," 472.

58. Chris McNickle, *To Be Mayor of New York: Ethnic Politics in the City* (New York: Columbia University Press, 1993), 51.

59. Ibid., 48–49.

60. Campbell J. Gibson and Emily Lennon, "Historical Census Statistics on the Foreign-Born Population of the United States, 1850–1990," Population Division Working Paper No. 29, U.S. Bureau of the Census, Washington, DC, February 1999, table 22, http://www.census.gov/population/www/documentation/twps0029/tab22.html, accessed October 1, 2010.

61. McNickle, *To Be Mayor of New York*, 52.

62. Charles Garrett, *The LaGuardia Years: Machine and Reform Politics in New York City* (New Brunswick, NJ: Rutgers University Press, 1961), 252–253.

63. Ibid., 271.

64. Edward L. Bernays, Recommendations to the O'Dwyer Campaign Committee, n.d. (1941?), ELB Papers, box 301.

65. Ibid.

66. Ibid.

67. Ibid.

68. Ibid.

69. Ibid. Using the gross domestic product (GDP) deflator, $100,000 is about $1.2 million in 2008 dollars. However, a more appropriate comparison for campaign expenditures might be the relative share of GDP, in which case $100,000 is equivalent to about $11.2 million in 2008 dollars (calculations using www.measuringworth.com). As a frame of reference, the Democratic candidate for New York City mayor in 2009, William Thompson, Jr., spent $9.4 million. His rival, Mayor Michael Bloomberg, spent $108 million, around 13 percent of which was spent on consulting and polling services (New York City Campaign Finance Board Searchable Database, available at http://www.nyccfb.info/searchabledb/, accessed October 13, 2010).

70. Financial statements 1941, O'Dwyer Campaign Committee, September 23, 1941: "For balance of fee in connection with survey and sampling public attitudes regarding candidates and issues in present city campaign, together with general recommendations . . . $1,750"; ELB Papers, box 5.

71. Garrett, *The LaGuardia Years*, 273.

72. McNickle, *To Be Mayor of New York*, 63.

73. Westbrook, "Politics as Consumption."

74. It is this reliance on academic knowledge that distinguishes political consulting from the craft work of the nineteenth-century party agents they displaced. Abbott, *The System of Professions*, 54–55.

Chapter 7. Accidental Hegemony

This essay is largely based on chapter 3 of Yoshiko M. Herrera, *Mirrors of the Economy: National Accounts and International Norms in Russia and Beyond* (Ithaca, NY: Cornell University Press, 2010).

1. In Russian the term is "balance of the national economy" (*Balans narodnogo khoziaistva*) but it is translated as MPS in international publications. The countries using the MPS were the Soviet Union, Albania, Bulgaria, Cambodia, China, Cuba, Czechoslovakia, the German Democratic Republic, Hungary, the Korean Democratic Republic, Laos, Mongolia, Poland, Romania, Vietnam, and Yugoslavia.

2. Michael Ward, *Quantifying the World: UN Ideas and Statistics* (Bloomington: Indiana University Press, 2004); Yoshiko M. Herrera, *Mirrors of the Economy: National Accounts and International Norms in Russia and Beyond* (Ithaca, NY: Cornell University Press, 2010).

3. Charles Ian Mead, Karin E. Moses, and Brent R. Moulton, "The NIPAs and the System of National Accounts," *Survey of Current Business*, December 2004.

4. Gary Herrigel, "Institutionalists at the Limits of Institutionalism: A Constructivist Critique of Two Edited Volumes from Wolfgang Streeck and Kozo Yamamura," *Socio-Economic Review* 3, no. 3 (September 2005): 565.

5. See Marilyn Waring, *Counting for Nothing: What Men Value and What Women Are Worth*, 2nd ed. (Toronto: University of Toronto Press, 2004).

6. William Alonso and Paul Starr, eds., *The Politics of Numbers* (New York: Russell Sage Foundation, 1987).

7. On the development of statistics in the twentieth century, see Stephen M. Stigler, *Statistics on the Table: The History of Statistical Concepts and Methods* (Cambridge, MA: Harvard University Press, 1999); David Salsburg, *The Lady Tasting Tea: How Statistics Revolutionized Science in the Twentieth Century* (New York: W. H. Freeman, 2001). On the history of modern national accounts and the SNA, see Paul Studenski, *The Income of Nations* (New York: New York University Press, 1958); Zoltan Kenessey, ed., *The Accounts of Nations* (Amsterdam: IOS Press, 1994); André Vanoli, *A History of National Accounting*, trans. Marion Pinot and Gayle H. Partmann (Amsterdam: IOS Press, 2005).

8. Kenessey, "The Genesis of National Accounts: An Overview," in Kenessey, *Accounts of Nations*, 6.

9. James Meade and Richard Stone, "The Construction of Trade Tables of National Income, Expenditure, Savings and Investment," *Economic Journal* 51, no. 202–203 (June–September 1941).

10. Stone was later knighted and awarded a Nobel Prize in Economics in 1984 for his work on the SNA.

11. For other key influences see Kenessey, "The Genesis of National Accounts," 2–5.

12. P. I. Popov, *Balans narodnogo khoziaistva SSSR 1923–24 goda*, vol. 29 (Moscow: TsSU, 1926).

13. UN Statistical Commission, *Report of the Statistical Commission to the Economic and Social Council* (New York: United Nations, 1946), E39. Twenty-four rotating member countries elected on the basis of geographical representation comprise the UN Statistical Commission, which is a functional commission of the UN Economic and Social Council. The commission oversees the work of the UN Statistical Division, which before 1989 was known as the UN Statistical Office.

14. Ward, *Quantifying the World*, 40.

15. Ibid., 77.

16. Richard Stone, *Definition and Measurement of the National Income and Related Totals: Appendix to the Report of the Sub-Committee on National Income Statistics for the League of Nations Committee of Statistical Experts* (Geneva: League of Nations, 1945); UN Statistical Office, *Report of the Sub-Committee on National Income Statistics*

for the League of Nations Committee of Statistical Experts: Measurement of National Income and the Construction of Social Accounts (Geneva: United Nations, 1947).

17. Frits Bos, "Constancy and Change in the United Nations Manuals on National Accounting (1947, 1953, 1968 and 1993)," in Kenessey, *Accounts of Nations*, 194, emphasis in the original.

18. Kenessey, "The Genesis of National Accounts," 12.

19. OEEC National Accounts Research Unit, *A Simplifed System of National Accounts* (Paris: Organisation for European Economic Co-operation, 1951); OEEC National Accounts Research Unit, *A Standarised System of National Accounts* (Paris: Organisation for European Economic Co-operation, 1952).

20. UN Statistical Office, *A System of National Accounts and Supporting Tables* (New York: United Nations, 1953), ST/STAT/ser.F/2.

21. For more on national contributions, see Kenessey, "The Genesis of National Accounts," and other individual chapters in Kenessey, *Accounts of Nations*.

22. UN Statistical Office, *A System of National Accounts and Supporting Tables* (New York: United Nations, 1968), ST/STAT/ser.F/2/rev. 3.

23. See Ward, *Quantifying the World*, 78.

24. François Lequiller and Derek Blades, *Understanding National Accounts* (Paris: Organisation for Economic Co-operation and Development, 2006), 401.

25. The ESA was an adaptation of the 1968 SNA for Europe, and the European Community published guidelines for the ESA. See Statistical Office of the European Community Eurostat, *European System of Integrated Ecnomic Accounts (ESA)* (Luxemburg: Office for Official Publications of the European Communities, 1970).

26. T. P. Hill, *The Measurement of Real Product: A Theoretical and Empirical Analysis of the Growth Rates for Different Industries and Countries* (Paris: Organisation for Economic Co-operation and Development, 1971), 42.

27. Ward, *Quantifying the World*, 50.

28. Árvay, a Hungarian statistician, participated in all phases of the development of the MPS.

29. János Árvay, "The Material Product System (MPS): A Retrospective," in Kenessey, *Accounts of Nations*, 220, emphasis added.

30. Conference of European Statisticians, *Report of the Sixth Plenary Session* (1958), CES/94, cited in Árvay, "Material Product System," 221.

31. Árvay, "Material Product System," 221.

32. Ibid. The CES used the 1952 version of the SNA, series F, no. 2.

33. Árvay, "Material Product System," 221.

34. V.A. Sobol, *Ocherki povoprosam balansa narodnogo khoziaistva* [Essays on the Material Product System] (Moscow: Gosstatizdat, 1960).

35. Árvay, "Material Product System," 223.

36. Ibid.

37. For a detailed discussion of the 1969 MPS document, see ibid., 225–229.

38. UN Statistical Office, *Basic Principles of the System of Balances of the National Economy* (New York: United Nations, 1971), ST/STAT/ser.F/17.

39. The Soviet view of this process is described in Vestnik statistiki, "XVI Sessiia Statisticheskoi Komissii OON" [XVI Session of the UN Statistical Commission], *Vestnik statistiki* 5 (1971).

40. For a comparison of the MPS and the SNA, see Aleksei N. Ponomarenko, *Retrospektivnye natsional'nye scheta Rossii 1961–1990* (Moscow: Finansy i statistika, 2002); Vanoli, *History of National Accounting*.

41. Árvay, "Material Product System," 225–227.

42. Ibid., 224. Drechsler worked in Hungarian statistics and at the United Nations. He had been chairman of the International Association for Research in Income and Wealth . His 1961 Ph.D. thesis addressed the issue of international comparisons between the MPS and SNA, and he was widely considered an expert in this field.

43. Ibid., 231.

44. For a detailed description of the system, see János Árvay, *National Production, National Income, National Wealth* (Budapest: Publishing House of Economy and Law, 1973).

45. Árvay, "Material Product System," 231.

46. Ibid., 264.

47. UN Statistical Office, *Comparisons of the System of National Accounts and the System of Balances of the National Economy* (New York: United Nations, 1981), ST/ESA/STAT/SER.F/20 (part II).

48. Árvay, "Material Product System," 233.

49. UN Statistical Office, *Basic Methodological Principles Governing the Compilation of the System of Statistical Balances of the National Economy* (New York: United Nations, 1989), ST/ESA/STAT/SER.F/17/rev.1.

50. Anne Harrison, "The SNA: 1968–1993 and Beyond," in Kenessey, *Accounts of Nations*, 169.

51. Ward, *Quantifying the World*, 96–98.

52. Ibid., 100.

53. Ibid., 43.

54. Harrison, "The SNA," 170.

55. United Nations Economic Commission for Europe, "*Review and Development of the United Nations System of National Accounts.*" Report of the Expert Group Meeting, CES/WP.22/66 (New York: United Nations, 1982), cited in Harrison, "The SNA," 171.

56. Harrison, "The SNA," 172.

57. Ibid.

58. Ibid., 173.

59. Ibid., 176–178.

60. Ibid., 179–180.

61. A former director of the French Central Statistical Office and chairman of the Council of the International Association for Research in Income and Wealth; he has been president of the French National Accounting Association since its founding in 1983.

62. For a list of all meetings, dates, locations, and participants at each meeting, see Harrison, "The SNA," 191–193, annexes I–II.

63. Árvay, "Material Product System," 234, emphasis in original. Other accounts also point to Hungarians as being a driving force behind the move to integrate rather than to compare or link the two systems; see Vanoli, *History of National Accounting*.

64. UN Statistical Commission, *Report on the Twenty-fifth Session, Supplement No. 3* (New York: United Nations, 1989), 25, par. 61, E/1989/21, E/CN.3/1989/25.

65. Árvay, "Material Product System," 234–235.

66. Harrison, "The SNA," 182.

67. Ibid.

68. Bos, "Constancy and Change," 202.

69. Harrison, "The SNA," 183. For a complete list of changes from the 1968 to the 1993 SNA, see ibid., annex III. For further discussion of the content of the 1993 SNA, see John W. Kendrick, ed., *The New System of National Accounts* (Boston: Kluwer Academic, 1996).

70. Lequiller and Blades, *Understanding National Accounts*, 402–403.

71. On the bilateral and multilateral cooperation that led to the improvement of national statistics, see Siegfried K. Apelt and Andreas Kahnert, "Bilateral and Multilateral Cooperation in Statistics for the Improvement of Systems of National Statistics," in *Statistics in the Democratic Process at the End of the Twentieth Century: Anniversary Publication for the Fortieth Plenary Session of the Conference of European Statisticians*, ed. Egon Hölder, Carlo Malaguerra, and György Vukovich (Wiesbaden, Germany: Federal Statistics Office, 1992). On the diversity of people who contributed to the 1993 SNA, see Ward, *Quantifying the World*, 85.

72. Árvay, "Material Product System," 233.

73. Anne Harrison, "Discussion of Chapter 10: Adaptation of the SNA for Transition Economies by Y. Ivanov and T. Homenko," in Kendrick, *The New System of National Accounts*, 339.

74. Gosudarstvennyi komitet RSFSR po statistike Goskomstat RSFSR, *Narodnoe khoziaistvo RSFSR za 70 let: statisticheskii ezhegodnik*, ed. V. F. Tsvelikh (Moscow: Finansy i statistika, 1987), 15, cited in Barry Kostinsky and Misha Belkindas, "Official Soviet Gross National Product Accounting," in *Measuring Soviet GNP: Problems and Solutions, SOV 90–10038*, ed. CIA (Washington, DC: Directorate of Intelligence, United States Central Intelligence Agency, 1990), 183.

75. Gosudarstvennyi komitet SSSR po statistike Goskomstat SSSR, *Metodika ischisleniia valovogo natsional'nogo produkta SSSR* [Method of calculating the gross national product of the USSR] (Moscow: Goskomstat SSSR, 1988), cited in Kostinsky and Belkindas, "Official Soviet Gross National Product Accounting," 183.

76. Iurii Ivanov, B. Riabushkin, and M. Eidelman, "Ischislenie valovogo natsional'nogo produkta SSSR" [Calculating GNP of the USSR], *Vestnik statistiki* 7 (1988).

77. Derek Blades and Anne Harrison, "Statistics in Central and Eastern Europe: Past, Present, and Future," in Hölder, Malaguerra, and Vukovich, *Statistics in the Democratic Process*, 101.

78. Timothy E. Heleniak and Albert Motivans, "A Note on *Glasnost*' and the Soviet Statistical System," *Soviet Studies* 43, no. 3 (1991): 479–480; Leonid Nesterov, "National Wealth Estimation in the USSR and the Russian Federation," *Europe-Asia Studies* 49, no. 8 (December 1997). On availability of GNP data, see Kostinsky and Belkindas, "Official Soviet Gross National Product Accounting."

79. National wealth figures for all union republics appeared in the union-level yearbooks for 1989 and in the 1989 yearbook, Gosudarstvennyi komitet SSSR po statistike Goskomstat SSSR, *Narodnoe khoziaistvo SSSR v 1989 godu* (Moscow: Goskomstat SSSR, 1989).

80. Blades and Harrison, "Statistics in Central and Eastern Europe," 102.

81. Árvay, "Material Product System," 235.

82. Herrera, *Mirrors of the Economy*.

83. Inter-Secretariat Working Group on National Accounts (ISWGNA), "System of National Accounts 2008" (United Nations, New York, 2009), http://unstats.un.org/unsd/nationalaccount/docs/SNA2008.pdf, accessed April 8, 2013.

84. Reflecting its relationship to the 1993 version, it was initially called "1993 SNA Revision 1," but the name was later simplified to "2008 SNA" to reflect the year it was completed.

85. For the full list of AEG members, see ISWGNA, "System of National Accounts 2008."

86. Inter-Secretariat Working Group on National Accounts (ISWGNA), "The Full Set of Consolidated Recommendations: The Recommendations Made by the Advisory Expert Group for the Update of the System of National Accounts, 1993," background document for UN Statistical Commission, Thirty-eighth session, February 27–March 2, 2007.

87. Even fierce critics of GDP do not question the SNA itself as the basis for any future national accounting work. See Joseph E. Stiglitz, Amartya Sen, and Jean-Paul Fitoussi, "Report by the Commission on the Measurement of Economic Performance and Social Progress [CMEPSE]" (CMEPSE, 2009), http://www.stiglitz-sen-fitoussi.fr/documents/rapport_anglais.pdf, accessed April 8, 2013.

Chapter 8. The Fluidity of Labor Politics

1. Paul Kubicek, *Organized Labor in Postcommunist States: From Solidarity to Infirmity* (Pittsburgh: University of Pittsburgh Press, 2004), ix.

2. Teri Caraway, "Pathways of Dominance and Displacement: The Varying Fates of Legacy Unions in New Democracies," *World Politics* 64, no. 2 (2012): 278–305.

3. David Ost and Stephen Crowley, "The Surprise of Labor Weakness in Post-communist Society," in Crowley and Ost, eds., *Workers After Workers' States: Labor and Politics in Postcommunist Eastern Europe* (Lanham, MD: Rowman & Littlefield, 2001), 7.

4. For a comparative perspective that acknowledges cross-national variation while stressing labor weakness, see Kubicek, *Organized Labor.* On individual postcommunist countries, see Crowley and Ost, *Workers After Workers' States.* On Russia, see below (note 6).

5. See, however, the differentiated treatment of legacies in Calvin Chen and Rudra Sil, "Communist Legacies, Postcommunist Transformations, and the Fate of Organized Labor in Russia and China," *Studies in Comparative International Development* 46, no. 2 (2006): 62–87.

6. Sarah Ashwin, *Russian Workers: The Anatomy of Patience* (Manchester: Manchester University Press, 1999); Sarah Ashwin, "Social Partnership or a 'Complete Sellout'? Russian Trade Unions' Responses to Conflict," *British Journal of Industrial Relations* 42, no. 1 (2004): 23–46; Linda Cook, *Labor and Liberalization: Trade Unions in the New Russia* (New York: Twentieth Century Fund, 1997); Stephen Crowley, "The Social Explosion That Wasn't: Labor Quiescence in Postcommunist Russia," in Crowley and Ost, *Workers After Workers State;* Sue Davis, *Trade Unions in Russia and Ukraine: 1985–1995* (London: Palgrave, 2001); Paul Kubicek, "Civil Society, Trade Unions and Post-Soviet Democratisation: Evidence from Russia and Ukraine," *Europe-Asia Studies* 54, no. 4 (2002): 603–624.

7. For a more detailed examination of the years immediately following the Bolshevik Revolution, see Frederick I. Kaplan, *Bolshevik Ideology and the Ethics of Soviet Labor (1917–1920)* (New York: Philosophical Library, 1968); Carmen Sirianni, *Workers' Control and Socialist Democracy: The Soviet Experience* (London: New Left Books, 1982).

8. This description draws on excellent descriptions of Stalinist labor relations in Joseph Berliner, *Factory and Manager in the USSR* (Cambridge, MA: Harvard University Press, 1957); Donald Filtzer, *Soviet Workers and Stalinist Industrialization* (Armonk, NY: M. E. Sharpe, 1986); Hiroaki Kuromiya, *Stalin's Industrial Revolution* (Cambridge: Cambridge University Press, 1988).

9. Linda Cook, *The Soviet Social Contract and Why It Failed* (Cambridge, MA: Harvard University Press, 1993), 19–40.

10. On the Soviet Union's engagement with the ILO, see Christopher Osakwe, *The Participation of the Soviet Union in Universal International Organizations* (Leiden: Sijthoff, 1972).

11. Cook, *Soviet Social Contract*, 70–71.

12. Ibid., 73–74.

13. On labor unrest in the Gorbachev era, see Walter Connor, *The Accidental Proletariat: Workers, Politics, and Crisis in Gorbachev's Russia* (Princeton, NJ: Princeton University Press, 1991); Stephen Crowley, *Hot Coal, Cold Steel* (Ann Arbor: University

of Michigan Press, 1997); Peter Rutland, "Labor Unrest and Movements in 1989 and 1990," *Soviet Economy* 6, no. 4 (1990): 345–384.

14. Crowley's *Hot Coal, Cold Steel* captures the contrast between the growing radicalism of miners and the passivity of steelworkers in the late 1980s.

15. Caraway, "Pathways," 295–296.

16. See, e.g., Ashwin, "Social Partnership"; Crowley, "Social Explosion"; Cook, *Labor and Liberalization;* Davis, *Trade Unions.*

17. Sarah Ashwin and Simon Clarke, *Russian Trade Unions and Industrial Relations in Transition* (London: Macmillan-Palgrave, 2003), 95–98.

18. Noted in *Kommersant,* May 24, 2001; also cited in Kubicek, *Organized Labor,* 160.

19. Cook, *Labor and Liberalization,* 22–23.

20. Ashwin and Clarke, *Russian Trade Unions,* 86.

21. The Labour Statistics Database of the International Labor Organization (ILO), Geneva, http://laborsta.ilo.org/, accessed August 2, 2012.

22. Crowley, "Social Explosion," 201.

23. See, e.g., Ashwin, *Russian Workers;* Crowley, "Social Explosion," 201; Debra Javeline, *Protest and the Politics of Blame: The Russian Response to Unpaid Wages* (Ann Arbor: University of Michigan Press, 2003), 34–43. For a recent view that takes seriously local strikes and protests, see Samuel Greene and Graeme Robertson, "Politics, Justice, and the New Russian Strike," *Communist and Postcommunist Studies* 43 (2010): 73–95.

24. Labour Statistics Database of the ILO.

25. During 1996–1998, the average annual figures were 77.67 days for Russia, 50.05 for France, 25.47 for Britain, and 1.67 for Germany. See Labour Statistics Database of the ILO.

26. The classic study of protest waves is Edward Shorter and Charles Tilly, *Strikes in France, 1830–1968* (New York: Cambridge University Press, 1974). See also John Kelly, *Rethinking Industrial Relations: Mobilisation, Collectivism, and Long Waves* (London: Routledge, 1998), 83–107; Hanspeter Kriesi, Ruud Koopmans, Jan Willem Duyvendak, and Marco Giugni, *New Social Movements in Western Europe: A Comparative Analysis* (Minneapolis: University of Minnesota Press, 1995), 111–143.

27. Greene and Robertson, "Politics, Justice," 77–79.

28. On the first view, see Crowley, "Social Explosion"; for the second, see Javeline, *Protest and the Politics of Blame,* 104–159.

29. Moscow Federation of Trade Unions, "Extracts from the Draft Platform of the Moscow Trade Unions—On 'Economic Democracy' (December 1992–January 1993)," *Socialism and Democracy* 8, no. 2–3 (1994): 35–42.

30. Walter Connor, *Tattered Banners: Labor, Conflict, and Corporatism in Postcommunist Russia* (Boulder: Westview, 1996), 82–87; Rick Simon, *Labour and Political Transformation in Russia and Ukraine* (Aldershot, UK: Ashgate, 2000), 109, 134.

31. Reported in 2010 by the International Trade Union Confederation (Brussels), http://www.ituc-csi.org/ituc-mourns-the-passing-of-russian.html?lang = en, accessed August 1, 2012.

32. See Yury Tyurin, "Trade Union Leaders Accuse the Government of Breaking the System of Social Partnership, and Are Determined to Protect the Organizers of Coal Miners' Protests From Prosecution," *RIA Novosti*, 8 July 1998.

33. Ashwin and Clarke, *Russian Trade Unions*, 86, 202.

34. On the ineffectiveness of the Trilateral Commission, see Connor, *Tattered Banners*, 25–55.

35. See Andreas Bieler, *The Struggle for a Social Europe: Trade Unions and EMU in Times of Global Restructuring* (Manchester: Manchester University Press, 2007).

36. Simon, *Labour and Political Transformation*, 142.

37. Interview with Aleksandr Shepel, former president of KTR, Moscow, June 8, 2002.

38. Connor, *Tattered Banners*, 157.

39. See Ashwin and Clarke, *Russian Trade Unions*, 86; Crowley, "Social Explosion."

40. Interview with Vitali Bud'ko, late vice-chairman of FNPR, Moscow, June 6, 2002.

41. Elena Shershneva and Jurgen Feldhoff, *The Culture of Labour in the Transformation Process* (New York: Peter Lang, 1998), 70–72.

42. Miriam Golden, *Heroic Defeats: The Politics of Job Loss* (New York: Cambridge University Press, 1996).

43. For a detailed account of the politics behind the Labor Code, see Ashwin and Clarke, *Russian Trade Unions*, 60–70.

44. Interviews with Sergei Khramov, president of Sotsprof, Moscow, June 5, 2002; Viktor Gamov, vice president of Zashchita Truda, Moscow, June 7, 2002.

45. Ashwin and Clarke, *Russian Trade Unions*, 62–64.

46. Ibid., 68–72.

47. Ibid.

48. Interview with Bud'ko.

49. This was evident in a 2007 strike at a Ford plant outside St. Petersburg as well as a 2008 strike at Nestle-Perm.

50. Ashwin and Clarke, *Russian Trade Unions*, 106–130.

51. Interview with Boris Kravtchenko, international secretary of VKT, Moscow, June 10, 2002.

52. These patterns may be inferred from the history of labor relations in Britain, the United States, and Japan. See, respectively, Golden, *Heroic Defeats*; Melvyn Dubofsky, *The State and Labor in Modern America* (Chapel Hill: University of North Carolina Press, 1994); Andrew Gordon, *The Evolution of Labor Relations in Japan, 1853–1955* (Cambridge, MA: Harvard University Press, 1985).

53. Figures are based on the International Trade Union Confederation's list of affiliated unions (Brussels), http://www.ituc-csi.org, accessed August 2, 2012. See also Ashwin and Clarke, *Russian Trade Unions*, 86; and Chen and Sil, "Communist Legacies," 78.

54. This is based on surveys in the New Russia Barometer 4 (1995) and New Russia Barometer 10 (2001), both cited in Richard Rose and Neil Munro, *Elections Without Order* (New York: Cambridge University Press, 2002).

55. According to weekly surveys on "Ratings of Social Institutions," conducted by VTsIOM, the Russian Public Opinion Research Center, http://wciom.com/index .php?id = 123, accessed August 11, 2012.

56. Ashwin, "Social Partnership," 41.

57. Javeline, *Protest and the Politics of Blame*, 34–38.

58. See notes 23–25.

59. In addition to Bieler, *Struggle for a Social Europe*, see also Andrew Martin and George Ross, eds., *The Brave New World of European Labor* (New York: Berghahn Books, 1999).

60. For the view that legacies of early postcommunism are now more relevant than communist legacies, see David Ost, "The End of Postcommunism: Trade Unions in Eastern Europe's Future," *East European Politics and Society* 23, no. 1 (February 2009): 13–33.

61. Graeme Robertson, "Strikes and Protest in Hybrid Regimes," *American Political Science Review* 101, no. 4 (2007): 781–798, on 787–790. See also Greene and Robertson, "Politics, Justice."

Chapter 9. From Birmingham to Baghdad

1. See Aristide Zolberg, "Moments of Madness," *Politics and Society* 2, no. 2 (March 1972): 183–207; Frances Fox Piven and Richard Cloward, *Poor People's Movements: Why They Succeed, How They Fail* (New York: Vintage, 1978); James Scott, *Weapons of the Weak: Everyday Forms of Peasant Resistance* (New Haven, CT: Yale University Press, 1987).

2. See Karen Orren and Stephen Skowronek, *The Search for American Political Development* (New York: Cambridge University Press, 2004). This position undergirds much of the new institutionalist literature in political science.

3. Rice links Birmingham and Baghdad in the following speeches: Remarks by National Security Advisor Condoleezza Rice at 28th Annual Convention and Career Fair of the National Association of Black Journalists, Dallas, August 6–10, 2003. See press release, Office of the Press Secretary, August 7, 2003, http://www.whitehouse .gov/news/releases/2003/08/print/20030807-1.html, accessed July 5th, 2007; National Security Advisor's Remarks at Mississippi College Law Commencement, First Baptist Church, Jackson, Mississippi, May 16, 2003, Office of the Press Secretary, May 19, 2003. http://www.whitehouse.gov/news/releases/2003/05/print/20030519-7.html, accessed July 5, 2007; Remarks by the National Security Advisor Condoleezza Rice, Vanderbilt University, Nashville, May 13, 2004. Press news release, Office of the Press

Secretary, May 17, 2004; with United Kingdom Foreign Secretary Jack Straw, Frank A. Nix Lecture, Blackburn Institute, University of Alabama, Tuscaloosa, October 21, 2005, http://www.state.gov/secretary/rm/2005/55423.html, accessed July 5, 2007.

4. Joseph Lowndes, "From Founding Violence to Political Hegemony: The Conservative Populism of George Wallace," in *Populism and the Mirror of Desire*, ed. Francisco Panizza (London: Verso Books, 2005).

5. The four girls killed at the Sixteenth Street Baptist Church on September 15, 1963, were Denise McNair, aged eleven, Addie Mae Collins, aged fourteen, Cynthia Wesley, aged fourteen, and Carole Robertson, aged fourteen. Rice usually mentions her connection with McNair and Collins. For the Rice quote, see "Condoleezza Rice: True Believer," *60 Minutes*, CBS News, September 24, 2006, transcript, CBSNews.com, accessed April 15, 2013.

6. Quoted from "Condi: The Girl Who Cracked the Ice," (London) *Sunday Times*, November 21, 2004 (accessed April 14, 2013). In her interview with the *Sunday Times*, Rice also remarked about the Sixteenth Street Baptist Church bombings: "Those terrible events burned into my consciousness. I missed many days at my segregated school because of the frequent bomb threats. Some solace to me was the piano, and what a world of joy it brought me."

7. Rice, remarks, twenty-eighth annual convention.

8. See "Being Condoleezza," *Essence*, September 12, 2006.

9. Rice, remarks, twenty-eighth annual convention.

10. Rice received a Ph.D. in political science from the University of Denver, specializing in international relations.

11. "Condi."

12. Ibid.; Jonathan Freeland, "Madam Secretary," *New York Times*, July 1, 2006; See also Marcus Mabry, *Twice as Good: Condoleezza Rice and Her Path to Power* (New York: Rodale Books, 2007); and Tom Whipple, "The Girl Who Had to Be Twice as Good," *Timesonline*, October 1, 2006.

13. Rice, remarks, Nix Lecture.

14. Ibid.

15. Interestingly, Rice has given similar speeches while abroad. For example, see the address delivered at Sciences-Po, Paris, France, February 8, 2005.

16. One exception is the interview with Katie Couric on *60 Minutes*. See "Condoleezza Rice: True Believer," CBS News, *60 Minutes*, Washington, September 24, 2006.

17. Eugene Robinson, "What Rice Can't See," *Washington Post*, September 26, 2005; Eugene Robinson, "Baghdad Isn't Birmingham," *Washington Post*, October 26, 2005.

18. See Condoleezza Rice and U.K. foreign secretary Jack Straw, interview with Mary Orndorff of the *Birmingham News*, Birmingham, Alabama, October 22, 2005, www.state.gov/secretary/rm/2005/55426.html, accessed November 5, 2005; Condoleezza Rice, interview with Jon Sopel of the *Politics Show* on BBC-1, Birmingham,

Alabama, October 22, 2005, http://www.state.gov/secretary/rm/2005/55425.html, accessed July 5, 2007.

19. Rice, interview with Orndorff.

20. Condoleezza Rice, interview with Steve Weisman, *New York Times*, October 20, 2005, www.state.gov/secretary/rm/2005/55437.html, accessed November 5, 2005.

21. George W. Bush, nomination acceptance speech, Republican National Convention, August 2000, http://www.2000gop.com/convention/speech/speechbush.html, accessed January 20, 2011.

22. Bob Herbert, "In America, a Slick Mix," *New York Times*, August 3, 2000.

23. Chris Rock, "Chris Rock Visits 2000 Republican National Convention," http://www.youtube.com/watch?v=UKi2yi_zaFQ, July 21, 2007, accessed January 20, 2011.

24. Brent Staples, "The Editorial Observer: The Republican Party's Exercise in Minstrelsy," *New York Times*, August 2, 2000.

25. Steven Teles, "Compassionate Conservatism, Domestic Policy, and the Politics of Ideational Change," in *The Crisis of Conservatism? The Republican Party, the Conservative Movement, and Politics After Bush*, ed. Joel D. Aberbach and Gillian Peele (New York: Oxford University Press, 2011).

26. Gary Gerstle, "Minorities, Multiculturalism, and the Presidency of George W. Bush," in *The Presidency of George W. Bush: The First Historical Assessment* (Princeton, NJ: Princeton University Press, 2010).

27. Ken Mehlman, speech, NAACP convention, January 14, 2005, http://www.ken-mehlman.com/ken-mehlman-naacp-speech.html, accessed January 20, 2011.

28. President George W. Bush, speech, NAACP annual convention, Washington, D.C., July 20 2006.

29. Ibid.

30. Terry Cronk Moon, "King Might Understand Today's Wars, Pentagon Lawyer Says," American Forces Press Service, January 13, 2011, http://www.defense.gov/news/newsarticle.aspx?id=62448, accessed January 20, 2011.

31. Ashley Southall, "Republican Allen West Joins Congressional Black Caucus" *New York Times*, January 5, 2011, http://thecaucus.blogs.nytimes.com/2011/01/05/republican-allen-west-joins-congressional-black-caucus/, accessed Jaunary 20, 2011.

32. Martin Luther King Jr., "A Time to Break Silence" (1967), reprinted in *A Testament of Hope: The Essential Writings and Speeches of Martin Luther King, Jr.*, ed. James Melvin Washington (New York: Harper San Francisco, 1991), 232.

33. See Adam Fairclough, "Martin Luther King, Jr. and the War in Vietnam," *Phylon* 45, no. 1 (1984): 19–39, on 22, 26; Taylor Branch, *At Canaan's Edge: America in the King Years 1965–68* (New York: Simon and Schuster, 2006), chaps. 33–34.

34. Martin Luther King, "The Casualties of the War in Vietnam," (speech in Los Angeles), reprinted in *Nation*, February 25, 1967,

http://mlk-kpp01.stanford.edu/kingweb/publications/speeches/unpub/670225-001_eThe_Casualties_of_the_War_in_Vietnam.htmp1.

35. King, "Casualties," 1; Branch, *At Canaan's Edge*; William. F. Pepper, "The Children of Vietnam," *Ramparts*, Extra. January 1967.

36. King, "A Time to Break Silence," 231.

37. Ibid.

38. Ibid., 237.

39. Ibid., 233.

40. Ibid., 240.

41. Ibid., 240–243.

42. King, "Casualties," 7.

43. "Dr. King's Error," *New York Times*, Op Ed, April 7, 1967; "A Tragedy," *Washington Post*, OpEd, April 6, 1967; John Sibley, "Bunche Disputes Dr. King on Peace," *New York Times*, April 13, 1967; Bayard Rustin, "Dr. King's Painful Dilemma," *New York Amsterdam News*, March 3, 2007. See also Douglas Robinson, "Jewish Veterans Attack Dr. King's Stand on War," *New York Times*, April 6, 1967.

44. "Dr. King's Error"; "A Tragedy"; D. Robinson, "Jewish Veterans."

45. Paul David, "Clio and the Economics of QWERTY," *American Economic Review* 75, no. 2, (1985): 332–337; Paul Pierson, "Increasing Returns, Path Dependence, and the Study of Politics," *American Political Science Review* 94, no. 2 (1992): 251–267.

46. Ellen Immergut and Karen Andersen, "Historical Institutionalism and West European Politics," *West European Politics* 31, nos. 1–2 (2008), 345–369; Daniel Carpenter, *The Forging of Bureaucratic Autonomy* (Princeton, NJ: Princeton University Press, 2001).

47. Adam Sheingate, "Political Entrepreneurship, Institutional Change and American Political Development," *Studies in American Political Development* 17 (Fall 2003): 185–203.

48. Andrew Polsky, "The 1996 Elections and the Logic of Regime Politics," *Polity* 30, no. 1 (1997): 153–166; John Aldrich, *Why Parties? The Origin and Transformation of Political Parties in America* (Chicago: University of Chicago Press, 1995); David Plotke, *Building the Democratic Political Order: Reshaping American Liberalism in the 1930s and 1940s* (New York: Cambridge University Press, 1996).

49. Stephen Skowronek, "The Reassociation of Ideas and Purposes: Racism, Liberalism, and the American Political Tradition," *American Political Science Review* 100, no. 3 (2006): 385–402; Edsall and Edsall, *Chain Reaction*; Nancy Fraser, *Unruly Practices: Discourse and Gender in Contemporary Social Theory* (Minneapolis: University of Minnesota, 1996); Gary Gerstle and Steven Fraser, eds., *The Rise and Fall of the New Deal Order* (Princeton, NJ: Princeton University Press, 1989).

50. Joan Scott, *Gender and the Politics of History* (New York: Columbia University Press, 1989); Judith Butler, *Bodies That Matter: On the Discursive Limits of "Sex"* (New York: Routledge, 1993); William Connolly, *The Ethos of Pluralization* (Minnesota: University of Minneapolis Press, 1995); Wendy Brown, *States of Injury* (Princeton, NJ: Princeton University Press, 1995); Ernesto Laclau, *Emancipation(s)* (New York: Verso, 1996).

51. Karen Orren and Stephen Skowronek, "Beyond the Iconography of Order: Notes for a 'New Institutionalism,'" in *Dynamics of American Politics: Approaches and Interpretations*, ed. Lawrence C. Dodd and Calvin Jillson (Boulder, CO: Westview Press, 1994).

52. Ibid.; Sheingate, "Political Entrepreneurship"; Desmond King and Rogers Smith, "Racial Orders in American Political Development," *American Political Science Review* 99 (February 2005): 79–92.

53. Victoria Hattam, *In the Shadow of Race: Jews, Latinos and Immigrant Politics in the United States* (Chicago: University of Chicago Press, 2007); Victoria Hattam and Joseph Lowndes, "Shifts Beneath Our Feet: Language, Culture, and Political Change," in *Formative Acts: Politics in the Making*, ed. Stephen Skowronek and Matthew Glassman (Philadelphia: University of Pennsylvania Press, 2007); Joseph Lowndes, *From the New Deal to the New Right: Race and the Southern Origins of Modern Conservatism* (New Haven, CT: Yale University Press. 2008).

Chapter 10. The Trouble with Amnesia

1. Numerous scholarly works have built their analyses on the notion of time as a construct. Political scientist Stephen Skowronek devises the notion of political time as the structuring context within which U.S. presidents seek to govern; see his *The Politics Presidents Make: Leadership from John Adams to Bill Clinton*, rev. ed. (Cambridge, MA: Belknap Press of Harvard University Press, 1997). Anthropologist Johannes Fabian examines how the construct of time has been deployed in his discipline to demarcate self from other; see his *Time and the Other: How Anthropology Makes Its Object* (New York: Columbia University Press, 2002). In my own work, I have posited that U.S. discourse located indigenous sovereignty in "colonial time," seemingly too archaic to be an active part of contemporary political life; see *The Third Space of Sovereignty: The Postcolonial Politics of U.S.-Indigenous Relations* (Minneapolis: University of Minnesota Press, 2007).

2. In "What Is a Nation?" nineteenth-century scholar Ernest Renan provided the canonical articulation of the argument that forgetting is central to nation making: "Forgetting, I would even go so far as to say historical error, is a crucial factor in the creation of a nation. . . . Indeed, historical enquiry brings to light deeds of violence which took place at the origin of all political formations." Ernest Renan, "What Is a Nation?" in *Nation and Narration*, ed. Homi Bhabha (London: Routledge, 1990), 11.

3. Thomas McCarthy, "Coming to Terms with Our Past, Part II: On the Morality and Politics of Reparations for Slavery," *Political Theory* 32, no. 6 (December 2004): 753.

4. Thomas McCarthy, "Vergangenheitsbewaltigung in the USA: On the Politics of Memory and Slavery," *Political Theory* 30, no. 5 (October 2002): 639, 640.

5. McCarthy "Coming to Terms with Our Past," 767, emphasis original.

6. Ibid.

7. Marita Sturken, *Tangled Memories: The Vietnam War, the AIDS Epidemic, and the Politics of Remembering* (Berkeley: University of California Press, 1997), 2.

8. George Shulman, *American Prophecy: Race and Redemption in American Political Culture* (Minneapolis: University of Minnesota Press, 2008), 243.

9. Giorgio Agamben, *Homo Sacer: Sovereign Power and Bare Life*, trans. Daniel Heller-Roazan (Stanford, CA: Stanford University Press, 1998), 109, emphasis original.

10. William Faulkner, *Requiem for a Nun* (New York: Vintage International, 1994), act 1, scene 3.

11. Paul Ricoeur, *Memory, History, Forgetting*, trans. Kathleen Blamey and David Pellauer (Chicago: University of Chicago Press, 2004), 24.

12. Henri Bergson, *Matter and Memory* (Mineola, NY: Dover Philosophical Classics, 2004), 87.

13. Ricoeur, *Memory, History, Forgetting*, 25

14. Ernst A. Kantorowicz, *The King's Two Bodies: A Study in Medieval Political Theology* (Princeton, NJ: Princeton University Press, 1957), 286.

15. Ibid.

16. Eviatar Zerubavel, "Calendars and History: A Comparative Study of the Social Organization of National Memory," in *States of Memory: Continuities, Conflicts, and Transformations in National Retrospection*, ed. Jeffery Olick (Durham, NC: Duke University Press, 2003), 316, 322, 330.

17. E. J. Dionne, "This Memorial Day, Honoring a Military That's in Isolation," *Washington Post*, May 31, 2010, A5.

18. Walter Benjamin, "Theses on the Philosophy of History," in *Illuminations*, ed. Hannah Arendt, trans. Harry Zohn (New York: Schocken Books, 1968), 261–262. The English translation is the verbatim translation from the footnote to this quote in the Benjamin text; see 262, fn*.

19. Russell M. Peters, "Comments on the Day of Mourning," *Pilgrim Hall Museum: American Museum of Pilgrim Possessions*, http://www.pilgrimhall.org/day mourn.htm, accessed May 27, 2010.

20. "Thanksgiving: The National Day of Mourning. Text of the 1970 Speech by Wampsutta, an Aquinnah Wampanoag Elder," *Black Commentator*, November 23, 2006, http://www.blackcommentator.com/207/207_day_of_mourning_wampsutta .html, accessed May 27, 2010.

21. United American Indians of New England/LPGS, "40th National Day of Mourning Flyer," http://www.uaine.org/, accessed May 27, 2010.

22. Peters, "Comments."

23. United American Indians of New England, "Background Information: UAINE and the History of National Day of Mourning," 2009, http://www.uaine.org/uainemai .htm, accessed June 6, 2010.

24. George W. Bush, "Rebuilding After New Orleans," speech, New Orleans, September 15, 2005, http://www.presidentialrhetoric.com/speeches/09.15.05.html, accessed, June 7, 2010.

25. Simon Stow, "Do You Know What It Means to Miss New Orleans? George Bush, the Jazz Funeral, and the Politics of Memory," *Theory and Event* 11, no. 1 (2008), emphasis original.

26. Stow, "Do You Know What It Means to Miss New Orleans?"

27. Bush, "Rebuilding After New Orleans."

28. W. J. Booth, "Communities of Memory: On Identity, Memory, and Debt," *American Political Science Review* 93, no. 2 (1999): 259. He gleans this notion from Nicole Loraux's *The Invention of Athens: The Funeral Oration in the Classical City* (Cambridge, MA: Harvard University Press, 1986), 3.

Chapter 11. Interest in the Absence of Articulation

1. Algerian scholar Luis Martinez has noted that pro-democracy forces in Algeria had supported the state and the repression of Islamists during the civil war; mistrust remained. Quoted in Adam Nossiter, "Amid a Sea of Upheaval, Algeria Is Still," *New York Times,* February 19, 2011, A4.

2. Robert P. Parks, "Arab Uprisings and the Algerian Elections: Ghosts from the Past?" jadaliyya.com, April 10, 2010, 2012.http://www.jadaliyya.com/pages/index/4979/arab-uprisings-and-the-algerian-elections_ghosts-f, accessed July 8, 2012.

3. Support for Islamists from those excluded from state benefits is well documented. See John Phillips and Martin Evans, *Algeria: Anger of the Dispossessed* (New Haven, CT: Yale University Press, 2008); Luis Martinez, *La guerre civile en Algérie, 1990–1998* (Paris: Karthala, 1998). For the claim of opportunism, see Hugh Roberts, *Battlefield Algeria, 1988–2002* (New York: Verso, 2003), 82–104.

4. Mustafa Al-Ahnaf, Bernard Botiveau, and Franck Frégosi, "La loi et le marché," in *L'Algérie par ses islamistes* (Paris: Editions Karthala, 1991), 153–203. These scholars discuss the issue generally as well as present extracts from political pamphlets and the press. See also Aziza Boucherit, *L'arabe parlé à Alger* (Algiers: ANEP, 2006). She presents texts from a sermon and radio program from the early 1990s that are preoccupied with the experience of political and economic corruption (235–274). Economic discussions mix colloquial Arabic and French; religious discourse on economic and political oppression mixes colloquial Arabic and formal Arabic to gain moral authority.

5. Ziya Oniş, "The Political Economy of Turkey's Justice and Development Party," in *The Emergence of a New Turkey: Democracy and the AK Party,* ed. M. Hakan Yavuz (Salt Lake City: University of Utah Press, 2006), 203—234.

6. Material, structural, and cultural analyses are used to explain stability; discursive formations, too, can be seen as structures. Benjamin Smith, *Hard Times in the Lands of Plenty: Oil Politics in Iran and Indonesia* (Ithaca, NY: Cornell University Press, 2007); Timothy Mitchell, *Rule of Experts: Egypt, Techno-Politics, Modernity* (Berkeley: University of California Press, 2002); Lisa Wedeen, *Ambiguities of Domination: Politics, Rhetoric, and Symbols in Contemporary Syria* (Chicago: University of Chicago Press, 1999); Jason Brownlee, *Authoritarianism in An Age of Democratization* (Cambridge: Cambridge University Press, 2007).

7. My fieldwork began in 1992 and 1993, with two research trips to Algeria made possible by the Social Science Research Council Pre-dissertation Grant, and then with a small but welcome grant from the American Institute for Magrib Studies. When the

fighting was largely over, I was able to return for short research trips in 2008, 2009, 2010, and 2012. Research in 2008 was generously funded by a Bryn Mawr College International Studies grant.

8. Ahmed Henni, *Essai sur l'économie parallèle: Cas de l'Algérie* (Algiers: ENAG Editions, 1991).

9. M. Hakan Yavuz, *Islamic Political Identity in Turkey* (New York: Oxford University Press, 2003), 5.

10. Lloyd I. Rudolph and Susanne Hoeber Rudolph, *The Modernity of Tradition: Political Development in India* (Chicago: University of Chicago Press, 1967).

11. Mustafa Emirbayer and Ann Mische, "What Is Agency?" *American Journal of Sociology* 103, no. 4 (January 1998), 962–1023.

12. Jacques Derrida, *Of Grammatology*, trans. Gayatri Chakravorty Spivak (Baltimore: Johns Hopkins University Press, 1997), 200. Derrida does not offer the example of Jell-O, to which many things can be added: raisins, marshmallows, shredded carrots, etc. The addition of pineapple dissolves Jell-O; the addition of nonelite voters to an expanding democratic system may transform politics into something radically different.

13. Alev Çinar, *Modernity, Islam, and Secularism in Turkey: Bodies Places and Time* (Minneapolis: University of Minnesota Press, 2005).

14. Gauthier de Villers, *L'état demiurge: Le cas algérien* (Paris: L'Harmattan, 1987).

15. Adlène Meddi, *La prière du maure* (Blida, Algeria: Editions Barzakh, 2008).

16. Miriam Lowi, *Oil Wealth and the Poverty of Politics: Algeria Compared* (New York: Cambridge University Press, 2011). Lowi commits to a determinedly structuring-unstructuring position, assigning significance to structural weight but also to the importance of decisions from within the regime.

17. Henni, *Essai sur l'économie parallèle*, 12, emphasis original.

18. Louis Althusser, *Pour Marx* (Paris: Editions F. Maspero, 1965).

19. Deborah Harrold, "The Menace and Appeal of the Informal Economy in Algeria," *Middle East Report*, January 1995.

20. Michel de Certeau, *The Practice of Everyday Life*, trans. Steven Rendell (Berkeley: University of California Press, 1988), 29–32.

21. Ibid., 41.

22. François Burgat, *The Islamic Movement in North Africa*, with William Dowell (Austin: University of Texas Press, 1993), 247–305; Mark Tessler, "The Origins of Popular Support for Islamist Movements: A Political Economy Analysis," in *Islam, Democracy and the State in North Africa*, ed. John P. Entelis and John O. Voll (Bloomington: Indiana University Press, 1997), 93–126.

23. Timur Kuran, *Islam and Mammon: The Economic Predicaments of Islamism* (Princeton, NJ: Princeton University Press, 2005).

24. Roberts, *Battlefield Algeria*; also, Lowi, *Oil Wealth*.

25. Born in British India in 1903, Mawdudi sought to embed economics within an Islamic worldview, using language and arguments that could address those with

modern education for whom Islam was in danger of becoming irrelevant. Sayyid Abdul A'la Mawdudi, *First Principles of Islamic Economics* (Islamic Foundation, 2009 [1930s–1960s]).

26. Sayyid Qutb, *Social Justice in Islam*, ed. Hamid Algar, trans. John B. Hardie (Berkeley, CA: Islamic Publications International, 2000 [1949]).

27. Richard P. Mitchell, *The Society of the Muslim Brothers* (London: Oxford University Press, 1993).

28. Ellis Goldberg, "Muslim Union Politics in Egypt: Two Cases," in *Islam, Politics, and Social Movements*, ed. Edmund Burke III and Ira Lapidus (Berkeley: University of California Press, 1990), 228–243.

29. Alan Richards and John Waterbury, *A Political Economy of the Middle East*, 3rd ed. (Boulder, CO: Westview Press, 2008), 372–373.

30. See Jamal Ad-Din Al-Afghani, "Lecture on Teaching and Learning" [1882], trans. Nikki R. Keddie and Hamid Algar, in Nikki R. Keddie, *An Islamic Response to Imperialism: Political and Religious Writings of Sayyid Jamal ad-Din "al-Afghani"* (Berkeley: University of California Press, 1983), 101–108; Albert Hourani, *Arabic Thought in the Liberal Age, 1798–1939* (London: Oxford University Press, 1967). Today, the term *salafi* is often used by members of armed groups with little connection to the intellectual movement of the late nineteenth century and early twentieth century. The new use claims the intellectual standing and prestige of the earlier movement.

31. Afghani's friend and student Muhammad Abduh directed his energies to educational and legal reform in Egypt, combining rationalism with piety and an appreciation for humbler faith. While Abduh visited North Africa and met with enthusiastic supporters, other scholars encountered the salafi movement though pilgrimages of study and subsequent journals. See Hourani, *Arabic Thought*.

32. Ali Merad, *Le reformisme musulman en Algérie de 1925 a 1940: Essai d'histoire religieuse et sociale* (Paris: Mouton, 1968).

33. The first explicitly nationalist movement for Algeria was formed in France, and the efforts of liberal nationalists were overtaken by political marginalization and the emergence of the underground Algerian nationalist movement.

34. Fanny Colonna, "Cultural Resistance and Religious Legitimacy in Colonial Algeria," *Economy and Society* 3, no. 3 (August 1974): 233–252.

35. John Waterbury has noted the problem with terminology; for the Middle East, this term is just a description of what the state seems to be doing now. See John Waterbury, *Democracy Without Democrats: The Renewal of Politics in the Muslim World*, ed. Ghassan Salam (London: I. B. Tauris, 1994).

36. Clem Henry devised the term "bunker state" to describe the Algerian state. See Clement M. Henry and Robert Springborg, *Globalization and the Politics of Development in the Middle East* (London: Cambridge University Press, 2001), 99–133.

37. Luis Martinez, *The Algerian Civil War, 1990–1994* (New York: Columbia University Press, 2000).

38. Martinez, *Algerian Civil War*.

39. Phillips and Evans, *Algeria: Anger of the Dispossessed*.

40. The Front des Forces Socialistes, with major support from Kabyle Berbers and as a party that was partly a modern party and partly the vehicle of a great man, supported the FIS's right to take its place in the National Assembly. Algeria's communist, the Parti des Travailleurs (PT), also supported the FIS's right to take its seats and the continuation of open politics. Louisa Hanoune, head of that party at the time, sent roses to FIS leadership in jail in solidarity; she had been imprisoned in Algeria in the past.

41. Interviews in Algeria, 2009, 2010, 2012.

42. Martinez, *Algerian Civil War*; Henry and Springborg, *Globalization and the Politics of Development* ; Phillips and Evans, *Algeria: Anger of the Dispossessed*.

43. Henry and Springborg, *Globalization and the Politics of Development* ; see also Bradford Dillman, "Review: Reassessing the Algerian Economy: Development and Reform through the Eyes of Five Policy Makers," Journal of Modern African Studies 35, no. 1 (March 1997): 153–179.

44. Henry and Springborg, *Globalization and the Politics of Development*.

45. Mahfoud Bennoune, *The Making of Contemporary Algeria, 1830–1987: Colonial Upheavals and Post-Independence Development* (Cambridge: Cambridge University Press, 1988).

46. Burgat, *Islamic Movement in North Africa*.

47. Tahir Wattar, *The Earthquake*, trans. William Granara (London: Saqi Books, 2000). This novel from Algeria's most famous author writing in Arabic follows an opponent to land reform as he roams Constantine looking for relatives in whose name he can inscribe his property. According to translator and scholar William Granara, he is one of the least sympathetically presented characters in Arabic literature: avaricious and cut off from reality, eventually mad.

48. Ahmed Rouidjia, *Les frères et la mosquée* (Paris: Karthala, 1990).

49. Burgat, *Islamic Movement in North Africa*; Rouidjia, *Les frères et la mosquée*.

50. Bradford L. Dillman, *State and Private Sector in Algeria: The Politics of Rent-Seeking and Failed Development* (Boulder, CO: Westview Press, 2000).

51. Burgat, *Islamic Movement in North Africa*.

52. Many Algerians who gained the title of "mujahid" as a result of their service during Algeria's war for independence have greater access to the state's resources.

53. Rouidjia, *Les frères et la mosquée*.

54. Rachid Tlemçeni, *Etat, bazar et globalization: L'aventure de l'infitah en Algérie* (Algiers: El Hikma, 1999).

55. Martinez, *Algerian Civil War*, 26–28.

56. *Trabendo*, the Algerian term for smuggled goods from the Spanish *contrabando*, reminds us of the Spanish colonial presence in western Algeria, and that the region of the western border with Morocco remains a strategic part of the Algerian informal economy.

57. Martinez, *Algerian Civil War*, 27.

58. I heard this critique many times from small operators in 1992 and 1993.

59. Harrold, "Menace and Appeal."

60. Martinez, *Algerian Civil War*.

61. Mamaar Boudersa, *La ruine de l'économie Algérienne sous Chadli* (Algiers: Editions Rahma 1993), a socialist critique of the reforms.

62. Dillman notes that shifting the discourse might be the only accomplishment of the liberal economic reforms. See Dillman, *State and Private Sector*, 161.

63. M. L. Benhassine, M. Medjitena, and M. El-Faiz, *Essais de pensé économique Arabo-Musulmane* (Algiers: Editions El-Adib Editions Aurès, 1991).

64. Henry and Springborg, *Globalization and the Politics of Development*, 115–116.

65. Smail Goumeziane, Le mal algérien: Économie politique d'une transition inachevée (Paris: Fayard, 1994).

66. Benjamin Stora, *A Short History of Algeria, 1830–2000* (Ithaca, NY: Cornell University Press, 2001). These markets have been frequently noted but seldom described.

67. FIS and Hamas *economic* policies did not differ; they were both liberal and reformist. Real differences emerged in political style and also class support; Hamas appears to have more middle-class, FIS more mass support.

68. Terry Karl, *The Paradox of Plenty: Oil Booms and Petro-States* (Berkeley: University of California Press, 1997).

69. Gizem Zencirci, "The Limits of Welfare: Governing Social Assistance in Turkey," paper presented at the Middle East Studies Association meeting, Washington, D.C., December 2, 2011.

70. This information circulated widely in Algiers in 2010.

71. Amel Boubekeur, "The Future of Algeria's Islamist Parties," *Magreb Center Journal* 1 (Spring 2010), 1–12, pp. 5, 6.

Conclusion

1. For classic new institutionalist texts, see Stephen Skowronek, *Building a New American State: The Expansion of National Administrative Capacities, 1877–1920* (New York: Cambridge University Press, 1982); Suzanne Berger, ed., *Organizing Interests in Western Europe* (New York: Cambridge University Press, 1983); James G. March and Johan P. Olsen, "The New Institutionalism: Organizational Factors in Political Life," *American Political Science Review* 78, no. 3 (September 1984): 734–49; and Peter Evans, Dietrich Rueschemeyer, and Theda Skocpol, eds., *Bringing the State Back In* (New York: Cambridge University Press, 1985).

2. Stephen Skowronek and Matthew Glassman, eds., *Formative Acts: American Politics in the Making* (Philadelphia: University of Pennsylvania Press, 2007); Mark Blyth, *Great Transformations: Economic Ideas and Institutional Change in the Twentieth Century* (Cambridge: Cambridge University Press, 2002); Craig Parsons, *A Certain Idea of Europe* (Ithaca, NY: Cornell University Press, 2003); Adam Sheingate, "Political

Entrepreneurship, Institutional Change and American Political Development," *Studies in American Political Development* 17 (2003): 185–203; Hokyu Hwang and Walter W. Powell, "Institutions and Entrepreneurship," in Sharon Alvarez, Rajshree Agarwal, and Olav Sorenson, eds., *Handbook of Entrepreneurship* (New York: Springer, 2005), 179–210; Bruce Miroff, "Leadership and American Political Development," in Skowronek and Glassman, *Formative Acts*, 32–51; Daniel J. Tichenor, "Leaders, Citizenship Movements, and the Politics Rivalries Make," in Skowronek and Glassman, *Formative Acts*, 241–268.

3. Gerald Berk and Dennis Galvan, "How People Experience and Change Institutions: A Field Guide to Creative Syncretism," *Theory and Society* 38, no. 6 (2009): 543–580; Victoria Hattam and Joseph Lowndes, "The Ground Beneath Our Feet: Language, Culture, and Political Change," in Skowronek and Glassman, *Formative Acts*, 199–222; Victoria Hattam, *In the Shadow of Race: Jews, Latinos, and Immigrant Politics in the United States* (Chicago: University of Chicago Press, 2007); Joseph Lowndes, *From the New Deal to the New Right: Race and the Southern Origins of Modern Conservatism* (New Haven, CT: Yale University Press, 2009); Sheingate, "Political Entrepreneurship."

4. On the "fit" between background and actor features, see Daniel Kryder, "Organizing for Disorder: Civil Unrest, Police Control, and the Invention of Washington, D.C.," in Skowronek and Glassman, *Formative Acts*, 105–125; James Mahoney and Kathleen Thelen, eds., *Explaining Institutional Change: Ambiguity, Agency, and Power* (New York: Cambridge University Press, 2009).

5. Mustafa Emirbayer, "Manifesto for a Relational Sociology," *American Journal of Sociology* 103, no. 2 (1997): 281–317.

6. Ruth Berins Collier and David Collier, *Shaping the Political Arena: Critical Junctures, the Labor Movement, and Regime Dynamics in Latin America* (Princeton, NJ: Princeton University Press, 1991); Gregory Luebbert, "Social Foundations of Political Order in Interwar Europe," *World Politics* 39, no. 4 (July 1987): 449–478; Paul Pierson, "Increasing Returns, Path Dependence, and the Study of Politics," *American Political Science Review* 94, no. 2 (June 2000): 251–267.

7. Paul DiMaggio and Walter W. Powell, introduction to Walter W. Powell and Paul DiMaggio, eds., *The New Institutionalism in Organizational Analysis* (Chicago: University of Chicago Press, 1991), 1–40; Pierre Bourdieu, *Outline of a Theory of Practice* (Cambridge: Cambridge University Press, 1977 [1972]); Paul Pierson, *Politics in Time* (Princeton, NJ: Princeton University Press, 2004).

8. See Mahoney and Thelen, *Explaining Institutional Change*; Wolfgang Streeck and Kathleen Thelen, eds., *Beyond Continuity* (Oxford: Oxford University Press, 2005).

9. See Walter Dean Burnham, "The Changing Shape of the American Political Universe," *American Political Science Review* 59, no. 1 (1965): 7–28; Philip E. Converse, "Change in the American Electorate," in Angus Campbell and Philip E. Converse, eds., *The Human Meaning of Social Change* (New York: Sage, 1972), 263–337; Walter Dean Burnham, "Theory and Voting Research: Some Reflections on Converse's

'Change in the American Electorate,'" *American Political Science Review* 68, no. 3 (1974): 1002–1023; Philip E. Converse, "Comment," *American Political Science Review*, 68, no. 3 (September 1974): 1023–1027; Walter Dean Burnham, "Rejoinder," *American Political Science Review*, 68, no. 3 (September 1974): 1050–1057.

10. For the importance of proximate causes, see Raymond E. Wolfinger and Steven J. Rosenstone, *Who Votes?* (New Haven, CT: Yale University Press, 1988); Converse, "Change in the American Electorate." Compare these with Walter Dean Burnham, "The Appearance and Disappearance of the American Voter," in Richard Rose, ed., *Electoral Participation: A Comparative Analysis* (Beverly Hills, CA: Sage Publications, 1980), 35–73. For the impact of spatially and temporally distant social forces, see Theda Skocpol, *States and Social Revolutions: A Comparative Analysis of France, Russia and China* (New York: Cambridge University Press, 1979); Stephen Skowronek, *Building a New American State* (New York: Cambridge University Press, 1982); and especially Karen Orren, *Belated Feudalism: Labor, the Law, and Liberal Development in the United States* (New York: Cambridge University Press, 1992). See also the classic work on transnational movements such as Paul Gilroy, *The Black Atlantic: Modernity and Double Consciousness* (Cambridge, MA: Harvard University Press, 1993); Daniel T. Rodgers, *Atlantic Crossings: Social Politics in a Progressive Age* (Cambridge, MA: Harvard University Press, 1998; Amy Kaplan, "Left Alone with America: The Absence of Empire in the Study of American Culture," in Amy Kaplan and Donald E. Pease, eds., *Cultures of United States Imperialism* (Durham, NC: Duke University Press, 1993).

11. See Jasbir Puar, *Terrorist Assemblages: Homonationalism in Queer Times* (Durham, NC: Duke University Press, 2007).

Contributors

Stephen Amberg is associate professor of political science at the University of Texas at San Antonio. He received a Ph.D. from the Massachusetts Institute of Technology. In 2009–2010 he was a Fulbright Professor at the Copenhagen Business School. He has published widely on American political development, U.S. automobile industry industrial relations, and evolving labor market policies in the American states. He is currently writing about social learning in active labor market policy in Denmark and the uses of multiparty politics for collaborative employment regulation in New York.

Chris Ansell is a professor of political science at the University of California, Berkeley. He is the author of *Schism and Solidarity in Social Movements* (Cambridge University Press, 2000) and *Pragmatist Democracy: Evolutionary Learning as Public Philosophy* (Oxford University Press, 2011) and co-editor of *Restructuring Territoriality: Europe and the U.S. Compared* (Cambridge University Press, 2004) and *What's the Beef: The Contested Governance of European Food Safety* (MIT Press, 2006). Since 2010, he has been the U.S. editor of *Public Administration: An International Journal*, and he was an associate editor of the *Encyclopedia of Governance* (Sage, 2007).

Gerald Berk is professor of political science at the University of Oregon. His work on historical alternatives to corporate capitalism and redistributive regulation in the United States is realized in two books: *Alternative Tracks: The Constitution of American Industrial Order, 1870–1914* (Johns Hopkins University Press, 1994), which was awarded the American Political Science Association's J. David Greenstone Prize for the best book in politics and history, and *Louis D. Brandeis and the Making of Regulated Competition, 1900–1930* (Cambridge University Press, 2009). In 2012, he received a National Endowment for the Humanities Research Fellowship to work on a book entitled *Rationality and Improvisation in the Cold War State*, which will trace the passage of systems analysis from the RAND Corporation in the 1950s to weapons procurement, fiscal management, and the Great Society in the 1960s.

Kevin Bruyneel is associate professor of politics at Babson College. He wrote *The Third Space of Sovereignty: The Postcolonial Politics of U.S.-Indigenous Relations* (University of Minnesota Press, 2007), and is presently researching and writing on the relationship between race, colonialism, and collective memory in the United States.

Dennis C. Galvan is professor of political science and international studies and vice-provost for international affairs at the University of Oregon. Galvan received his Ph.D. from the University of California, Berkeley, and his B.A. from Stanford. He has conducted field research since 1988 in West Africa (primarily in rural Senegal) and since 1999 in Indonesia (primarily in central Java). In 2009–2010, he was a Fulbright Scholar in Senegal, at the Université Cheikh Anta Diop de Dakar. Central to all his work is a concern for how ordinary people adaptively transform the nation-state, markets, law, local government, and natural resource management systems to suit their changing and mutable notions of heritage, identity, and political morality. His books include *The State Must Be Our Master of Fire: How Peasants Craft Culturally Sustainable Development in Senegal* (University of California Press, 2004), which won the 2005 Best Book Award from the African Politics Conference Group, and *Reconfiguring Institutions Across Time and Space: Syncretic Responses to Challenges of Political and Economic Transformation* (Palgrave Macmillan, 2007). His articles on institutional change, peasant adaptation of property regimes, social capital and democratization, sustainable development, and grassroots patterns of nation building have appeared in *Theory and Society, Journal of Democracy, Journal of Modern African Studies, Cahiers d'Etudes Africaines, Electoral Studies,* and *African Economic History.* He is completing *Everyday Nation Building,* an exploration of the experiential roots of ethnic cooperation, religious tolerance, and national belonging in Senegal and in central Java, Indonesia.

Deborah Harrold has taught in the Department of Political Science at Bryn Mawr, as well as the University of Pennsylvania, Drexel University, and the University of Austin at Texas. Her Ph.D. is from the University of Chicago.

Her interests are at the intersection of political economy and political culture in the Middle East and North Africa. She has written on the culture of the economy, gender issues and economic change, and the informal economy.

Victoria Hattam is professor of politics at the New School for Social Research, working on American culture and politics. Hattam is currently exploring questions of visuality and politics through a variety of collaborations with faculty from the Parsons School of Design. Hattam has been a visiting scholar at the Russell Sage Foundation and a member at the Institute for Advanced Study at Princeton. Hattam has worked extensively on issues of immigration and race politics in the United States. Recent publications include *In the Shadow of Race: Jews, Latinos, and Race Politics in the United States* (University of Chicago Press, 2007), which was awarded the Ralph Bunche Prize from the American Political Science Association in 2008; "From Immigration and Race to Sex and Faith: Rethinking the Politics of Opposition," *Social Research* 77, no. 1 (Spring 2010): 133–162, coauthored with Carlos Yescas; and "Ethnicity and the American Boundaries of Race," *Daedalus* 134, no. 1 (Winter 2005): 61–69. Hattam served as the president of the Politics and History Section of the American Political Science Association in 2006–2007 and as chair of the Politics Department at the New School for Social Research from 2005 to 2009.

Yoshiko M. Herrera graduated from Dartmouth College, earned a Ph.D. in political science from the University of Chicago, and currently is associate professor in the Department of Political Science and director of the Center for Russia, East Europe and Central Asia at the University of Wisconsin-Madison. She is the author of several articles as well as *Imagined Economies: The Sources of Russian Regionalism* (Cambridge University Press, 2005) and *Mirrors of the Economy: National Accounts and International Norms in Russia and Beyond* (Cornell University Press, 2010), and coeditor of *Measuring Identity: A Guide for Social Scientists* (Cambridge University Press, 2009).

Gary Herrigel is professor of political science and the college at the University of Chicago. He is the author of *Manufacturing Possibilities: Creative Action and Industrial Recomposition in the U.S., Germany and Japan* (Oxford University Press, 2010) and *Industrial Constructions: The Sources of German Industrial Power* (Cambridge University Press, 1996). He has published widely in the areas of comparative political economy, economic sociology, industrial relations, and business history.

Joseph Lowndes is associate professor of political science at the University of Oregon. His research interests include political institutions, culture, and identification. He is the author of *From the New Deal to the New Right: Race and the Southern Origins of Modern Conservatism* (Yale University Press, 2008) and coeditor (with Julie Novkov and Dorian Warren) of the volume *Race and American Political Development* (Routledge, 2008).

Ato Kwamena Onoma is the author of *The Politics of Property Rights Institutions in Africa* (Cambridge University Press, 2009) and the forthcoming book *The Politics of Encounters: Knowledge, Violence and Refugee-Host Relations in Africa* (Cambridge University Press). He holds a bachelor's degree in philosophy from the University of Ghana, Legon and a doctorate in political science from Northwestern University. He was a postdoctoral fellow at the Niehaus Center for Globalization and Governance, Woodrow Wilson School of Public and International Affairs, Princeton University, from September 2006 to June 2007. From July 2007 to December 2011 he was assistant professor of political science at Yale University. In January 2012 he joined the Institute for Security Studies as a program manager in its Addis Ababa office.

Adam Sheingate is an associate professor in the Department of Political Science at Johns Hopkins University. He is the author of *The Rise of the Agricultural Welfare State: Institutions and Interest Group Power in the United States, France, and Japan* (Princeton University Press, 2001) as well as a number of articles and book chapters on American political development and comparative public policy. His current work examines processes of political and institutional transformation in American politics. One project examines the origins and development of the political consulting profession during the twentieth century; a second project examines the political obstacles to and opportunities for a new politics of food in the United States.

Rudra Sil is professor of political science at the University of Pennsylvania. His scholarly interests encompass Russian and postcommunist studies, comparative labor politics, institutional analysis, and philosophy of social science. He is author of *Managing "Modernity": Work, Community, and Authority in Late-Industrializing Japan and Russia* (University of Michigan Press, 2002) and, with Peter Katzenstein, of *Beyond Paradigms: Analytic Eclecticism in the Study of World Politics* (Palgrave Macmillan, 2010). His articles have appeared in such journals as *Journal of Theoretical Politics, Perspectives on Politics,* and *Post-Soviet Affairs.* He is also coeditor of several anthologies, including *The Politics of Labor in a Global Age* (Oxford University Press, 2001).

Ulrich Voskamp has been a long-term industrial researcher at the Soziologisches Forschungsinstitut at the Georg-August University in Göttingen, Germany. He has published numerous articles on outsourcing and offshoring, the restructuring of global supply chains, and the enlargement of the European economy.

Volker Wittke was professor of sociology in the Department of Sociology at the Georg-August University in Göttingen, Germany. He was also chief director of the SOFI Institute for Sociological Research in Göttingen. He published very widely on the global transformation of German and U.S. industries, in particular in the electronics, telecommunications, new media, automobile, and machinery sectors. He was author of many books and articles; most recently he was coeditor (with Klaus Dörre and Dieter Sauer) of *Kapitalismustheorie und Arbeit: Neue Ansätze soziologischer Kritik* (Campus, 2012).

Index

Acknowledgments

This project began in a series of wide-ranging conversations among the editors, the contributors, and others, which revealed some surprising but rather inchoate similarities among a diverse group of scholars. We continued to develop our ideas through several American Political Science Association panels and follow-up discussions, a two-day workshop at the University of Oregon, and the process of putting together this volume. Some of the participants in those discussions stuck with us throughout; others joined later and became contributors to this volume. And so, in addition to the contributors (whom we acknowledge at length in the introductory chapter), we are extremely grateful to the many participants in those venues who helped us clarify our goals, sharpen our ideas, and build a more creative and coherent volume. We especially thank Dan Tichenor, Craig Parsons, Janice Fine and Nida Alahmad. We are ever grateful to Karen Orren and Stephen Skowronek. This project builds directly on their work alone and together, they participated at several stages in its development, and this book would not exist in its current form without their careful thought and criticism. We're grateful to our colleagues at the University of Oregon, Priscilla Southwell and Lars Skalnes. As associate dean and Political Science Department head, respectively, they saw the promise in this project at its early stages and funded the workshop, "Unstructuring Politics."

Many other people have helped and influenced this project through their relationships with us individually or collectively. We're especially grateful to Shana Agid, Brian Balogh, Richard Bensel, David Brody, Elizabeth Clemens, Clive Dilnot, Babacar Fall, Robin Jacobson, Bill Keith, Colin Koopman, Nora Krug, Jie-Hyun Lim, Jim Livingston, Richard Locke, Ned Lorenz, Alf Lüdtke, Tim Marshall, Carol Nackenoff, Anne Norton, Julie Novkov, Jeff Ostler, Michael Piore, Charles Sabel, Marc Schneiberg, Phil Scranton, George Shulman, Rogers Smith, Ann Snitow, Fred Thompson, Jilly Traganou, and Jonathan Zeitlin.

We're grateful to our editor at the University of Pennsylvania Press, Peter Agree, for his unwavering support, good humor, and sage advice. We've been lucky to work with him from the outset of the project. He helped us convene a better workshop, organize a more coherent volume, and write more useful supporting chapters. It was a pleasure to work with the staff at the University of Pennsylvania Press: Rachel Taube, Noreen O'Connor-Abel, and Melissa Marshall. We're grateful to two anonymous reviewers for their insightful suggestions about how to rethink the Introduction and Conclusion.

As ever, partners and family were supportive and patient with our endless conversations over Skype, confusions with the material, and clumsy efforts to weather the vicissitudes of collaboration with equanimity. We're delighted to be able to thank Tom, Emily, and Robert; Karen and Jeep; and Kirsten, Ben, Sam, and Spats.